THE CHANGING
WORLD MARKET
FOR IRON ORE
1950–1980

THE CHANGING WORLD MARKET FOR IRON ORE 1950–1980

An Economic Geography

GERALD MANNERS

Published for Resources for the Future, Inc.
by The Johns Hopkins Press, Baltimore and London

RESOURCES FOR THE FUTURE, INC.
1755 Massachusetts Avenue, N.W., Washington, D.C. 20036

Resources for the Future is a nonprofit corporation for research and
education in the development, conservation, and use of natural resources
and the improvement of the quality of the environment. It was established
in 1952 with the cooperation of the Ford Foundation. Part of the work of
Resources for the Future is carried out by its resident staff; part is supported
by grants to universities and other nonprofit organizations. Unless otherwise
stated, interpretations and conclusions in RFF publications are those of
the authors; the organization takes responsibility for the selection of
significant subjects for study, the competence of the researchers, and their
freedom of inquiry.

This book is one of RFF's energy and mineral studies, which are directed by
Sam H. Schurr. The author, who is Reader in Geography at University
College London, University of London, did most of the research for his study
while on leave from his university as a visiting scholar with Resources for the
Future. The manuscript was edited by Adele Garrett. Illustrations were drawn
by Mary Hayward, in the Cartographic Unit of the Department of Geography,
University College. The index was prepared by L. Margaret Stanley.

RFF Editors: Henry Jarrett, Vera W. Dodds, Nora E. Roots, Tadd Fisher.

The Johns Hopkins Press, Baltimore, Maryland 21218
The Johns Hopkins Press Ltd., London

Library of Congress Catalog Card Number 70–146734
ISBN-0-8018-1308-5

FOREWORD

When speculation about prospective developments in an industry is based only on an examination of its present situation, the result often is not very useful because it fails to reflect proper perspective. This can be gained only by an analysis of the underlying forces at work in an industry over a period long enough to reveal changes caused by them. Gerald Manners has performed this task in a very thorough fashion. The bulk of his study is a careful examination of the forces influencing the demand for and the supply of iron ore over the period 1950–65. Building on this foundation, he proceeds to indicate some of the likely developments in the years to 1980.

The course of the iron ore industry from 1950 to 1965 has been determined to a marked degree by technological changes. New methods of making steel have influenced the demand for ore in important ways; on the supply side, every phase of the long process—from the finding of ore deposits to delivery of ore to the blast furnace—has been changed by the imperatives of technique. The swift spread of radically different practices in ore mining, preparation, and transport have brought about complex changes in the scale and locational pattern of activities. It is noteworthy that this procession of changes, far from being haphazard, has been quite systematic and orderly. Consequently, when viewed broadly, the process of finding and developing iron ore deposits cannot be viewed as something haphazard—no matter how much the individual exploration geologist may feel himself to be at the mercy of chance.

Technology, however, does not provide the whole explanation for the dynamic way in which the spatial market for iron ore has developed. Technology itself has been channeled by national policies that are based on political as well as economizing considerations. It is the latter, however, that may be considered the dominant element determining the locational and other equilibratory factors among the forces of change.

Manners' approach is that of the economic geographer; nevertheless, those readers who study the iron ore industry from the viewpoint of industrial organization will feel themselves at home in this study and will find that it illuminates many of the questions that are of interest to them.

During a reading of this study, it will be clear that an examination of the iron ore industry in just one country would serve only very limited objectives. The view that the market must be studied in its entirety even though this may involve the entire world is also exemplified in other RFF studies. Two of these are *Trends in the World Aluminum Industry* (1967), and *Energy in the World Economy*, to be published toward the end of 1971.

ORRIS C. HERFINDAHL
Associate Director
Energy and Minerals Program
Resources for the Future, Inc.

8 December 1970

A NOTE ON STATISTICAL SOURCES

United Nations. The United Nations *Statistical Yearbook*, published annually, contains world data on a national basis concerning apparent steel consumption, steel and pig iron output, and iron ore production in tons of contained iron. The *Monthly Bulletin of Statistics* contains more current data, albeit for rather fewer countries, on steel, pig iron, and iron ore production; the ore figures are in actual tons. *Statistics of World Trade in Steel* records the volume of steel product exports and imports on a national basis. The *Yearbook of International Trade Statistics* has data on the volume and value of steel, pig iron, and iron ore imports and exports throughout the world; the ore figures are in actual tons. These data are also available in *Commodity Trade Statistics.*

Economic Commission for Europe (ECE). This regional commission of the United Nations deserves special mention, since it has been particularly concerned with the ferrous industries for many years. Its *Quarterly Bulletin of Steel Statistics for Europe* contains data on steel, pig iron, and iron ore production (actual tons) for the countries of Western and Eastern Europe; the more recent issues also include data for the United States and Japan. Three ECE studies contain valuable summaries of data: *Long-Term Trends and Problems of the European Steel Industry* (1959), *The World Market for Iron Ore* (1968), and *World Trade in Steel and Steel Demand in Developing Countries* (1968).

Organization for Economic Cooperation and Development (OECD). Like its predecessor, the Organization for European Economic Cooperation (OEEC), the OECD publishes annually *The Iron and Steel Industry*, which contains data on steel and pig iron output in its member countries.

Statistical Office of the European Economic Community (EEC). This office publishes *Iron and Steel* (bimonthly), which contains a wealth of statistical data concerning the iron and steel and iron ore industries of the member countries of the Common Market.

Official national sources. The United States Bureau of Mines publishes world data on a national basis for steel, pig iron, and iron ore (actual tons) production in its annual *Minerals Yearbook.* More current data on mineral production and trade are published in the Bureau's monthly *Mineral Trade Notes.* The Mineral Resources Branch of the Department of Energy, Mines and Resources in Ottawa (formerly the Department of Mines and Technical Surveys) each year publishes *Primary Iron and Steel* and the *Canadian Iron Ore Industry,* both of which contain comparative international data. The *Statistical Summary of the Mineral Industry,* published annually by the Mineral Resources Division of the Institute of Geological Sciences in London, contains data on a national basis concerning world steel, pig iron, and iron ore (actual tons) production and international trade in iron ore (actual tons).

Industry sources. The American Iron and Steel Institute publishes an *Annual Statistical Report,* which relates principally to the North American industry but also includes world statistics, by country, on steel, pig iron, and iron ore (actual tons) production. The American Iron Ore Association publishes *Iron Ore Industry of the United States and Canada* annually; this also includes data on world iron ore production and trade by countries. The British Steel Corporation (and earlier the British Iron and Steel Federation) publishes an annual *Statistical Handbook* and a monthly *Iron and Steel Monthly Statistics,* sections of which have international data on steel, pig iron, and iron ore (actual tons) production. Statistisches Bundesamt, Düsseldorf, publishes *Eisen und Stahl,* which contains world data, by countries, on iron and steel production. *Trades of World Bulk Carriers* is published annually by the Fearnley & Egers Chartering Co., Ltd. of Oslo; it contains a valuable section on the world seaborne trade in iron ore.

CONTENTS

Part II. Trends in the Supply of Iron Ore, 1950–1965

Part III. The Market Prospects for Iron Ore: Forecasts to 1980

Part IV. Summary

LIST OF TABLES

Table

Table

Table

CHAPTER 1

Introduction

Conceived in the first instance as part of a much wider program of research into the problems associated with the growing volume of international trade and investment in minerals and energy raw materials, this study has its roots in certain fundamental questions concerning the changing magnitude and geographical characteristics of the world iron ore industry. What changes have taken place in the location of iron ore production during the recent past, and are they likely to continue in the near future? Are the geological resources of iron ore large enough to meet the prospective growth in demands both globally and regionally? And what are the implications of new technological developments in iron ore mining and preparation? In what ways have the trading patterns in this raw material, whose availability is basic to the successful growth of modern industrial societies, altered in response to both new market situations and recent advances in the technology of bulk commodity transport? What associated changes have there been in the nature and structure of the iron ore industry? What developments can reasonably be expected in the size and location of demands for iron ore in the light of past experience? Is it reasonable to expect that the many recent changes in the industry will continue into the future, or are some developments subject to checks and limitations?

In order to answer these questions, directed primarily toward the iron ore industry, it is imperative to be able to respond with confidence to a number of questions relating to the changing economic geography of the iron and steel industry and to its markets. Only rarely today is iron ore consumed in exactly the same form in which it is recovered from the earth. Invariably it is subject initially to some form of preparation, which can range from simple screening and washing to complex concentration and agglomeration procedures. Nevertheless, it is at the next stage of the ore transformation process—when it is reduced into pig iron—that the level and location of ore demands are primarily determined, and it is the spatial distribution of blast furnaces that affords the major control over the geography of iron ore demands. Small quantities of ore are, of course, directly reduced to sponge iron and consumed as such. Equally small quantities are used in certain steelmaking processes as a refining agent.

1

And even smaller demands for ore originate from the chemical, and especially the paint, industry. However, most iron ore (after preparation) is fed into blast furnaces for conversion into pig iron.

Some of this pig iron is used directly in foundries. Some enters international and interregional trade. Much the greater part is yet further refined into steel by one of several processes that are located either in works geographically separate from the blast furnace or more usually in an integrated plant. Not all steel is made from pig iron, of course. Some is made from scrap. As a consequence, the spatial patterns of pig iron production, pig iron demand, and steel production are by no means identical. Nevertheless, a general coincidence, plus a close and important set of relationships, exists between all three. As a broad generalization, therefore, the geographical distribution of iron ore demands throughout the world is in large measure a function of the map of iron and steel production. And insofar as the pattern of steel production stems from, and cannot be understood without reference to, the location of steel demands, it is the markets for steel that provide the starting point in any realistic examination of the markets for iron ore.

Historically, the markets for steel, the iron and steel industry, and the production of iron ore have been remarkably mobile on the world stage, despite the fact that the iron and steel industry has frequently been characterized by economic geographers and economists alike as an industry that is powerfully subject to forces of inertia (Estall and Buchanan, 1961, p. 187). Although steel was still a rare commodity in 1870, the world production of pig iron had reached a level of 12 million tons (Table 1). Over one-half

TABLE 1. WORLD PRODUCTION OF PIG IRON AND CRUDE STEEL, BY REGIONS, 1870–1950

(Thousands of tons)

Region	1870	1913	1920	1939	1945	1950
PIG IRON						
World	12,040	79,090	62,640	101,960	78,330	133,650
North America	1,700	32,490	38,550	33,210	51,600	62,500
Western Europe	}10,340	46,100	21,500	41,910	12,370	39,180
Eastern Europe			1,280	18,510	9,660	23,830
Asia and Oceania		500	1,300	7,750	3,660	6,150
Latin America			10	280	480	1,220
Africa and Middle East				300	560	770
STEEL						
World	510	76,900	72,580	137,800	114,670	191,580
North America	40	32,860	43,930	49,310	75,020	93,030
Western Europe	}470	43,740	25,140	54,230	18,910	52,540
Eastern Europe			2,210	24,170	14,150	35,540
Asia and Oceania		300	1,270	9,510	5,660	8,270
Latin America			30	210	390	1,320
Africa and Middle East				370	540	880

Source: United Nations, 1964-A, 1968-A.

Note: Blank spaces in this table and subsequent ones indicate that data are not available or not applicable, or that the amount is negligible or nil.

of this pig iron was smelted in Britain. The United States, with 14 percent of the world output, Germany with 12 percent, and France with 10 percent were Britain's nearest rivals. During the next forty years, the inventions of Bessemer and Siemens were relentlessly exploited in what were then the most advanced industrialized countries of the world; and, although the iron and steel industry remained exclusively on both sides of the North Atlantic, the relative importance of its several major producers changed. By 1913, a year in which the production of steel ingots had almost reached the same level as that of pig iron for the first time, the United States had clearly emerged as the most important national steel producer, and was pouring one-third of the world total.

In the interwar years, the geography of the world steel industry continued to change as production very nearly doubled from 73 million tons in 1920 to 138 million tons in 1939. North American and Western European output still dominated the world industry, but significant changes were occurring elsewhere on the globe. The Soviet Union increased its steelmaking from one-third of a million tons to 17 million tons. Japan's output expanded steadily, and by 1939 it had reached 6 million tons. India, South Africa, Mexico, and Brazil, among other industrially less developed countries, began producing small quantities of steel; in the future, their output was to become significant. Although World War II ended with steel production in the United States towering far above that of any other country (it accounted for over half of the world's production in 1945), and although Western Europe made a spectacular recovery from the ravages of war to give it and North America together over three-quarters of the 192 million tons of world output in 1950, the seeds had been sown for a far-reaching dispersal of steel production facilities throughout the world.

The mining of iron ore has exhibited equally dramatic geographical shifts over the years. Before World War I, pig iron and steel production had invariably been based on the use of domestic and frequently local iron ores. Geographical changes in pig iron manufacture and steelmaking were therefore closely reflected in the distribution of iron ore production. By the interwar years, however, another factor entered into the situation. This was the declining reserves of high-grade and economical ores in a number of key steel-producing countries. Within Western Europe, for example, Britain, Germany, Belgium, and Luxembourg found it necessary to supplement their own iron ore production with imports from Sweden, Spain, and North Africa. By 1929, Germany was importing two-thirds and Britain one-third of their ore requirements in terms of their iron content. Even in the resource-rich United States, concern was being expressed over the adequacy of domestic ore reserves, and in the thirties the steel industry turned to Canada and Latin America for supplementary supplies. From the very first, of course, Japan had to rely largely on overseas sources of ore in order to support its iron and steel industry. Since the twenties, but more especially since 1945, the owners of many blast and steel furnaces throughout the world have been looking further and further afield for additional (and very often superior) supplies of their basic raw material.

The present study is concerned with the most recent—and the immediately prospective—developments in the location of the iron and steel and the iron ore industries, and with their interaction through the market for iron ore. Its main objective is to examine the economic, technological, sociological, and political forces that have gripped the two industries in recent years. These forces have revolutionized the financial and geographical relationships between the two industries; they have developed new technologies and opportunities for the production and processing of manufactures and raw materials; they have transformed the scale and the organization of the transport systems used by the steel and the ore industries; they have demanded a relocation of facilities; and they have produced a new spatial pattern of the two industries throughout the world.

Part I analyzes the principal forces playing upon the location of the demands for iron ore. It is broadly concerned with the changing economic geography of the world iron and steel industry. Since the questions to which answers are ultimately sought relate essentially to the iron ore industry, the discussion of other steelmaking raw materials (such as coking coal, limestone, and scrap) is kept to a minimum. Part II examines the forces affecting the supply of iron ore and analyzes changes in both the market for ore and the means whereby it is satisfied. Parts I and II conclude with summary chapters on global and macroregional changes in the demand for, and the supply of, iron ore.* Part III makes some forecasts of the spatial shape of the iron and steel and the iron ore industries.

The year 1950 was taken as a convenient starting point for the present study, since by that time the extreme distortions in the world's economic geography caused by World War II had been erased, although Western European steel production was still below that of 1939. Another reason for choosing 1950 was that the preceding year had seen the devaluation of sterling and the associated currency readjustments, which injected a little more realism into international trading relationships. For projections into

---

* For further details supplementing Parts I and II, the reader is referred to my manuscript dealing with the spatial distribution of the iron and steel and the iron ore industries between the years 1950 and 1965. This manuscript, which is organized on a country-by-country basis and formed part of the research resulting in the present book, is in the files of University Microfilms, Ann Arbor, Michigan, under the title *The Changing World Market for Iron Ore: A Descriptive Supplement Covering the Years 1950–1965.* Bound Xerox copies may be purchased from University Microfilms. For a listing of the countries and regions covered by this supplement, see Appendix B.

the future, 1980 was taken as the forecast year, since events beyond that date could not reasonably be anticipated at the time of writing. And 1965 afforded a convenient mid-point in this 30-year period. In addition, 1965 was the year before certain key international currencies again came under severe strain; this led to a second postwar devaluation of sterling. It was also one of the last years for which a reasonably complete set of production and trade statistics were available on a worldwide basis. Some slightly later data are presented in Appendix A.

All the measures in the study are in metric units. All the values are in U.S. dollars. Some iron ore data are recorded in actual tons ("a" tons), but most data are in tons of contained iron ("c" tons), which are normally preferable for comparative purposes.

part I

Trends in the demand for iron ore, 1950–1965

CHAPTER 2

The Location of Demand in Market Economies

The location of demand for iron ore is primarily a function of the geography of iron and steel production. The iron and steel industry is one in which several bulky raw materials, in addition to iron ore, are assembled and processed, and from which heavy and frequently awkward products are transported to their markets. In 1964, for example, the British iron and steel industry consumed 31 million actual tons of iron ore, 22 million tons of purchased coal and coke, 15 million tons of ferrous scrap, 4 million tons of limestone and dolomite, 4 million tons of oil, and 6.5 million tons of other materials—all to produce about 26 million tons of ingots and 20 million tons of finished steel. Some iron and steel producers, using higher-quality ores or a greater percentage of scrap, need to amass a rather smaller volume of raw materials in relation to their output; yet others, using lower-grade ores and alternative technologies, assemble even more, sometimes up to five or six tons of raw materials in order to produce one ton of finished steel.

Naturally the best location for an iron and steel industry is a site where all its principal raw materials are to be found not only in close proximity to each other but also near the major markets for its products. Since the industry's several raw materials are hardly ever to be found in the same locality, however, and since most iron and steel works in reality tend to satisfy the needs of several geographically separate markets, such an ideal location for the industry simply never exists. And even if, by chance, it did exist at one particular moment in time, the changing availabilities and economics of raw-material supply, together with the persistent spatial shifts in the markets for iron and steel products, would soon result in its being only temporarily so. Therefore, while those responsible for locating steelmaking capacity in theory would search for *least-cost* sites under an

9

average set of economic and technological conditions throughout the life of the plant, in reality they have to recognize the changing nature of the space economy and have to be content with *low-cost* sites. The geography of such sites stems from the nature and structure of the iron and steel industry's costs. It is to these that we first turn.

THE STRUCTURE OF COSTS IN IRON AND STEEL PRODUCTION

A first step toward understanding the major components in the costs of iron and steel production can be taken by examining a largely hypothetical example. Table 2 is based on a study, conducted by the Economic Commission for Latin America (United Nations, 1964-A), which sought to examine the possibility of profitable iron and steel production in certain parts of Latin America. The cost breakdown in this example relates to the production of flat products in an integrated plant with an annual capacity of 1.5 million tons. The figures are based on "reasonable" prices for raw materials and other inputs and on an assumption that the plant is operated under optimum conditions. Consequently, the costings are considerably below those normally encountered by most Latin American (and, indeed, many other) producers. Moreover, at each stage of production, an output of 1.5 million tons per year is assumed. But since only 0.75 tons of pig iron are used to produce 1 ton of (in this case open-hearth) steel, and since 1.39 tons of ingot steel are used to produce 1 ton of flat products, a corollary assumption of the costings must be that full use can be made of the blast-furnace and rolling-mill facilities by sales of pig iron and purchases of ingots elsewhere. The table must be interpreted with care. Nevertheless, the figures are based on careful and detailed engineering and economic studies, and they throw much light on the structure of costs in contemporary steelmaking using a conventional blast furnace, open-hearth furnaces, and rolling mills.

The total cost of producing and delivering one ton of steel is shown to be $110. Of this, just under 6 percent—that is, $6.56—is the cost of delivering the steel from the integrated works to its market. The cost of transporting raw materials, on the other hand, is much higher. To assemble the inputs of the blast furnace costs $14.37, and a further $2.77 is spent on the haulage of scrap to the steel furnaces. In a strict sense, yet further transport costs should be added, for no separate figure is provided in the table for the costs of transporting the other materials used in iron and steel production, such as the iron ore used in the open-hearth furnaces, the ferro-alloys, the fuel oil, the refractories, and the like. Therefore the listed costs of assembling raw materials and delivering the steel products, which amount to 21.6 percent, must be regarded as a low figure for total transport costs in this case. Their sum is only slightly less than the costs

TABLE 2.   HYPOTHETICAL COSTS OF PRODUCING ONE TON OF FLAT PRODUCTS IN A PLANT WITH 1.5 MILLION TONS CAPACITY

(*Dollars at 1962 prices*)

Stage of production	Cost/ton material	Cost/ton pig iron	Cost/ton ingot	Cost/ton product	Cost/ton product c.i.f.	
RAW MATERIALS						
Ore f.o.b.	4.50*	7.10	5.32	7.40	7.40	6.7%
transport	5.00*	7.80	5.85	8.13	8.13	7.4
c.i.f.	9.50	14.90	11.17	15.53	15.53	14.1
Coal f.o.b.	11.00*	6.75	5.06	7.04	7.04	6.4
transport	7.00*	4.31	3.23	4.49	4.49	4.1
c.i.f.	18.00	11.06	8.29	11.53	11.53	10.5
Limestone f.o.b.	2.00*	0.67	0.50	0.70	0.70	0.6
transport	5.00*	1.67	1.25	1.74	1.74	1.6
c.i.f.	7.00	2.34	1.75	2.44	2.44	2.2
Total raw materials						
f.o.b.		14.52	10.88	15.14	15.14	13.8
transport		13.78	10.33	14.37	14.37	13.1
c.i.f.		28.30	21.21	29.50	29.50	26.8
BLAST FURNACE						
Raw materials		28.30	21.21	29.50	29.50	26.8
Labor		0.77	0.57	0.80	0.80	0.7
Process and other raw materials		3.24	2.43	3.38	3.38	3.1
Capital charges		4.35	3.26	4.54	4.54	4.1
Pig iron		36.66	27.47	38.22	38.22	34.7
OPEN-HEARTH FURNACE						
Pig iron			27.47	38.22	38.22	34.7
Scrap f.o.b.	25.75*		8.23	11.43	11.43	10.4
transport	6.25*		2.00	2.77	2.77	2.5
c.i.f.	32.00		10.23	14.22	14.22	12.9
Ferro-alloys and iron ore			4.72	6.54	6.54	5.9
Total raw materials			42.42	58.96	58.96	53.6
Labor			2.56	3.56	3.56	3.2
Process			12.41	17.25	17.25	15.7
Capital charges			2.75	3.82	3.82	3.5
Steel ingot			60.14	83.59	83.59	76.0
ROLLING MILL						
Steel ingot				83.59	83.59	76.0
Labor				3.30	3.30	3.0
Process				8.84	8.84	8.0
Credits (scrap)				−9.66	−9.66	8.8
Capital charges				17.37	17.37	15.8
Finished steel				103.44	103.44	94.0
DELIVERY						
Finished steel f.o.b.					103.44	94.0
transport					6.56	6.0
c.i.f.					110.00	100.0

Source: Based on United Nations, 1964-A, pp. 104–7.
* Author's estimate.

of the principal raw materials (iron ore and coking coal) at their respective sources. The two major raw materials cost $14.44 per ton of finished steel; with limestone and scrap, the cost of raw materials at source is $26.57, or 24.1 percent. Among other major items in the cost of steel production are the processing costs, including the cost of energy, which represent about 27 percent of the total; the capital charges, 23.4 percent; and the cost of labor, about 7 percent.

Hypothetical though the figures are, the structure of the costs in Table 2 is by no means out of accord with reality. In the European Economic Community (EEC) in the late fifties, the freight component of finished steel (ex-works and other than the costs of internal handling) averaged between 20 and 25 percent of total costs (Housz, 1960). And some British evidence (Waring and Dennison, 1962) suggests that circa 1960 the delivered cost of raw materials and energy in steelmaking averaged about 40 percent of the total. Nevertheless, it is equally important to recognize that the cost structure of the iron and steel industry is subject to considerable variation. Two broad categories can usefully be distinguished:

1. *Technological cost variations.* The cost variations resulting from the application of different types of iron and steelmaking technology are exemplified in the Linz-Donawitz (L.D.) basic oxygen converter which shows considerable savings in its process costs, its capital charges, and its labor expenses by comparison with the more traditional open-hearth furnace. Other things being equal, the effect of these economies is to increase the relative importance of raw-material costs in the total costs of steel production. In Table 7, for example, the cost of pig iron and ferro-alloys in open-hearth steel production is just over 70 percent, whereas it is over 80 percent in the case of the L.D. furnace. Technological cost variations also result from engineering advances. A modern blast furnace is a case in point. With its high top pressure and fuel oil injection, it is capable of producing pig iron with much greater efficiency and at lower costs than an older furnace. And the widest variations in costs occur at the finishing end of steelmaking operations, where the capital and process expenses of manufacturing—for instance, bars on the one hand and hot-rolled sheet on the other—are very different. Bars, by 1965, had a delivered value in the United States of about $150 per ton; hot-rolled sheet, $190. Tinplate, galvanized sheet, special alloy steels, and the like involve even more expensive processes; yet their raw-material inputs and very often their works-to-market transport costs are much the same as more ordinary steel products.

Another aspect of technological cost variations stems from the economies associated with large-scale production. Table 7 illustrates something of their magnitude. On its assumptions, steel costs over $20 per ton more to manufacture in plants with a capacity of 0.1 million tons per year compared with those of 1.5 million tons; and the relative importance of processing, capital, and labor costs appears to diminish in each type of steelmaking technology as the scale of production is increased. It would, however, be unwise to press this observation into too broad a conclusion; for the possibility of assembling the iron and steelmaking raw materials for larger plants with greater efficiency and lower costs by exploiting scale economies in transport (see Chapters 9 and 10) is not recognized in the figures. Another dimension is the fact that these (and many other) cost breakdowns of the iron and steel industry are based on an assumption of a high degree of plant use. In reality, the load placed on any particular piece of equipment varies hourly, daily, weekly, and annually with fluctuations in the demand for steel. The cost structure of steel production at a works with a high load factor will clearly have a smaller proportion of capital charges than that of a comparable facility suffering from wide fluctuations in demand. Wylie and Ezekiel (1940) showed from data of the United States Steel Corporation that one of the most important factors in the cost variations of that firm was the degree to which its capital equipment was utilized. While such variations might most frequently be a response to changing market conditions, they are also influenced by such matters as labor efficiency, the quality of management, decisions about pricing, and other commercial policies.

2. *Locational cost variations.* This category stems from spatial differences in the price of transport, raw materials, and other factor inputs. When a steelworks is situated close to its market, the cost of distributing its products might be only 2 to 4 percent of the delivered cost. More usually it lies somewhere between 4 and 8 percent. But if a steelworks is located some considerable distance from its market, or if its transport arrangements are inefficient, the distribution cost can be twice as much. The Chiba works of Kawasaki by Tokyo Bay, for example, is able to ship a large proportion of its products by small boat to the adjacent market of metropolitan Toyko; and the cost per ton lies in the order of a mere $2 to $3. Even lower is the distribution cost of the Fuji Iron and Steel Company plant at Kamaishi, which is able to supply the Keihin area with steel products by sampan at a cost of about $1 per ton, which is equivalent to 0.7 percent of the price of heavy plate (Murata, 1962, p. 33). On the other hand, the Conference freight rate (see Chapter 4) for moving structural steels from the United States to Western Germany is over $30 per ton (U.S. Joint Economic Committee of Congress, 1963, p. 569)—over 25 percent of the market price—and Latin American importers often have to pay even higher freight rates from Western Europe.

Variations in the costs of transporting iron and steelmaking raw materials can be almost as wide. In part, they are a function of the iron and steelmaking technology adopted (see Chapter 3). During the mid-fifties, for example, in making each ton of finished product, the French iron and steel industry assembled more than twice the weight of raw materials used by its Italian counterpart (Table 3). This variation was in large measure a function of the heavy reliance of the French industry on the low-grade iron ore of Lorraine, in contrast to the extensive use then made of scrap for steel manufacture in Italy. This did not mean that steel production was cheaper in Italy than in France; on the contrary, the high price of scrap at the time helped to place the Italian industry's costs among the highest in Western Europe. More generally, and irrespective of the quantities employed, it is clear that the location of iron and steel production in relation to the sources of raw materials will powerfully influence the aggregate delivered costs at the furnace. When the industry is sited close to its principal raw materials, the assembled cost of the materials can be as low as 15 to 20 percent of the cost of the finished product. In most instances, longer hauls and rather higher transport charges on the raw materials raise their delivered costs to 25 or 35 percent of the total. And still higher percentage costs result either from inefficient and expensive raw-material transport arrangements or simply from a bad production location.

Such variations in the costs of raw-material transport must be distinguished from the variations in the costs of raw materials f.o.b., which themselves exhibit a considerable range (see Chapter 7). The cost of winning ore, for example, can vary between $0.25 per ton in an easily worked open

TABLE 3.   QUANTITY AND COST OF RAW MATERIALS PER TON OF FINISHED STEEL IN SELECTED AREAS, 1956

Raw material	Germany	Saar	France	Belgium	Luxembourg	Italy	Britain	U.S.A.
	QUANTITY (tons)							
Coal and fuel......	1.665	1.884	2.166	1.750	1.710	1.325	1.963	1.451
Iron ore...........	1.571	3.070	3.541	2.329	4.037	0.727	1.862	1.497
Purchased scrap....	0.307	0.105	0.300	0.231	0.009	0.623	0.356	0.308
Limestone.........	0.344	0.154	0.202		0.151		0.309	0.389
Total.........	3.887	5.213	6.209	4.310	5.917	2.675	4.490	3.645
	COST (dollars)							
Coal and fuel......	20.85	27.70	35.55	26.85	31.65	24.40	25.10	14.55
Iron ore...........	21.95	19.00	13.25	23.70	18.15	7.20	20.00	20.65
Purchased scrap....	16.95	5.75	13.15	13.70	9.55	38.60	13.50	16.45
Total...........	59.75	52.45	61.40	64.25	59.35	70.20	58.60	51.65
Other metallics (+ or −).......	+1.60	+7.00	−1.00	+9.25		+8.80	+4.40	
Total.........	61.35	59.45	60.40	73.50	59.35	79.00	63.00	51.65

Source: Lister, 1960, pp. 60–61.

pit to as much as $5 or $7 per ton in difficult underground conditions. And the costs of preparing the ore for the blast furnace range from a few cents in the case of some simple screening processes to perhaps $4 or $5 per ton when more complex beneficiation techniques are applied. Similarly, coking-coal costs and prices vary enormously from place to place. American and Australian coals won by large-scale opencast methods are very much cheaper than French or British coals extracted from thin underground seams. Such a situation compounds the geographical complexity of the steel industry's raw-material costs and their variable importance in the delivered costs of steel products.

Labor and capital costs, too, exhibit noticeable spatial differences. Something of their diversity in the industry's cost structure was illustrated in a pioneer study of eight hypothetical plants in Latin America and the United States in 1948 (United Nations, 1954-A, p. 112). The study assumed rather small plants of 0.25 million tons ingot capacity per year, the application of comparable technology at each site, and the use of the cheapest available raw materials (Table 4). It showed how the cost of making one ton of finished steel could vary from a little over $76 at Belencito (Colombia) to $100 at Sparrows Point (United States) and $128 at San Nicolás (Argentina). At these three locations the share of delivered raw-material costs was 20, 34, and 55 percent, respectively. Variations in the absolute and proportionate cost of wages and salaries were not so great; they ranged from under $8 (9.5%) in the case of Chimbote (Peru) to nearly $30 in the case of Sparrows Point (30% of total costs). Capital charges showed even less absolute variation between the locations; yet their percentage variation, from 26 to 48.5, was considerable. These figures do no more than hint at the spatial variety in the magnitude and structure of steelmaking costs under identical technical and economic assumptions. They illustrate well the difficulty of generalizing about the breakdown of costs in iron and steel production. In no sense, however, can they be taken to indicate the best locations for the industry, since they neglect both the differences in the size of steel markets in the several countries concerned and the costs of transporting the finished steel to the markets.

With the structure of the iron and steel industry's costs subject to numerous technological and spatial variables, plant managements are frequently able to offset one relatively expensive factor of production against other comparatively low-cost inputs. In the discussion of the industry's locational behavior, however, analysts have traditionally paid most attention to only one variable—namely, transport costs. They have argued that, while other elements in the cost structure of the iron and steel industry can frequently be decisive in molding its geography, the industry's most profitable locations will tend to be influenced most powerfully by the expense

TABLE 4. COST STRUCTURE OF IRON AND STEEL PRODUCTION AT SEVERAL HYPOTHETICAL WORKS, 1948

(Dollars per ton of finished steel)

Plant	Raw materials		Wages and salaries		Capital charges		Other costs		Total costs
San Nicolás, Argentina[a]	70.04	54.6%	11.12	8.7%	36.09	28.2%	10.89	8.5%	128.14
San Nicolás[b]	51.48	46.9	11.12	10.1	36.09	32.9	11.09	10.1	109.78
San Nicolás[c]	47.08	44.7	11.12	10.6	36.09	34.2	11.05	10.5	105.34
Volta Redonda, Brazil	45.62	44.7	10.04	9.8	35.58	34.9	10.84	10.6	102.08
Huachipato, Chile	29.03	34.7	8.35	10.0	35.58	42.6	10.66	12.7	83.62
Belencito, Colombia	15.41	20.2	10.77	14.1	36.82	48.5	13.12	17.2	76.12
Monclova, Mexico	33.31	37.0	9.57	10.6	36.10	40.2	10.93	12.2	89.91
Chimbote, Peru	24.55	30.0	7.76	9.5	35.58	43.5	13.90	17.0	81.79
Barcelona, Venezuela[d]	28.31	27.5	24.47	23.7	35.58	34.6	14.68	14.2	103.09
Barcelona[e]	33.23	32.0	24.51	23.6	35.58	34.3	10.49	10.1	103.81
Sparrows Point, U.S.A.	33.68	33.6	29.75	29.7	26.37	26.3	10.45	10.4	100.25

Source: United Nations, 1954-A, p. 102.
Note: Capacity of 0.25 million ingot tons per year is assumed for the hypothetical works.
[a] Zapla ore.
[b] Itabira ore.
[c] Sierra Grande ore.
[d] Coke from asphalt or petroleum residues.
[e] Coke from imported coal.

16

of transporting their raw materials on the one hand, and by the rates for distributing their finished products on the other.

LOCATIONAL ANALYSIS

In earlier periods, when even larger quantities of raw materials were required for the production of iron and steel than today, and when their transport costs were particularly high, it was generally most advantageous for the industry to be located near those raw materials. In the nineteenth century, when up to eight tons of coking coal were often used to produce one ton of pig iron, it was not unnatural for ironmasters to seek out locations where coking coal (or charcoal) and iron ore were to be found in close proximity. As a consequence, the industry had to accept the inevitability of a generally long product haul to its markets. Or, alternatively, the metal-consuming industries elected to locate themselves close to the mills.

With time, the changing technology of iron and steel manufacture reduced the volume of raw-material inputs, the transport costs of raw-material assembly fell, and a gradual reappraisal of the best location for the industry took place. As early as 1928, two American geographers were pointing to the falling costs of transport and to the growing advantage of *market* locations for iron and steel production (Hartshorne, 1928, 1929; White, 1928). While recognizing, in classical Weberian fashion, the "pull" of raw materials on the industry and continuing attraction of a coal- or ore-field location, Hartshorne declared that in the emerging geography of the industry the market factor is of greater importance than the others.

This concept was furthered by Isard (1948) and Isard and Capron (1949), who drew attention both to the importance of scrap supplies in reinforcing the spatial "pull" of markets and to the fact that many regions (such as the Ruhr), which had formerly attracted the iron and steel industry through their supplies of raw materials, especially coal, subsequently retained their attractiveness as a result of the markets for steel that had grown up there. Isard and Capron demonstrated for the first time, with 1939 data, the transport cost advantage of iron and steel manufacture at market locations in the United States. Barloon (1954-A) and then Craig (1957) showed that in 1950 only a narrow gap existed between the costs of assembling the raw materials and the costs of shipment to markets in American iron- and steel-making centers (Table 5). By implication, the lowest total transport costs would be recorded by those producers who were able to minimize the expense of product shipments by locating close to their markets. Craig also showed how the distribution of steelmaking plants in the United States had changed considerably over the previous twenty years. The eastern seaboard and the Cleveland-Detroit districts had increased their share of the country's capacity, while the Pittsburgh-Youngstown district had exhibited

TABLE 5. COST OF ASSEMBLING RAW MATERIALS FOR PIG IRON MANUFACTURE AT SELECTED BLAST-FURNACE LOCATIONS IN THE UNITED STATES, 1950

(*Dollars per ton*)

Location	Ore		Coal		Limestone		Total delivered cost of raw materials per ton of pig iron
	Cost of mining and beneficiation	Cost of transportation	Cost of mining and preparation	Cost of transportation	Cost of quarrying and preparation	Cost of transportation	
Chicago..........	4.92	5.02	7.87	5.53	0.26	0.41	24.01
Pittsburgh.....,...	4.73	9.07	7.89	0.86	0.26	0.75	23.57
Buffalo..........	4.92	5.05	8.16	4.39	0.28	0.90	23.69
Duluth...........	6.42	2.18	7.52	5.02	0.31	0.47	21.92
Ohio River.......	5.81	9.48	7.87	2.07	0.30	1.10	26.64
Granite City, Ill....	5.93	5.49	7.09	4.15	0.29	2.25	25.19
Bethlehem........	7.34	6.27	5.08	5.08	0.17	0.24	24.19
Baltimore........	3.74	7.61	4.09	4.77	0.23	0.61	21.85
Birmingham......	9.89	1.04	13.70	0.82	0.14	0.18	25.77
Houston.........	5.84	5.49	8.86	6.86	0.77	0.92	28.74
Lone Star, Tex....	9.03		9.75	2.95	1.03	1.18	23.95
Geneva, Utah.....	3.76	3.81	6.75	3.62	0.25	0.44	18.63
Fontana, Calif....	3.88	3.97	7.02	8.20	0.25	0.30	23.63

Source: Barloon, 1954-A, p. 17.

a marked relative decline. The inference was drawn that this shifting geography of American iron and steel production represented the industry adjusting its location to the geography of markets and electing not to make major reinvestments in plants with a raw-material orientation. Certainly, in transport-cost terms, the logic of iron and steel manufacture at the market was clear. Yet the absence of an adequate set of spatial data on the markets for iron and steel products in the United States left this thesis unproved. The suggestion made by Craig that the capacity for iron and steel production and the size of the markets for iron and steel products in the Midwest were approximately in balance was simply not verified.

In 1954 Chauncey Harris published a seminal paper on the geography of markets as a factor in the location of industry. He was concerned with quantifying the locational pull of markets on the manufacturing industry in general. Through his index of "market potential" (an abstract index of accessibility to all markets from any given center), he sought to describe geographical variations in the proximity of places to aggregate consumer demands. His paper indicated a means of measuring the spatial dimension of demand. Yet it was nearly ten years before this lead was followed up and an attempt was made to apply a quantitative test to the market-location hypothesis. This was achieved by Fink (1963-A, 1963-B), who worked with the Pittsburgh Regional Planning Association (1963). If the assumption is valid that a market location, *ceteris paribus*, affords the lowest transport costs for iron and steel production, and if transport costs are the industry's major spatial cost variable, then it presumably follows that those plants and firms that are most advantageously located to satisfy the demand for iron and steel products will be the most profitable. It was Fink's singular achievement to demonstrate quantitatively the validity of this proposition.

His study assumed that, by and large, very little distinction is made in the American market between the virtually identical products of different steel firms. Buyers normally purchase their requirements from the mill or mills offering the lowest combination of f.o.b. price and transport rates— that is, the lowest c.i.f. price. Although the aggregate demand for steel is relatively insensitive to changes in price, individual buyers are very aware of any differentials in the delivered price of products. Yet open price competition has never been a feature of the American iron and steel market. The huge investments required by the industry make it advantageous for producers generally to stabilize or neutralize the price dimension of competition. For many years, therefore, steel companies in the United States (and elsewhere) have tended to quote identical lists of prices and extras for their products; and, following the decision of the Supreme Court in the Cement Institute case in 1948, their quotations have been on an ex-works basis. It has been the consumer who has decided upon and paid for the mode of transport. The antitrust laws, however, have permitted steel companies to meet each other's delivered prices by means of "freight absorption" in those cases where firms with differential delivery costs are competing for business. In effect, this has meant that the delivered price of steel in any location has been the f.o.b. price at the nearest steel plant plus the cheapest means of transport to consumers there. More distant works, by absorbing freight, have been able to compete in that market, but (assuming equal production costs) only by accepting a lower net return on their product. If the market price for a particular sheet-mill product is, say, $150 per ton, and the cost of producing that product is $125 per ton, a company selling in a nearby market to which transport costs are $10 will have an f.o.b. mill net return of $15, or 11 percent of the f.o.b. price. But if the mill elects to sell to a customer located nearer another plant by absorbing freight, that $15 can very quickly be reduced. In such a situation, all other things being equal, the more freight a steelworks has to absorb in order to maintain a high level (or at least a reasonable level) of production, the less profitable will that works prove to be; and the less likely will the industry be inclined to invest capital in installing additional capacity in the existing works or in replacing obsolete plant.

Using the best statistical evidence available on the location of iron and steel production capacity, on the geography of steel markets, and on the transport costs for steel products, Fink was able to simulate the industry's product movements as a transport-problem linear program. Given the existing geography of production facilities and markets, he sought to establish the most efficient way in which these demands could be satisfied, and the load that this would place on different plants and steelmaking districts. His program showed that an optimum solution to the transport problem would necessitate considerable variations in the use of different iron and steel plants. While the works at Bethlehem, Fontana, Cleveland, and Detroit would be utilized at full capacity, those at Pittsburgh, Wheeling, and Youngstown would only be working at 16.5, 12, and 7 percent, respectively, of their capacity (Table 6). Crude though the data (on steel markets and, especially, transport costs) may have been, the low level of activity allocated by the linear program to the latter three districts suggested that their operating rates would only be marginally altered by the use of more precise statistics or more sophisticated statistical analyses. In order to maintain reasonable levels of production in relation to their capacity, the works at Pittsburgh, Wheeling, and Youngstown in particular would have to absorb a considerable amount of freight on a large proportion of their sales.

Additional evidence demonstrated that although there were regional variations in the operating rates of different plants and districts, they did not accord with the "optimum." Fink therefore examined the geography of profitability in steelmaking, and he established two specific items of evidence germane to the locational issue. First, he showed that notwithstanding the variety of factors that can affect the costs and profitability of a particular steel company—the attitudes of labor, the quality of management, and the wisdom of investment decisions—there was a clear relation-

TABLE 6. OPTIMUM OPERATING RATES AND OTHER DATA FOR U.S. STEELMAKING CENTERS, 1954

Steelmaking centers	Estimated optimum operating rates, 1954 (*percent of capacity*)	Actual operating rates, 1954 (*percent of capacity*)	Crude index of rates of return, 1954	Percent change in ingot capacity, 1954–60
Baltimore........	93.7		0.0645	43
Bethlehem.......	100.0			
Birmingham.....	61.8	72.2	0.0480	24
Buffalo.........	48.5	73.1	0.0495	17
Chicago.........	83.8	73.5	0.0534	20
Cleveland.......	100.0	71.0	0.0620	30
Detroit.........	100.0	78.5	0.0628	22
Fontana........	100.0	75.5	0.0656	35
Geneva.........	50.0			
Johnstown......	7.0			
Houston........	100.0			
Middletown.....	100.0			
Morrisville......	100.0			16
Pittsburgh.......	16.5	73.0	0.0319	17
St. Louis........	100.0	61.0		
Wheeling........	12.0	70.0		
Youngstown.....	19.5	66.4	0.0293	13

Source: Fink, 1963-A, 1963-B.

ship between the "optimum" operating rates and the estimated rates of return on the capital invested in the various steelmaking centers of the United States. Second, he demonstrated that there was a high degree of positive correlation between the expected profitability (in the light of his earlier analysis) of the steelmaking centers and changes in their capacity between 1954 and 1960 (Table 6).

The Pittsburgh Regional Planning Association was particularly concerned with the prospects of that district as an iron- and steel-producing center. Its recent experience had been far from encouraging. While at the turn of the century it could boast over 30 percent of the country's ingot capacity, by 1960 its share had fallen to 15 percent. In its 1963 report, the Association concluded that "Pittsburgh's loss of access advantage for a large part of the United States market, in conjunction with the fact that locational considerations other than access to markets have gradually dwindled in significance, constitutes the main explanation of this area's failure to share substantially in the continued growth of the American steel industry" (pp. 289–90). The report suggested that the Pittsburgh district, with its much reduced share of national steelmaking capacity, was singularly cramped in the matter of market accessibility. Only about 5 percent of American steel demands were located within easy reach of the district by land transport, and perhaps a little more if cheap Ohio water transport was taken into consideration. Such a disparity between its capacity and its "natural markets" implied that the iron and steel producers of the district as a whole had to accept both a high level of freight absorption and relatively low profit margins in order to utilize their capacity at a reasonable rate. An improvement in the situation could only follow from the evolution of a closer accord between the geography of the markets for steel and the location of production facilities.

In sum, the evidence suggests that, within a market economy like that of the United States, the most advantageous location for iron and steel production tends to be either at or near the markets for steel. The thesis rests on the following three basic assumptions:

1. While spatial variations do exist in the several cost elements in iron and steel production, the element most subject to geographical variation is total transport cost. A major goal of management in location decision-making must therefore be the minimization of transport expenses. The extent to which some plants are poorly located to serve their markets and experience relatively high transport costs, yet at the same time remain reasonably profitable, immediately suggests the limitation of this assumption (see pp. 23–26).

2. The costs of assembling the several raw materials for iron and steel manufacture do not vary significantly between the alternative potential

centers of production. The evidence of Barloon and Craig suggests that this was the case in the fifties. But where a large inland market has to be satisfied by iron and steel manufactured from largely imported raw materials (either ore and coking coal, or possibly even ore alone), simple Hooverian location theory suggests that the point of lowest transport costs will often be the point of entry into the country (Hoover, 1948, p. 38). In such circumstances, the market orientation of the iron and steel industry will tend to express itself in a location at the break-of-bulk point near the market, rather than at the market itself. This is clearly the case in Western Europe. A contemporary study of raw-material assembly costs for the American industry, recognizing in particular the rapid fall in ocean freight rates, would almost certainly show east coast locations to have significant cost advantages over Appalachian centers; and the future iron and steel demands in the southern and southeastern sections of the United States would appear most likely to be satisfied from coastal plants.

3. The market is large enough to justify a size of plant that will afford scale economies sufficient to ensure competitive iron and steel production. This assumption is crucial to an understanding of the pattern of steel production in the western United States, just as it is the crux of the problem of the economics of iron and steel manufacture in the developing countries of the world. The size of market required varies with the iron and steel production technology adopted (and hence the costs of production), the costs of transport from the nearest alternative center of manufacture, and the costs of production at that center (see Chapter 4). It also varies with the institutional characteristics of the market. Alexandersson (1961) has shown how an understanding of the patterns of plant ownership is important in interpreting the geography of iron and steel production in the United States. The emerging shape of British steel production under the corporate plans of the British Steel Corporation is clearly very different from what might have resulted from continuing investments by the many separate managements of the companies vested in the nationalized Authority.

To the extent that these assumptions are not fulfilled, the realities of iron and steel production will tend to diverge from this market-oriented model.

The principal literature on the location of the iron and steel industry in a market economy has predictably emerged largely from the United States. But Canadian and Japanese thinking and experience confirm the validity of the market-orientation thesis (Elver et al., 1963; Murata, 1962).

The first Canadian plants, established in the nineteenth century, were located near their raw materials—both scrap and iron ore. And the first integrated works to be built, following the decision of the Canadian Federal Government in 1879 to protect its iron and steel industry, was located in Nova Scotia on tidewater near a source of coal and within easy access to Newfoundland ore and limestone. It was a raw-material–oriented plant par excellence. Later, the Canadian industry became increasingly attracted to locations near its markets. It has relied to a large degree on the import of both iron ore and coking coal from the United States. Canada's second integrated plant, located at Hamilton, Ontario, was strategically placed to serve the main Canadian markets. Using some local ores at first, it has subsequently been fed largely with ore imported from the United States. The third integrated plant was located in western Ontario. Although slightly eccentric to the main Canadian markets at the time, it was well placed to serve the expanding agricultural areas to the west. The fourth integrated plant, like the second, was also built in Hamilton. In phase with the Canadian market, the industry grew relatively slowly throughout the first forty years of the present century. Then, paralleling the unprecedented growth of the Canadian manufacturing industry, iron and steel production capacity expanded rapidly, and it was in those plants best suited to serve the domestic market that the greater part of the new investment was placed. Looking back over the industry's geographical evolution, Buck and Elver in 1963 could confidently assert: "The most important consideration in determining the location of successful Canadian steel plants has been the size, nature, and location of the present and future market for primary steel shapes and for secondary products made principally of steel" (p. i).

In Japan, too, it has been seen that "since the 1930s, the location of blast furnace changed its orientation and settled in market or its vicinity [sic]" (Murata, 1962, p. 17). The oldest Japanese works may have been drawn toward their raw materials—the Kamaishi Iron Works to a source of iron ore, and the Yawata Works to a source of coal. But from 1936, when the Nippon Kokan Iron Works was located in the Keihin industrial area, and three years later when the Hirohata Iron Works selected a site near the Hanshin industrial area, the Japanese industry has been clearly oriented toward its markets. With virtually no domestic raw materials for iron and steel production in their country, the Japanese chose sites (even reclaimed coastal land) near the major industrial centers. Thus there emerged in Japan one of the world's classic market-oriented iron and steel industries.

LOCATIONAL PERSPECTIVES

While it is likely that the management of a modern iron and steel industry will seek out market-oriented locations having efficient transport arrangements, the variable cost structure of the industry also permits other factors sometimes to play an equally decisive role. For example, the industry has to operate within a multivariate framework of its own shifting locational forces, which in turn respond to a changing geography of both markets and resources. A site that might afford the industry low total transport costs at one point in time can sometimes become a relatively high-cost location. However, the considerable capital investment on that site often denies the industry the opportunity of locational adjustment, for it is many times too costly either physically to move or alternatively to write off the plant already constructed. Frequently the industry continues to produce at the "obsolete" site (Rodgers, 1952-A, 1952-B). It can do so competitively for two reasons in particular.

One of the larger items in steel production costs (see Table 2) is the interest charges on capital. It represents over 23 percent of the delivered cost of steel (see the hypothetical figures on page 12). An older works, with the value of its plant completely or even partly amortized, is often able to compete with a new works that is more advantageously located to serve a particular market, since the lower capital charges of the older works can compensate for its rather higher transport costs. Moreover, in an existing works there are usually a number of production capacities that are different for each stage of the steelmaking process, and only rarely are these exactly in balance. It is frequently possible to increase the capacity of a works inexpensively by replacing, enlarging, or improving those items of equipment that make for the underutilization of other stages in the production process. The introduction of an oxygen lance into an open-hearth furnace, for example, can significantly increase a works' steelmaking capacity; this in turn can mean that, under certain circumstances, any previously underutilized blast-furnace or finishing-mill capacity can be more fully exploited. By such means, iron and steel production at an older works in an "old" location can often be increased at costs considerably below those required to start up production on a "green field" low-cost site. In the early fifties, the United States Steel Corporation spent about $256 per ingot ton of capacity to construct a new plant on the east coast—the Fairless Works, at Morrisville near Philadelphia—whereas the Bethlehem Steel Corporation, by extending its existing plants between 1946 and 1953, was able to add an equivalent volume of capacity at an average cost of $112 per ingot ton (Warren, 1959). Obviously, there comes a time when an existing works cannot be economically extended, owing to limitations at its site, the distance from its proposed markets, or the need for extensive modernization of its equipment. Moreover, in the longer run, new plants sited at more advantageous locations afford (in addition to their immediate transport economies) much more profitable opportunities for expansion. The exact timing of the geographical adjustment of steel production to changing patterns of demand and new locational forces, however, is a delicate matter; we turn to it again in Chapter 5.

Competitive iron and steel production can also take place at locations with relatively high transport costs, when there are labor and process costs of an advantageous nature. Sometimes these derive from a plant's technological characteristics, sometimes from low-cost factor inputs. And occasionally factors other than cost influence the industry's spatial behavior. Even in the market economies, the role of political factors in location decisions must be acknowledged as being capable of going well beyond the provision of tariffs to protect the home market. To some extent they reinforce historical forces compounded with sociological pressures, which may make for the industry's inertia. The attempts made to prolong, through various subsidies, the life of the Dominion Steel Company's plant at Sydney (Nova Scotia) in order to maintain employment in a district unable to offer alternative jobs, fall into this category.

Political forces are also capable of pressing for and achieving a new location that contravenes the pull of market forces. The Duluth plant of the United States Steel Corporation, for example, was built in response to regional political pressures, although the corporation has partly overcome the comparatively high costs of location by allocating to the plant those orders that can best withstand a relatively high transport cost to their markets. In 1965 there were similar pressures in the Province of Quebec, pressures which sought to realize quickly a somewhat premature proposal to build a new integrated iron and steel works on the St. Lawrence River between Montreal and Quebec City.

During wartime, the political element in location decisions tends to be particularly powerful. In the United States two integrated steelworks were located in the Western States primarily for strategic reasons. The Geneva plant of the United States Steel Corporation at Provo, Utah, was originally built by the Federal Government to serve the war industries on the Pacific coast, while the Fontana (California) plant of the Kaiser Steel Corporation was sited some distance inland for purely strategic reasons.

In Japan the relationship between the iron and steel industry and both the national and local governments is, to say the least, a little opaque. However, political factors have been known to influence the geography of the industry, not so much modifying in any significant way the location of plants, but rather influencing the exact timing and phasing of investment projects in different sites and areas. The parallel development in the mid-sixties of two new integrated works by the Yawata Iron and Steel Company, at Sakai and Kimitsu, appears to be essentially a response to local political leverage in a country where steelwork sites are at a premium. The economics of the industry would suggest the advantage of developing a single plant to a reasonable size before constructing another.

Such political pressures in the market economies are quite weak, of course, compared with the strength of political factors in the location of the iron and steel industry in both the fully planned and the mixed economies. (See Chapter 5 for a more complete discussion.)

In sum, the location of demand for iron ore in the market economies must be understood against a background of the variable structure of the costs of iron and steel production, the changing locational preferences of the industry, and the diverse set of factors that explain its spatial behavior. This analysis rests, of course, on certain broad assumptions concerning the technology of iron and steel production. Consequently, a fuller understanding of the geography of iron ore demands requires a more thorough examination of the industry's basic technology. This is the purpose of the next chapter.

CHAPTER 3

Technological Changes in Iron and Steel Production

Throughout the period under review, the technology of the iron and steel industry was subject to constant change. In the early fifties, the industry was possibly most affected by the spreading abroad of the North American wide-strip mill. Later in that decade the size and efficiency of the blast furnace were radically increased, with first Russian and then Japanese technology setting the pace. In the early sixties, the major change affecting steelmaking was the diffusion of the basic oxygen converter from its Austrian birthplace. And by the mid-sixties, the industry appeared to be on the threshold of major developments using the technology of continuous casting. Each of these new processes had its implications for the geographical pattern of the industry.

The classical process of iron and steel manufacture involves three distinct stages of production (Figure 1): (1) The manufacture of pig iron in a blast furnace; (2) the making of steel by the Bessemer, open-hearth, or electrical processes; and (3) processing in the finishing mills.

The blast furnace, in effect, is a vertical steel cylinder lined with protective refractories. While iron ore, coke, and limestone are fed into the top of the furnace stack, hot air is blown in through the tuyeres at the bottom. A small quantity of fuel oil, pulverized coal, or natural gas may be injected through the tuyeres as well. The oxygen in the air causes the coke and injected fuel to burn fiercely, generating both heat and a large volume of reducing gas which moves up through the stack. This gas is subsequently cleaned and used for heating the air blast, for raising steam, for firing coke ovens, and for heating the reheating furnaces. As the coke burns away, the various raw materials (the "charge") descend through the furnace. The gas and the heat act on the ore, reducing the iron oxides to metallic iron, which picks up carbon from the coke and melts. Most of the impurities in the ore,

28

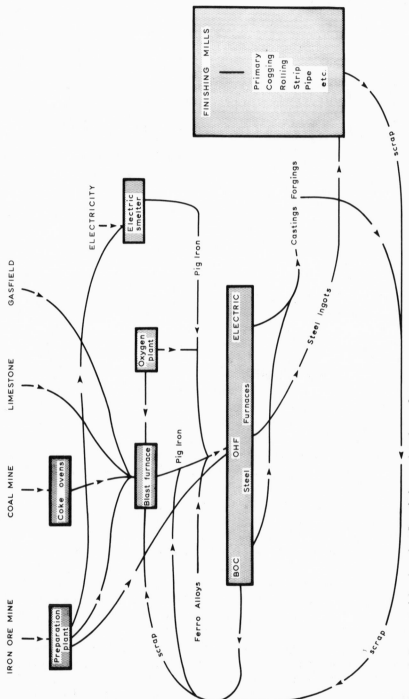

FIGURE 1. **Raw material and product flows in iron and steel manufacture.**

together with ash from the coke, are fluxed by the limestone to form a liquid slag. The two immiscible liquids drop to the bottom of the furnace, while the less dense slag floats on top of the iron and is removed separately. The whole process is continuous as long as the refractory lining to the furnace remains intact. When the lining wears thin, the furnace has to be emptied and re-lined, a process that might take as long as three months.

Some of the pig iron produced in the blast furnace is used for foundry purposes; in a solid state it is sent to a special furnace in order that it may be further refined and its composition adjusted for making iron castings. Most of the pig iron, however, is moved on to the second stage of the production process, the making of steel.

Pig iron contains a considerable amount of carbon, which it has absorbed in the blast furnace. Normally the percentage ranges from 3 to 4. It also contains quantities of silicon, sulfur, phosphorus, and manganese in varying proportions. During the steel manufacturing process, these "impurities" are partly removed, usually by a process of oxidation. For example, in the acid Bessemer process, a traditional and somewhat inflexible though very fast method of producing steel, the oxidation is achieved by simply blowing air through molten iron. The Bessemer converter consists of a cylindrical body of steel plates lined with silica; it has air holes in the bottom. Molten pig iron is added, and air blown in from the bottom causes the silicon, manganese, and carbon in the pig iron to oxidize, generating considerable heat. Within about twenty minutes all the carbon has been removed, and the process is complete except for the addition of ferromanganese (to remove excess oxygen introduced toward the end of the "blow") and, if required, a small amount of carbon.

Open-hearth steelmaking, on the other hand, is a much slower process. A "heat" takes between ten and twenty hours. The quality of the steel can be more accurately controlled than in a converter, and the process can utilize considerable quantities of scrap. The use of scrap means that what is essentially a refined metal is being fed into the steel furnace, so that the time spent removing impurities (through the addition of iron oxides) is somewhat reduced. Scrap also has the following advantage: In replacing pig iron, it reduces the amount of blast-furnace capacity required; and, since the blast furnace is one of the more expensive pieces of equipment in an iron and steel works, scrap in effect reduces the amount of capital required for the steelmaking operation. It can also be argued that the use of scrap helps to conserve the resources of ore and coking coal available to a country or region. On the other hand, it must be noted that the replacement of molten pig iron by cold scrap increases the charging time, and also the time taken to melt the metal prior to refining; and the heat needed to liberate the oxygen from the iron oxides used in refining must be supplied by burning more fuel.

The creation of scrap begins at the very moment pig iron is tapped from the blast furnace. From then on, and throughout the rest of the steelmaking process—at the pouring of the ingots, during the rolling and cropping of the slabs, and with the trimming of the bars and sheets and other products of the mills—more and more "works," or "circulating," scrap is created. All modern steelworks in this way create a significant proportion of the scrap they use, perhaps up to 50 percent of their needs. Additional scrap, of course, arises at the engineering or manufacturing plants in which steel is used. This is normally returned immediately to the steelworks, often in the same freight cars or trucks that deliver further supplies of steel. It is known as "process" or "prompt industrial" scrap. The quantities of this type of scrap available for a steel industry are naturally very closely related to the level of current steel production. Much more variable, however, is the availability of another type of scrap—namely, steel products at the end of their useful life, which are known as "capital" or "obsolete" scrap. The quantities available in this category are related to the use of steel perhaps twenty or twenty-five years earlier. Some steel goods, of course, have a shorter life cycle than this, while others are expected to last many more years. But, insofar as the consumption of steel historically has been subject to significant variations—for instance, in the downturn of demand during the recession years of the early 1920s and during the Great Depression of the 1930s following the Wall Street collapse of 1929—it is inevitable that during any subsequent period of steadily expanding steel production there are liable to be variations in the quantities of obsolete scrap available. This, in turn, demands some flexibility in the steel production process. Moreover, inasmuch as the geography of steel consumption has steadily changed, the spatial coincidence of obsolete scrap availability and contemporary steel production may not always occur. As a result, there emerges a need for the transport of some obsolete scrap toward those steel markets in which demand has grown rapidly—markets in which a steel industry has been established but in which little obsolete scrap is yet available. Japan is a case in point. (See Fig. 7, p. 127.)

The open-hearth furnace consists of a shallow bath with a back wall, doors in the front wall, and a roof over the top. In order to withstand the tremendous heat, the furnace is built with special bricks in a steel casing, and it may be either fixed or arranged for tilting. At each end there are openings—on the one end for the passage of heated air for the combustion of the oil, tar, pitch, or natural gas fuels injected into the furnace, and on the other end for the escape of the burned gases to a chimney by way of the regenerators. The air is preheated below the furnace in these regenerators, which absorb heat from the burned (and otherwise waste) gases. At regular intervals the direction of gas and air flow is reversed, so that each regenerator in turn is made to absorb and give out heat. In a typical operation, steel scrap is charged first, together with some limestone and iron ore. The furnace is then strongly heated; and when the steel scrap is just starting to melt, the molten pig iron is poured in. Silicon, manganese, some carbon, and some phosphorus are removed from the metal in the violent reaction that follows. The remaining phosphorus, plus a certain amount of sulfur and carbon, are subsequently removed by further additions of iron ore and limestone. It is possible to carry out chemical analyses of the metal and slag during the refining period and, with careful control, to "catch" the carbon and produce directly a steel of any specified carbon content.

For higher-quality products, the industry for many years has used another steelmaking process: the electric furnace. The furnace is heated by means of carbon electrodes, which carry an electric current from a supply transformer to the steel charge in the bath of the furnace. When the circuit is made, the electrodes are withdrawn slightly from the steel so that the current jumps from the electrode tips to the steel, and an electric arc is struck between the metal and the electrodes. Called the electric arc method, the process generates a temperature of some 3400°C. The charge generally consists of steel scrap with a small proportion of pig iron. It is melted down and refined first under oxidizing conditions, using lime and iron ore or mill scale to produce the necessary slag. Carbon is removed at this stage. Then, after about one and a half hours, the slag is skimmed off with most of the silicon, manganese, and phosphorus. A second reducing slag is next formed with the addition of lime, fluorspar, and carbon or powdered ferrosilicon, which both deoxidizes and desulfurizes the steel. Finally, alloy additions give the steel its desired composition.

Once it has been made, steel is sometimes cast directly into molds for shapes that are too large or too complex to be obtained by forging. Usually, however, it is poured into ingots ready for the third stage of manufacture—namely, processing in the finishing mill. The main ways of working steel into its final shape are by hammering, pressing, and rolling. In each case, the prime requirement is that the steel should be sufficiently hot to allow manipulation, and this is achieved in the soaking pit. For rolling, a temperature of some 1200°C must be attained. The ingot is first passed through a cogging mill. It is then sheared into blooms or slabs ready for the finishing mills. And then the steel is rolled into billets, small sections, bars, rods, and wide strips and sheets in either a continuous or a noncontinuous mill.

In a continuous mill, stands of rolls are placed in line so that the steel may pass through them all in succession. By this means the slab may be quickly rolled down to the finished product in one forward operation. As the product greatly increases in length during its progress, each stand of rolls must be adjusted to run faster than the one before it, and the product, still red-hot, usually emerges from the final stand at high speed. Some continuous mills have up to twenty stands of rolls according to the product for which they are designed. They work faster than the noncontinuous mills; and for a sufficient product tonnage of one size, they work more economically. But for comparatively small product demands or special sizes or quality, the noncontinuous mill is economically more advantageous. The products of both types of mill are cut to the required size by saw, flying shears, or guillotine, or else coiled by machine. They are then allowed to cool; or they are heat-treated before the next stage in their processing.

Billets, rails, bars, and some rods are usually cut into standard lengths, whereas plates are cut to specification. Billets can be re-rolled as bars, "pierced" for the manufacture of tubes or pipes, or made into such things as motor axles by means of forging or drop-forging. Bars are made into nuts and bolts, precision parts for typewriters, automobile parts, bicycles, and machinery. Many tons of bars are used every year in reinforced concrete. Larger bars may be machined to make shafts and gears, and a large tonnage is used in the manufacture of seamless tubes. Rods may be drawn into many types of wire, which in turn may be manufactured into rivets, needles, springs, and the like. Plates are extensively used in the engineering and shipbuilding industries and also for tubemaking. Wide strip may be sheared into sheet; after being treated, annealed, and tinned, it provides the food industry with tinplate for canning purposes. Other wide strip is pressed into shape for car bodies, while narrow strip is used in the light engineering industries. Pipes are produced by the bending over and welding of strip, sheets, or plates; or they may be rolled from pierced or solid billets and bars.

Such, then, are the various stages in the traditional steelmaking process. At each stage of manufacture, rather large technological changes were made in the 1950–65 period. The changes did not affect iron and steel production throughout the world uniformly, for technological change is, in part, a function of local conditions. Developments in iron and steelmaking technology tend to be pioneered and adopted where the need for them is greatest. Thus, L.D. steelmaking was developed first in Austria, where the pig iron made from the local ores contains insufficient phosphorus for the basic Bessemer process, yet too much phosphorus for the acid process. Simultaneously, a national shortage of scrap made the open-hearth process rather uneconomical when used with a high percentage of hot metal of medium phosphorus content. In no other steel-producing country did the conditions for the development of a new process apply with such force.

Again, ability to take advantage of technical innovations is also a function of the rate of growth of steel demand—and hence of production—in particular parts of the world. The Japanese steel industry had many more opportunities during the 1950–65 period to invest in new technology than did, say, the British industry with its rather slower rate of growth. Moreover, the need to take advantage of technological advances also has a distinctive geography. The Canadian iron and steel industry showed itself to be singularly adventurous in adopting new technology, in order to reduce its costs and so be better able to withstand the perennially severe competition it faced from nearby American plants with their greater economies of scale.

A point of emphasis in the present chapter is the falling level of iron and steelmaking costs, but the interpretation of costs calls for caution. Tech-

TABLE 7. COST COMPARISONS OF VARIOUS STEELMAKING PROCESSES FOR OPERATIONS OF DIFFERENT ANNUAL CAPACITIES

(Dollars at 1962 prices)

Process and cost items	Annual production in thousands of ingot tons						
	100	200	400	500	800	1,000	1,500
OPEN-HEARTH FURNACE							
Molten pig iron[a]	$36.99	$33.25	$30.64	$29.75	$28.76	$28.23	$27.47
Scrap[a]	14.26	12.82	11.82	11.48	11.09	10.89	10.23
Iron ore[a]	0.76	0.76	0.76	0.76	0.76	0.76	0.76
Iron and ferro-alloys	55.61	50.43	46.82	45.59	44.21	43.48	42.42
Salaries and wages	8.07	6.98	4.10	3.73	3.28	3.08	2.56
Other conversion costs	14.46	14.21	13.41	13.09	12.75	12.61	12.41
Total direct costs	78.14	71.62	64.30	62.41	60.24	59.17	57.39
Capital charges[b]	6.74	6.24	5.34	4.80	3.86	3.37	2.75
Total costs	84.88	77.86	69.67	67.21	64.10	62.54	60.14
ELECTRIC STEEL FURNACE							
Molten pig iron[c]	35.71	32.09	29.57	28.72	27.76	27.25	26.51
Scrap[c]	13.77	12.38	11.41	11.08	10.71	10.51	10.23
Iron ore[c]	1.15	1.15	1.15	1.15	1.15	1.15	1.15
Iron and ferro-alloys	52.88	47.87	44.38	43.20	41.87	41.16	40.14
Salaries and wages	6.50	5.23	3.06	2.78	2.42	2.26	1.97
Other conversion costs	12.75	12.55	11.75	11.45	11.15	11.05	10.95
Total direct costs	71.73	65.65	59.09	57.43	55.44	54.77	53.06
Capital charges[b]	5.78	5.34	4.73	4.26	3.54	3.21	2.71
Total costs	77.51	70.99	63.92	61.69	58.89	57.68	55.77
L.D. PROCESS							
Molten pig iron[d]	38.92	34.98	32.24	31.29	30.25	29.70	28.90
Scrap[d]	15.11	13.26	12.51	12.49	11.75	11.53	11.22
Iron and ferro-alloys[d]	57.18	51.39	47.90	46.93	45.15	44.38	43.27
Salaries and wages	5.38	4.62	2.84	2.54	2.20	2.07	1.75
Other conversion costs	8.53	8.30	7.46	7.14	6.77	6.61	6.36
Capital charges	4.52	4.10	3.44	3.12	2.58	2.26	2.00
Total costs	75.61	68.41	61.64	59.73	56.70	55.26	53.38

Source: United Nations, 1964-A, p. 105.

[a] The charge of all open-hearth furnaces has been assumed to be 0.749 tons of hot metal, 0.321 tons of scrap, and 80 kilos of high-grade lump ore.

[b] Capital charges are estimated at 9% annually on the investment in the steel shop and do not include taxes, profits, etc.

[c] The charge of all electric steel furnaces is estimated to be 0.723 tons of hot metal, 0.31 tons of scrap, and 120 kilos of high-grade lump ore.

[d] The charge of the L.D. converters has been assumed to be 0.788 tons of hot metal and 0.34 tons of scrap.

nical studies of the various processes of iron and steel manufacture often concentrate on the implications of an improvement in one part of the system rather than the system as a whole. They tend to assume that all other things remain the same, in particular, that the prices of the various inputs remain unchanged; and they fail to weigh the fact that changes at one stage of the production process can have a significant effect on the costs of associated processes. Improvements in technology usually raise the physical efficiency of a particular process: a given set of outputs can result from a smaller quantity of inputs; alternatively, with a given set of inputs, a new and larger set of outputs can be achieved. In other words, the very nature of technological advance means that relationships within the whole production system—the inputs, the production itself, and the outputs—are changed, with the result that all the costs and prices within the system will change as well. Yet engineering cost studies tend to focus solely on changes in production efficiency and to neglect the implications of the changes for the input and output prices. Hence the need to handle costs with care. For example, the costings in Table 7 give the impression of an increasing relative importance of raw-material costs with larger-scale production. The costings, however, while useful for some purposes, were based on the questionable assumption of constant iron ore and other raw-materials input prices. Technological change clearly leads to greater efficiency in resource and input use, and causes a changing mix of product outputs; but its full effect on system costs and prices is much more difficult to establish. Costing studies as a result should be interpreted as a guide to the magnitude of changing efficiency, costs, and prices, rather than as accurate statements about them.

Changes in Blast-Furnace Technology

Although a few blast furnaces in 1950 were producing 1,500 tons of pig iron each day, a typical well-managed furnace in the United States was producing between 800 and 1,000 tons. With a hearth diameter of perhaps 7 meters and an operating temperature of between 500 and 550°C for making each ton of pig iron, the furnace burden would be composed of 1.7 actual tons of direct shipping ore, 0.8 tons of coke, and 0.45 tons of limestone. By 1965, however, as a consequence of a succession of technical advances, an increasing number of blast furnaces in the world were producing between 3,000 and 4,000 tons of pig iron each day (some were even planned for 5,500 tons per day), and their raw-material inputs per unit of production were very much smaller. Under certain conditions the amount of ore for each ton of pig iron had fallen to less than 1.4 tons, and the coke and limestone requirements were down to 0.5 and 0.2 tons, respectively (Table 8).

TABLE 8. HYPOTHETICAL TRANSPORT COSTS TO ASSEMBLE RAW MATERIALS FOR PIG IRON PRODUCTION, ASSUMING TYPICAL BLAST-FURNACE BURDENS, CIRCA 1950 AND 1965

	Circa 1950			Circa 1965			
Raw material	Raw material required per ton of pig iron: direct-shipping ore (tons)	Cost per ton of raw material (dollars)	Cost per ton of pig iron (dollars)	Raw material required per ton of pig iron: coarse ore (tons)	Raw material required per ton of pig iron: pellets (tons)	Cost per ton of raw material* (dollars)	Cost per ton of pig iron* (dollars)
Ore (actual tons)	1.70	7.50	12.75	1.50	1.35	4.50	6.08
Coking coal	1.10	5.00	5.50	0.83	0.68	5.50	3.74
(Coke)	(0.80)			(0.67)	(0.50)		
Limestone	0.45	4.00	1.80	0.26	0.22	5.00	2.05
Total	3.25		20.05	2.59	2.25		11.87

Sources: Joseph, 1946; Graff and Bouwer, 1965. For transport cost assumptions, see text, p. 43.   * Assuming pellet burden.

Undoubtedly the most important development in blast-furnace technology stemmed from the improvement of the burdens, and in particular from the sizing, the agglomeration, and the beneficiation of the ores (see Chapter 8). The efficiency of a blast furnace improves considerably if its iron ore is limited to pieces ranging from about 10 to 30 mm (Kikuchi, 1967). A wider size range reduces the permeability of the burden, gives rise to an uneven distribution in the furnace, and so causes the reducing gases to be channeled irregularly upward. Larger pieces of ore take much longer to reduce. A carefully graded furnace feed, therefore, permits a smooth movement of gas up through the furnace and an efficient transfer of heat within it. The volume of coke needed for the reduction process is thereby lowered, and a greater productivity of the furnace is assured. Larger pieces of ore can be crushed down to the right size; and various processes were developed to agglomerate the small, fine pieces of ore that result from the mining and beneficiation operations. Sintering, for example, had been used on a small scale for many years, but it was only when the practice of screening the sinter (just before use) was started in the mid-fifties that its full potential was realized. Wittur (1964, p. 43) has recorded the conditions under which the sinter content in a blast furnace was increased from nil to 80 percent; output was increased by more than 40 percent; and the rate of coke consumption fell by nearly 30 percent. Even more advantageous than ordinary sinter, from the viewpoint of blast-furnace productivity, is a self-fluxing sinter (containing limestone). Not only is the output of the sinter plant increased, but, more important, the fluxed sinter has a greater strength at high temperatures; this is a matter of increasing importance (see page 38). Equally attractive to the blast-furnace manager are pellets. Remarkably uniform in their chemical composition and in size, they distribute themselves evenly in the blast furnace, are reduced rapidly, and allow a much closer control of the composition of the pig iron being produced.

Frequently the production of agglomerated sinter and of pellets is accompanied by the beneficiation of the ore—that is, the raising of the percentage of iron in each ton of ore. Together with the use of ores that are naturally of higher iron content than many of those traditionally used, this also raises the productivity of the blast furnace considerably. Smaller quantities of purely waste material have to pass through the blast furnace, the volume of slag produced falls, and a smaller tonnage of coke is required. There is a fairly clearly defined relation between the amount of slag produced in a blast furnace and the quantity of coke consumed. While it is possible to use very low-grade ores of perhaps 24 to 28 percent iron in the furnace, they yield perhaps 1.2 tons of slag for each ton of pig iron, and use at the very least 0.65 tons of coke. A higher-grade ore, on the other hand, will produce only 0.35 to 0.4 tons of slag, and its coke consumption will be down to approximately 0.5 tons.

Some quite dramatic improvements in the productivity of blast furnaces have resulted from the use of all these types of improved burdens, particularly from the use of pellets. The Armco Steel Corporation at Middletown, Ohio, once introduced a 100 percent pellet burden into its 1,530 m^3 furnace instead of using a direct shipping ore. As a result, iron production rose from 1,326 to 2,669 tons per day; coke consumption dropped from 787 to 632 kg/ton; the amount of ore charged into the furnace fell by 356 kg/ton; and limestone consumption fell by 118 kg/ton (Olt, 1962; Voskoboinikov, 1963).

Graff and Bouwer (1965) attempted to cost the effect of improving the quality of blast-furnace burdens, even going beyond ordinary pellets to examine the cost advantages of using fluxed and prereduced pellets. Although demanding skeptical interpretation, since neither fluxed nor prereduced pellets have yet been produced on a commercial scale (Britain, Iron and Steel Institute, 1967), their findings were impressive (Table 9). They showed how at existing ore prices the major cost savings resulting from the use of better burdens are (1) the reduction in coke consumption; and (2) the greater productivity of the blast furnace, which allows the capital costs of the furnace to be spread over a greater tonnage of output. With a new (1963) 3,000-tons-per-day blast furnace in the United States costing about $19 million (plus or minus 15%); with the associated sinter and coke plants costing $10.5 million and $24 million, respectively; and with other facilities costing $22 million—in other words, with the whole blast-furnace complex costing about $75 million—the enormous economic advantages of increasing the productivity of the blast furnace are all too obvious.

Another major development in blast-furnace technology during the 1950–65 period was the use of larger units of equipment. In 1950, many

TABLE 9. ESTIMATED COSTS (EXCLUDING DEPRECIATION) OF PRODUCING PIG IRON WITH DIFFERENT ORES, 1965

(*Dollars per ton*)

Item	Natural ore	Coarse ore	Sintered fines	Pellets	Fluxed pellets	Pre-reduced pellets
Ore......................	14.04	14.65	14.92	15.04	16.26	17.65
Coke.....................	12.75	10.05	9.23	8.25	7.50	4.50
Stone....................	0.59	0.52	0.55	0.44		0.41
Sintering................			3.84			
Handling flue dust...........	0.49	0.05	0.02	0.02	0.03	0.02
Furnace processing..........	6.57	5.71	5.44	5.12	4.89	4.09
Total...................	34.44	30.98	34.00	28.87	28.68	26.67

Source: Graff and Bouwer, 1965.

authorities thought that the blast furnace was approaching its maximum practical size (United States, President's Materials Policy Commission, 1952, p. 31). Yet, in fact, the size of furnaces has steadily increased. Hearth diameters have increased to 9 and 10 meters; the height of furnaces has grown to 31–33 meters; their capacities have been increased to 2,000 and 2,300 m^3; and their daily output to well beyond 3,000 tons. Scale economies in pig iron production are in fact, under the right conditions, evident up to at least 5,000 tons per day, and stem from both the lower processing costs and the lower unit capital charges of the larger plants. In Table 10 some costings of the Economic Commission for Latin America are reproduced for blast furnaces with capacities ranging from 0.1 to 1.5 million tons per year. They hint at—and if anything underestimate—the magnitude of the savings to be derived from large-scale production.

Still another improvement during the period was the increase in blast-furnace temperatures from about 500–550°C to 900–1150°C. This was made possible by the development of better refractory materials, the use (to heat the blast) of furnace gases that might otherwise have been wasted, and the injection of moisture and fuel through the tuyeres. Moisture injection permits better temperature control in the furnace. Fuel injection (natural gas, fuel oil, and powdered coal have all been used) allows higher-quality and/or lower-priced fuels to replace coke in its heat-creating role, and may reduce the amount of slag (since coke contains a certain amount of ash). More room is thereby made for iron ore, and the productivity of the furnace is thereby increased. Oxygen injection makes the fuel burn faster, the furnace much hotter, and the rate of iron production higher. All these developments permit a further reduction in the consumption of coke. A final important development in blast-furnace efficiency has been the raising of the top pressure to 4 kg/m^2 or thereabouts; as a result, the output that can be obtained from the furnace is significantly increased.

The total effect of all these changes has been a considerable reduction in the weight and volume of the raw materials needed to manufacture one ton of pig iron. In 1950, a typical blast furnace in Cleveland, Ohio, might have assembled 1.7 tons of ore, 1.1 tons of coal (to make 0.8 tons of coke), and 0.45 tons of limestone to produce each ton of pig iron—the total weight of these three raw materials amounting to 3.25 tons. By 1965, however, the use of fairly high-grade coarse ores and superior blast-furnace technology could have reduced the weight of the three materials to 2.59 tons per ton of pig iron; and the use of pellets could have reduced the weight even further, to 2.25 tons (see Table 8). This is a 30 percent reduction from the 1950 figure.

All iron- and steel-producing countries benefited from the improvements in blast-furnace technology, but none perhaps quite so rapidly as Japan.

TABLE 10. ESTIMATED IRON ORE REDUCTION COSTS IN HYPOTHETICAL LATIN AMERICAN STEEL PLANTS

(Dollars per ton of pig iron at 1962 prices)

Reduction system and item of cost	Capacity in thousands of tons of pig iron or sponge iron per year							
	100	200	300	400	500	800	1,000	1,500
COKE BLAST FURNACE								
Assembly costs	$28.30	$28.30		$28.30	$28.30	$28.30	$28.30	$28.30
Salaries and wages	5.18	2.83		1.53	1.13	0.99	0.95	0.77
Fuel and power	1.00	1.00		1.00	1.00	1.00	1.00	1.00
Oxygen	0.62	0.60		0.58	0.57	0.53	0.51	0.45
Other supplies	5.73	3.87		2.72	2.48	2.38	2.18	1.79
Total direct cost	40.83	36.61		34.13	33.48	33.20	32.94	32.31
Capital charges[a]	8.56	7.78		6.78	6.24	5.20	4.75	4.35
Total cost	49.39	44.39		40.91	39.72	38.40	37.69	36.67
DIRECT REDUCTION[b]								
Assembly costs	26.27	26.27	26.27					
Salaries and wages	1.85	1.22	0.85					
Other conversion costs	5.32	3.56	1.88					
Total direct cost	33.44	31.05	29.00					
Capital charges[a]	4.16	3.41	3.16					
Total cost	37.60	34.46	32.16					

Source: United Nations, 1964-A, p. 104.
[a] Taken as a straight 9% on the invested capital, not considering taxes, profits, etc.
[b] Theoretical data checked with Hojalata y Lámina at Monterrey, Mexico.

TABLE 11. SOME OUTSTANDING BLAST FURNACES, CIRCA 1965

Works	Blast Furnace — Hearth diameter (m)	Blast Furnace — Useful volume (m³)	Burden	Slag (kg/ton of pig)	Coke rate (kg/ton of pig)	Iron production per day (tons)
Chiba, Kawasaki (Japan)	10.00	2,142	52% sinter, 4% pellets	292	494	3,845
Cherepovets (U.S.S.R.)	9.75	2,002	100% sinter	585	525 +35m³ n.g.*	3,520
Krivoy Rog (U.S.S.R.)	9.75	2,002	100% sinter self-fluxing	685	522 +71m³ n.g.*	3,100
Broken Hill Pty., Port Kembla (Australia)	8.84		90% sinter / 10% ore	400	625	2,802
Bethlehem Steel Co., Bethlehem (U.S.A.)	8.76		65% pellets / 22.5% sinter	268	586	2,696
Armco Steel Corp, Middletown (U.S.A.)	8.53	1,530	88% pellets	380	652	2,669
Youngstown Sheet & Tube Co., Indiana Harbor (U.S.A.)	8.53		83% pellets	328	611	2,427
Great Lakes Steel Corp, Detroit (U.S.A.)	8.84		100% pellets	307	528 +50m³ n.g.*	2,229
Ford Motor Co., Detroit (U.S.A.)	8.84		60% pellets / 40% sinter	339	609	2,127
USINOR, Dunkirk (France)	8.50	1,282	90% sinter / 10% ore	440	597	1,930
Phoenix Rheinrohr, Duisburg (W. Germany)	7.50		55% sinter	361	562	1,601
Hoesch AG, Westfalenhütte (W. Germany)	7.50		60% sinter	382	513	1,461
Amagasaki (Japan)	6.00	674	100% sinter	1,080	609 +37 kg fuel oil	1,124
La Providence, Rehon (France)	5.30	632	100% sinter	439	548	610
Kokura (Japan)	5.57	457	90% sinter / 10% ore	1,005	587 +32 kg fuel oil	555
SIDELOR (France)	5.00	567	100% ore			470

Sources: United Nations, 1966, p. 72; Kikuchi, 1967.

* Natural gas.

In 1955 it used on average 0.71 tons of coke (to make each ton of pig iron); ten years later, the average figure was 0.5 tons, and some furnaces were using only 0.43 to 0.45 tons. Some Japanese blast-furnace performances in the mid-sixties are given in Table 11, which records data for works in five other countries as well.

Locationally, these changes in blast-furnace technology and practice meant that a smaller tonnage of raw-material inputs would be assembled for each unit of iron and steel output. Consequently, the geographical pull of raw materials for the location of production was considerably lessened. Movements in the freight rates charged for the transport of raw materials reinforced this trend.

RAW-MATERIAL TRANSPORT COSTS

Trends in the costs of, and the rates charged for, iron ore transport are discussed in some detail in Chapters 9 and 10. The years 1950–65 witnessed many major improvements in the efficiency of both ocean and inland transport, especially the former. The result was a general downward movement in ocean freight rates, and the bargaining of an increasing number of low rail charges. For an iron and steel works located on the coast, with port facilities capable of handling vessels of up to 80,000 dwt, a decline in freight rates of well over 50 percent was recorded during the period, certainly for the longer hauls. For an integrated works sited inland, rate reductions of nearly 25 percent were frequently associated with the introduction of large-unit trains.

On the whole, the speed of improvement in the efficiency and rationalization of ocean shipments of coking coal and scrap was slower than in the case of ore. The major flows of coal were from the United States to Western Europe and Japan. There were also shipments from the U.S.S.R. to Japan and, toward the end of the period, from Australia to Japan. Most of the coal was carried in small tramp vessels of 10,000 to 15,000 dwt, chartered on the open market. Considerable fluctuations occurred in the rates charged for shipments. The rate for the North Atlantic run from Hampton Roads to Rotterdam moved between a high of $15 per ton in 1956 to less than $3 per ton at other times. Toward the end of the period, an increasing number of tramp vessels were chartered on long-term contracts (which stabilized their rates), and larger ships also came to be used. An increasing number of 40,000-dwt vessels were built solely for the coal trade; and when coal shipments were combined with other bulk commodity movements, vessels of 60,000 dwt and over were sometimes employed. The coal transport rate for these larger vessels was much lower than for the smaller ones. In 1965 the movement of coking coal from Hampton Roads to Japan was fixed at $5.50 per ton for vessels of over 50,000 dwt, compared with $6.50 per ton for ships of 37,500 dwt. This combination of longer charters and larger ships made a considerable impact on the delivered price of coking coal in Japan. In the early sixties the average rate for coal shipments between Australia and Tokyo Bay, by small tramp vessels chartered on the open market, was $3.70 to $3.80 per ton. The introduction of specialized bulk carriers of 40,000 dwt reduced the rate to $2 per ton. The result, together with a more competitive market for coking coal following the opening up of the Australian fields, was that the value of coking coal delivered to Japan fell from about $16 per ton to $11–$12 per ton (Nippon Kokan's *Japan Steel Notes*, February 1965).

On the other hand, the ocean transport of scrap—the most important shipments of which were from the United States to Western Europe and Japan (see Fig. 7, p. 127)—continued to remain almost entirely in the hands of the tramp market. Because of the awkward nature of scrap cargoes, plus the damage that the loading of scrap can do to ships, the rates charged tended to be higher per ton-kilometer than for either ore or coking coal. Relatively small vessels with fluctuating rates tended to be employed by the scrap trade throughout most of the period, but in 1965 a 32,000-dwt vessel was chartered for the first time to move scrap from the east coast of the United States to Japan. The charter was subsequently repeated, which would suggest a possible shift downward in the rates for ocean scrap movements prospectively.

The reduction of rail rates for the movement of bulk commodities in unit trains was pioneered for the transport of American coal—in response to the highly competitive primary fuels market created by the electricity-generating industry. And by the early sixties the iron and steel industry had won a number of special bulk freight concessions also. Unit trains were introduced on a few lines, such as the Santa Fe Railroad which hauls New Mexico coking coal to Kaiser's Fontana (California) iron and steel plant. The result was a significant reduction in Kaiser's raw-material transport costs—a reduction that was echoed in many other parts of North America and the world.

Similar discounts were negotiated for large regular movements of scrap. However, the chief point to note about scrap transport by rail is its relatively high rates per ton-kilometer compared with other bulk commodities. In 1965 the rate for single-car scrap movements between Detroit and Birmingham, Alabama, was $12.48 per ton; from San Francisco to Portland and Seattle, $9.35; and from New York to Pittsburgh, $9.75. This latter figure was not very much lower than the rates charged for moving steel products in the other direction, and was considerably higher than the $3.76 rate per ton for hauling iron ore between the east-coast ports and Pittsburgh. These high scrap freight rates were due to the much greater wear and tear on rolling stock occasioned by the loading and unloading of scrap. They meant that the interregional flow of scrap within the United States was somewhat "sticky," and they resulted in a lower ocean freight rate for shipping scrap between American east-coast ports and Japan than from those same ports by rail to Pittsburgh.

Together, these downward movements in the rates charged for transporting raw materials, plus the changes in the nature of blast-furnace burdens, meant that the reduction in the raw-material transport costs per ton of pig iron (or steel) was quite considerable between 1950 and 1965. For a hypothetical blast furnace on the eastern American seaboard— drawing its iron ore from an overseas source 8,000 kilometers away, hauling its coking coal from domestic mines, and getting its limestone from nearby quarries—raw-material transport costs in the early fifties could well have been over $20 per ton of pig iron. The cost of railing ore even a short distance from an inland mine to the port of export and loading it on board a 10,000- or 15,000-dwt vessel would be perhaps $1 per ton; sea freight and unloading expenses might be $6.50. Thus the total transport cost for ore would be at least $7.50 per ton, which, at an estimated burden in 1950 of 1.7 tons of raw ore for each ton of pig iron, gives a raw-ore transport cost of $12.75 per ton of pig iron produced (see Table 8). Rail freights on coal would be about $5 per ton, and on limestone (a shorter but less efficiently organized haul) $4 per ton. The transport costs of these two raw materials per ton of pig iron would therefore be $5.50 and $1.80 per ton. Total raw-material transport costs in 1950 might have been $20.05.

Let us assume that the same raw-material sources were being used in 1965, with the exception that a pellet plant had been constructed at the mine. The cost of hauling the prepared ore to the coast would in all probability have increased slightly, minor improvements in rail efficiency being more than offset by inflation. A rate of $1.50 per ton of ore can be suggested as not unreasonable. The ocean freight, however, might have fallen to $3 per ton, including unloading charges, as a result of the introduction of 60,000-dwt bulk carriers on term charters. The total transport cost on each ton of pellets, therefore, would be $4.50, and ore transport costs per ton of pig iron $6.08. Transport costs on coking coal by conventional means would undoubtedly have risen as a result of inflation. However, with unit trains a rate of $5.50 per ton of coal could still reasonably be assumed; coking-coal transport costs per ton of pig iron would therefore be $3.74. The rail rate on limestone might have crept up to $5 per ton. In sum, despite inflation, the total raw-material transport costs per ton of pig iron by 1965 would have fallen to $11.87, compared with a cost of $20.05 ten or fifteen years earlier.

By no means were all of the world's iron and steel works able to record such large changes in their raw-material transfer costs. Where the technology of pig iron manufacture remained unchanged, or where inefficient rail systems were used for transport, raw-material assembly costs almost certainly increased. Nevertheless, many iron and steel works were able to achieve comparable economies. And where both the iron ore and the coking coal came to be imported in large ocean carriers—as in the case of many iron and steel works in Japan and Italy—even greater savings were recorded. To these transport savings could be added, certainly in the sixties, a marked weakening in the market price of both iron ore (see Chapter 12) and coking coal. And to the extent that all these economies were grasped, the pull of raw materials as a factor in locating iron and steel production was weakened.

ALTERNATIVES TO BLAST-FURNACE REDUCTION

There are circumstances in which the blast furnace is perhaps not the most economical process by which iron ore can be reduced. Alternative technologies appear particularly feasible in those parts of the world where coking coal is more expensive than other forms of energy, such as hydroelectricity, oil, and natural gas. A number of processes have been developed to produce pig iron, sponge iron, or "reduced agglomerates" by techniques other than the classical blast furnace—but, while these processes have produced a mountain of literature and raised many hopes, their commercial application has been singularly limited. Of the 300 or so million tons of pig iron produced each year, toward the end of the period only 7 million tons or so were produced in furnaces other than the blast furnace (Hyde and Bliss, 1964).

After the blast furnace, the most widely used method of making pig iron is by means of an electric furnace. This is a process used for many years in such countries as Norway, Sweden, and Italy, which are, or in the past have been, rich in low-cost hydroelectric resources. It has these disadvantages: output has to remain on a relatively small scale (up to perhaps 200 tons per day), and the amount of energy consumed in the furnace per ton of pig iron is rather higher than in a conventional blast furnace. On the other hand, it has certain advantages: its unit capital costs are lower than those of the blast furnace; its coke consumption is less by perhaps 50 percent; and its coke quality requirements are rather less rigorous (it being possible to use the more weakly caking varieties). Its disadvantages persisted. The advantages of electric smelting, on the other hand, lessened as improved blast-furnace technology lowered coke rates. Compared with the situation in 1950, the 370 kg of coke and coke breeze used in an electric furnace to produce one ton of pig iron was not particularly striking by 1965.

After World War II, new techniques to manufacture pig iron in low-shaft furnaces were developed. By 1965 a fairly large number of these furnaces were still in use (essentially they were experimental) in the United States, West Germany, Italy, East Germany, and India. Even though the low-shaft furnace could make use of noncoking coals, it had much lower outputs and a considerably higher fuel consumption than the conventional blast furnace. As a consequence, interest in the low-shaft furnace tended to fade.

On the other hand, the desire to produce iron "directly" from ores continued and even quickened. Of the several techniques developed, the oldest is the Krupp-Renn process; it was pioneered before 1939 in Germany, and exploited particularly in Czechoslovakia after 1945. It is a process well suited to locations in which low-grade ores and low-cost solid fuel or fuel oil are readily available. It yields a 92 percent iron product called "luppen," which is suitable for use in the steel furnace. Undoubtedly the most successful of the direct-reduction processes is the Hy-L technique used at Monterrey, Mexico. It is certainly the largest production unit, with two plants producing 214,000 tons of sponge iron in 1965 for several electric steel furnaces; and a third plant, integrated with steelmaking and with an annual capacity of 165,000 tons, has been built at Veracruz (United Nations, 1968-B, p. 188). In the Hy-L process, natural gas is both the source of heat and the reductant, and it must be available at a specially low price.

Several other direct-reduction processes have interested the oil industry, partly because they might offer means of making use of its surplus products. Indeed, so many interests are anxious to promote the several direct-reduction processes—either because of the equipment they already manufacture or hope to manufacture, or because of the surplus fuels they happen to have available—that it is virtually impossible to obtain a technical and economic assessment of the processes that have been produced independently of the vested interests.

In all the direct-reduction processes there are two sets of problems. The first relates to the efficiency of the technology. All of the processes appear to offer lower capital costs per ton of product than the conventional blast furnace when small quantities of sponge iron are being produced. But there is no evidence that they can compete with either the unit capital or the processing costs of the conventional blast furnace when large-scale production is needed. A suitable locality for their use might be found in the more remote regions of technologically advanced countries, but the most likely localities would be in the developing world, where the markets for iron and steel products are quite small. A major obstacle, however, faces the developing world in the application of direct-reduction technology, which is still to a large extent experimental. There are problems enough involved in transferring an *established* technology from the advanced countries into the developing ones, but there are even more problems in transferring a *new* technology.

The second set of problems relates to the need to find markets for the resultant products—sponge iron or comparable reduced ore. Metallurgically, the nearest equivalent to these products among the various feedstocks of the steel furnace is heavy melting scrap, and therefore sponge iron and reduced ore must be made available at their potential markets at prices approximately the same as those of scrap. Possibly they could be sold at prices a little above those of scrap, since their iron content tends to be more finely controlled, and since they are much less likely to be subject to the violent price fluctuations that characterize many scrap markets. (In 1959 a ton of No. 1 heavy melting scrap in Pittsburgh cost $40.75; in 1962, it was $24.)

Toward the end of the 1950–65 period small quantities of sponge iron and other reduced agglomerates were being marketed in the developing world, principally as a feedstock for small-scale steelmaking in electric furnaces. For limited quantity production, they obviously had some advantages over blast furnaces with the same capacity. When scrap prices were high and fluctuating, steel producers occasionally used sponge iron as a supplementary feed in both blast and steel furnaces. However, this was hardly a suitable basis on which to make major investments in new direct-reduction plants. The larger the market and the scale of production envisaged, the less certain became the economics of direct-reduction technology, and the more attractive appeared the conventional blast furnace. By 1965, a future for direct-reduction processes was still highly uncertain. As Hyde and Bliss (1964) put it, "Much depends upon the acceptance by the steelmakers of such material [reduced agglomerates] as a superior blast furnace feed ideal for periods when the demand for hot metal is unusually high in relation to the number of blast furnaces in operation at the time. Even more important in attaining acceptance will be the ability of the proponents of direct reduction to produce an acceptable product and deliver it to steelmakers at prices competitive or near those of heavy melting scrap" (p. 272). Of course, should the agglomerates ever begin to make inroads into the scrap market, the price of scrap would fall, and further sales would as a result be more difficult to obtain.

Nonconventional methods of reducing iron ore have had very little impact on the overall geography of iron ore demands. And there appears little likelihood of any significant change in this state of affairs in the foreseeable future. Geographically, unintegrated processes are invariably drawn toward the sources of their raw materials—that is, to the ore plus the fuel—or to a nearby break-of-bulk point. The Orinoco Mining Company, for example, decided to construct a direct-reduction plant at Puerto Ordaz (Venezuela), where local ore and low-cost natural gas, as well as a port for the briquette exports, were readily available. Similarly, the ESSO oil company at one time suggested Goa as a good location for a reduction plant which could use local iron ore and cheap Middle Eastern oil and serve the Japanese market with the resulting "piglets." Such decisions and suggestions stem both from the fact that the reduction process causes a considerable loss of weight in the iron-bearing material, and from the feasibility of shipping pig iron, sponge iron, reduced agglomerates, etc., in bulk. With suitable transport arrangements, freight rates for these materials need only be slightly above those for shipping ore in similar-sized vessels. In the case of integrated reduction and steelmaking plants, raw-material–oriented locations have frequently been chosen. The past expense of transporting electrical energy to the markets for steel has caused a number of integrated works to use electric reduction furnaces in locations near their raw materials. It is noteworthy, however, that the second center for Hy-L production in Mexico is market-oriented. And it is not inconceivable that the use of reduced agglomerates in the developing world as a scrap replacement could also call for a market orientation of production, provided the energy and the ore could be transported to the markets for steel with comparative ease.

Changes in Steelmaking Technology

In 1950 the open-hearth furnace was central to steelmaking throughout the world. It accounted for about 80 percent of total production. Throughout the rest of the decade, its supremacy remained unchallenged. Although its capital costs were high—since the furnace, with its downtakes, checker chambers, flues, and stack, is a large and rambling structure requiring large quantities of refractory material and steel in its construction—it produced large tonnages of high-quality steel at low cost from a highly flexible combination of pig iron and scrap. And the efficiency of the process was improved steadily following the replacement of coke-oven gas by fuel oil, tar, or natural gas, the construction of progressively larger furnaces with their economies of scale, and the use of oxygen for flame enrichment and direct decarbonization.

As early as 1949, a new steelmaking process, which was eventually to spread throughout the world, was undergoing trials in Austria. This was the L.D. basic oxygen converter, an adaptation of the original Bessemer process, which waited upon the availability of "tonnage" oxygen. The new converter offered the advantages of a relatively simple, flexible, and speedy operation, which was equally well suited to 5-ton vessels as to 300-ton units. Moreover, it had a cycle time lasting only about 40 minutes—5 minutes to charge, 30 (or even 20) to process, and 5 on average for delays—compared with the 8 hours of an accelerated open-hearth furnace. At first it seemed that the basic oxygen converter would only be suitable for a charge largely composed of molten pig iron. But by 1965 it was technologically possible to use 50 or even 60 percent scrap by adding calcium carbide to provide the extra heat needed for melting the metal. A "heat-refining nozzle," which injects fuel plus oxygen into the converter to melt the charge, was developed by VOEST (an Austrian association of iron and steel works); and the British Iron and Steel Research Corporation patented the F.O.S. (fuel-oxygen-scrap) process. Both techniques allowed the converter to operate on entirely cold materials. The principal advantage of the L.D. process was that, compared with the open-hearth furnace even in its most advanced form, it offered considerable economies both in capital charges and in processing costs (United Nations, 1962-B, chap. 5, and 1964-A, p. 105; Battelle Memorial Institute, 1964). In furnaces producing 1.5 million tons of steel per year, the converter offered savings of up to $7 per ton of ingot, nearly 12 percent of the steelmaking costs in an open-hearth furnace (see Table 7).

Rather faster than most technological innovations, the basic oxygen converter took only about a decade to make a significant impact on the world steelmaking community. At the end of 1965, the total world capacity of L.D. converters—quite apart from the various modifications, such as the L.D.-A.C., the Kaldo, and the V.L.N. converters—had reached some 102 million tons. And it was reliably expected that their capacity would reach 160 million tons within another three years (*Metal Bulletin*, October 22, 1965). It appeared unlikely that any new open-hearth furnaces would ever be built again.

The country that seized most eagerly on the technical and economic advantages of the L.D. process was Japan. By 1966, in response to its burgeoning markets, Japan's iron and steel industry had installed 33 million tons of converter capacity, some 60 percent of its total steelmaking plant. The iron and steel industry of the United States, on the other hand, partly in response to the comparatively slow rate of its market growth, had shown itself initially to be rather more conservative in the adoption of the technique; by 1966, however, it had installed about 34 million tons of L.D. capacity. The Soviet Union was even more cautious; it had invested in only 5 million tons or so of L.D. plant.

An important aspect of the basic L.D. process from the viewpoint of ore demand is its requirement for iron ores with a phosphorus content of less than 0.8 percent. But since, in many parts of the world, high-phosphorus ores had traditionally been used for steelmaking, it was natural that an attempt should be made to adapt the new process to them. The O.L.P. (Oxygène Lance Poudré) process was developed by IRSID, the French metallurgical research association; and the L.D.-A.C. process was pioneered in Belgium. The rotary Kaldo steelmaking process, capable of producing steel to a wide range of specifications, was developed in Sweden to make high-quality steels from phosphoric pig iron. Efficient though all these processes, and other variants of the converter, might be in engineering terms, the basic L.D. process itself was the most successful commercially. The steel industry throughout the world adopted it readily, and it has bene- fited from the greatest technical development. As a consequence, a new and considerable premium came to be placed on low-phosphorus ores, and this has played an important part in helping to mold the changing geography of iron ore supplies (see Part II).

The conventional Bessemer furnace gradually fell out of favor as a result of the high sulfur, phosphorus, and nitrogen content of its pig iron; its production declined both absolutely and relatively. The electric steel fur- nace, on the other hand, grew substantially in importance. Although, generally speaking, electric steelmaking is rather more expensive than L.D. steelmaking (see Table 7), there are localities where the combination of scrap and electricity prices (compared with the costs of making or pur- chasing pig iron) make the electric furnace a more economical process. Dur- ing the period 1950–65, the real costs of electric steelmaking fell consider- ably—partly as a result of the construction of larger furnaces with capaci- ties of up to 200 tons, and, by 1965, talk of a 400-ton furnace. Additionally, the decline in costs resulted from the development of more efficient refrac- tories, from the fact that the real cost of electricity tended to fall rather faster than that of the other fuels used in steelmaking, and from the appli- cation of larger quantities of oxygen to speed up the smelting process. The attractions of electric steelmaking were also enhanced by the growing sophistication of steel markets, especially the tighter specifications that accompanied steel demands and the widening outlets for alloy and stain- less products. To some extent, these demands have been met by develop- ment of vacuum degassing systems for the converter process. However, by virtue of its outstanding process control whereby almost any grade or composition of steel can be made, the electric furnace is even better suited to satisfy many of the steel markets. As a result, its role in the technologi- cally advanced economies has widened considerably.

By 1965, electric furnaces were used to produce rather more than 10 per- cent of all the steel made in the United States (Battelle Memorial Institute, 1964, chaps. 8 and 9) and in the European Economic Community. In the developing regions and countries, the fact that the process is traditionally based on cold metal—scrap, reduced agglomerates, or pig iron—is a distinct advantage, particularly when the market is not large enough to warrant the construction of a blast furnace. Moreover, in some developing countries electrical energy is both relatively cheap and indigenous. Eco- nomically and politically, therefore, it naturally suggests itself as a desirable source of heat for steelmaking, the more so since the electric furnace can be scaled down fairly efficiently to produce relatively small tonnages. In 1962 about one-fourth of all the steel manufactured in Latin America was poured from electric furnaces, and in individual countries the proportion was very much higher.

To a large degree, geographical variations in the attractiveness of electric steelmaking are strongly affected by the price and the quality of scrap metal in relation to the costs of making pig iron in the same district. The somewhat volatile price of scrap in many markets in the early fifties undoubtedly restrained the expansion of electric steel production for a while. By the early sixties, however, the price of scrap in the developed economies had become more stable as a consequence of the increasingly capital-intensive nature of the scrap industry. In the United States, huge scrap processing plants were built in several metropolitan areas at a cost of approximately $2 million each. They were able to handle 1,400 cars each week, and produced between 0.25 and 0.5 million tons of shredded scrap each year. The value of their highly consistent product was somewhat higher than ordinary bundles of mixed scrap; but its price was steadier. In addition, where scrap was produced in the course of operations within an integrated works (the so-called circulating scrap), a very stable price could be allocated to it by the accountants. Therefore it is not surprising that many of the world's largest integrated iron and steel works include an electric smelter in their equipment.

The major geographical implications of these changes in steelmaking technology—apart from the new premium placed on low-phosphorus ores and the advantages of larger-scale production (see Chapter 4)—were twofold. In the first place, the distinctly lower costs of L.D. steelmaking meant that those countries or regions that were able to adopt it on a large scale had a significant competitive advantage. Certainly older, open-hearth furnaces might for a time be able to produce steel at unit working costs equal to the unit total costs of a new converter; but this advantage was short-lived. Any industry that equipped itself for L.D. steelmaking was thus able simultaneously to arm itself with lower marginal costs than could be obtained by open-hearth or electric steelmakers, and as a result could gain considerable marketing advantages. The Japanese steel industry stood in this position in 1965.

In the second place, the new steelmaking technology could be transferred rather more easily to developing countries and regions than could the open-hearth furnace. Both the L.D. and the electric furnace could be scaled down to produce small tonnages of steel relatively efficiently, and their operational simplicity was a distinct advantage for an inexperienced management and labor force. This did not mean, of course, that the developing world was able immediately to attract a large number of new steel plants; it simply slightly lessened their difficulties in attracting such investment (see Chapter 4).

CHANGES IN FINISHING TECHNOLOGY

In large measure because of the size, the demands, and the opportunities of its domestic market, the iron and steel industry of the United States has for many decades tended to pioneer the improvement of steel-finishing processes. From the strip mill, which was developed there in the thirties and only spread overseas in the postwar years, to the application of the computer controls throughout the rolling mills, American companies have set the pace of finishing-mill development. Perhaps some of their technology has been too readily adopted in parts of the world where market conditions do not fully justify its introduction. Whereas the installation of double-reduction tinning mills—to satisfy demands and meet competition in the beer can, frozen fruit juice, and motor oil container markets—made economic sense in the United States, it was by no means certain that Western European markets were ready for such facilities by the mid-sixties. Yet the technology-proud managements of a number of Western European iron and steel companies decided to install these mills irrespective of their commercial prospects.

Between 1950 and 1965, there were no really revolutionary changes made in the rolling operations of the steel industry. Rather, there was a steady modification and improvement of existing technology and its gradual diffusion throughout the world. The result was a gradual raising of the level of the industry's efficiency and an improvement in the quality of its products. The more exacting demands for steel plates, for example, were met by the replacement of 2-high by 4-high rolling mills. In the light-product sector, high-capacity multistrand continuous mills were able to manufacture rods, bars, and strip to higher standards of precision and finish than those manufactured in older mills. In nearly all types of mills, automation and the application of computer technology permitted more accurate control of, for example, the gauge of strip in the hot and cold mills, or the thickness of tin and zinc in the electrolytic tinning and strip-galvanizing plants. As a result, the productivity of both men and machines was improved. Equally noteworthy was the tendency for mills to become both larger and faster and so to exploit the advantages of large-scale production, which are demonstrated in Table 12. Considerable savings can be made by rolling flat products in a mill with an annual capacity of 1.5 million tons as against one of 0.5 million tons—a saving of $28 per ton, or the value of a ton of scrap in many parts of Western Europe and the United States at the

TABLE 12. Estimated Cost of Rolling Flat Products in Hypothetical Plants of Different Sizes[a]

(Dollars at 1962 prices)

Cost item	Annual capacity of plant in thousands of tons of finished products							
	100	200	400	500	800	1,000	1,500
Ingot steel	$140.92	$129.25	$105.20	$101.49	$92.95	$86.39	$83.59
Fuel (blast-furnace gas or equivalent purchase)	2.01	2.01	1.48	1.48	1.67	1.54	1.54
Credit for scrap	−22.22	−19.97	−14.10	−13.69	−11.68	−9.94	−9.66
Cost of ferrous material	120.71	111.39	92.58	89.28	82.94	78.53	75.47
Salaries and wages	15.52	12.60	6.22	5.62	4.51	3.92	3.30
Other conversion costs	12.30	11.25	10.67	10.60	8.60	7.75	7.30
Total direct cost	148.53	135.24	109.47	105.50	96.05	90.20	86.07
Capital charges[b]	43.46	38.60	29.70	25.85	19.80	17.92	17.37
Total costs	191.99	173.84	139.17	131.35	115.85	108.12	103.44

Source: United Nations, 1964-A, p. 107.

[a] On the basis of the best possible yield of the equipment selected for each size of plant, the physical input per ton of finished products for a plant with an annual capacity of 100,000 tons of finished products is 1.66 tons; with a 200,000-ton capacity, 1.66 tons; with a 400,000-ton capacity, 1.51 tons; with a 500,000-ton capacity, 1.51 tons; with a 800,000-ton capacity, 1.45 tons; with a 1,000,000-ton capacity, 1.39 tons; and with a 1,500,000-ton capacity, 1.39 tons.

[b] Nine percent on the capital invested in the rolling and roughing mill without considering taxes, profits, etc.

time. Such statistics underline the economic advantages of those works that are able to utilize large units of production.

A major new technology did emerge at the primary stage of the finishing operations. This was the continuous-casting process (Britain, Iron and Steel Institute, 1965; OECD, 1964; Association of Iron and Steel Engineers, 1964). Instead of pouring an ingot of 10 tons or more, letting it cool, bringing it to a uniform temperature in a soaking pit, and then passing it through a primary mill, the continuous-casting plant accepts molten steel in a water-cooled mold. It then allows the steel to be continuously withdrawn from the bottom of the mold, as soon as a sufficiently strong shell has frozen, in the form of an endless cast. With the help of water sprays, this cast completely solidifies shortly after leaving the mold. Subsequently it is cut into the exact lengths required for further processing. At root, the technique means that an uninterrupted steelmaking process replaces a batch process, with all the economies such a change affords.

Continuous casting began on quite a small scale—in the tonnages handled, in the number of plants constructed, and in the size of the products cast. For some years, slabs proved especially difficult to pour; and certain grades of steel, particularly rimming steel, seemed unsuited to the process. However, by 1965 there were, throughout the world, well over one hundred plants continuously casting steel. They were pouring sections as small as 5 cm^2, and slabs as large as 150 cm wide; and they were handling a wide variety of steels, including rimming and stainless steel. The U.S.S.R. invested most heavily in the process, but by 1965 Britain and West Germany together had more plants than the U.S.S.R.

The advantages offered by continuous casting over conventional equipment are lower investment and operating costs. Particularly is this the case when smaller tonnages are being produced. These economies derive basically from a much improved ingot yield. Whereas up to 15 or even 20 percent of an ingot is wasted and recycled as scrap with conventional finishing technology, only 2 to 6 percent is "lost" in continuous casting. Further economies result from the fact that a continuous-cast slab or billet demands less rolling, and claims have been made that the surface quality of the steel is better. Continuous casting also affords considerable savings of physical space in an iron and steel works. Some costings appear in Table 13.

The apparent advantages of continuous casting under many economic conditions, particularly in the regions and countries with small demands, meant that its development was greeted with enthusiasm by those concerned with the introduction of steelmaking into the developing world (United Nations, 1964-A). Yet by 1965 there was still no unanimity among steelmakers concerning the advantages of the technology as the *principal* finishing facility in large integrated mills. There were two reasons for this

TABLE 13. ESTIMATED COST OF ROLLING MERCHANT BARS AND LIGHT PROFILES IN PLANTS OF DIFFERENT TECHNOLOGY AND SIZE

(Dollars at 1962 prices; tons of finished merchant bars)

Cost item	Open hearth and blooming mill (capacity of plant in 1,000 tons)			L.D. and continuous casting (capacity of plant in 1,000 tons)		
	100	200	300	100	200	300
Steel ingots[a].................	$104.83	$96.16	$91.02	$83.04	$74.90	$71.27
Fuel (blast-furnace gas)........	1.11	1.11	1.11			
Credit for scrap..............	−7.82	−7.03	−6.74	−4.89	−4.39	−3.83
Total raw materials...........	98.12	90.54	85.39	78.15	70.51	67.44
Salaries and wages...........	6.00	4.58	3.87	7.80	5.47	4.37
Other conversion costs........	8.40	7.85	7.40	7.30	6.10	5.95
Total direct cost.............	112.52	102.97	96.66	93.00	82.68	77.91
Capital charges[b]..............	12.18	11.26	10.39	8.05	7.27	6.83
Total costs...............	124.70	114.23	107.05	101.05	89.95	84.79

Source: United Nations, 1964-A, p. 107.

[a] In the classical case, 1,235 tons of ingot per ton of finished product; 1,145 with continuous casting.
[b] Nine percent on the capital invested in the rolling and roughing mill without considering taxes, profits, etc.

lack of certainty: (1) it remained impossible to produce, with sufficient reliability, the perfect surface finish that is required for many steel sheets; and (2) whereas ingot casting requires a major disaster to make it quite impossible to dispose of a complete batch of steel, the failure of a continuous-casting plant presents the steelmaker with major problems (and high costs) if standby facilities are not available. Although a growing number of continuous-casting plants were installed as supplementary finishing lines—as a means of *increasing* the capacity of a steelworks at the primary stage of rolling—major investment decisions were still generally being made against the adoption of the technology as the core of finishing operations. In the United States and Japan alike, traditional primary rolling facilities were still being ordered for new, large integrated works. However, it appeared to be only a matter of time before experience, reliability, and confidence allowed continuous casting to move to the center of the steel-finishing stage.

THE TOTAL PRODUCTION SYSTEM

A consistent feature of the industry throughout the 1950–65 period was the continuing and decisive economic advantage of integrated production —whenever the market was large enough to justify the installation of a blast furnace. This was as true in the fully planned economies (Bannyy *et al.*, 1960) as it was in the market and mixed economies. The advantages of integrated production stemmed in particular from economies in the use of heat and movement of scrap, and the ease of management. The demand for iron ore increasingly reflected the geography of integrated iron and steel production as a result.

Perhaps the principal economy of integrated production stems from the ability to balance the heat and energy availabilities and requirements within a works. Within an integrated works the waste gases from the coke ovens and blast furnaces can be used to heat the soaking pits in the hot-metal shops and the reheating chambers at various stages of the rolling operations. The same gases can be used to generate electricity (which in turn is needed to power the production processes) and to heat the coke ovens. If there are chemical works associated with the iron and steel works, it may be possible to use the same gases for chemical manufacture. Production in an integrated works also saves in the actual quantity of heat required, by using the minimum amount of cold metal in the various stages of the production process.

Integrated plants offer additional savings in the matter of scrap movements, especially as a result of the physical juxtaposition of the finishing operations and the actual steel production. Sometimes nearly one-half of all the scrap used in a steel furnace originates from within the steelworks itself. Poorly made ingots, badly shaped slabs, crop ends from bars and sheets, and the trimmings from the strip mill can all be fed back into the steel furnace as "process" or "circulating" scrap. To transport this scrap within an integrated works is clearly both easier and cheaper than to transport it between unintegrated works.

Another advantage of integrated iron and steel production is that a single management controls the total production system, and is afforded many opportunities to reduce costs which are denied to the balkanized managements responsible for different plants. With single management, the possibilities of disrupted raw-material and product flows are reduced, and new opportunities are created for the better timing of additional investments in the several stages of the steel production process.

However, circumstances do exist in which unintegrated production is both desirable and economical. Sometimes the most efficient means of meeting small and geographically isolated demands for steel is to locate a rolling mill at the market and feed it with semifinished steel from larger and more distant works, especially since freight rates on billets are sometimes one-half of those on finished products. The demands of many of the small isolated markets in prairie and western Canada are satisfied in this way. Occasionally, too, it is advantageous both to manufacture steel and to roll ingots at a market, without integrating back into pig iron production. Based upon supplies of locally produced scrap, as well as its own "circulating" scrap, an electric furnace and rolling mill can economically produce, say, 250,000 tons of products each year; investments of this type have been made in some of the larger cities in the Great Plains and Far West of the United States. Where steel demands are satisfied in this fashion, there is, of course, no associated local demand for iron ore. It would be impossible to justify economically the backward integration of such an operation into pig iron production in a small blast furnace. The advantage of small market-oriented mills and furnaces stems in part from the ability of their management to gain detailed knowledge of local demands and to have the operational flexibility required best to serve them. At the same time, a plant in such a location is frequently well placed to integrate back into pig iron production once the market has grown to justify this development.

A large integrated works takes several years to build, and a question naturally arises as to the best timing for the construction of its various parts. One solution that has proved highly satisfactory is for the rolling mills to be installed first of all. Temporarily, these can be fed with slabs or ingots from existing works elsewhere. The construction of the steel furnaces then follows, with pig iron being supplied either hot or cold from other works. Finally, integration is completed with the erection of the necessary blast furnaces. This approach was adopted by the Bethlehem Steel Corporation at its "green field" Burns Harbor site in Indiana. Plate, cold-rolled steel and tinplate, and hot-sheet mills were constructed first of all, with a combined capacity for rolling nearly 2 million tons of finished products each year. They were fed in the first instance by slabs transported 800 kilometers (at $5.25 per ton) from the company's huge Lackawanna works in New York State; the slabs were handled hot in specially equipped 80-wagon unit trains, and they were still warm on arrival. In this way the finishing facilities could be steadily run in without the management's simultaneously having to face the complexities of constructing and running in the steel and blast furnaces. As a result, the works could be better assured a smooth takeoff. In such circumstances, the demand for steel in Greater Chicago was temporarily reflected in enlarged iron ore demands in upper New York State until the L.D. and blast-furnace plants were installed at Burns Harbor. Such a construction procedure is doubly useful if surplus steel and pig iron capacity is conveniently available at nearby existing plants.

Unintegrated operations can serve as short-term means of balancing out steel-rolling and steelmaking capacity in different locations; they can also serve to balance up pig iron and steelmaking capacities when they are geographically out of phase. Traditionally, pig iron has nearly always been shipped cold between works. But in recent years it has become possible to transport molten pig iron over increasing distances. In the United States, hot pig iron was for a while transported 24 kilometers between the Interlake and Acme plants in Chicago, following the merger of these two companies and a shortage of blast-furnace capacity at the latter works. In Belgium, pig iron has been more regularly transported as a hot metal by rail in thermos wagons between Seraing and Chertal, a distance of 22 kilometers; the company concerned, Espérance-Longdoz, has also made experimental runs from Chertal to Couillet (a distance of 110 km) and from Chertal to Arbed in Luxembourg (248 km). In the latter case, the shipment was in transit for twelve hours, during which the temperature of the pig iron only fell from 1334°C to 1227°C. This suggests the technical possibility of transporting hot pig iron over perhaps 300 or 400 kilometers. However, technical possibilities and financial advantage are quite different things, and until more costings on such movements have been published, an economic judgment of their worth must be suspended.

The greater part of pig iron transfers are still in the form of cold metal. In the form of small bars, it can be handled in bulk; and, although the handling charges are very much higher than those of iron ore, the actual line-haul rates are only a little higher than the rates for small-scale movements of iron ore. Most of the pig iron transported between works is the surplus metal of integrated operations, for, as several Russians have put it, "Plants engaging in blast furnace production alone are irrational as in such cases the power resources are not adequately utilised" (Bannyy et al., 1960, p. 112). The exceptions, such as the unintegrated blast furnaces at Port Kembla in Australia, at Newcastle in Natal, and at Ostkombinat in East Germany, are a response to unusual geographical circumstances, political pressures, or mistaken locational decisions. Their survival may be made possible by endemic shortage of blast-furnace capacity in several steel-producing centers; but their expansion would be unlikely to meet with commercial success. Their existence, however, does bear upon the geography of iron ore demands.

A final circumstance in which unintegrated operations can prove to be advantageous is during a period of locational rationalization. As noted in Chapter 4, the changing economic and geographical forces molding the iron and steel industry in the older steel-producing countries have necessitated reshaping the distribution of production. To achieve this end, some stages of an integrated operation in one place need to be phased out as part of a program for gaining scale economies elsewhere. A small blast furnace might be closed down in one location, an outdated rolling mill in another. Such programs inevitably mean that imbalances of capacity within a works have to be rectified by the haulage of pig iron, ingots, slabs, etc., from other plants.

Notwithstanding the existence and occasional importance of unintegrated operations, the overall preference of the iron and steel industry for integrated operations remains. Closely related to this feature of the industry's system technology is another feature—namely, the gradual movement toward continuous rather than batch production. The initial success of continuous casting has been discussed. In addition, a new continuous process—spray steelmaking—was developed in Britain to reach the semicommercial pilot plant stage. In spray steelmaking, molten pig iron and flux from a tundish are broken up by jets of oxygen from an atomizer ring as they are poured into a receiving ladle. Steel is produced basically by removing the carbon, silicon, manganese, etc., from pig iron by oxidation. The rate at which it can be done depends largely on the rate at which oxygen can be brought into contact with the unrefined metal. The L.D. process is quicker than the open-hearth process, simply because large quantities of oxygen are injected into the metal. Spray steelmaking carries this principle one stage further by atomizing the hot pig iron and surrounding the small particles with the oxidizing agent. Its potential success raises the possibility of engineering a continuous flow of hot metal from a blast furnace or a direct-reduction plant, through a spray steelmaking unit and into a continuous-casting plant for manufacture into, say, billets.

If such a set of processes could be satisfactorily developed on a reasonable scale, it would immediately offer steel producers better quality control, for, once steady states have been achieved, the end products gain a far more consistent quality. The quality of billets, for example, would show considerable improvement, since batch production, with the temperature of the metal unavoidably higher at the beginning than at the end of the operation, inevitably leads to differences in their physical properties. The engineering simplicity of the several continuous processes also offers the prospect of both lower capital and process costs. The continuous production of iron and steel was certainly not a feature of the industry between 1950 and 1965; its arrival by 1980, however, cannot be discounted. Implicit in the technology is a closer spatial accord between steel production and iron ore demands.

The system technology of the period tended to give encouragement to those who were concerned with helping the developing countries of the world to establish iron and steel manufacture. Again and again it was suggested that technological innovation was making it easier to locate iron and steel plants in regions with small and unsophisticated markets and to provide those regions with works that could compete with the larger plants of the technologically advanced countries (United Nations, 1964-A). Continuous casting, like direct reduction and the L.D. processes before it, was hailed as a major step in solving the economic problems of iron and steel manufacture in countries with severe shortages of capital and a need for relatively small quantities of steel. In the short run, such observations were probably valid. New technologies are inevitably developed on a small scale in the first instance and by definition are more efficient than older techniques in plants of comparable size. Before the new processes have been scaled up, there is often a period during which small-scale production based on new technology in a developing country has a chance to compete with large-scale production using conventional technology in the advanced economies. In the longer run, however, successful new processes tend to be adopted by the iron and steel industries of the developed countries, and are scaled up, with the result that the apparent opportunity for competitive production in the smaller markets is quickly eroded away. In addition, there remains the problem (mentioned earlier in the case of direct reduction) of transferring a new technology to, and helping to develop it in, the relatively alien environment of the developing world. Experience suggests that the impetus for the development of iron and steel production in the developing economies—and hence any growth of their iron ore demands— came more from purely political and political-economic forces than from technological developments (see Chapter 5).

Perhaps the most important feature of the changing technology of iron and steel production between 1950 and 1965—a feature quite alien to the needs of the developing world—was the scaling up of operations within the whole system and the derivation therefrom of substantial economies. In 1952 the Anglo-American Council on Productivity suggested that there were few scale economies to be derived from plants above 0.75 to 1 million ingot tons. In 1956, J. S. Bain argued that the optimum size of an integrated strip mill was between 1 and 2.5 million ingot tons. But by 1965 it was widely recognized that a useful initial size for an integrated works was between 4 and 5 million ingot tons. Such a plant enabled one modern primary rolling mill of optimum capacity to be utilized effectively; and it could be associated satisfactorily with four large blast furnaces and perhaps three large oxygen converters. Provided the market and the raw-material circumstances were right, works of 8 to 10 million ingot tons capacity were regarded as both technically feasible and economically desirable (Dastur and Lalkaka, 1964). And serious consideration was being given to works of up to 15 million tons.

Throughout the period, and worldwide, iron and steel plants were built larger and larger, and plans existed to make them larger still. By 1965 the Bethlehem Steel Corporation at Sparrows Point (near Baltimore) had 10 blast furnaces, 35 open-hearth furnaces, and an ingot capacity of over 8 million tons per year; its other works, at Lackawanna, New York, was slightly smaller; and its new plant at Burns Harbor, Indiana, was planned for an eventual capacity of at least 10 million tons. In the U.S.S.R., the Magnitogorsk works had an ingot capacity of 8.5 million tons per year, and works of 6 million and 6.5 million tons were planned for Cherepovets and Novo-Lipetsk, respectively. In Czechoslovakia, the new Kosice works was laid out for an ultimate capacity of 8 million tons. And in Japan the same trend toward larger plants prevailed. The combined capacity of the adjacent and integrated Yawata and Tobata plants on the island of Kyushu was 7.7 million in ingot tons in 1965. The newest plant of Nippon Kokan at Fukuyama was laid out for a planned capacity of 8 million tons per year. And the new Mizushima works of Kawasaki, the Oita works of Fuji, and the Kashima works of Sumitomo were each designed on the assumption that they would eventually produce 12 million ingot tons of steel.

Although there are several facets to the matter of scale economies (see Chapter 4), central to them all is the greater technical efficiency of larger plants. With relative prices constantly changing and with inflation affecting all costings, accurate data cannot be produced on the total economic effect of the technological advances made during the 1950–65 period. Some measure of the changes has been suggested by Cartwright (1964) in his consideration of sheet and tinplate production in Britain. He noted that in the early sixties a domestic and overseas market for rather less than 6 million tons of products was satisfied from five plants with a combined capacity of 8 million ingot tons (Table 14). With 15 blast and 46 steel furnaces, 5 slabbing mills, and 5 strip mills, the works originally cost $1,733 million and would have cost much more to replace. While most of the equipment was little more than ten or fifteen years old, the geographical distribution of the investment and its division between five separate works dated back to 1937 (see Chapter 5). By adopting good modern practice, these five works could be replaced by two. Six new blast furnaces could do the work of the existing 15; six L.D. steel furnaces could replace the existing 46; and 2 large slabbing mills and 2 hot-strip mills could achieve the required 6 million tons of product. Moreover, the 1964 capital costs of the two replacement plants would have been less than the original costs of the existing five; and their process costs would also have been lower through the economies of large-scale production, the smaller unit consumption of coke, scrap, and electricity (only partly offset by higher ore and oil costs), and the huge gains that larger works offer in labor productivity. Enormous though these gains in efficiency might be, it is not unreasonable to suggest that even more scale economies could probably be grasped by having only one works rather than two.

The implications of the effect of technological change on the production system as a whole are clear. During the 1950–65 period, the number of iron and steel works in the world grew much more slowly than the rate of increase in steel demands. In fact, in certain countries a growth of demand went hand in hand with a contraction in the number of iron and steel plants. With the industry concentrating spatially on progressively fewer

TABLE 14. COMPARISON OF EXISTING AND OPTIMUM FLAT-PRODUCT PRODUCTION FACILITIES IN BRITAIN, CIRCA 1964

Item	Existing, 1964	Optimum
FACILITIES		
Annual ingot capacity.......	8 million tons	8 million tons
Number of works...........	5	2
Coke ovens...............	945	520
Blast furnaces.............	15	6
Hearth diameter..........	7.25 to 9.50 m	9.75 m
Steel furnaces		
Open-hearth.............	34 ⎫	
L.D. & LDAC...........	8 ⎬ 46	6 L.D. (300 tons capacity)
V.L.N..................	4 ⎭	
Slabbing mills.............	5	2
Hot-strip mills.............	5	2
Cold mills................	11	6
CAPITAL COST		
Total ($ million)...........	1,733*	1,469
Per annual ton ($)..........	216	196

INPUTS

	Per year (*millions*)	Per ton of finished product	Per year (*millions*)	Per ton of finished product
Coking coal...............	5.7 tons	0.965 tons	4.2 tons	0.712 tons
Oil in blast furnaces........			1.01 tons	0.171 tons
Iron ore..................	9.55 tons	1.62 tons	10.0 tons	1.69 tons
Scrap.....................	3.46 tons	0.585 tons	2.12 tons	0.426 tons
Fuel oil for steel plant.......	1.18 tons	0.20 tons		
Electricity................	2,770 kwhr	47 kwhr	2,120 kwhr	36 kwhr
Man-hours................	143	24.2	45	7.6

Source: Cartwright, 1964, pp. 26–27.
* Original deflated cost.

locations for a given volume of production (this in turn having a comparable spatial effect on the demand for iron ore), it became increasingly imperative that the right, low-cost locations be chosen for iron and steel manufacture.

In sum, changes in the technology of iron and steel production during the period under review placed a new premium on low-phosphorus ores; they promoted the emergence of important new and rapidly growing markets for ore; they encouraged the development of large centers of demand within those markets; and they helped to reorientate the demands for ore toward the countries and regions with substantial steel consumption. In the next chapter, the behavior of the iron and steel industry in those markets will be examined more closely.

CHAPTER 4

Size and Distribution of Iron and Steel Works

In preceding chapters the weakening locational attractions of raw materials for iron and steel production and the trend toward more market-oriented production were noted, but the specific nature of the market's pull on the industry in its locational decisions was not explored. In reality, the markets for steel, as expressed geographically, are a complex "palimpsest" of large and small purchasers. They are scattered unevenly between and within towns and cities, and they represent varied qualitative demands. The role of the market in the geographical behavior of the iron and steel industry—and hence in the spatial characteristics of ore demands—is examined more fully in this chapter.

The primary forces influencing the locational pattern of iron and steel production *within* any particular market are the scale economies of manufacture and the costs of transporting the finished steel products. Where the economies of scale in production are large and the product transport costs small, the ideal locational response of the industry will be to dispose a few large works throughout the market area. On the other hand, where the scale economies of production are small and product transport costs high, the industry's most appropriate locational response will be to construct a large number of small works.

SCALE ECONOMIES IN IRON AND STEEL PRODUCTION

Scale economies embrace three quite distinct sets of gains: (1) technological, (2) internal, and (3) external economies. The purely *technological* scale economies are the unit cost reductions that follow from the use of larger pieces of equipment. They are made possible by the division of labor, the integration and simultaneous performance of formerly separate processes, and the mechanical advantages of large items of machinery

63

(United Nations, 1964-B). The gains tend to be greatest at the lower end of the scale when relatively small-capacity equipment and works are replaced by larger ones. Table 15 demonstrates how a theoretical increase in the scale of integrated steel production (in 1948) from 250,000 tons per year to 500,000 tons reduced the total cost of a ton of finished steel by over $20. However, a further doubling of the scale of production reduced costs by only $10 per ton. No matter how small the marginal gains, there would still appear to be technological scale economies available in works of 4 or 5 million annual tons and over. Associated with these are certain unique advantages to very large iron and steel works, which are not fully revealed in a normal set of engineering cost estimates, such as appear in Table 15. Only very large works can afford to install modern automation and computer equipment, which not only increase productivity and reduce costs but also permit higher standards of process control and product quality. A further technical (and economic) advantage to large integrated works is that fuller use can be made of the by-products at the intermediate stages of manufacture. The construction of a chemical plant to process the by-products of the coke ovens is an example.

The *internal* economies of scale in iron and steel production are essentially locational economies, as exemplified in the savings made in standby plant at larger iron and steel works, the administrative economies of larger plants, and the gains stemming from the provision of common works services such as workshops, research facilities, canteens, health facilities, and playing fields. Internal scale economies originate fundamentally from the ability to spread the economic and social overheads of a plant over a larger volume of production. The costs of marketing finished

TABLE 15.   ESTIMATED COST OF MANUFACTURING FINISHED STEEL AT DIFFERENT SCALES OF PRODUCTION, LATIN AMERICA, 1948

(*Dollars per ton*)

Item	Capacity of plant in thousands of tons/year			
	50	250	500	1,000
Raw materials........................	$ 33.84	$ 31.26	$ 31.26	$ 25.68
Labor.................................	32.00	15.20	8.57	6.60
Capital charges.......................	122.93	101.20	87.10	85.05
Maintenance, etc......................	20.59	11.11	10.57	9.83
Total.............................	209.36	158.77	137.50	127.16
Investment/ton.......................	492.00	405.00	348.00	340.00

Source: United Nations, 1961, p. 44.

Note: The costs were taken from engineering calculations for hypothetical integrated plants at Sparrows Point, Maryland. However, in order to reflect Latin American conditions, the estimates on labor costs were figured at 50% of those in the U.S.A., and capital charges at 25%.

products, the staff needed to maintain machinery and equipment, the bulk purchase of raw materials, advertising, specialized management, and the like, all come within this category. One source has suggested that "economies of scale realized through facilities for economic overheads seem to be at least as important as technological economies of scale in a large number of industries" (United Nations, 1964-B, p. 55).

The *external* economies of scale are those that accrue to works sufficiently near to other steelworks to take advantage of shared services. The common use of a port, educational facilities serving a district with several steelworks, the agglomeration of industrial services, advertising agencies, the representatives of machinery manufacturers, and the like, all represent part of a specialized industrial and regional growth process and afford economic advantages to the individual firms. Such external economies are abundantly available to iron and steel works in, say, Chicago and the Ruhr, but clearly denied to the Taranto steelworks in southern Italy and most of the plants in the developing world.

Scale economies are important to the profitability of the iron and steel industry, but of the three sets of gains not all have been (and perhaps cannot be) measured with the same degree of thoroughness. While quantitative evidence is widely available on technological economies, only a limited amount of data can be obtained on internal economies, and virtually none on external economies. This does not mean, however, that internal and external economies of scale in integrated steel production are unimportant. It simply reflects the difficulties that stand in the way of accurate measurement. The costings available on what are essentially technological economies of scale understate the advantages to large works, especially groups of large works, in the production of low-cost iron and steel. Thus, while the figures in Table 15 embrace the impact of technological scale economies (as reflected in lower unit costs of capital and labor at larger steel production plants) the internal scale economies of the industry are only partly mirrored in the figures. The lower raw-material costs, for example, are doubtless in part a reflection of the advantages of bulk purchasing; and the improved maintenance costs of the larger works are a measure of the greater use to which they can put their skilled labor, engineering workshops, and the like. Yet nowhere in the costings is there any recognition of the lower unit expenses to the large iron and steel works of, say, advertising and selling, or the provision of social overheads. And external scale economies are completely neglected in the costings.

The separate cost breakdowns in Tables 7, 10, and 12 for pig iron production, steel production, and steel finishing, respectively, reveal that at every stage of the manufacturing process economies are available in both labor and capital costs with an increase in size of plant. These cost breakdowns support the view that, regardless of any geographical variations in factor prices, big plants are inherently more efficient than small ones (Figure 2). The costings also indicate that large-scale operations offer greater relative savings in the costs of labor than in the costs of capital. In Table 15 an increase in plant capacity from 0.25 to 1 million tons reduces labor costs by nearly 57 percent, whereas capital charges fall by only about 16 percent. The exploitation of scale economies is therefore a matter of greater importance in the developed economies (where hourly labor rates are high) than in the developing ones. However, such an observation must not be taken to imply that the iron and steel industry can remain indifferent to the matter of scale economies in the developing world. Quite the contrary is in fact the case (see Chapter 5).

Perhaps the most interesting point about technological scale economies in iron and steel production is the fact that the optimum scale of output at each stage of the production process appears to be achieved at a different level. It follows that it is impossible to construct an integrated works in which equipment of an optimum size can be used throughout. For example, by 1965 there was evidence that, under identical burden conditions, the blast furnace with the lowest unit costs was one with an output of about 5,000 tons per day—that is, a production of perhaps 1.8 million tons per year. However, apart from the need for insurance against mechanical

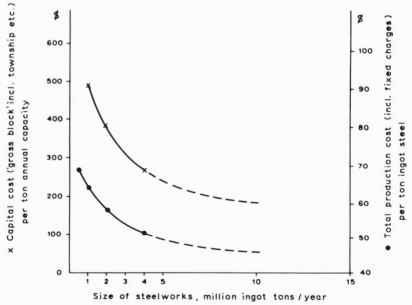

FIGURE 2. Scale economies in iron and steelmaking: variations in capital and total production costs with size of works, circa 1962. (From the British Iron and Steel Institute, 1964.)

breakdown, the management of an integrated works would be reluctant to rely on a single furnace, since provision has to be made for continuity of steel production while that furnace is being re-lined. Two such furnaces would thus be required, and, from the viewpoint of pig iron manufacture, the technologically optimum size of an integrated works would be one capable of consuming about 3.5 million tons of pig iron each year. At the same time, there was evidence that for L.D. steel production 300-ton converters offered the lowest unit costs. Two of these, with only one being used at any one time while the other was being re-lined, would have an annual output of about 3.5 million ingot tons of steel. With at least 20 percent, and possibly 30 percent, of the metallics coming from scrap, it would be impossible for these two L.D. furnaces to utilize fully all the pig iron of the two blast furnaces. Yet a third 300-ton converter would create surplus steelmaking capacity.

Furthermore, the primary rolling mill is one of the more expensive pieces of equipment in an integrated works. Geared to the needs of, say, a strip mill producing a 200-cm continuous wide strip, a plant of technically optimum size would be capable of rolling 4 million tons of slabs or blooms per year; these in turn would need approximately 4.5 million tons of ingots. As to the other possible finishing mills, rather smaller tonnages of steel would be required. A billet mill in 1965 reached its most desirable economic size at about 1.25 million tons; a semicontinuous light-plate mill, at 0.75 million tons. Other mills reached their optimum size rolling smaller tonnages: an ideal (four-stand) wire-rod mill would have a capacity of 0.55 million tons, a heavy-section mill 0.6 million tons, a rail mill 0.5 million tons, and a light-section or bar mill 0.35 million tons. Therefore, with all the rolling mills (except the strip mill) achieving their optimum performance at such small tonnages, it was not surprising that most integrated works tended to be multiproduct works; they could thereby take advantage of large-scale production in the making of pig iron and steel and at the same time fully utilize low-cost finishing mills. It also followed that the geographical distribution of bar, section, and rod production throughout the world was much more scattered than that of wide-sheet production. The advantages of balancing the several optima in rolling operations with the lowest-cost pig iron and steel production are obvious.

Differentials in the characteristics of technological scale economies at each stage of the iron and steel production process make the search for the "ideal" size of either integrated or unintegrated works somewhat fruitless. In London, the Benson Committee (British Iron and Steel Federation, 1966-A) made some interesting assessments of the most satisfactory size of works under foreseeable British conditions. They concluded that in the matter of wide-strip production, economies in the blast furnace should marginally be forgone in favor of maximizing the throughput of the primary (slabbing) mill. Anticipating the development of larger converters, the committee argued that an optimum scale of steel production could be envisaged in such a works. The most economical primary mill for strip production in 1965 was judged to have a product capacity of 4.25 million tons. It required 4.9 million tons of ingots and (assuming the use of 1.6 million tons of scrap) 3.8 million tons of pig iron. Two 350-ton converters were thought to be the cheapest means of producing the steel. Pig iron was thought to be best produced in three blast furnaces, each with a diameter of 8.84 meters, with an output of 3,800 tons per furnace-day, a somewhat smaller and a slightly more costly scale of production than the optimum.

For the manufacturers of other products, the Benson Committee considered that the most appropriate size of primary mill was 3 million tons. This would require 3.6 million tons of ingots and (assuming the use of 1.2 million tons of scrap) 2.8 million tons of pig iron. Compared with the strip mill, smaller steel furnaces but larger blast furnaces could best be associated with such a primary mill. The suggestion was made that the 3.6 million tons of required ingots could be most economically produced in two 275-ton converters, while the pig iron could be smelted in two furnaces of 9.5-meters diameter with a daily output of 4,200 tons each. And in the case of a nonintegrated works, the Committee suggested that the key determinant of size was usually the billet mill. Ideally, it would require between 1 and 1.5 million tons of steelmaking capacity, and this could best be provided by the installation of four or five electric-arc furnaces using large quantities of locally available scrap.

Such assessments of the optimum size of iron and steel works are subject to considerable historical, technological, and geographical variations. In 1950 the optimum size of a continuous-wide-strip mill appeared to have a capacity of 1 million tons per year, while the most economical section mills and heavy-plate mills had outputs of 0.2 and 0.4 million tons, respectively (United Nations, 1950-B, pp. 37–38; Burn, 1961, p. 272). Since 1950, however, there has been a persistent tendency for the optimum size of plant to increase. And it is not unreasonable to assume that in the future—particularly with the control of large units of production becoming technically easier through the use of computers—there will be a continuing upward movement of the optimum size of plant. Technological variations in the optimum size of iron and steel works are equally obvious. The solutions offered by the Benson Committee generally assumed the use of conventional blast furnaces, the L.D. converter, and traditional primary mills. If, on the other hand, direct reduction, the electric furnace, and continuous casting had been chosen to produce, say, bars and rods, the ideal scale of production would certainly have been different.

This matter of optimum plant size has geographical implications. In the developing world, the best solution to a steel production problem may be found in the installation of an older second-hand plant. Such a plant, although large enough to satisfy local demands, would have a rather small output, relatively large labor inputs, and small capital charges. This kind of mix is best suited to the economic conditions pertaining in a low-income country. When the Huachipato iron and steel plant was built in Chile in 1950, it was decided initially to use old hand-mills for the production of sheet and plate. At first, these were satisfactory, but as the Chilean market grew in size and as its demands became more sophisticated, they gradually had to be replaced by more sophisticated semicontinuous equipment with a larger output. The fully continuous mill, however, has yet to arrive.

This Chilean solution raises a question concerning the most advantageous size of plant to install in a location that has a steadily expanding market for steel products. It exposes the steelmaker's dilemma of how much surplus capacity should be built into a plant in anticipation of future growth of the market. In theoretical terms, the optimum scale of plant is presumably set at the point where the discounted value of production over time exceeds the discounted costs of production (including depreciation) by the greatest amount. To calculate a solution, a considerable number of assumptions must be made. In particular, the rate of growth of the market and a realistic rate at which capital should be discounted must be hypothesized. Slow growth and high discount rates on capital will tend to make for a small surplus being built into the initial capacity of the works, and vice versa. But such assumptions are difficult to quantify with precision.

Similarly, many investment decisions concern not so much the optimum size of plant but rather the most appropriate scale of incremental production facilities. Capital charges can represent a considerable proportion of the total costs of iron and steel production. Consequently, small and old steelworks are often able to compete with larger modern ones, since through inflation their initial capital costs were relatively small, and in any case much of their equipment has been wholly or partly amortized. The operational problem facing the management of existing works is normally what to scrap and how best to add to existing, less efficient, but nevertheless competitive facilities in order to yield the maximum return on investment. Decisions on the most appropriate scale of plant to install will in many cases be far removed from the ideal.

The play of scale economies on investment decisions concerning iron and steel plants within a market area is an important component in the evolution of the geography of the industry. Interacting with scale economies are the costs of transporting steel products from the works to the consumer.

THE COSTS OF TRANSPORTING FINISHED STEEL

On leaving the finishing mills, steel is transported to its markets by road, rail, or water. The choice of medium is a function of the facilities available, the distances involved, and the rates charged. The distances over which finished steel is transported range from a few to several thousand kilometers. The rates charged can vary between perhaps $3 and $50 per ton.

With the steel industry increasingly market-oriented, and with the distances over which steel companies have to transport products to their customers tending to decline, road transport has increasingly won favor in many countries—particularly where road systems have been improved to high-capacity standards and larger-sized vehicles have become available. In 1965, approximately 70 percent of Swedish and Italian steel products left the mills for their markets by road; in Belgium, 40 percent; and in West Germany, 30 percent. The major advantage of road transport is its geographical and load flexibility. Products can be delivered without transshipment to many more markets than they can by either railway or waterway. And since the proportion of running costs to capital costs is higher for road transport than for other transport media (wages, maintenance, and fuel costs are the largest outgoings in the operation of a road fleet), road transport is well adapted to hauling loads that are irregular throughout the week or year. Moreover, road transport has the advantage of relatively low handling and transshipment charges. Whenever terminal charges represent an appreciable part of the total cost of haulage (this means short hauls in particular), it becomes advantageous to use road vehicles. However, short distances in a North American context can mean up to perhaps 600 kilometers.

Over such distances, and often over shorter ones, railways can be a highly competitive form of land transport for steel products. Better suited than road haulage to the movement of large tonnages, they have traditionally been the principal means used for steel distribution. In France, the railways handle between 70 and 80 percent of steel shipments each year; in Belgium and West Germany, 60 and 40 percent, respectively. Although they have rather higher loading and transshipment costs than road transport, railways can claim to have appreciably lower line-haul costs; hence they offer considerable advantages for medium- and long-distance shipments. By no means have all railway managements been able to take full advantage of the potentials of their systems, but where they have provided regular and speedy services between the steelmaking centers and their major customers, their ability to attract traffic has been unquestioned. Toward the end of the 1950–65 period, British Rail moved trainloads of 700 to 800 tons of steel daily from South Wales, northeast England, and other steelmaking districts to their principal markets in the Midlands and the Greater London areas. In other parts of Western Europe, trainloads of up to 2,000 tons were moved; and in the United States, even larger shipments.

In contrast to roads and railways, inland waterways offer what is often a somewhat circuitous mode of transport. Export shipments of steel from the works of Lorraine via the port of Antwerp are moved by barge down the Moselle and the Rhine, and then by Dutch and Belgian waterways—a much longer haul than the direct rail route. To compete in such circumstances, barge operators must be prepared to accept considerably lower ton-kilometer freight rates than their railway competitors. They must also be prepared to offer a lower tonnage rate than the railways in order to compensate for their rather higher loading and unloading charges. This they are prepared to do, since their line-haul costs tend to be exceptionally low in comparison with land transport. In the United States, the Pittsburgh steelmakers are able to sell large quantities of their products in the Midsouth, and even as far away as Texas, largely as a result of the low rates charged for moving steel down the Ohio-Mississippi water system. In a country like the Netherlands, where there is an abundance of waterways, approximately 70 percent of all steel shipments use this method of transport. In Germany (30 percent) and France (10–15 percent), the proportions are lower. Barges are also used occasionally for relatively short-distance coastwise movements of steel. In Japan, 45-ton pusher barges are used to move groups of three 400-dwt barges carrying pipes and tubes between Chiba and Ichikawa across Tokyo Bay.

Over longer distances coastwise, movements tend to be in more conventional though still small vessels. Ocean shippers of steel have traditionally used liner services. The major advantage of the latter is their exceptionally low ton-kilometer costs and rates, though these are frequently offset by very high handling and other port charges. In recent years the Japanese steel industry has pioneered the use of ships solely for the transport of steel. By taking over or chartering vessels of up to about 10,000 dwt, Japanese exporters have been able to achieve substantial savings in their trans-Pacific and Japan-to-Europe freight expenses on sheet steel in particular.

In the case of each of the alternative media used to move steel products from the works to the consumer, transport costs are almost invariably shared with other commodities. As a result, the rates charged for moving steel are based partly on what the traffic will bear, partly on what alternative facilities are available for its shipment, and partly on such obvious criteria as distance and line-haul costs. For each of the media there is a considerable range of rates both per ton and per ton-kilometer, which can only be explained by reference to the individual circumstances of the routes to which they relate. The lowest ranges are charged for ocean shipments.

The international ocean freight rate situation is a complicated tangle of legal cartels, complex rate schedules, and often complicated subsidies. In most instances, the rates are settled by Liner Conferences, whose objective is to reflect in the rates an amalgam of factors—such as the value of the service to the shipper, the availability of shipping space, port conditions, operating costs, the value of the merchandise and its stowage and handling characteristics, the volume in which it moves, and the regularity of movement. Frequently the rate for transporting steel along a particular route varies not only with each product but also with the direction of movement. On the North Atlantic, the 1962 rate for shipping structural steels from North European ports to the United States was $19.75 per ton, while the rate for moving the same product from the United States to Europe was $31.25 per ton. Most varieties of steel were in fact transported more cheaply in an east-to-west direction. Steel sheets, however, the one product that was regularly exported from the United States to Western Europe, had a cheaper rate in an easterly direction—namely $13.25 per ton compared with $18.04 per ton for European exports. Similar variations are found in the conference rates between the United States and Japan (Table 16). Outside of the major shipping routes, the rates for transporting steel by ocean liner are higher. While the rate for moving bars from Rotterdam to New York in 1962 was $19.75 per ton, the comparable rate from New York or Rotterdam to Rio de Janeiro ranged between about $23 and $25 per ton; and the rates from the same two exporting ports to Chile were $35 and $40 per ton. It would be difficult to substantiate the charge that freight rates for steel shipments were arranged deliberately to discriminate against particular steel flows. The pattern was explicable in other terms. However, it certainly limited the market opportunities of some producers, and tended to help existing exporters maintain their overseas sales.

Throughout the period, inflation tended to increase the level of ocean freights on steel. In 1950 the rate on bars from Northwest Europe to the United States (between $9 and $12 per ton) stood at about half the level of ten or so years later. The major exception to this upward drift in rates was achieved by the Japanese, who, in pioneering the use of vessels solely for steel exports, were able to make dramatic reductions in their freight charges. The conference rates for the shipment of steel plate and sheet from Japan to Rotterdam in 1964/65 were in the order of $18 to $20 per ton; in the opposite direction they were about $15 per ton. However, by using its own vessels rather than the conference lines, the Japanese steel industry was able to reduce these rates to $7.50 per ton. Although only feasible

TABLE 16. Comparison of Conference Ocean Freight Rates Effective March 1962 on Iron and Steel Products for Three U.S. Foreign Trade Routes

Route / Products	U.S. North Atlantic ports and West Germany[a]		U.S. Gulf ports and North Atlantic French ports[b]		U.S. Pacific ports and Japan[c]	
	Freight rate on U.S. exports	Freight rate on U.S. imports	Freight rate on U.S. exports	Freight rate on U.S. imports	Freight rate on U.S. exports	Freight rate on U.S. imports
Angles, beams, girders (structurals)	$31.25	$19.75	$28.50	$17.00	$28.10	$15.50
Bolts	31.25	24.00	28.50	20.50		
Castings and forgings	44.25	29.25	40.25	34.00		
Billets and blooms			13.25	17.00	30.35	15.50
Rails	36.75	19.75	33.50	17.00		
Wire rods (plain)	29.50	18.25			28.25	15.50
Screws	46.00	24.00				
Pipes (15-cm diameter)					30.35	21.00
Barbed wire	28.50	23.00	28.50	19.00		
Reinforcing bars		19.75			28.10	
Oilwell casings					33.60	21.00
Shapes (not fabricated)					28.10	
Rods					28.25	15.50
Sheet	13.25	18.04	13.25	19.00		

Source: United States, Joint Economic Committee of Congress, 1963, pp. 501, 569.
[a] North Atlantic Continental Freight Conference tariffs.
[b] Gulf-French Atlantic Hamburg Range Conference and Continental U.S.A. Gulf Westbound Conference.
[c] Pacific Westbound Conference and Trans-Pacific Freight Conference of Japan.

where large quantities of steel could be marketed, such a transformation in the freights for moving steel over considerable ocean distances—together with improvements in the speed and reliability of ocean vessels and in international communications generally—was bound to have long-term repercussions on the pattern of steel production and trade throughout the world.

Even the much higher conference rates for ocean transport of steel represented a very low ton-kilometer cost by comparison with other media (Table 17). However, this basic advantage of sea transport was offset by the high (though quite variable) terminal charges. The cost of handling a ton of steel at Tokyo-Yokohama in 1964 was only $2.54; at Rotterdam it was $5.67; and at New York it was $12.88. Such charges had an influence on the patterns of steel trade.

Barge transport had to bear substantial terminal charges, though these were lower than for ocean vessels. The 1960 cost of loading steel products onto barges at Pittsburgh was $0.90 per ton, and the cost of unloading downriver was sometimes as high as $1.55 per ton. Rail and road handling charges were smaller. According to O'Connor (1966, p. 203), the average water rate for moving tinplate in Western Europe was 39 percent cheaper than the average road rate, but he concluded that additional cranage, inventory, and other minor costs associated with water hauls reduced this advantage to a mere 2 percent.

Barges, railways, and road transport have just as variable a set of line-haul rates as ocean transport. For the short-distance movement of steel products across Tokyo Bay by barge, the rate in 1964 was approximately $3 per ton. For the much longer haul from Pittsburgh downstream to New Orleans, the 1960 rate was $7.34 per ton, and the rail rate for the same haul was $21 per ton, or about twice the rate for barge transport including handling charges. Even for the shorter haul from Pittsburgh to Cincinnati, the barge rate at $2.34 per ton was approximately one-fourth the railway rate ($8.80 per ton). Clearly, the American railways had elected not to compete on this route. But in other circumstances, the two media compete vigorously for traffic, and the reduction of rates charged by one meets with a response of rate reductions by the other. With the opening of the Moselle Canal and the quickening flow of Lorraine steel by waterway into South Germany, the German railways immediately cut their Ruhr-to-Karlsruhe steel tariffs by as much as $4 per ton.

Similarly, whereas road transport offered only limited competition to railways and waterways at the beginning of the period, by 1965 it was challenging them increasingly. Road haulers were not only able to offer a more direct and speedier service, but also, through the introduction of larger vehicles and the growing efficiency of the industry's organization, able to keep their costs remarkably stable throughout most of the period.

TABLE 17. FREIGHT RATES ON SELECTED STEEL PRODUCTS

Date	From	To	Product	Rate/ton (*dollars*)	Approx. rate/ton-km (*cents*)
OCEAN RATES					
1962...........	Rotterdam	New York	Bars	19.75	0.37
1962...........	Rotterdam	Rio de Janeiro	Bars	23.00	0.25
1962...........	Rotterdam	Chile	Bars	35.00	0.26
1962...........	New York	Rio de Janeiro	Bars	25.00	0.33
1962...........	New York	Chile	Bars	40.00	0.48
1965...........	Rotterdam	Japan	Sheet	15.00	0.06
1965...........	Japan	Rotterdam	Sheet	20.00	0.08
1965...........	Japan	Rotterdam	Sheet	7.50*	0.03
1965...........	Yawata	Tokyo	Tinplate	2.80	0.29
BARGE RATES					
1960...........	Pittsburgh	Cincinnati		2.34	0.31
1960...........	Pittsburgh	New Orleans		7.34	0.25
1960...........	Pittsburgh	Louisville		2.90	0.30
1960...........	Pittsburgh	Evansville		3.29	0.26
1965...........	Aliquippa	Baton Rouge	Pipes	12.80	0.45
RAIL RATES					
1956...........	Hamilton	Toronto	Bars, sheet	2.87	4.00
1956...........	Buffalo	Toronto	Bars, sheet	9.30	1.55
1956...........	Pittsburgh	Toronto	Bars, sheet	17.00	2.70
1957...........	Oberhausen	Paris		11.02	1.84
1957...........	Belval, Lux.	Rotterdam		8.22	2.20
1960...........	Pittsburgh	Cincinnati		8.80	1.50
1960...........	Pittsburgh	New Orleans		21.00	1.05
1965...........	Pittsburgh	Erie	Sheet	5.50	2.60
1965...........	Pittsburgh	Philadelphia	Sheet	10.30	1.84
1965...........	Aliquippa	Baton Rouge	Pipe	17.00	0.85
1965...........	Pittsburgh	Birmingham	Pipe	17.80	1.32
1965...........	Germany	France		9.13	1.74
1965...........	France	Netherlands		7.60	1.59
1965...........	Belgium	Italy		15.42	1.68
1965...........	South Africa, 160 km			4.00	2.50
1965...........	South Africa, 800 km			13.23	1.66
1965...........	Rhodesia, 160 km			7.00	4.37
1965...........	Rhodesia, 1,120 km			16.27	1.45
1965...........	Nigeria, 1,120 km			18.62	1.66
ROAD RATES					
1965...........	Pittsburgh	Erie	Sheet	6.00	2.90
1965...........	Pittsburgh	Philadelphia	Sheet	10.00	2.08
1965...........	South Wales	London	Sheet	6.00	2.20
1965...........	South Wales	Birmingham	Sheet	4.00	2.50
1965...........	South Wales	Birmingham	Billets	3.60	2.20
1965...........	South Wales	Sheffield	Billets	6.00	2.00

Sources: Canada, Royal Commission on Canada's Economic Prospects, 1957, Table 23; Murata, 1962; United States, Joint Economic Committee of Congress, 1963; Transport Division, European Coal and Steel Community, High Authority; Canada, Department of Energy, Mines and Resources; steel company sources.

* Specialized steel carrier.

By 1965, for distances up to, say, 600 kilometers in North America, and rather less in Western Europe, road rates tended to set the pace of inland steel transport charges. Thus, the road rate for hauling cold-rolled sheets from Pittsburgh to Philadelphia in 1965 was $10.30 per ton. The road rate for moving sheet between South Wales and London was $6 per ton. The railways had to meet these rates if they were to obtain the traffic. Road transport also became increasingly competitive as new steel warehouses moved out of city centers and relocated near the interchanges of major motorways, and as a greater proportion of industry came to be sited away from the main railway lines.

Road haulers could not, however, offer the same volume rate reductions as the railways. The 1965 road rate for hauling cold-rolled sheets from Pittsburgh to Erie was $6 per ton and the normal rail rate $6.90 per ton, but the railways also offered a rate of $5.50 for lots of 40 tons and over and even further reductions for very large loads. In Britain, one could think in terms of at least a 10 percent reduction in the tonnage rate when whole trainloads of steel were moved. Thus, while road haulers could adapt themselves profitably to the needs of the small- and medium-sized consumer, the railways had every opportunity to retain steel traffic to the really large markets and purchasers, and to the ports. This keen competition between the several forms of inland transport in most technologically advanced countries restrained the upward drift of actual freight rates on steel products between 1950 and 1965. In real terms, the costs of steel distribution fell.

There were a great many other variables in the complex structure of inland transport rates for moving steel. The tariffs naturally varied with the distance of the haul, the regularity of the traffic, and the handling characteristics of the product concerned. Steel strip, for example, presents greater difficulties in shipment than do merchant bars or structural steel. As a result, strip tended to be charged a somewhat higher tariff. The structure of transport rates was also considerably affected by the value of the product being moved and by the related assessment of what rates the traffic could bear. Tinplate valued at $185 per ton could clearly carry a higher rate than reinforcing bars priced at $130 per ton. Occasionally it was in the interests of a transport company to offer low rates to certain steel producers in order to enable them to compete in particular markets. The ability of the Ontario steel industry to compete in British Columbia was primarily the result of the railways agreeing to an especially low set of rates in return for a guarantee by the steel industry that a high percentage of its shipments would be sent by rail. Similarly, with about 30 percent of the U.S. west coast market being satisfied by Japanese imports, it was natural that in 1966 domestic (particularly Midwest) steel producers negotiated a reduction in rail rates by as much as $15 per ton in an attempt to win back at least some of the market.

Even when railways are not publicly owned, their rates are normally subject to some form of public supervision. Thus they are subject to manipulation to serve public objectives, which can include the spatial behavior of the steel industry. In the Soviet Union, rates are fixed with the deliberate intention of moving most steel products by rail. In India, the difference between the price paid for steel by the consumers (within a system of uniform delivered prices) and the price received by the steelworks is allocated to a freight equalization fund. This fund was originally established to equate the price of domestic and foreign steels; subsequently it came to be used to subsidize those works and products that had a long and expensive haul to their markets (Johnson, 1964).

The sum effect of the changes in, and the variety of, the freight rates charged for hauling steel products during the period 1950–65 was twofold: (1) Where transport conditions were moderately or highly competitive, there was a marked propensity for the efficiency of haulage operations to increase, either through superior organization or through the use of larger items of equipment. As a consequence, the real costs of steel distribution tended to fall. Thus it became possible for many iron and steel works to widen their market areas and so to exploit more fully the economies of scale in production. (2) The continuing and considerable variety of the rates charged for the transport of steel products, interacting with the complexity of steel production economics, meant that the disposition of both the size and geography of iron and steel production facilities within the markets for steel was subject to another somewhat erratic variable. So, too, as a result, was the geography of iron ore demands.

PATTERNS OF THE INDUSTRY

Where the markets for steel are relatively isolated and above a minimum size, the economics of production plus the high costs of product transport create a situation in which the demands can generally best be satisfied by small-scale local production. The construction of first unintegrated, and then integrated, iron and steel production facilities can then most advantageously be phased with the growth of the market. New Zealand is a case in point. A small country with a population of 2.5 million people, it has traditionally imported most of its steel needs from overseas, in particular from Britain and Australia. By the early sixties, however, the growth of demand to about 450,000 tons per year, plus its prospective expansion, suggested that the domestic production of at least some steel products was becoming economically possible. The New Zealand Steel Investigating Company, Ltd. (*Report*, 1963; Dick, 1963) was established by the government to consider the creation of a domestic steel industry (in addition to the small existing bar mill producing about 50,000 tons per year from local scrap). The size of the market ruled out the possibility of wide-strip production for years to come, and it seemed that the specialized manufacture of narrow strip could not be contemplated before the late seventies. For the immediate future, however, the Steel Investigating Company suggested that (with mild government infant-industry protection) the manufacture of flat and corrugated galvanized sheets from imported coil would be economical. Plans were therefore formulated for this to start in 1967. In 1968 it was proposed that billets and wire rods should be produced (in a continuous-casting plant). It was expected that the market would become large enough by the early seventies to justify the construction of a New Zealand welded-pipe mill (using imported strip), and that hot-rolled coil and tinplate production could be started by 1976. Meanwhile, iron and steel manufacture could begin, based at first on local raw materials (employing a direct-reduction process on the titaniferous iron sands), with the use of both electric and oxygen furnaces.

What emerges from an examination of the prospects of the nascent iron and steel industry in New Zealand is the severe limitation imposed by the size of the domestic market on the prospects for economic production, even given the relative isolation of the country some 2,000 kilometers from its nearest existing producer (in Australia) and thousands more kilometers from its more traditional suppliers (in Britain). In spite of the industry's advantageous proximity to resources of iron ore, coal, and half the New Zealand market (all within 120 kilometers of each other), and in spite of the prospect of tariff protection for seven years, the difficulties facing the New Zealand Steel Company (Provisional Board Report, 1965), as it embarks on a modest scale of iron and steel production, are considerable. The demand prospects for iron ore are also modest.

Where the interaction of steel demands, production scale economies, and product transport rates make for large markets and market areas, the resulting pattern of iron and steel plants, and of iron ore demands, is much more complex. In such a situation, a considerable variety of works, both in size and in output, come to be built. Some of these plants are very large, but many are quite small. In the U.S.S.R., which has laid considerable stress in the past on the need to exploit scale economies by the development of very large integrated plants, some 8 percent of all rolled products and 20 percent of merchant sections come from nonintegrated operations with capacities of between 150,000 and 200,000 tons per year (Dastur, 1963). Although a number of these plants serve small regional markets that are ill suited to integrated production, the greater number are in fact to be found in the principal iron and steelmaking districts in the most industrialized parts of the country, where they meet the demands of the engineering industry in particular. Some estimates of the size frequency of steelworks in other industrially advanced economies are shown in Table 18.

These estimates, calculated by the British Iron and Steel Federation, illustrate how even in a national market that affords the greatest opportunities for the exploitation of scale economies and can boast a highly efficient internal transport system—namely, the United States—half of the country's ninety-four major steelworks were capable of producing less than 1 million tons per year in 1965. Over 70 percent were in this category in the EEC and Britain, and only slightly less in Japan. At the same time, there was considerable variation in the way in which different countries were able to construct very large works and took the opportunity to do so. In 1965, Britain had only three works with an annual capacity of over 2 million tons; Japan had seven.

Not only are works of different sizes able to survive within a country, but they are also capable of existing almost adjacent to each other. Near the huge 8-million-tons-per-year Bethlehem Steel Corporation plant at Sparrows Point is the Alan Wood steelworks with an annual ingot capacity of 1.25 million tons. At Hamilton, Ontario, close to the 3-million-tons-per-year plant of the Steel Company of Canada, a small company with an electric furnace of 50,000-tons capacity remains competitive by satisfying small and specialized demands. And in South Wales, within 5 kilometers of the 3-million-tons-per-year British Steel Corporation plant at Port Talbot, an unintegrated steelworks one-tenth the size manufactures angles, bars, and sections for the engineering industry. In most of the technologically advanced countries, with their large and complex markets, there remain ample opportunities for plants much smaller than the technological optimum to survive and flourish.

TABLE 18.   SIZE FREQUENCY OF STEELWORKS IN SELECTED COUNTRIES, 1965

Capacity range (*million tons/year*)	Britain		EEC		Japan		U.S.A.	
	No. of works	% of capacity	No. of works	% of capacity	No. of works	% of capacity	No. of works	% of capacity
Totals	41	100.0	106	100.0	49	100.0	94	100.0
Below 0.5	20	21.0	46	23.1	31	14.7	32	8.4
0.5 to 1	9	19.7	31	21.2	4	6.5	15	7.2
1 to 2	9	40.0	16	21.0	7	17.0	17	19.0
2 to 3	2	14.0	11	24.0	2	16.0	16	14.0
3 to 4	1	10.0	1	4.0	3	15.0	7	11.0
Over 4			1	5.0	2	11.0	7	23.0
1965 output (*million ingot tons*)	27		86		41		119	

Source: Steel Review, October 1966.

Nevertheless, as steel demands have increased over the years, as technology has changed, and as the uses for steel strip and heavy structural sections have multiplied (faster than for other products), the advantages of reducing the number while increasing the size of steelworks in advanced countries have become clearer. In 1946, 93 percent of British capacity was in plants of less than 1 million tons per year, compared with 38 percent twenty years later. Yet the capital sunk in existing British works, as in the plants of other older steel producers, plus important sociological pressures to preserve employment in traditional steelmaking centers, prevented a speedy response to these pressures. The steel industry in such a situation has attempted to gain new economies of scale in production without closing down too much old plant, through various attempts at operating and investment rationalization. For example, by the late fifties a movement toward intercompany cooperation began in West Germany. Under a 1959 agreement between Hoesch Westfalenhütte and Dortmund-Hörder Hüttenunion, the slabs of one company are rolled on the hot-strip mill of the other (which, as part of the bargain, deferred its plans to construct its own strip mill for at least ten years). In 1962, Hüttenwerk Oberhausen, August Thyssen-Hütte, and Mannesmann signed an eight-year agreement under which Oberhausen and Mannesmann canceled their plans for building a hot-strip mill, and Thyssen agreed to roll semis for them. Subsequent agreements linked other West German firms, and the process spread to other West European countries.

There was a tendency at first for the agreements to be concerned with the rolling of flat products and wire rods. These sectors of the market had previously forgone considerable scale economies. In most of the early arrangements the cooperating firms tended to be located fairly close to each other. With time, however, almost all types of rolling operation came to be affected, and the linkages between plants became longer. In 1965, four companies in the Ruhr (Dortmund-Hörder Hüttenunion, Hoesch, Hüttenwerk Oberhausen, and Mannesmann) established a central office for the receipt of orders for bars and sections. Orders for the same specification were then combined and allocated to one of the fifteen rolling mills of the participating companies. In 1967, the whole of the West German steel industry agreed to organize its sales on the basis of four regional units. By these means, longer runs could be achieved at the individual mills, and the expectation was that the scheme would reduce costs by up to 15 percent. One of the later French agreements associated Usinor and Lorraine-Escaut, some 110 kilometers away, in order to make fuller use of the more modern facilities at the new coastal plant at Dunkirk. The not inconsiderable transport costs involved in the movement of slabs over that distance were presumably more than offset by the increased efficiency of the Dunkirk rolling operations.

Such cooperation between two or more geographically separated works was enormously facilitated by the speed and efficiency of modern communications. It became possible to transmit at high speed, and with high resolution, facsimiles of orders between a coordinating center and several widely scattered works. The same techniques allowed the large American steel corporations, with works located at different points in the manufacturing belt, to make much better use of their facilities. And such techniques were not unrelated to the success that the Japanese steel industry was able to record in expanding its overseas sales.

After the cooperative agreements came the mergers. One of the biggest, after many years of negotiation, was the Thyssen-Phoenix-Rheinrohr group, which in 1965 had a combined capacity of 8.87 million tons, and in 1967 sought to join with Hüttenwerk Oberhausen to provide steelmaking facilities well in excess of 10 million tons under one management. In 1966 the French industry, backed by the government, was thrown into a major reorganization—Le Plan Professionel—out of which two large groups emerged: De Wendel-Pont-à-Mousson and Usinor-Lorraine-Escaut, with capacities (in 1965) of nearly 8 and 7.4 million tons, respectively. In 1966 also came the first international merger; this was between the Dortmund-Hörder-Hoesch group in the eastern Ruhr and the Netherlands producer, Hoogovens. With a total capacity of over 10 million tons (though a rather lower production in 1965), it became one of the largest steel groups in Western Europe (Table 19). In Britain, meanwhile, the renationalization of most of the steel industry (completed in 1967) created a corporation with a production of over 22 million tons. These developments brought the size of a number of Western European steel groups up to that of many American and some of the larger Japanese producers. (The Japanese were simultaneously being encouraged from some quarters to merge into two main producing units.) Even so, the gradual remolding of the Western European industry still left its largest units much smaller than the two largest corporations of the United States. More important from the viewpoint of the present study, there remained in Europe many more small centers of iron and steel production than in America, and hence more loci of iron ore demand.

Financial integration and the successful and efficient integration of production are quite different undertakings. While the former presents considerable difficulties, the complete integration of the administration and operation of geographically separate works is only occasionally possible. When the works are only a few kilometers apart (as were the three plants

TABLE 19. ESTIMATED OUTPUT OF LEADING STEEL PRODUCERS IN NORTH AMERICA, WESTERN
EUROPE, ASIA, AND OCEANIA, 1965

Producers	Millions of ingot tons
U.S. Steel Corporation.	29.6
British Steel Corporation.	22.1
Bethlehem Steel Corporation, U.S.A.	19.1
Republic Steel Corporation, U.S.A.	9.0
Thyssen group, W. Germany	8.4
Hoogovens–Dortmund-Hörder-Hoesch.	8.1
De Wendel–Pont-à-Mousson.	8.1
National Steel Corporation, U.S.A.	7.7
Yawata, Japan.	7.7
Finsider, Italy.	7.1
Fuji, Japan.	7.1
Armco, U.S.A.	7.0
Usinor–Lorraine-Escaut, France.	6.3
Jones & Laughlin, U.S.A.	6.6
Broken Hill Proprietary, Australia.	5.9
Inland Steel, U.S.A.	5.9
Youngstown Steel & Tube, U.S.A.	5.4
Kawasaki, Japan.	4.1
Sumitomo, Japan.	4.1
Krupp group, W. Germany.	3.9
Arbed, Luxembourg.	3.6
Steel Company of Canada.	3.5
Hindustan Steel, India.	3.4

Sources: Iron Age, June 23, 1966; and others.

Note: Some of these "producers" were the result of mergers between 1965 and 1967. In 1968, Yawata and Fuji announced their intention to merge (1965 production was 14.8 million tons), while an earlier agreement between Thyssen and Hüttenwerk Oberhausen (combined 1965 output was about 10 million tons) remained to be ratified by the High Authority of the European Coal and Steel Community.

of Nippon Kokan in the Tokyo-Yokohama area, which were integrated in 1965/66 into a single 5.2-million-ton unit), the production control is much easier than when they are separated by 100 kilometers or more. It became only too obvious by the end of the period that the desire of the iron and steel industry (especially in Western Europe) to exploit to the full the advantages of production scale economies would need more drastic action than simply cooperative agreements and financial integration. And it was in response to this situation that many advocated a fuller public involvement in the industry.

CHAPTER 5

Political Influences

The iron and steel industry, more perhaps than any other in the manufacturing sector, is frequently considered to be "clothed with the public interest." In most parts of the world, as a result, it has increasingly been subject to a variety of political influences, which have affected both its markets and its locational characteristics. Naturally, the degree of political involvement varies considerably from country to country. At one extreme of the spectrum lie the market economies, in which public policies affecting the industry tend to be restricted to the imposition of protective or revenue tariffs, to some supervision over pricing policies, and perhaps to an occasional plant location decision during wartime. In the middle are the mixed economies, in which there is some degree of public ownership (with governments frequently providing the industry with low-interest loans), and in which there tends to be a fairly regular political involvement in the locational decisions of the industry. At the other end of the spectrum are the fully planned economies, in which the industry's investment and locational decisions are influenced by a completely different set of economic and political criteria.

Political intervention in the locational affairs of the iron and steel industry can range from the use of indirect influences on the geography of its market areas on the one hand, to complete governmental control over both the markets for steel and the means of its production on the other. It can be seen at nearly all levels of political organization—from the local municipality offering cheap land and tax exemptions in order to attract a plant, to international agencies making capital available to establish steel production in the developing world. It is sometimes overt, as in the activities of the High Authority of the European Coal and Steel Community. It is more frequently covert, as in the relations between the Japanese government, its Ministry of International Trade and Industry, and the iron and steel producers of Japan. The motives of political intervention are quite mixed—

sometimes economic, sometimes sociological, and sometimes strategic. Sometimes they are incomprehensible.

POLITICAL INFLUENCES ON THE MARKETS FOR IRON AND STEEL

While it is possible for local markets for steel to be subject to political influences—for example, the states of California and Washington prohibit the use of foreign steel in any construction projects they finance—it is at the national level that steel markets are most frequently subject to political manipulation. In fully planned economies, all imports are, of course, strictly controlled. And the administered nature of both prices and the market allows (in theory at least) a readier exploitation of scale economies than in the market economies, where competition and the imperfections of the market generate multiple cross flows of identical steel products. The governments of the mixed and market economies, on the other hand, although they occasionally impose quotas on steel imports, more usually afford their domestic steel industries some form of tariff protection. In the early sixties, the unweighted average of tariffs on products entering the EEC was 10 percent, the United States 13 percent, and Britain 14 percent. These percentages were considerably above the usual share of, say, product transport costs in the delivered costs of steel. In a detailed study of the Western European tinplate industry, O'Connor (1966, p. 270) concluded that "tariffs were the most important single influence in determining market areas," since they effectively prevented the penetration of low-cost foreign suppliers into most national markets. A reduction of tariffs—for example, after the Kennedy Round—is likely to trigger off considerable changes in the patterns of steel trade. By the same token, differential tariffs on steel imports, varying with the country of origin, can powerfully affect the geography of market areas and trade. This could be seen within the British Commonwealth at the beginning of the period; by the late fifties and sixties, however, the margins of preference for Commonwealth trade had fallen appreciably and the geography of trade shifted accordingly (see Chapter 6).

There are, of course, differences in the role of tariffs within the advanced and the developing countries. In the former they afford some measure of protection for the existing iron and steel industries against lower-cost producers, and against marginally priced exports from countries with surplus capacity. In the developing countries, however, the role of tariffs must generally be to increase the costs of product transfer from other countries to a level where domestic production becomes profitable. In such a situation, the economy has to bear rather higher steel prices than might otherwise be the case. On the other hand, the country gains employment opportunities for its people and often some valuable savings in foreign exchange. There can be no doubt that the costs of producing steel in the developing world are frequently very high indeed. To the inevitably high costs of small-scale production must be added the considerable expense of learning how to produce steel. It is not unusual to find that perhaps one-third of the equipment within a plant in a developing economy requires replacement within twelve months or so, as a result of inexperienced and faulty use. Yet figures can be produced to show that it is worthwhile for a developing country to establish an iron and steel industry.

In a survey by the United Nations (1964-A), an attempt was made to quantify the foreign exchange advantages of encouraging iron and steel production in various countries of Latin America. To some extent, the savings depend on the proportion of the raw-material inputs that are available from domestic sources. In Table 20 several situations are postulated and their foreign exchange expenditures costed. The table sets forth the estimated expenditures of foreign exchange resulting from the production of flat products and of bars and profiles under a variety of conditions. The two basic variables are the scale of production and the source of the raw materials. Estimates are given at various levels of output for those circumstances in which both ore and coal are imported, for those in which only coal is imported, and for those in which steel production is possible with entirely domestic raw materials. Also shown are estimates of the savings afforded by domestic production under assumptions of, first, rather high cost imports, and, second, a more realistic level of import prices in the light of experience in the mid-sixties. The foreign exchange savings are not inconsiderable, even in the latter case. For a country importing all its raw materials, the saving is nearly 30 percent in a plant of 500,000 tons per year producing flat products; and for a country using local raw materials, the saving can be as high as 75 percent in the case of a plant twice that size.

The table is based on somewhat optimistic assumptions about production costs. The combination of processes used in the calculations are relatively rare in Latin American circumstances. The assumed levels of productivity are somewhat high for a developing country. And the raw-material costs are lower than is likely to be the case in many locations. Nevertheless, the clear opportunities for substantial savings of foreign exchange cannot be neglected by the governments of the developing countries, since shortages of hard currency are often a major obstacle to their aspirations for economic growth. It is therefore important to estimate the length of time over which the foreign currency component of an investment in an iron and steel plant could be amortized with the annual savings in foreign exchange expenditure as a result of local production.

Some estimates concerning this matter are given in Table 21—for two types of product and at several scales of production. It is assumed that two-thirds of the cost of the iron and steel plant has to be paid for in foreign

TABLE 20. Estimated Expenditure and Savings of Foreign Exchange in Hypothetical Plants in Latin America, 1962

(Dollars per product ton)

Annual capacity of plant (thousands of tons)	Expenditure of foreign exchange in domestic steel production						
	Foreign exchange inputs			Total foreign exchange expenditure			
	Spare parts and sundries[a]	Iron ore[b]	Coking coal[c]	Capital charges[d]	Importing ore and coal	Importing coal only	With local ore and coal
FLAT PRODUCTS							
100	$22.97	$23.50	$14.80	$41.80	$103.07	$80.20	$64.77
200	19.30	23.50	14.80	37.30	94.90	71.40	56.60
400	12.32	22.40	13.50	28.70	76.92	54.52	41.02
500	9.76	22.40	13.50	25.40	71.06	48.66	35.16
800	6.84	20.50	13.00	19.70	60.04	39.54	26.54
1,000	5.30	20.00	12.40	18.80	56.50	36.50	24.10
1,500	4.59	20.00	12.40	16.90	53.89	33.89	21.49
BARS AND PROFILES							
100	14.00	16.30	10.60	13.80	57.40	38.40	27.80
200	12.93	16.30	10.60	12.70	52.53	36.23	25.63
300	11.95	16.30	10.60	11.85	50.70	34.40	23.80

Saving of foreign exchange resulting from local steel production facing high-cost imports

Annual capacity of plant (thousands of tons)	Steel cost at plant	Price of imported steel (delivered)	Saving of foreign exchange			Two-thirds of the investment estimated to be in foreign exchange
			Importing ore and coal	Importing coal	With local raw materials	
FLAT PRODUCTS						
100	$182.71	$182.00	$ 78.93	$101.80	$117.23	$464.00
200	165.35	182.00	85.10	110.60	125.40	414.00
400	134.41	182.00	105.08	127.48	140.98	317.00
500	127.23	182.00	110.94	133.54	146.84	290.00
800	113.47	182.00	121.96	142.64	155.46	219.00
1,000	106.61	182.00	125.50	145.50	157.90	208.00
1,500	102.65	182.00	128.11	148.11	160.51	187.00

100	101.05	141.00	83.60	102.60	113.20	168.00
200	98.95	141.00	88.47	104.77	115.37	140.00
300	84.79	141.00	90.30	106.60	117.20	130.00

Saving of foreign exchange resulting from local steel production facing low-cost imports

Annual capacity of plant (*thousands of tons*)	Steel cost at plant	Price of imported steel (delivered)	Saving of foreign exchange			Two-thirds of the investment estimated to be in foreign exchange
			Importing ore and coal	Importing coal	With local raw materials	
FLAT PRODUCTS						
100	$182.71	$100.00	−$ 3.07	$ 19.80	$ 35.23	$464.00
200	165.35	100.00	5.10	28.60	43.40	414.00
400	134.41	100.00	23.08	45.48	58.98	317.00
500	127.23	100.00	28.94	51.34	64.84	290.00
800	113.47	100.00	39.96	60.46	73.46	219.00
1,000	106.61	100.00	43.50	64.50	75.90	208.00
1,500	102.65	100.00	46.11	66.11	78.51	187.00
BARS AND PROFILES						
100	101.05	78.00	20.60	39.60	50.20	168.00
200	89.95	78.00	25.47	41.77	52.37	140.00
300	84.79	78.00	27.30	43.60	54.20	130.00

Source: United Nations, 1964-A, pp. 107, 109, 110.

Note: Types of plant: (1) Production of flat products in coke blast furnace, L.D. converter, rolling mill. (2) Production of light bars and profiles in coke blast furnace, L.D. converter, continuous casting, rolling mill.

a Spare parts, refractories, and sundries.

b Imported ore at $14 per ton at plant. Consumption varies with the yield of the rolling equipment.

c 100 percent coal imported at $18 per ton at plant. Consumption varies with the yield of the rolling equipment.

d Covers interest and amortization on two-thirds of the investment, which are assumed here to have been obtained abroad.

TABLE 21. ESTIMATED NUMBER OF YEARS IN WHICH THE SAVING IN FOREIGN EXCHANGE
           COULD EQUAL THE FOREIGN EXCHANGE COMPONENT OF THE INVESTMENT IN A
           STEEL PLANT

(Dollars at 1962 prices)

		High-cost imports		
		Years in which investment will be returned by savings in foreign exchange		
Plant capacity *(thousands of tons/year)*	Price of steel *(dollars/ton landed)*	Importing ore and coal	Importing coal	With local raw materials
FLAT PRODUCTS				
100..........................	182	5.8	4.6	4.0
200..........................	182	4.9	3.8	3.3
400..........................	182	3.0	2.5	2.2
500..........................	182	2.6	2.2	1.7
800..........................	182	1.8	1.5	1.4
1,000........................	182	1.7	1.4	1.3
1,500........................	182	1.5	1.3	1.2
BARS AND PROFILES				
100..........................	141	2.0	1.6	1.5
200..........................	141	1.6	1.3	1.2
300..........................	141	1.4	1.2	1.1

		Low-cost imports		
		Years in which investment will be returned by savings in foreign exchange		
Plant capacity *(thousands of tons/year)*	Price of steel *(dollars/ton landed)*	Importing ore and coal	Importing coal	With local raw materials
FLAT PRODUCTS				
100..........................	100		23.5	13.1
200..........................	100	81.0	14.5	9.6
400..........................	100	13.7	7.0	5.4
500..........................	100	10.0	5.6	4.5
800..........................	100	5.4	3.6	3.0
1,000........................	100	4.8	3.3	2.8
1,500........................	100	4.1	2.9	2.4
BARS AND PROFILES				
100..........................	75	7.3	4.2	3.4
200..........................	75	5.5	3.4	2.7
300..........................	75	4.7	3.0	2.4

Source: United Nations, 1964-A, p. 110.

exchange. Two sets of import prices are assumed. They reflect, on the one hand, a situation of high tariffs; and on the other, the low price at which steel can be purchased on the world market. The writers of the United Nations document (1964-A, p. 110) judged that "since international credit is usually given for a longer term than would be required by most of the situations . . . it may be concluded that the prospects for new ventures are not quite desperate." Moreover, it has to be remembered that in the real world of international finance and intergovernmental loans, it is usually very much easier to borrow money to build a steel plant than to borrow money to purchase steel imports. To be sure, much depends on the use to which the steel imports are to be put; yet the bias toward the construction of a plant is only too obvious.

These remarks should not be interpreted to mean that the construction of an iron and steel plant is invariably the most advantageous course of action for a developing country with modest steel demands. In a world of falling steel export prices (see Chapter 6), the limited amounts of foreign capital available to such a country might be better spent in another sector of the economy. The steel industry should certainly not be thought of as a national status symbol. Nor should it be regarded as the developing world's economic salvation, nor as inevitably bringing wide-ranging economic growth in its wake. Instead, it should be seen for what it is—namely, a possible but dispensable element within a broad economic strategy of national development. In many countries of the developing world, the national market is simply not large enough (foreign exchange savings or no foreign exchange savings) to justify local iron and steel production even with substantial tariffs. Particularly is this true in the case of products, such as sheets and plates, whose production costs respond dramatically to the economies of scale. It is for this reason that a good deal of attention has been given in recent years to the possibility of enlarging the markets of the developing world through common market agreements. In such arrangements, governmental initiatives and sometimes supragovernmental political initiatives are critically important.

In 1964, the Economic Commission for Africa (ECA) proposed that the whole of West Africa should be associated economically as a common market. Only in this way could a viable iron and steel industry of any consequence—to say nothing of other industries—be developed. The most optimistic figures for West African steel demands in 1970 showed a need for rather more than 1 million tons of products, a market that immediately precluded the possibility of heavy-section and wide-strip production. Moreover, the distances and communications in the region were such as to necessitate the construction of two plants, one to serve inland markets and the other located on the coast. The Commission's report (United Nations, 1964-C) suggested the advantages of Gouina in Mali as the inland site, and proposed a small electric reduction plant there. In addition, the report suggested that the major works, an integrated plant rolling annually about 0.5 million tons of products, should be in Liberia. While there was no dissension over the Gouina proposal, the Liberian project met with strong opposition. Nigeria pointed out that it already had a plant in the advanced planning stage; Mauretania demanded that Port Etienne be studied as an alternative site; and Gabon stated that, come what may, it too would build a plant. The debate about the exact location of the works is less important in the present context than a growing realization that, in the words of a United Nations document (1963-B, p. 43), "There is a strong case for only one . . . plant, serving a substantial proportion of the needs of the whole West African region. This in turn would require cooperation between African countries in the financing and setting up of the plant, together of course with support from non-African countries, and also an agreement among the countries of the sub-region to ensure markets for the products of the plant." But international rivalry for the location of the production facilities will be a difficult issue to resolve.

Of somewhat greater potential impact on the geography of the iron and steel industry are those common markets contemplated between countries that already have some steelmaking facilities and already know the costs of small-scale and relatively inefficient production. An attempt was made in the mid-sixties to rationalize production in the several steel plants of the Maghreb, in order to facilitate specialization and permit rather longer production runs in the existing mills. Even more symbolic was the emerging Latin American Free Trade Association (LAFTA), formed in 1960 with Argentina, Brazil, Chile, Colombia, Ecuador, Mexico, Paraguay, Peru, and Uruguay as its constituent members (United Nations, 1965). Following LAFTA's decision to impose a common external tariff against third countries and gradually to remove the existing tariff barriers between member nations, theoretically the existing steel works will be able to begin rationalizing their production through a greater degree of plant specialization and trade. Greater use could thus be made of their existing plant. Even more important in the long run, the rationalization of investment plans could lead to substantial savings of capital for the member countries. For example, in one estimate (United Nations, 1964-A; Aguirre, 1963), it was suggested that by 1975 the total production of LAFTA will have risen to 15 million tons. By cooperation and investment rationalization, capital savings in the order of $3,700 million possibly could be made. This is the difference between the cost of an investment program in which each country seeks to meet its own needs and the cost of a program in which optimum investments are made within the framework of a Latin American common market. In addition, savings in production costs could be as high as $400 million in the same year, 1975.

The immediate problems of establishing such a Free Trade Association are enormous. There are still considerable advantages for any one country to import steel from the industrially advanced economies, which tend to offer better credit terms and frequently afford lower transport costs. There is also the problem of the poverty of transport facilities and the high transport rates within and between the countries of LAFTA, to say nothing of difficulties presented by unstable currencies and the varying tax arrangements in the member countries. Moreover, there remains an urgent need for a Latin American equivalent to the High Authority of the European Coal and Steel Community—a body that can coordinate, examine, and report on the advantages and disadvantages of investment proposals. Apart from these problems, the creation of a common market in Latin America, together with the enlargement of the markets of its domestic iron and steel producers, offers the region exceptional opportunities for the expansion of steel manufacture on a sound economic basis.

The enlargement of market areas through political agreement is not, of course, limited to the developing world. In fact, the most notable achievement in this direction was in Western Europe, where the creation of the European Coal and Steel Community led to considerable changes in the geography of its iron and steel industry. After 1953 the patterns of product distribution, the location of production, and the raw materials used to produce the pig iron and steel, all shifted in response to the new market situation. It is, of course, difficult to distinguish with precision between the influence of the changing economic circumstances of an industry and its technology on the one hand, and the effects of politically changed market circumstances on the other. The many shifts that occurred in the geography of iron and steel markets and trade in Western Europe after 1953 cannot possibly all be ascribed to the effects of the creation of the European Coal and Steel Community. Nevertheless, the considerable penetration of the market of southern Germany by the producers of eastern France, and the satisfaction of some northern French demands with Belgian steel, from the late fifties onward, would have been unlikely to occur without the Common Market. And this in turn had its effects on the geographical pattern of investment in new iron and steel production facilities—and hence the changing spatial characteristics of ore demands—in all the member countries. It is to this matter of the effect of political behavior on the location of steel production that we next turn.

LOCATIONAL ANALYSIS IN THE MIXED ECONOMIES

To a small degree, as has been noted, political forces have played a part in helping to mold the geography of iron and steel production in such market economies as the United States—just as the effects of market forces have penetrated into the locational processes and the pattern of Soviet industry. It is, however, more useful to approach the question of the effects of political behavior on the geography of iron and steel manufacture by considering the role of politics in those parts of the world where a blend of market and political forces is more openly admitted to exist. At root, the locational factors of the iron and steel industry in the mixed economies must be interpreted as being essentially the same as those in the market economies. However, in the mixed economies, the state—through direct ownership of the industry or through deliberate policy decisions or through indirect action—can considerably influence the behavior of the industry.

In Western Europe, something like one-fifth of steel output in 1965 came from plants that were either wholly or partly owned by governments. In Scandinavia, there are two state-owned companies. Italy's Finsider is part of a larger state holding agency—the Istituto per la Ricostruzione Industriale (I.R.I.). The Salzgitter works in West Germany is government owned. The Dutch government holds a 26 percent share in the Royal Dutch steelworks at Ijmuiden. And by 1967 the greater part of the British steel industry was brought under public ownership. In many parts of the world outside of Western Europe, the same phenomenon can be seen. Half of India's steel industry is owned by the government; the South African government owns Iscor (as a result of the early commercial failure of a private steelmaking venture); and in Latin America many of the iron and steel industries are either wholly or partly government owned.

Remarkably loose and variable though the relationships between most of these steel producers and their owner-governments might be, the fact remains that a large share of the world's iron and steel industry is not in private hands, and accordingly its locational behavior can be considerably affected by public policy. An initial understanding can best be approached through examples.

In Scandinavia, the Swedish and Norwegian governments have built small and uneconomic iron and steel plants in their northern territories at Luleå and Moirana, respectively, which can only be interpreted as efforts to create employment in peripheral and underdeveloped, yet strategically important, localities. As Alexandersson (1956, p. 41) put it, "If they meet with economic success, a reevaluation must be made among economic geographers about the importance of different locational factors in the steel industry." The geography of the Indian steel industry cannot be fully understood without some recognition of the desires of certain Indian States to have a steelworks, and the pressures they brought to bear on New Delhi in order to achieve their objectives. A particularly interesting case of the steel industry being obliged to respect the broader objectives of a government's regional economic policies in its locational decisions is to be found in Italy.

The rapid expansion of steel production in Italy after 1945—based almost entirely on imported raw materials—was concentrated at the Finsider coastal works, sited at break-of-bulk points near the markets for steel in the north of the country. Since Finsider is owned by a state corporation, and because the state has elected to pursue a regional economic policy that seeks to raise the living standards in the south of the country by stimulating industrial developments there, the Italian steel industry has been required to locate its latest integrated works in the south at Taranto (Italsider, Sp.A., 1967). Technologically, it was one of the most modern plants in Western Europe in 1965, and plans existed for the eventual expansion of its capacity to 5 or possibly even 7 million ingot tons per year. Yet the plant initially faced a glaring locational disability—the absence of a reasonably large local or regional market for its products. There were hopes that the plant, with its low process costs (stemming from its advanced technology) would allow for penetration into the markets of North Africa and the Middle East. And its coastal site meant that there were opportunities to transport some of the mill products relatively cheaply to the ports of northern Italy by sea. However, the plant's eccentric location plus its high unit capital charges (Taranto was a "green field" site, and several of its expensive items of equipment, such as the primary rolling mill, had to remain underutilized for a number of years) meant that its economic prospects initially appeared somewhat gloomy. In the longer run, the profitability of the plant rested heavily on the success or failure of the agencies of the Italian government to attract new industries, especially metal-consuming industries, into the south of the country.

There is an assumption in some economic and geographical writing—an assumption that has only too readily been accepted by politicians and planners—that a large iron and steel plant will automatically attract a number of satellite industries into its locality and so serve as the keystone of a regional development program. Yet there is very little evidence to confirm this view. French and British experience in, say, Lorraine and South Wales (Manners, 1964-B) tends to deny it. A few steel users are inclined to take advantage of locations near a steelworks, but most manufacturers are more powerfully influenced by other locational factors—in particular, the geography of their own markets. In the mixed economies, any decision to locate the iron and steel industry away from its markets should therefore be accompanied by a vigorous program aimed at relocating, in the same vicinity, some of the industries that form its major markets. To some extent, this was recognized in Italy.

Paralleling the establishment of the iron works at Taranto, the *Casa per il Mezzogiorno*, which is responsible for economic development in the south (Lutz, 1962), made a major effort to establish an important "pole" of economic growth in the Taranto-Bari region, which included a wide range of metal-consuming industries. But by 1965 its success was still open to question. If such industries could be bullied, bribed, or by various devices induced to locate in the south—if, in other words, the markets could be shifted to the steel mills and if they could be expanded to the point of using

much of the steel produced at Taranto—the political decision to build a
large integrated works in the south would be vindicated. Taranto would
then be of considerable influence in the formulation of regional planning
schemes elsewhere in Western Europe, and indeed the world. However, if
only a few metal-consuming industries are steered into the region (and in
the mixed economies deliberate industrial movement by governments has
nowhere proved easy), most of the production of Taranto for a long time
will have to be transported a considerable distance to its markets. The
plant's management will then have to accept a permanently high-cost location, and it will be forced to concentrate production on those higher-value
products that are best able to absorb relatively high product-transport
costs; possibly, too, it will have to accept a lower return on capital than
works in more advantageous situations.

Taranto, in conclusion, can best be interpreted as a clear and bold political locational decision taken within the context of a broad strategy of regional development. It is a decision that makes economic and social sense
provided a reasonable chance exists for the *total* regional strategy to be
fulfilled. In many other instances, however, the role of political decisions
and influences on the geography of iron and steel manufacture within the
mixed economies is more difficult to isolate, and the logic of political objectives is less easy to follow. Within the older industrial economies of Western Europe—particularly in Britain, France, and West Germany—complex historical and sociological forces bear upon the geography of the
industry and are very difficult to separate from political factors. In these
countries, the iron and steel industry first developed when its technology
and costs encouraged the use of locations near the sources of its raw materials. Despite some signs of spatial readjustment, a substantial component
of the industry has continued to remain in such places through both non-
political and political forces of inertia. Quite apart from the economic
dilemma of choosing the right moment to shift investment to a new location (see Chapter 2), several other types of inertia are also experienced.

Over the years, there has been a certain conservatism of thinking on the
part of those responsible for the industry's locational behavior. While at
the international level, market-oriented iron and steel manufacture was
taken for granted, at the national scale in Western Europe it was often
argued by managements making locational decisions (even between 1950
and 1965) that a continuing orientation of iron and steel production toward its raw materials remained economically advantageous. It is important to respect their views; it is equally imperative to question vigorously
their locational wisdom. Mounting evidence confirms that many considerations affecting the location of steel production were in fact only rarely
studied seriously by those production-oriented metallurgists, engineers,

and managers in whose hands lay the responsibility for the industry's investment decisions. The type of pre-investment question that would normally be raised by a location economist or economic geographer aware of the changing spatial forces affecting the industry was therefore generally ignored. With the ownership of the Western European industry highly balkanized, of course, the options of many steel firms were either to invest further in their existing facilities and plant or not to invest at all. With the construction of a completely new works beyond their financial resources, many firms could not possibly include a geographical variable in their investment considerations.

The locational continuity of much of Western Europe's iron and steel manufacture also stemmed from the fact that distances within the subcontinent, which were never very long, in effect became very much shorter with improvements in communications. Although major steel-consuming industries did not develop close to the principal integrated works, many of the industry's raw-material sites were in fact by 1965 reasonably near the markets for steel. The final explanation of the conservative spatial behavior of the iron and steel industry in the older industrial economies was essentially political. Undoubtedly, pressure was exerted by many governments to keep the industry in its established locations, in order to avoid the social problems and distress that would have accompanied relocation.

While the variety of forces encouraging the spatial inertia of the Western European iron and steel industry is clear, it is difficult to establish with confidence which of the forces was primarily responsible in any particular case. Britain affords a typical example. Having inherited a large number of rather small works sited primarily in response to historical locational priorities, the British industry has for many years been faced with the economic and sociological dilemma of resolving the most advantageous time to relocate its facilities in the light of changing geographical conditions. Its response has followed from a distinctive blend of private enterprise and public activity. Until 1967, the British steel industry was largely in private hands, except for a brief spell of nationalization in the early fifties and the continuing public ownership of one large firm, Richard Thomas and Baldwins Ltd. Nevertheless, throughout the period the government reserved the right broadly to supervise the major investment programs of the industry through the Iron and Steel Board (Britain, 1955, 1957, 1961, 1964), and on a number of occasions became intimately involved in location decision-making.

The locational dilemmas of the British industry can be illustrated initially by the history of the Consett Iron Company in the northeast, which in 1946 had a capacity of 0.5 million ingot tons. Near the western margin of the coalfield, on a relic site of the coke-iron industry's early days, the plant used coking coal hauled some distance from newer pits 30 kilometers to the east, and ore imported from overseas via the Tyne, some 37 kilometers away. Assuming that a case could be made for iron and steel production in northeast England (it certainly could not be taken for granted in the light of the geography of British markets), a steel industry locating in the region *de novo* would obviously prefer a coastal site or sites. This was realized by many in 1946, and by a few even before that date. Some argued that a locational shift of the industry to the coast should be effected immediately (in much the same way that the Dowlais Iron Company in South Wales had moved from the northern edge of that coalfield to the coast at Cardiff in the late nineteenth century). The view of those who disagreed was accepted—on the grounds that the incremental costs of expansion at Consett would be less than on a "green field" site, and that the sociological case for locational inertia was strong, since the local prospects for attracting alternative employment were singularly poor. In postwar years, successive development programs at Consett were approved. By 1965 the works had a capacity of nearly 1.5 million tons, a third L.D. furnace was planned for 1967, and a proposal for further expansion of the works was being canvassed on the grounds that the incremental costs of new capacity there would be lower than at alternative sites.

Whatever the comparative production costs of iron and steel manufacture at Consett in 1965, three points should be made about the works there at that time: (1) The cost of production was without doubt higher than if the plant had been relocated on the coast in 1945 (or even earlier). (2) By 1965 the industry was faced with the dilemma of whether or not to phase out an ill-located works with a capacity approaching 2 million tons. This was a much more formidable task than if the works had been phased out twenty years earlier. (3) While both the local management and political pressures together ensured the continuing expansion of the plant, it is not clear which of the two was primarily responsible.

The British steel industry as a whole from 1950 to 1965 was faced with the Consett problem writ large. Although many small iron and steel works were closed down, progress toward a more profitable geography of production was very slow indeed. Even apparently firm intentions to rationalize the spatial pattern of manufacture all too frequently evaporated. Under the postwar plan for the industry from 1945–50, both the Skinningrove and the South Durham works on Teesside were scheduled for closure. Yet by 1965 they were both still in production, modernized and enlarged. In addition, a new and rather inconvenient "green field" site had been developed by the South Durham Steel Company for small-scale integrated production. As Burn (1961, p. 250) has noted, virtually all the plans for the rationalization and concentration of the industry were in effect largely deferred. Consequently, the average size of furnaces was kept down, rolling mills were underutilized, and scale economies in production were denied the industry. And many of the industry's historical and high-cost sites remained centers of production. In 1965, to produce just over 27 million ingot tons of steel, the industry had twenty-one integrated and thirteen nonintegrated works; their size frequency is recorded in Table 18.

As a consequence of its past investments, the British iron and steel industry inevitably exhibited some characteristics of geographical inertia in regard to both the number and the location of its production facilities. But there were other reasons for its inertia as well. For example, many of those concerned with running the industry proved singularly unadventuresome in their thinking about locational matters. Throughout the classic account by Burn (1961) of the industry between 1939 and 1959, there runs a theme of conservative geographical thinking on the part of the industry's management. And when the government involved itself in the investment decision-making process of the industry, it too displayed a remarkable ignorance of the shifting locational advantages of iron and steel production. In vetting the industry's investment priorities and programs, the Iron and Steel Board left any questions on where the expansion should occur discreetly alone. In the words of Burn (1961, p. 80), "The decision to build a further strip mill was treated as a South Wales question from the first—the Principality's exclusive right to make tinplate was deemed axiomatic." The net result of such attitudes was that the regional distribution of steelmaking in Britain throughout the postwar years remained very much the same as it had been during the thirties.

While there were some grounds for Smith (1949, p. 316) to argue, from largely prewar evidence, that "the location of an iron and steel industry, using relatively low grade materials in bulk, is modelled largely on the provenance of its raw materials . . . the initial stages of manufacture being influenced more profoundly than the latter," by the fifties a somewhat different interpretation of the industry and its geographical priorities would undoubtedly have been more in order. Yet even at the end of the period, the official journal of the industry was prepared to argue that "the industry works with a ratio of more than 4 tons of raw materials to 1 ton of finished steel; so it is clear that, other things being equal, plants will tend to be located closer to the sources of raw material than to the final destination of the finished product" (British Iron and Steel Federation, *Steel Review*, October 1965-B). One year later the Benson Committee, considering the reorganization of the industry, found itself inclined to the view that "given the limited size of Britain, close proximity to markets should not be taken as the major factor determining steelworks locations" (British Iron and Steel Federation, 1966-A, p. 59).

The Benson Committee went on to point to yet another reason for the industry's characteristic of geographical inertia. It noted: "Any U.K. works which is well located from a raw materials point of view would, in practice, have a market for the bulk of its production within a 100-mile (160 km.) radius; and at current freight rates, the difference in cost between delivering within a 50 mile and a 100 mile radius is of the order of only 8s ($1.12) a ton." While an additional cost of $1.12 per ton would represent an extra $17 million to the 1965 industry as a whole—a sum that would not necessarily be offset by lower raw-material costs—a more general point must be made. The growing efficiency of both rail and road transport within the country, toward the end of the period, considerably reduced any disadvantage the industry formerly experienced from not having good access to the Great London and West Midlands markets. However, this improving efficiency of transport in no way ameliorated the parallel problem of the industry's output being divided between too many small works.

Woven into, and at times indistinguishable from, the geographical inertia of plant and works, and the less admissible inertia of spatial thinking, was the influence of more direct political pressures and decisions on the distribution of the industry. In virtually all major locational decisions concerning new sites for British wide-strip mills and their associated iron and steelmaking plant since the thirties, political considerations have played a part. On the whole, they intensified the inertia of the industry. For welfare and sociological motives, and possibly with some real savings in social costs, the government as early as 1937 helped to convince a private steel company to locate its new integrated strip mill on an old steelmaking site in a cramped and relatively isolated Welsh coal-mining valley. This was Ebbw Vale. In the late forties the government persuaded another company, the Steel Company of Wales, to separate by several kilometers its tinning plants from its new integrated works and strip mill in the Swansea area. In 1958 it insisted that the third strip mill in South Wales should be kept artificially small in order that another (very reluctant) company could be persuaded to build a small strip mill in Scotland. It is not a tale of the most enlightened political pressures. To be fair, however, since the necessary research has yet to be attempted, it is still not known in quantitative terms exactly what the costs and benefits (private and public, economic and social) of the several conservative elements in the iron and steel industry's locational decision-making have been. And even if they were known, it would be impossible to isolate the effects of political influences from the several other forces that have helped to give the British iron and steel industry a somewhat historical geography—and have left a pattern of ore demands urgently in need of revision (Manners, 1968-A).

Elsewhere in the older industrial economies of Western Europe (particularly in France, to a lesser extent in West Germany), the same imprecise blend of geographical inertia, conservative locational thinking, and political involvement in the spatial behavior of the iron and steel industry can be traced. In the developing mixed economies, on the other hand, the political element in the emerging geography of the iron and steel industry is clearer. At the international scale, the importance of "soft" low-interest loans from the World Bank, from the Development Assistance Committee of the Organization for Economic Cooperation and Development (OECD), and from national governments cannot be overstressed as a decisive factor in the evolving world geography of iron and steel production. British, French, West German, and Soviet aid to India, Japanese aid to Singapore, American aid to Latin American countries, and the like, were fundamental to the establishment and expansion of the steel industry in those developing nations. In the *Congressional Record* (August 12, 1963) it is reported that funds from the United States passing through the Agency for International Development between 1945 and 1962 helped to build or expand some 179 foreign steel mills at a cost of about $2 billion. Sometimes the loans were offered without qualification. Sometimes, and increasingly, they were given on condition that the steelmaking equipment be purchased in the donor countries. Occasionally the loans were negotiated on the basis that specified trade relationships would be developed between the donor and the recipient. The Japanese, for example, frequently associated their financial and technical assistance for steel-finishing mills in the developing world with agreements ensuring that the mills would use Japanese semifinished steel. Whatever their basis, there can be no doubt that these largely politically inspired loans have been a key factor in the diffusion of iron and steel manufacture throughout the world.

In the developing countries, locational decisions concerning steelmaking have been as varied as in the advanced industrial economies. In many of them a market-oriented strategy has been followed. The major steelworks in Pakistan are at Karachi; in Malaysia, at Singapore; in Egypt, at Cairo. Particularly when the industry has established itself through the construction of finishing mills in the first instance, and then integrated backward into steel and pig iron production, market orientation has predominated. In other circumstances, a parallel to the Italian Taranto case is to be found. The Guayana-Orinoco iron and steel complex in Venezuela was developed in the mid-sixties in what was until recently an almost unpopulated region. It took advantage of the huge iron ore deposits of the area, and of the very low-cost power available from the Caroni-Orinoco hydroelectric project. And it was intimately associated with the government's broader industrial development and diversification plans, which provided for the construction of a new city (with an initial population of some 250,000) and the establishment of a number of metal-transforming industries and other steel markets in the district. A similar development was proposed for North Patagonia in Argentina, associated with the rich deposits of the Sierra Grande iron ore and a Rio Negro hydroelectric project.

Occasionally a situation arose in the developing world where the capacity of the transport system was insufficient to permit the long-distance movement of large quantities of raw materials, and where capital was not available for expansion of the system. As a result, raw-material orientations have sometimes been chosen for the steel industry in order to minimize the strain on the transport system. In India, apart from political considerations affecting the location of works, the steel production industry has been expanded near its raw materials, partly in order to avoid overburdening the country's railways with large tonnages of raw materials moving toward market-oriented plants. In Brazil, the Volta Redonda plant (with a 1965 capacity to produce 1.25 million tons) is ideally located to serve the markets of both São Paulo and Rio de Janeiro, the country's two largest consumer centers. This plant has very good transport links with the inland iron ore deposits at Lafayette, and in 1965 the company wanted to expand there. Whether the transport system on which the works relied could support such an expansion was questionable. It was suggested that if the railway facilities were inadequate and could not be expanded by the government, an entirely new plant would have to be built to the north of Rio de Janeiro at Vale de Parapoeva.

Political decisions that defy reasonable explanation can also be found in the geography of the iron and steel industry in the developing world. The plans for a small integrated steelworks in northeast Brazil, and plans for a plant in the Mexican state of Sonora, come to mind. Such proposals represent either a misinterpretation of the locational requirements of iron and steel manufacture, or simply a response to the crudest of political forces. Such forces are relevant to an understanding of the geography of iron and steel production, and of iron ore demands, in the developing world.

LOCATIONAL ANALYSIS IN THE FULLY PLANNED ECONOMIES

The political factor as a locational force in the iron and steel industry reaches its fullest expression in the fully planned economies. In such economies the ideas and principles of classical economics have only a limited relevance to an understanding of the values used in economic—including locational—decision-making. There are, of course, certain common denominators affecting the geographical characteristics of the industry in both types of economic system. It is obvious from Soviet literature that as high a degree of cost consciousness exists in the ranks of Soviet managerial and technical personnel as in, say, the United States. In the Soviet

Union, however, detailed studies of the costs of pig iron and steel production are published for different locations in a way that is unknown in North America or Western Europe. In the U.S.S.R., as Clark (1961) put it, "administrative decree[s] . . . took the secrecy wraps off the publication of detailed cost data" (p. 24). The technology of iron and steel manufacture in both the fully planned and the market economies has common roots. It is not surprising that in both economic systems the ability to produce concentrated ores and sinter has reduced the iron ore and coke requirements of pig iron production and so lowered the costs of assembling raw materials at a blast furnace. Similarly, in both systems it has been found that, in general, integrated iron and steel production has cost advantages to offer over unintegrated production, but that for small and isolated market areas it is often advantageous to establish unintegrated works based on scrap to satisfy local demands. However, the basic investment criteria of the two types of economic system are quite different. In the one case, the objective is the maximization of profit, modified by certain institutional, sociological, and political factors. In the other, it is described in such terms as "the systematic territorial distribution of enterprises . . . with a view to including the natural and labour resources of all the economic regions into the process of expanded socialist production" (Bannyy et al., 1960, p. 170). As a consequence, some divergence in the locational patterns of their respective iron and steel industries and in the patterns of ore demand is to be expected.

There has yet to appear, in English publications at least, a fully satisfactory interpretation of the geographical criteria governing investment decision-making in the Soviet iron and steel industry. In one exposition of the *Economics of Iron and Steel in the U.S.S.R.* (Bannyy et al., 1960, pp. 169–75), it is argued:

One of the basic laws of a socialist society is the law of systematic and proportional development which came into being as a counterbalance to the anarchy and competition of the capitalist world. . . . The major purpose of the distribution of industry in a socialist society is to secure an all round systematic and rapid development of a country's productive resources, the fullest utilisation of the resources of all the economic regions and, finally, a reduction in the use of labour for the creation of material wealth. The distribution of industry in the U.S.S.R., including ferrous metallurgy, is governed by the following basic principles: 1. A systematic territorial distribution of the enterprises in the country with a view to including the natural and labour resources of all the economic regions into the process of expanded socialist production. . . . 2. Locating the enterprises close to the sources of raw material and fuel as well as to the consumer areas. . . . 3. The all-round economic development of the erstwhile backward areas and national republics. . . . 4. The systematic and complex development of the economic regions. . . . and 5. Strengthening the country's independence and defensive capacity.

Unresolved in such a set of principles are the appropriate locational strategy and investment criteria where there happens to be no geographical coincidence of the markets for steel products and the raw materials used in iron and steel manufacture. To quote Bannyy *et al.* (p. 174) once again, "The location of the [iron and steel] industry close to the sources of raw materials and fuel is one of the most important principles of the socialist distribution of industry." Yet only a few paragraphs earlier (p. 173) they argue that "it is also important to have the metallurgical enterprises close to the areas consuming the finished metal product which usually have large quantities of scrap metal. If a plant is located far from its iron ore and coal sources but close to the metal consuming areas with their large reserves of scrap metal, the cost of its metal products to the consumer may be lower than that of the metal shipped in from far away." When future economic, regional, and physical plans are being drawn up by Soviet planners, the matter can presumably be easily resolved by regarding "markets" as a locational variable that can be moved to, or developed in, districts with the necessary steelmaking raw materials. This, more than in Italy, would be regarded as a perfectly legitimate exercise within the fully planned economy of the U.S.S.R. But where markets already exist away from those raw materials—as they in fact do in the Soviet Union—there would appear to be an unresolved contradiction in the Soviet writings on the steel industry's locational problem.

In reality, on the other hand, an examination of the geographical shifts in the Soviet industry suggests that, as in the market economies, the locational attraction of markets for iron and steel production has been increasing. During the first five-year plans, the Soviet iron and steel industry was expanded almost entirely near the source of its raw materials, such as the coal and ore of the Ukraine or the iron ores of the Urals. Subsequently, however, large and growing investments have been made in what can only be described as increasingly market-oriented plants, such as Novo-Lipetsk (near Moscow) and Cherepovets (near Leningrad). "Oriented" is, of course, a relative term. Novo-Lipetsk is some 350 km away from Moscow, and Cherepovets over 400 km from Leningrad. On the other hand, the iron ore and coking coal for the Cherepovets plant have to be railed over very much greater distances from the Kola Peninsula (1,500 km) and the Pechora Basin (1,900 km), respectively. Moscow and Leningrad, in addition, have small unintegrated works, which rely heavily on scrap and either electric or open-hearth furnaces to produce special steels or products for associated engineering works.

Behind this changing locational pattern lay some quite fundamental changes in the railway freight rate policy of the country. Within the Soviet economic system, it has historically been argued that the means and the costs of transport should not be allowed to determine the location of industrial activity. Instead, it was suggested that a geographical pattern of industrial development should be served by a transport system constructed and priced for its successful completion and operation. Freight rates, therefore, both for the movement of raw materials and the finished steel products, are administered by the central planning authorities in order to help bring about the desired pattern of industrial development.

During the first two five-year plans, it was the objective of economic and regional planning to expand iron and steel production at the source of its raw materials, both in European Russia and in Western Siberia. To achieve this end, the freight rates allocated to the movement of finished steel were relatively low, while those on raw-material shipments were generally higher than in the market economies. The major exception concerned the famous iron ore and coking-coal shuttle service between the Urals and the Kuzbas. In that case, the extremely long haul of raw materials demanded low transport rates in order to justify the whole industrial location decision. As a result, the ton-kilometer rates allocated in 1928 were approximately one-third of those charged for coal shipments generally throughout the Soviet Union, and about one-half the average rate for ore movements. The arrangement was eventually subject to severe criticism. It was argued that the actual costs of the operation were more than twice the rates charged, and that the Urals and Kuzbas iron and steel industries were being subsidized by the rest of Soviet industry. Nevertheless, the general levels of freight rates on finished products and raw materials before World War II meant that the regional planning objectives of developing a raw-material–oriented iron and steel industry appeared to be economically advantageous. The penalty, of course, was the steady increase in the length of haul needed to get steel products to their markets—787 km in 1931 and 1,019 in 1938.

After the second five-year plan, in contrast, the gigantomania of the early Communist years gave way to a search for a new geography of industrial development incorporating a greater degree of regional self-sufficiency. Soviet ideas on the regionalization of economic activity thus came to be of growing importance to the distribution of iron and steel production between the regions, and steps were taken under the third five-year plan to build a number of small steelworks at, and to serve, the more remote centers of demand. It was at this time that works were planned for Transcaucasia and in Azerbaijan to serve the local Baku oil industry. This was also the time when the decision to build a steel plant at Komsomolsk was taken—a decision for which a rational explanation evades most Western observers, since it affords easy access to neither sources of raw materials nor a regional market. Simultaneously, it was decided to construct three or four major steel-consuming enterprises near the existing large centers of iron and steel production—a decision, in other words, to move at least some of the markets close to mills.

In line with these developments, it was recognized during the third five-year plan that transport costs could no longer be regarded as matters of secondary importance, but must assume a more central place in economic and locational decision-making. In 1939, therefore, in order to encourage a reduction in the burden to the economy of the long-distance hauls of both steel products and at times raw materials, all freight rates were raised to more nearly cover their costs. The ton-kilometer rates for the transport of steel products were raised to about the same level as those for ore, and above those for coal (Hunter, 1957).

The new freight rate structure clearly increased the locational attractions of markets for iron and steel production, and this trend was even further emphasized in 1950 when for the first time the administered price of iron and steel was quoted c.i.f., and the cost of moving the finished products to market became significant in the accounts of the industry. While the Soviet Union has continued to expand and modernize its iron and steel production at many raw-material–oriented locations since World War II, a tendency has emerged to invest increasingly in plants with a good or reasonable access to their markets. Some of the older raw-material–oriented centers of production, such as the Ukraine, were by 1965 located within regions of considerable steel demands; they were well placed to serve their markets. In addition, there has been a rapid expansion of iron and steel production of an essentially market-oriented character in central European Russia. By 1965 that region produced approximately 11 percent of the country's steel, and plans were well advanced for the further expansion of its capacity on a significant scale.

Dialectical considerations apart, the spatial behavior of the iron and steel industry in the fully planned economies appears to have paralleled to some degree developments in the market economies as an increasing proportion of capacity came to be located primarily to ensure good market access. The major difference between the two economic systems is that in the planned economies the location of markets is subject to a considerable degree of spatial manipulation by the economic planning authorities (they frequently regarded the iron and steel industry as a primary lever in manipulating the geography of their markets), whereas in the market economies the distribution of steel demands is accepted as the outcome of largely unalterable market forces.

This thesis is confirmed in one sense by an examination of developments in the iron and steel industry of Middle Europe. Naturally, some variations in the siting characteristics of the industry can be noted. In Poland and Czechoslovakia, for example, there has been a tendency to erect new plants to serve various regional planning objectives; yet, viewed in the context of the Eastern European economic system, they were all essentially market-oriented plants. Drawing on Russian and other foreign supplies of iron ore —and sometimes also importing the coking coal they required—the iron and steel industries of these countries were at root a response to the domestic market opportunities that were opening up.

In sum, any interpretation of the changing world geography of the iron and steel industry in the second half of the twentieth century must above all point to the strength of the locational pulls toward its markets. Under all economic systems at the international level, the market orientation of the industry was taken for granted, but it was increasingly recognized at the national level too. Technological, historical, transport, political, and sociological factors were by no means irrelevant, of course, to the geographical behavior of the industry. But as the changing distribution of the demand for, the trade in, and the production of iron and steel between 1950 and 1965 is examined (see Chapter 6), the all-important attraction of the industry's markets is repeatedly underlined. Only on this foundation can an understanding of the geography of iron ore demands be built.

Changing Patterns of Iron Ore Demand

THE DEMAND FOR IRON ORE IN 1950

Although the world had progressed a long way by 1950 toward its recovery from World War II, the pattern of crude steel consumption throughout the world was still stamped with the impress of a conflict that had left the United States by far the most powerful nation. Out of a total apparent steel consumption of 192 million ingot tons, over 47 percent was used in North America, and nearly 45 percent—just under 86 million tons—in the United States (Table 22; see also Table A-1). In Western Europe, with the help of American aid programs, great strides had been made toward economic rehabilitation. Even so, the apparent consumption of steel per head in each European country was less than one-half of that in the United States, with the result that the much larger European population was able to generate a demand for only 44 million tons of crude steel, less than one-quarter of the world market. Similarly in Eastern Europe, but in this case within a closed economy, the Soviet Union and its Middle European neighbors were rebuilding their war-torn economies. By 1950 sufficient progress had been made for their steel needs to have risen to about 27 million tons in the U.S.S.R. and a further 8.5 million tons in the rest of the region; together these represented 18.3 percent of the apparent world steel consumption. Finally, throughout the rest of the world—in Asia, Oceania, Africa, the Middle East, and Latin America—poverty and technological backwardness dominated a scene in which less than 10 percent of world steel consumption was to be found. Countries of relative affluence, such as Australia, New Zealand, and South Africa certainly used considerable amounts of steel per head, but their relatively small populations meant that they made little impact on the magnitude and the importance of the "region" as a whole.

107

TABLE 22.   WORLD APPARENT CONSUMPTION OF CRUDE STEEL, BY REGIONS, 1950 AND 1965

Region	Total apparent consumption (*thousands of ingot tons*)		Percentage	
	1950	1965	1950	1965
Total...............................	191,575	455,656	100.00	100.00
North America.........................	90,139	138,099	47.05	30.31
Western Europe........................	45,031	115,076	23.51	25.26
Eastern Europe........................	35,100	117,438	18.32	25.77
Asia.................................	7,953	52,802	4.15	11.59
Oceania..............................	2,512	6,473	1.31	1.42
Latin America.........................	3,681	11,307	1.92	2.48
Africa and Middle East.................	3,309	8,509	1.73	1.87
Unallocated production.................	3,850	5,952	2.01	1.31

Source: United Nations, *Statistical Yearbook;* and author's estimates. See Table A-1 for consumption by countries.

At the level of both these macroregions and their constituent countries, most of this demand for steel was met by local production. International trade in steel products in 1950 amounted to 15.8 million product tons, an equivalent of 20.5 million ingot tons or 10.7 percent of production. The major exporters (Figure 3) were several Western European countries—later, members of the European Economic Community (France and West Germany in particular)—Britain, and the United States. The exports of the Western European countries were strongly oriented toward their former colonial territories, while those of the United States were mainly destined for Latin America and Canada. About one-quarter of the trade was between the exporting countries themselves. The relatively small volume of total steel trade, however, meant that the geography of steel demand was fairly closely mirrored in the spatial pattern of steel production (see Figure 6 and Table 28; also Table A-2). North America once again dominated the pattern, with 48.6 percent of the world total. Western Europe, with 27.4 percent, produced rather more than its share of consumption. Eastern Europe was essentially self-sufficient with 18.6 percent. And the rest of the world produced a mere 10 million ingot tons, or 5.5 percent of the world total. Nationally, the largest producers were the United States (90 million tons) and the U.S.S.R. (27 million tons). Britain with 17, West Germany with 14, and France with 9 million tons were the only other countries with outputs above 5 million tons, although Japan nearly produced that volume with 4.8 million tons.

The quantitative relationship between pig iron demand and steel production is a close but variable one. It is influenced in part by the amount of scrap used in the manufacture of steel (see Chapter 3), and (since in a

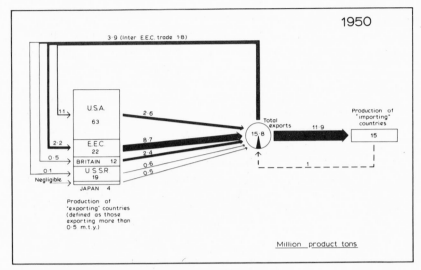

FIGURE 3. Pattern of international steel trade, 1950.

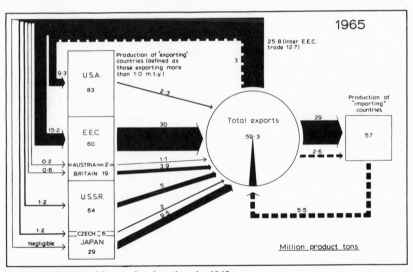

FIGURE 4. Pattern of international steel trade, 1965.

number of developing countries there is a tendency for cast iron to be used for a variety of manufactures) in part by the stage of a country's economic development. On a world basis in 1950 some 90 million tons of scrap were used in steel production, and about 29 million tons of pig iron were smelted in foundries. The apparent consumption of pig iron as a result stood at about 134 million tons. With only 2.7 million tons of this demand being satisfied through international trade, its spatial distribution generated as a result an almost identical geography of pig iron production (see Table 29; also Table A-3). Once again, the largest share of the world's output was in North America, which accounted for 46.8 percent. The Western European share was 29.3 percent, slightly greater than its share of the world's steel production; this was largely a response to the region's considerable production of Bessemer steel with its relatively small scrap input. Eastern Europe produced just under 18 percent of the world total. And the rest of the world, with China and India in particular using considerable quantities of pig iron for unsophisticated manufactured products, smelted just over 6 percent. On a national basis, the United States produced the most pig iron, 60 million tons; the countries of the (then forthcoming) European Economic Community had an output of 26 million tons; the U.S.S.R. made 20 and Britain 10 million tons. The other significant pig iron producers, such as Japan, Canada, Czechoslovakia, India, and Poland, all had outputs of about 2 million tons.

The relationship between pig iron production and the demand for iron ore expressed in terms of actual tons is naturally subject to considerable fluctuation, as a result of the different qualities and, in particular, the variable iron content of the ores used. But even the relationship between pig iron output and iron ore demand measured in terms of iron content is subject to a certain amount of variation. The ratio between the two can vary between the 1 : 0.52 of West Germany (in 1950), to the 1 : 0.85 of the United States (in 1950) and the ratio of approximately 1 : 1 reported for the U.S.S.R. throughout most of the postwar years. These variations are a function of the quantity of scrap (circulating and purchased) used in pig iron production, the general level of blast-furnace efficiency, and the nature of the ferro-alloys produced in the furnace.

The world demand for iron ore in 1950 was 116 million "c" tons (see Figure 10 and Table 30; also Table A-4). Of this amount, North America consumed 55 million "c" tons, 47.4 percent of the total, and about the same proportion as the region's share of pig iron production. Western Europe, on the other hand, accounted for only 25 percent of the world's iron ore demands, compared with its 29 percent share of the world's pig iron output. Its relatively small consumption of iron ore, 29 million "c" tons, was a function of the exceptionally high rate of scrap consumption in its blast-furnace practice (especially in West Germany), and its considerable output of ferro-alloys. In Eastern Europe and the rest of the world, iron ore consumption was relatively greater than the regional share of pig iron output. Eastern Europe afforded a market for 25 million "c" tons of ore (21.2 percent of the world total); and the rest of the world consumed 7.5 million "c" tons (6.5 percent). On a national basis, the United States

(52.7 million "c" tons) and the U.S.S.R. (20.4 million "c" tons) were the two largest markets; future European Coal and Steel Community (ECSC) countries consumed 18 million "c" tons, with French demands for ore (unlike their production of pig iron) standing slightly above those of West Germany; and Britain consumed nearly 9 million "c" tons. The other notable centers of iron ore demand were India, Czechoslovakia, Australia, Poland, and Japan, each of which used between 1 and 2 million "c" tons of ore.

Such, then, was the broad geography of iron ore demands in 1950. It was, of course, the distinctive product of the immediate postwar years. It was a pattern in the process of being changed.

CHANGING DEMANDS FOR IRON AND STEEL

The consumption of iron and steel in any country or region is closely related to the living standards attained there. As national or regional incomes rise, so, by and large, does the demand for steel and pig iron (United Nations, 1954-A, p. 44). The relationship is by no means linear, since the rate of growth of demand for steel in the industrially mature economies tends to be rather slower than that in countries still in the early stages of industrial development. And the relationship is by no means uniform, since there are some countries whose industrial structure makes for rather heavier iron and steel demands than are to be found in countries with comparable living standards. Nevertheless, the relationship generally holds true. As a result, the transformation of the world economy and living standards during the years between 1950 and 1965 was of paramount importance to the geography of iron and steel consumption.

In a changing order, the economic dominance of the United States in the world was gradually reduced. Although its population grew steadily and its living standards continued to rise (and still remained unequaled in 1965), in a rapidly expanding world economy it was inevitable that the American share of global wealth should be reduced. In Western Europe a vigorous and diversified economy affording a rapidly rising income per head was built on the ruins of World War II. By 1965, Western Europe's average standard of living certainly had not reached North American levels, and there remained extensive pockets of poverty both nationally and regionally. Yet the growing affluence of the continent left a firm impress on the world pattern of iron and steel demands. From much poorer beginnings, in the fully planned economies of Eastern Europe the foundations were successfully laid for the development of technologically advanced societies, and the basic infrastructure was acquired for yet further economic growth. Their progress may have expressed itself somewhat differently from the pattern of economic development in the market and mixed economies of the West. Nevertheless, toward the end of the period the economic achievements of Eastern Europe were being reflected in higher levels of personal consumption, which in turn affected the quality as well as the quantity of steel demands. Throughout the rest of the world as well, although there remained vast areas of desperate poverty, certain countries—such as Japan, Australia, Mexico, and South Africa—exhibited either dramatic or continuing progress in the improvement of their living standards. As elsewhere, their economic progress was directly reflected in their needs for iron and steel.

From a level of 191 million tons in 1950, the world apparent consumption of steel rose to 456 million ingot tons in 1965 (Table 23; see also Table A-1). This was an increase of nearly 150 percent, and an annual average (compound) growth rate of 6 percent. Pig iron consumption similarly rose from 134 to 335 million tons, an almost identical rate of expansion. And with these changes in demand came radical shifts in the geography of the markets for iron and steel throughout the world. In the United States, for example, the consumption of iron and steel grew only slowly. The apparent consumption of steel there was 90 million tons in 1950. Yet, although the American economy continued to grow at a moderate pace, and the country's population increased from 152 to 194 million, consumption fluctuated around the 90 to 100 million tons range throughout most of the period. Only in 1964/65 did it leap up to new record levels of just under 128 million tons. Pig iron demand followed suit. In 1950 it stood at 60 million tons; by 1965 it had increased by about 20 million tons.

There were several reasons for this relatively slow growth of the American market for iron and steel products: First, consumption per head of iron and steel in the United States at the beginning of the period was far above that of any other country, and the American economy did not have to experience a postwar recovery comparable to that which transformed demand throughout most of Western Europe, Eastern Europe, and parts of the Far East, especially Japan. Second, competition from alternative

TABLE 23. STEEL PRODUCTION, BY PROCESS, IN SELECTED COUNTRIES, 1966

(Percentage of total output)

Country	Open hearth	Bessemer	Electric furnace	Basic oxygen (L.D. and similar)
Britain........................	59.1	5.3	13.8	21.9
France........................	22.9	52.4	8.5	14.4
Japan.........................	18.0		19.3	62.7
U.S.A.........................	63.4		11.1	25.3
U.S.S.R.......................	84.3		9.2	3.8
West Germany.................	39.2	27.8	8.7	24.3

Source: United States, Senate Committee on Finance, 1967, p. 20.

industrial materials, such as plastics, glass, paper, and aluminum, gained strength and succeeded in capturing some of the traditional markets of the iron and steel industry. While steel continued to be a basic material for the American economy and remained entrenched in its main markets, peripheral substitution took place all the time. And third, partly in response to this competition, and partly as a result of technological progress, the quality of steel improved. Thus smaller tonnages per unit of output were required in particular industries (the motor car industry used thinner sheets for its bodies, and the construction industry used smaller tonnages of more specialized steels for its buildings and bridges). In fact, consumption per head in the United States actually fell between 1950 and 1963. By 1965, however, it had reached a new American record of 656 kilograms per head, a figure that was exceeded only by Sweden. These were the trends and problems that the iron and steel industries of all advanced countries would have to face sooner or later as their technology and steel requirements became more sophisticated.

The Canadian economy was at a much earlier stage of development in 1950. As a consequence, Canada's demand for iron and steel during the following fifteen years was not subject to the same restricting forces as were operating in the United States. Steel consumption rose steadily to reach 10.4 million tons by 1965, more than twice the 1950 demand of 4 million tons. North America as a whole, therefore, increased its apparent consumption of steel during the period from 90 to 138 million tons. Its share of the world market, on the other hand, fell from 47 to 30 percent.

Throughout the fifties, the demand for iron and steel in Western Europe surged upward, with the countries of the European Economic Community (especially West Germany) setting the pace. Steel needs grew from 45 to 96 million tons during the decade to 1960, and in the latter year Western European requirements temporarily exceeded those of North America. This growth reflected the rapid recovery and the exciting transformation of the Western European economy from the destruction and dislocation of the war. Indeed, the figures for the individual countries show a clear relationship between the intensity of wartime destruction and the rate of recovery, including growth in demands for steel. Thus the market for steel in West Germany rose nearly threefold, from 10 to 29 million tons, whereas demand in Britain grew from 14 to only 22 million tons, a 50 percent increase.

By the early sixties, however, the rate of growth of iron and steel demand throughout the region as a whole had begun to show clear signs of slackening, and successive obstacles were presented to the Western European countries in their quest for further rapid economic growth. The levels of steel consumption per head were steadily approaching the near-saturation levels of the two North American economies (see Table A-1), and by 1961 demand per head in West Germany temporarily exceeded that of the United States. Competition from substitute materials increased in intensity, and there was a growing use of higher-quality steels. By 1965, therefore, the demand for steel in Western Europe had moved up 19 million tons in five years, to 115 million tons. Some 23 million tons less than that of North America, it now represented a quarter of the world market.

In Eastern Europe the apparent consumption of iron and steel expanded both faster and more consistently than that of Western Europe. Between 1950 and 1965 steel requirements rose from 35 to 117 million tons to create a market slightly larger than that of Western Europe. There were some signs in the early sixties that the rate of growth of demand was to some extent slowing down. This was, however, only a relative slackening, since the consumption of steel per head of the population still remained low by North American standards. Some countries in Eastern Europe, such as Czechoslovakia and East Germany, as a result of their industrial structures, had a particularly high consumption of steel per head. Middle Europe, where only 8.5 million tons of steel were being used at the beginning of the period, nearly quadrupled its needs to 31 million tons in 1965. Poland and Czechoslovakia were the main centers of demand, and Middle Europe's apparent consumption of steel in that year was almost as large as that of West Germany. However, the greater part of the region's use of steel continued to be located in the U.S.S.R., which by 1965 afforded a market for 87 million tons.

The changing pattern of iron and steel consumption in the rest of the world defies generalization. In some regions and countries the growth of demand was quite dramatic; in others it barely changed throughout the fifteen years. Undoubtedly, the outstanding development occurred in Japan, where a war-shattered economy consuming a mere 4 million tons of steel in 1950 was transformed into a growing industrial power using 29 million tons in 1965. Although the available statistics are notoriously unreliable, during the same period the use of steel in China probably increased from just over 1 million tons to somewhere in the region of 11 million tons; and in 1965 pig iron consumption there was very much higher at about 18 million tons. In India, the other major market of Asia, progress was rather less spectacular; nevertheless, the demand for steel increased from less than 2 million tons to nearly 7.5 million. Three other countries consumed more than 3 million tons of steel in 1965: Australia (5.8 million tons), South Africa (4.2), and Brazil (3.1). Although the tonnages of iron and steel used in other countries of Asia, Latin America, and Africa remained relatively small, the *rate* of growth of demand throughout these developing continents as a whole was significantly above that of North America and of Europe.

The Construction of New Capacity

The first response to these changes in the demand for iron and steel was a rush to expand existing iron and steel works and to build entirely new works throughout the world. Most of the new capacity was located in the countries and regions with the largest and fastest-growing markets—that is, in Western Europe, Eastern Europe, and Japan. In addition, especially during the last eight years of the period, the developing world was also able to boast an increasing number of relatively small iron and steel works. By 1965, many countries that fifteen years earlier had relied entirely on imports had become small producers. In Latin America, Colombia, Chile, Peru, Uruguay, Venezuela, Cuba, and Puerto Rico were in this category (see Table A-2). Altogether about seventy countries were making steel in 1965, about twice the number making it in 1950.

This proliferation of new iron and steelmaking facilities permitted and even encouraged technological diffusion, experimentation, and advance throughout the world. The spectacular changes in the technology of the industry between 1950 and 1965 (see Chapter 3) could only have been achieved within a framework of rapidly growing markets and continuing investment in new plant. The fifteen years were also characterized by the rapid growth of technical literature on iron and steel production, and its speedy communication to the industry throughout the world. The technical conference, the study tour, and the exchange visit were all means whereby developments in any one part of the world were quickly made known and exploited elsewhere.

There were, however, spatial differences in the rates at which the new technology with its lower costs could be, and was, accepted. Its diffusion was a function of economic necessity and opportunity. American iron and steel producers, with their large markets and scale economies, could afford to neglect many new developments in a way that Canadian manufacturers, with smaller markets and inherently higher costs, could not. As a consequence, the iron and steel industry of Canada was technologically more adventuresome than its United States counterpart in introducing, for example, refinements in its open-hearth furnaces and in adopting continuous casting. And in those parts of the world where demand expanded particularly rapidly—West Germany in the fifties, Japan in the sixties—the introduction of new technology was infinitely easier than in countries experiencing slower rates of growth. A situation thus emerged in which a much larger proportion of the iron and steelmaking facilities of these "growth" countries was new and modern in comparison with others. By 1965 the Japanese steel industry was able to boast a much larger share of its steel-making capacity in L.D. converters than any other major producing country (see Table 23). Herein was a source of a new set of differentials in the international costs of making iron and steel. There were others, too.

The changing delivered price of raw materials differed from country to country. The variable nature of their transport costs is exposed in Chapters 9 and 10, and something of the range of delivered ore prices is recorded in Chapter 12. The cost of coking coal to the steel industry also displayed considerable international differences, with some Western European producers paying heavily for the various measures designed by their governments to protect their coal industries. International differences in iron and steelmaking costs also stemmed from variable opportunities and willingness of producers to exploit the economies of scale in production (four examples are shown in Table 18) and in the costs of labor. Hourly steel labor costs in the United States in 1964 were $4.63, compared with $1.68 in West Germany, $1.58 in Italy, $1.23 in Britain, and only $0.64 in Japan. Meanwhile, output per man-year in Britain was only one-half of that being achieved in Japan.

One country's cost advantage in the matter of one factor input was frequently offset by its disadvantage in another. The American industry's economies of scale were offset by comparatively high labor costs; low raw-material costs in India were offset by relatively high process costs. Theoretically, it would be instructive to make a detailed comparison of various national steelmaking costs and their changes through time, but the comprehensive cost data that would be required are not available publicly. There is a good deal of evidence, on the other hand, to suggest that, on average, Japanese steelmaking costs in 1965 were substantially below those of the United States iron and steel industry, and that Western European costs by and large lay somewhere between the two. Some estimated values

TABLE 24.   ESTIMATED AVERAGE PRODUCTION COST AND DELIVERED PRICE TO U.S. CONSUMERS OF ONE TON OF CARBON STEEL PRODUCTS, CIRCA 1965

	Source		
Item	U.S.A.	Japan	Western Europe
Average cost, f.o.t. mill.	$133	$100	$116
Average U.S. freight rate.	10	5	5
Ocean freight.		15	15
Average tariff.		7	7
Average cost c.i.f.	143	127	143
Average delivered price.	163	143	143
Pretax profit.	20	16	0

Source: United States, Senate Committee on Finance, 1967, p. 24.

are given in Table 24; they are derived from work conducted on behalf of the American Iron and Steel Institute. In a sense they are symbolic, yet they undoubtedly point in the direction of reality. Indeed, for certain situations the figures understate the competitive position of Japanese producers in international markets. Not unnaturally, the broad pattern of international trade in steel products shifted in response to these new cost differentials.

THE "SURPLUS" OF STEELMAKING CAPACITY

The pattern and the magnitude of world trade in steel were also considerably affected by the changing relationship between steelmaking capacity and demand. Whereas in 1950 many parts of the world were suffering from a shortage of iron and steel products, and world consumption stood somewhere below the actual (but partly unsatisfied) demand, by 1965 many steelmakers were embarrassed by what was widely regarded as a considerable surplus of productive capacity. The term "surplus capacity" is all too easy to use; in reality, the concept is difficult to define with accuracy. It is even more difficult to quantify, since the amount of iron or steel that a given piece of equipment is capable of producing varies with the efficiency of its use, the length of unchanged production runs, and the number and duration of daily shifts. Consequently, data on the expansion of world iron and steelmaking capacity are available in only rather generalized terms. In 1950, world steelmaking capacity was something like 200 million ingot tons. This figure is slightly above the level of production in that year, since, although in many places there was a shortage of steel, some plants with surplus capacity in the United States could not economically meet unsatisfied demands elsewhere; and yet other plants could not be fully utilized because of raw-material shortages or inappropriate finishing facilities. By 1965, however, according to one estimate (Table 25), capacity had been increased to 525 million tons.

During the early years of the fifties, the growth of world steelmaking capacity, by and large, kept pace with the growth of steel demands. But after 1958 the construction of new facilities tended steadily to outstrip the

TABLE 25. ESTIMATED WORLD CRUDE STEEL CAPACITY AND PRODUCTION, 1950–1965

(Millions of ingot tons)

Item	1950	1955	1958	1960	1961	1962	1963	1964	1965
Estimated capacity..........	200	281	344	396	424	448	475	508	525
Production.................	192	270	274	339	353	360	385	435	456
Surplus capacity............	8	11	70	57	71	88	90	73	69
Percentage.................	4	4	20	14	17	20	18	14	13

Source: Norris Oakley Brothers, 1966, p. 43. Alternative estimates can be found in British Iron and Steel Federation, 1966-A, p. 26.

expansion of demand. The result was that while the margin between the two was about 8 million tons in 1950, it had widened to 88 million tons twelve years later. By 1965, following the upswing of American demands, the gap had narrowed slightly again, to 69 million tons. These figures would certainly not be accepted by steel industry statisticians in all countries. Some producers, for example, tend to maintain a certain amount of obsolete and written-down equipment to meet peak demands; and although this might represent about 10 percent of peak-year capacity, American producers are reluctant to include it in their capacity assessments for "normal" years. The Japanese, from their domestic experience, might be inclined to place higher capacity figures on Western European plants than their owners. And there are many who would doubt the ability of the U.S.S.R. regularly to produce steel (as is claimed) at 100 percent of its industry's capacity. Nevertheless, it is clear that on a world scale the capacity to produce steel in the late fifties and early sixties considerably outstripped the apparent ability to consume it. The reasons for this world surplus of capacity were fourfold:

1. From the mid-fifties onward, new steel industries were started in countries which traditionally had imported steel from Western Europe and North America. Part of the market supplied by these new works had previously been left unsatisfied for foreign-exchange reasons. Another part represented the growth in the developing countries' domestic needs. A third part, however, had formerly been satisfied by the traditional steel-exporting countries; and it proved difficult for these exporters to adjust both their thinking and their capacity to a revised market situation in which they were forced to concentrate their attention increasingly on purely domestic and regional demands.

2. Quite contrary to many expectations, the demand for iron and steel products in the technologically advanced economies did not increase at a rate comparable to its growth performance in the past. This was partly the result of domestic economies failing to expand as fast as had been expected. It was also the result of an unexpected weakening in the intensity of steel demand as technology advanced and steel came to be used with greater economy. In Britain's case, domestic steel requirements of the early sixties were projected in 1955 on the assumption of the continued growth rate of the Gross National Product at 3 percent per year. The growth rate actually achieved by 1962 averaged only 2.3 percent per year, with the result that steel production stood 5 million tons below the level that had been forecast. Between 1960 and 1966, however, when the country's GNP increased at a rate nearer to 3 percent per year and 17 percent over the six-year period, the steel intensity factor came to play a key role in restraining the growth of demand, and consumption increased by only 11 percent. This British

experience was not unique. Western Europe and North America had similar experiences. The result was an overprovision and underutilization of new steelmaking facilities.

3. The growing surplus of capacity also stemmed from the fact that technological advances seen in virtually all branches of the industry throughout the period offered lower unit production costs. Consequently, many manufacturers (especially those controlled by technology-minded rather than market-minded managements) were tempted to install new plant, and to install it with a capacity in excess of their existing requirements in order to gain further economies through larger-scale production. This would have been a successful strategy had only a few producers pursued it. In the event, many did, and their actions compounded the problem of surplus steelmaking capacity.

4. In many respects the most important reason for the overprovision of iron and steel plant stemmed from changes in the technology, transport costs, markets, and raw-material sources—indeed, the total locational economics—of the industry. Together, these changes created many new and economically attractive locations for iron and steel production. At the same time, they meant that an equally large number of existing locations for iron and steel manufacture became redundant through their high costs. Although new works and facilities were only too readily erected at new locations, the owners of plants situated on the high-cost sites were generally reluctant to close them down. As a consequence, there was a geography as well as a history to the emergence of a surplus capacity in the iron and steel industry.

While there might be some legitimacy in speaking about a *world* surplus of iron and steelmaking capacity in the early sixties, it is equally important to recognize that at the end of the period there were some markets in which a shortage of steel persisted, and some producers who were unable to meet all the demands made on them. In 1965, India's steel mills had order books that would keep them busy for several years to come. And in 1966 the Managing Director of Japan's Nippon Kokan Corporation found it necessary to reassure his company's overseas customers that, although in some instances domestic and overseas requirements exceeded the capacity of Japan's steel industry at that time, this situation was considered to be merely transitional and would be solved in the not-so-distant future (Nippon Kokan, December 1966). In fact, since it was desirable, even necessary, for the developing countries to install reserve capacity in excess of their immediate and rapidly growing demands, the surplus steelmaking capacity was largely a Western European, and to a lesser extent an American, problem.

The development of this surplus from the late fifties onward naturally led to a downward pressure on steel prices. The producers, faced with more plants than they could use and reluctant to close down their higher-cost units, had two basic alternatives. One was to operate their plants well below their design capacity, and so accept somewhat higher unit production costs and thereby smaller profits. Most companies in the United States and Britain opted for this alternative. The other alternative (the one adopted by most of the producers in the European Economic Community) was to run their steel plants as near to full capacity as possible by selling steel at reduced prices in overseas markets. Cold-rolled sheet, for example, priced at about $100 per ton f.o.b. Antwerp, was being sold for export at $40 per ton below the ruling domestic prices in several countries in 1965. With the demand for steel highly inelastic in the short run, this policy inevitably meant that producers and stockists were seeking outlets in basically unresponsive markets for growing quantities of unsold steel. Hence the steady decline in steel prices, as illustrated in Table 26.

The "surplus" steel was initially exported to the traditional importing countries, with their relatively high-cost production facilities. Their capacity to absorb additional steel was, of course, very limited. Once these markets showed no significant response to the lower prices, Western European producers turned to another outlet, in which sales (and hence profits) appeared possible—namely, the home markets of the leading producers themselves. These were the major centers of steel consumption, and they immediately offered considerable scope for imports. Shipments into the European Coal and Steel Community, Britain, and the United States rose from about 3 to nearly 12 million product tons between 1958 and 1965. These imports were naturally landed at the expense of some domestic production, which would have suffered more had not the home mills been willing to align their prices down to meet the challenge of imports. To the steel industry as an international whole, this chain of events presented an

TABLE 26. STEEL EXPORT PRICES IN THE EUROPEAN COAL AND STEEL COMMUNITY, 1960–1966
(*Dollars per ton, f.o.b. Antwerp*)

January	Wire rod	Reinforcing bar	Merchant bar	Sections	Hot-rolled strip	Plate 10 cm and over
1960...........	up to 104	108–10	110–14	101–2	110–12	110–12
1961...........	105–7	up to 96	99–101	94–95	109–11	99–100
1962...........	89	83	95	94	93	91
1963...........	82–83	71–71.5	78–79	78	93	88
1964...........	73–80	75/76–78	80–82	75–78	84	84–85
1965...........	89–90	81	91	84–86	96	99
1966...........	78–79	74	80–82	73–75	83–84	84

Source: *Metal Bulletin*, 1960–66.

ever-increasing financial nightmare, since the lower average prices at which its products were sold meant a lower aggregate revenue and a smaller return on capital. Between 1960 and 1963, gross profits on steelmaking fell by 53 percent in France and 35 percent in Belgium. Within another two years, the industries of both countries were making virtually no profits at all (Table 27).

The British Iron and Steel Federation began—and continued—to call for "some form of international action to stabilise the steel situation" (*Steel Review*, 1967). It was never very clear what this would be. The High Authority of the ECSC sought to impose tighter controls on the industry's investment programs. The British Government and the High Authority together agreed to form a committee to discuss the problem further. But the finances of the steel industry continued to deteriorate. In all the debate, one point seemed regularly to be missed—namely, that, once investments had been made in modern plant designed to make and roll large tonnages of steel, only a high degree of use could possibly make them profitable. The industry appeared to be thinking itself into a position where it would accept some form of market sharing. Indeed, in 1968 an agreement was reached, between the steel industries of Japan and the ECSC on the one hand and the steel industry and government of the United States on the other, to reduce the level and limit the rate of growth of imports into the latter country. Yet such market-sharing devices of themselves offered nothing to those countries (such as Japan and the Netherlands) that were able to make full use of their largely modern capacity, except perhaps the removal of a threat of more formal limitations to the rising level of American steel imports. Such devices still left most of the industry relatively unprofitable; and, like the International Steel Cartel of the thirties, they did nothing directly either to make production cheaper or to encourage producers to concentrate their activities at the most favorable and lowest-cost locations. In fact, toward the end of the period, only

TABLE 27. TRENDS IN THE PROFITABILITY OF SELECTED STEEL PRODUCERS, 1960–1964

(*Profits after taxes as percentage of total revenue*)

Country	1960	1961	1962	1963	1964
Belgium (3–5)	4.4	6.0	5.8	1.6	0.8
Britain (2–6)	13.8	9.7	2.8	2.7	1.1
France (14–15)	0.7	1.4	1.0	2.1	0.5
Italy (7)	4.4	5.0	9.3	5.7	10.9
Japan (6)	4.0	4.7	2.7	4.7	4.5
Luxembourg (1–2)		3.1	3.8	1.1	3.1
Netherlands (1–2)	19.3	15.4	14.1	10.3	11.1
U.S.A. (33)	6.0	5.3	4.3	5.6	6.0
West Germany (17)	3.7	3.7	1.7	1.6	2.1

Source: United States, Senate Committee on Finance, 1967, p. 448.
Note: Figures in parentheses indicate the number of reporting companies.

the deliberate and speedy closure of high-cost and ill-located plant could have resulted in bringing the industry's capacity into line with the opportunities of its markets and hence in improving the profitability of the remaining producers in those countries and regions particularly burdened by underutilized facilities. It was to the most satisfactory means of achieving this end, quickly and equitably, with the minimum social disruption, that the attention of those concerned with the future of the industry should have been directed.

By the end of 1965, it became increasingly doubtful whether the surplus problem was getting worse, and whether in the future it would make such a decisive impact on the pattern of international steel trade. The industry maintained that the surplus persisted, and there was no immediate challenge to the figure of about 66 million tons put forward by the OECD as the magnitude of the world's surplus steelmaking capacity in 1967 (Manners, 1969-B). Yet, with the upsurge of American demands in 1964 and 1965, the U.S. domestic iron and steel industry—despite the rising level of imports—was left with little or no spare capacity. Meanwhile, in Western Europe the rate of new investment had slowed down during the early sixties. At the same time, steel demands had edged slowly upward, and thereby some of its surplus capacity was absorbed. Indeed, by 1968 the British steel industry, with an improvement in its home market conditions, found itself with *too little* usable capacity, and the British Steel Corporation had to import a variety of steels in order to meet its market commitments. At least in some countries, therefore, the "surplus" was demonstrably becoming the normal reserve capacity that provident steelmakers try to hold in hand until the next major increment in demand. Explanations of the changing volume and pattern of international trade in steel, as a result, had to rest increasingly on an appreciation of the widening differentials in the costs of manufacture (Britain, National Board for Prices and Incomes, 1969, p. 7), and on general tendencies in the world market for steel that encouraged an increasing volume of international trade.

THE CHANGING GEOGRAPHY OF TRADE AND PRODUCTION

In the wake of falling tariff barriers, the expectation must be that delivered export prices will fall and that trade will increase. Steel is no exception (United Nations, 1968-B). In addition, the development of more efficient transport arrangements for the shipment of steel products (see Chapter 4) permitted a reduction in freight rates, enlargement of market areas, and a fall in delivered prices; as a consequence trade further increased. Moreover, in the face of growing competition, some steel producers undoubtedly became more willing to sell some of their steel at or near its marginal costs in order to increase their sales. Whether or not there was large-scale dumping is another matter, for, although the charge was frequently made, not one major case was in fact proved before the American courts.

The growth in the volume of international steel shipments can also be explained in part by the increasingly specialized characteristics of the markets for steel, and by the tendency toward international specialization in those product lines for which international demands remained relatively small in relation to a low-cost scale of production. As the emphasis of international trade shifted from such staple items as bars, billets, and angles, and increasingly comprised such expensive products as strip and coils, pipes and tubes, and high-quality alloys, so too did its broad geography change. Whereas in 1950 most international trade in steel was concerned with making up deficiencies in the ingot production and finishing facilities of steel-deficit economies, by the end of the period an increasing share of trade was conducted essentially on an exchange basis, in which specialized grades and types of steel were shipped between countries that had considerable steel-producing capabilities. Nearly one-half of the steel exports of 1965 were destined for the "steel exporters" themselves—a group then defined as those countries shipping annually more than 1 million tons of steel products overseas (see Figure 4).

The actual volume of international trade in steel products increased from less than 16 million tons to nearly 60 million between 1950 and 1965, an annual growth rate of more than 9 percent. The proportion of world steel production that was destined for overseas markets rose from about 10 to 17 percent. The changes in the geography of the trade in part reflected the relatively high costs of the American iron and steel industry in the sixties. Although the United States was still exporting 2.3 million tons of finished products in 1965 (most of it under aid programs to the developing world), it had by then become a major steel importer. In that year it purchased 9.3 million tons of products from overseas producers. The geography of trade also followed the final crumbling of the Western European empires. Britain, for example, which in 1950 had sent most of its exports to the countries of the Commonwealth, by 1965 was marketing over 70 percent elsewhere. Similarly, the steel trade of the EEC countries became increasingly intra-European, although together they still remained the largest exporting group in the world and shipped 30 million tons in 1965, of which rather more than half was to non-EEC countries.

The shifting pattern of trade in steel reflected the gradual emergence of new trade and political groupings. With time, the 1950 pattern of trade, in which the United States and certain Western European exporters shipped their products all over the world, came to be replaced by a pattern in which most steel trade was confined within distinct macroregional zones: the North Atlantic, South America, the Pacific, and Southeast Asia. The major

exceptions to this generalization were afforded by the Soviet Union and
Japan. The former continued to export primarily to the countries of
Middle Europe, and had increased the volume to 5 million tons by 1965.
The exports of Japan not only dominated Pacific and Southeast Asian
trade but also—having grown to 9.5 million tons and having become the
largest of any national producer—increasingly penetrated the markets of
the United States (in the East and the Midwest) and Western Europe.
These exports demonstrated the competitive strength of the Japanese
industry.

The resultant changes in the geography of steel production, in response
to the new pattern of markets and the shifting directions of trade, were
far-reaching (Figures 5, 6, 7, and Table 28; see also Table A-2). The over-

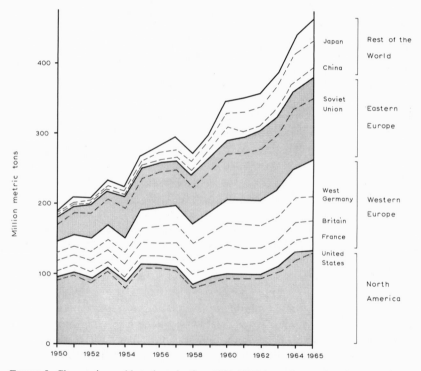

FIGURE 5. Changes in world steel production, 1950–1965, by regions and major countries.

all North American situation was dominated by developments in the
United States, where steel output between 1950 and 1963 fluctuated considerably and grew only sluggishly in response to a relatively stagnant domestic demand. Such a market inevitably posed a difficult reinvestment
problem for the American steel industry, since it limited the opportunities

TABLE 28. WORLD CRUDE STEEL PRODUCTION, BY REGIONS, 1950 AND 1965

	Production (thousands of ingot tons)		Percentage	
Region	1950	1965	1950	1965
Total....................	191,575	455,656	100.00	100.00
North America................	93,029	128,081	48.56	28.11
Western Europe................	52,538	129,429	27.42	28.40
Eastern Europe................	35,541	119,580	18.55	26.24
Asia.........................	6,994	61,321	3.65	13.46
Oceania.....................	1,275	5,496	0.67	1.21
Latin America.................	1,317	8,121	0.69	1.78
Africa and Middle East..........	881	3,635	0.46	0.80

Source: See Table A-2 which gives production by countries.

to construct new plant, with all the locational adjustments and technological innovations inherent in such construction. By 1966, only one-quarter of American steel was made in L.D. converters (see Table 23). To offset this disadvantage and its relatively high labor costs, the steel industry of the United States had all the opportunities of a uniquely large domestic market affording long production runs and economies of scale. It was also organized into large units, which gave the individual companies financial strength and ready access to new capital. And it could boast a technology in rolling and finishing operations which (largely a function of its home market) was second to none. However, by international standards the 1965 American steel industry was faced with relatively high overall costs. This showed up most clearly in the rising level of steel imports, which had reached about 10 million product tons by 1965 (and over 16 million tons three years later). As a consequence of its net import position by the end of the period, the output of the American steel industry over the fifteen years expanded rather more slowly than its domestic market. However, in 1964/65, following the sudden upsurge of home demand, production rose to new record levels, and in 1965 output stood for the first time at 119 million ingot tons.

The Canadian iron and steel industry contrasted with its United States counterpart. A much younger industry, it was able to take advantage of a rapidly growing home market (small as it was in comparison with that in the United States), and it succeeded in producing in its own mills many of the products that had previously been imported. It was also prepared to take technological initiatives. As a consequence of these factors, Canadian production was able to expand somewhat faster than Canadian demand. In the fifteen years it trebled to reach 9 million tons.

By 1965 the steel production of Western Europe had grown from its 52 million tons in 1950 to a level fractionally above North American output— that is, to just under 130 million tons. West Germany (37 million tons)

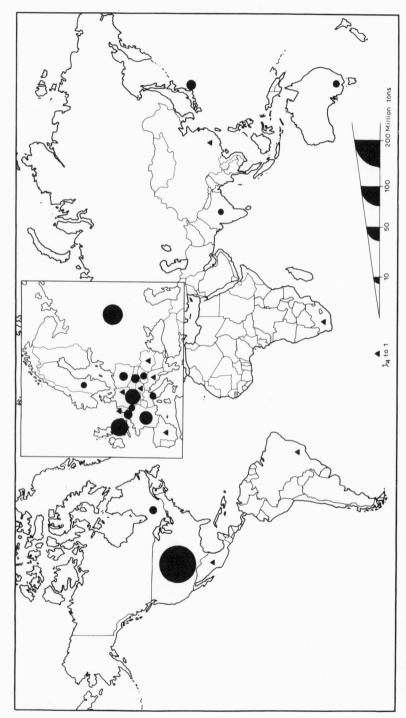

200 Million tons

100

50

10

¼ to 1

FIGURE 6. World steel production, 1950.

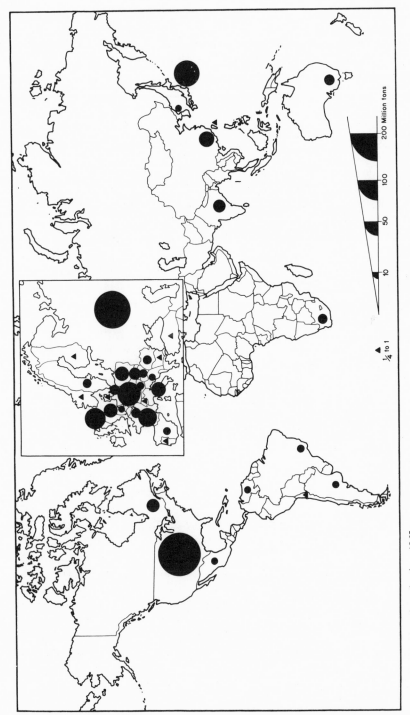

FIGURE 7. World steel production, 1965.

had overhauled Britain (27) as the largest national producer in the region, and Italy (13) had moved up to fourth position after France (20). Belgium (9 million tons) followed in fifth place. Sweden, Luxembourg, Spain, Austria, and the Netherlands were all producing between 3 and 5 million tons of steel annually by the end of the period. The sum effect of these national achievements was that production expanded rather faster in the European Economic Community than it did in the European Free Trade Association (EFTA). And whereas the output of the latter trading group had stood at two-thirds that of the EEC in 1950, it was less than half by 1965. Most of the expansion in Western European steel production took place in the fifties. Basically this was a reflection of the buoyancy of domestic demands during that decade. In addition, it was a function of a substantial expansion of extra-European exports. By the early sixties, however, the much slower expansion of Western Europe's domestic markets, together with a stiffening of competition in the export field (and, indeed, a growing volume of steel imports) left the iron and steel producers with a much slower rate of growth. Their problems, as a consequence, began to mount fast.

In strong contrast to its American counterpart, the relatively fragmented iron and steel industry in Western Europe faced a somewhat balkanized home market. The scale of its industrial organization was generally smaller; the size of steelmaking plant was usually more modest; the production runs were invariably shorter; the purchasers of steel had much smaller demands; and the market was significantly less transparent. Consequently, in spite of the much lower Western European labor rates, the costs of production and marketing were in places higher than in the United States. Moreover, during the boom years of the fifties the European industry had shown itself to be comparatively reluctant to adjust its locational pattern to contemporary geographical forces. The short-term advantages of expanding existing plant were often preferred to the long-term advantages of well-positioned "green field" sites. Also the fragmented pattern of mill ownership generally denied the possibility of large companies concentrating their expansion in the most favorable locations. Subsequently, in the relatively stagnant market conditions of the sixties, economic conditions were not ripe for the adoption of technological innovations and locational shifts, which were increasingly recognized as being imperative and which might have redressed somewhat the earlier failings of the industry.

Changes did, of course, occur, but many of them were a response to the producers' technological ambitions rather than their best economic interests. New plant was erected and new equipment installed, not infrequently in response to the whims and pride of engineers and metallurgists rather than to the needs of the market. The price that had to be paid by the industry for all these characteristics was a singularly poor return (sometimes simply no return) on the capital it had invested. The low profits in relation to total revenue in Belgium, Britain, France, Luxembourg, and West Germany is demonstrated in Table 27.

Although its trade with the rest of the world tended to increase in the later years of the period, Eastern Europe continued essentially as a closed economy. The growth in its demand for steel was almost exactly matched by the expansion of its steel production facilities. Output rose from 36 to 120 million tons. The types and the quality of the industry's products reflected the region's relatively immature stage of economic development, its lower living standards, and the comparative absence of the consumer durable manufactures found in Western Europe and North America. During the early years of the period there was something of a tendency for steel production in the U.S.S.R. to outstrip that of its Middle European partners. But by the early sixties this was offset by the rather faster rates of expansion experienced by the industry in the latter economies. In 1965, Middle European production stood at just under one-third of that of the U.S.S.R.—a proportion similar to that pertaining fifteen years earlier. The Soviet Union succeeded in raising its steel output from 27 to 91 million tons. The main producers in Middle Europe in 1965—as in 1950—were Poland and Czechoslovakia, each of which had an output of about 9 million tons, having increased their production threefold during the period. In addition, East Germany (4.4 million tons), Rumania (3.4), and Hungary (2.5) produced noteworthy quantities of steel.

Elsewhere in the world, Japan towered above all other countries in its feats of steel production. Output rose from a mere 5 million tons in 1950 to 41 million in 1965. It was a performance without equal, the equivalent of an annual growth rate of more than 15 percent. At the root of the achievement was the country's booming domestic market for steel, which justified the rapid construction of new and technologically advanced production facilities in good locations. To this was added a fairly long history of steelmaking and technological education; an ability to adapt and improve upon iron and steelmaking experience from all over the world; a shrewdness in raw-material purchases; a high degree of skill in plant management; a steady supply of American capital; and an outstanding efficiency in salesmanship. It was a set of circumstances that appeared unlikely to be repeated. The result was unusually low-cost steel production by international standards (see Table 24) and an ability to compete with growing success in export markets. Japanese steel output thus outstripped even the high growth rate of the country's home demands, and by the end of the period the rising volume of steel exports (nearly 10 million product tons in 1965) came to represent over 30 percent of total production.

China also increased its steel production at an exceptionally high rate, and by 1960 was claiming a decade of expansion even faster than that of Japan. While its 1950 output stood at a mere 0.6 million tons, ten years later Chinese official statistics recorded a production of 18.5 million tons of steel. This latter figure, however, was based on an unsuccessful attempt to accelerate the national rate of economic growth in "the great leap forward," and in the following year steel production fell back to about 10 million tons. By the end of the period, although no official statistics were available, the tentative figure adopted by United Nations statisticians was 12 million tons (this statistic is adopted in the present study). Other sources, however, by no means unreliable, have suggested that by 1965 Chinese steel production was approaching a level of 15 to 16 million tons once again. Whatever the exact figure, there can be little doubt that at this time the growth of production was based on surer foundations. The considerable achievements of India in developing its steel industry were overshadowed by developments elsewhere in Asia. Indian output rose from 1.5 million tons in 1950 to 6.4 million in 1965, but this level of production still failed to meet home demands, and India remained a net importer of steel.

Similarly, none of the countries of Latin America were able to throw off their dependence on foreign steel by the end of the period. Although production in Brazil had reached nearly 3 million tons by 1965, expansion of capacity in the whole of Latin America moved only very slowly toward a position from which it could completely satisfy the steadily growing domestic demands. Australia and South Africa on the other hand were able to lessen their dependence on foreign mills, and their 1965 output of 5.5 and 3.2 million tons of steel, respectively, included a certain amount of net export tonnage. The sum effect of these changes was that Asia, Australasia, Africa, the Middle East, and Latin America together increased their share of the world's steel production from 6 percent in 1950 to over 17 percent in 1965.

The contribution that scrap made to steel production throughout the world increased from 90 to about 200 million tons during the period. From 1950 until about 1959 scrap was in short supply. But as pig iron capacity came to be expanded in the major producing countries, and as the hot-metal capacity of existing furnaces increased with improvements in technology, the situation eased considerably. The weakening of the scrap market was also influenced by the gradual adoption of the L.D. steel-making technology, with its smaller demand for scrap per ingot ton of steel, and by the growing production of flat steel products with their larger scrap arisings. The years after 1960 saw more capital scrap becoming available, and methods of collecting and preparing scrap becoming more sophisticated. The net effect was a fall in scrap prices. Heavy melting scrap in Pittsburgh fell from $40.75 in 1959 to $24 in 1962.

Several types of steel producer relied particularly on scrap as a source of metallics (Pounds, 1959). One type embraced the technologically developed countries or regions that had a market large enough to justify a steel industry but too small (or in too disadvantageous a location) to allow the construction of competitive blast-furnace capacity. Countries like Denmark, Switzerland, and Finland based their growing but still relatively small steel output on scrap, just as the industry in such regions as the Pacific Northwest, the Great Plains, and the Prairies in North America relied almost entirely on local or imported scrap. A second type relying heavily on scrap embraced countries that were at a low level of economic development and just embarking on the road to industrialization. They offered markets large enough for steel production but not for pig iron manufacture. In their case, reliance was placed largely on imported rather than domestic scrap. Ghana, Saudi Arabia, Ceylon, and Uruguay fell into this category at the end of the period. A third type of producer was to be found among the largest users of scrap—in those countries where a rapid expansion of steel demand and production created a growing need for metallics that could not be satisfied from domestic blast furnaces. Sometimes they imported pig iron. More usually, however, they relied on domestic and imported scrap to make good the deficiency. The Italian and Japanese steel industries fell into this category of scrap users. Such countries offered large export markets for scrap to some of the older industrial economies with a scrap surplus, the most notable of which was the United States (Figure 8). International trade in scrap stood at 13.6 million tons in 1965.

It was primarily the growing demand for metallics in steel production (less the portion of demands satisfied by the use of scrap) that determined the changing geography of pig iron demand and production. In addition, the distribution of pig iron production was marginally modified by the direct consumption of the metal for casting and foundry needs. Chinese and Indian developments were particularly outstanding in this regard. And a small quantity of pig iron still continued to move in international and interregional trade. In 1965, however, the former was still only about 6.5 million tons. The net effect of all these factors influencing the geography of pig iron production, and hence the distribution of ore demands, was a set of spatial trends remarkably similar to those of steel production. World pig iron production rose from 134 to 335 million tons (Figure 9 and Table 29; see also Table A-3). North American output fluctuated between about 60 and 75 million tons during most of the period, and then moved up rapidly in 1964 and 1965 to nearly 90 million tons in 1965. Of this total,

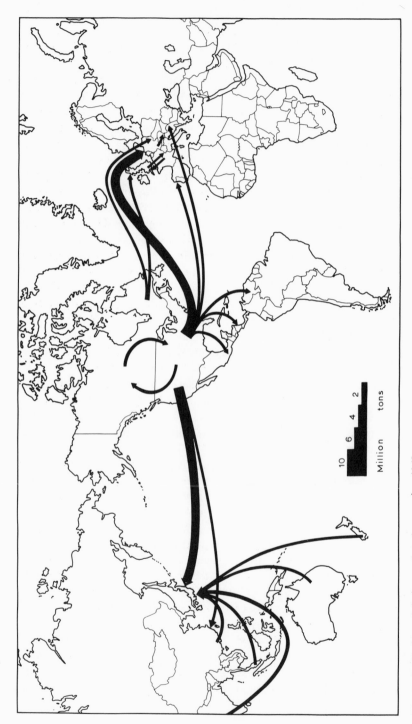

FIGURE 8. World trade in iron and steel scrap, circa 1965.

132

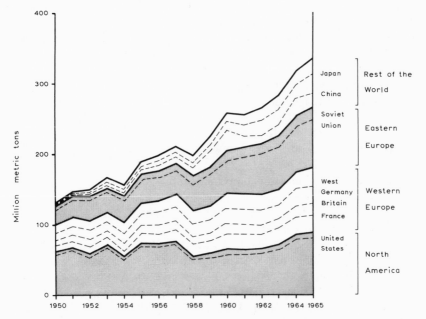

FIGURE 9. Changes in world pig iron production, 1950–1965, by regions and major countries.

the United States produced 82.6 million tons, and Canada 6.6. The North American share of world pig iron output, however, fell during the period from 47 to just under 27 percent.

The Western European proportion remained fairly stable, being 29 percent in 1950 and nearly 28 percent in 1965. As with steel, the largest producers were West Germany and Britain. Norway and Finland produced more pig iron than steel, largely in response to export opportunities. The shares of France, Luxembourg, and Belgium in West European pig iron

TABLE 29. WORLD PIG IRON PRODUCTION, BY REGIONS, 1950 AND 1965

	Production (thousands of tons)		Percentage	
Region	1950	1965	1950	1965
Total......................	133,651	335,419	100.00	100.00
North America.................	62,503	89,142	46.77	26.58
Western Europe................	39,183	92,415	29.32	27.55
Eastern Europe................	23,825	84,511	17.83	25.20
Asia..........................	5,035	56,032	3.77	16.71
Oceania......................	1,115	4,356	0.83	1.30
Latin America.................	1,223	4,910	0.92	1.46
Africa and Middle East..........	767	4,053	0.57	1.21

Source: See Table A-3 which gives production by countries.

output remained rather higher than their shares of steel production; this followed from the considerable number of Bessemer steel furnaces and the small scrap demand in these countries. Italy, Denmark, and Switzerland, on the other hand, made rather small quantities of pig iron in relation to their output of steel; they relied heavily or almost entirely on scrap for their steelmaking metallics. In sum, the total production of pig iron in Western Europe rose from 39 to 92 million tons between 1950 and 1965.

Output from the blast furnaces of Eastern Europe was raised from 24 to 85 million tons, and their share of world production increased from 18 to 25 percent. The blast-furnace technology of the Soviet Union commanded worldwide admiration throughout the late fifties; the size of the furnaces was increased; the burdens were improved; the pressures were raised; and the productivity of the furnaces reached new records. The Soviet Union's total output was increased from 20 to 66 million tons, but its share of the region's production fell slightly as the Middle European countries responded to their internal market opportunities, asserted their (limited) independence, and built up their pig iron capacity. But at the end of the period the U.S.S.R. was still producing nearly three-quarters of the region's output. Within Middle Europe the largest pig iron producer was Czechoslovakia (5.9 million tons in 1965), which maintained a slight lead over Poland (5.8 million tons).

The most rapid expansion of blast-furnace capacity occurred in Asia. The Japanese market for pig iron increased from 1.7 million to 30 million tons, and in 1965 over 28 million tons of this demand was satisfied by domestic furnaces as Japan for the first time took third place in the world's pig iron as well as steel production. The rate of growth of Chinese pig iron output was even faster. At an estimated 19 million tons in 1965, it was considerably larger than the country's steel output and was the fifth largest in the world—over 1 million tons higher than production in Britain. India's pig iron manufacture, too, continued throughout the period to be somewhat higher than its steel output, rising from 1.7 to 7.1 million tons between 1950 and 1965. Asia as a whole smelted 56 million tons of pig iron in 1965. This was 16.7 percent of the world total and contrasted vividly with that continent's 3.8 percent share fifteen years earlier. The largest producers in Oceania, Latin America, and Africa were Australia (4.4 million tons), South Africa (3.6), and Brazil (2.4). In all these countries favorable raw-material endowments and economic circumstances justified a small production, in excess of domestic demands, for export. Thus the "rest of the world"—that is, the world outside North America and Europe, both east and west—increased its importance for pig iron production between 1950 and 1965. While it accounted for a mere 6.2 percent of world output at the beginning of the period, fifteen years later it was responsible for over one-fifth. Such were the geographical shifts in an industry that was directly responsible for the greater part of the world's demands for iron ore.

NEW DEMANDS FOR IRON ORE

On a global basis, the ratio of pig iron production to the apparent consumption of contained iron ore is subject to a certain amount of historical and geographical variation, part of which is explained by the crude nature of the available iron ore statistics. In 1950, the ratio was 1:0.87. In 1964 (the last year for which a full set of international statistics is available at the present writing) the ratio was 1:0.93. However, in that same year there was an output of 0.8 million tons of contained iron ore that cannot be allocated to any particular market, and two years later the figure was 16.5 million contained tons (Table 30; see also Table A-4). Part of these figures undoubtedly represents changes in producers' stocks. Some of the tonnage can also be explained by a growth in the volume of ore at any one time in transit between the mines and their markets. But by far the largest element in any discrepancy may be explained by errors in the data for the production and consumption of iron ore on a contained iron basis.

In addition to the undoubted but ill-quantified temporal movements in the ratio, there also exist important national and regional differentials; these occasion a geographical distribution of iron ore requirements somewhat different from that of pig iron manufacture (Figures 10 and 11). In Western Europe, for example, proportionately less scrap was fed into the blast furnace, and the ratio rose from 1:0.74 in 1950 to 1:0.83 in 1964. The apparent consumption of ore, therefore, increased rather faster than pig iron production, reaching a level of 73.5 million "c" tons in 1964. On

TABLE 30. WORLD APPARENT DEMAND FOR IRON ORE, BY REGIONS, 1950, 1964, AND 1965

Region	Demand					
	1950	1964	1965*	1950	1964	1965
	(thousands of contained tons)			(percent)		
Total..................	115,582	288,681	310,594	100.00	100.00	100.00
North America.............	54,940	71,931	75,610	47.53	24.92	24.34
Western Europe.............	28,969	73,537	76,956	25.06	25.47	24.78
Eastern Europe.............	24,558	86,911	92,317	21.25	30.11	29.72
Asia......................	4,015	42,788	53,671	3.47	14.82	17.28
Oceania...................	1,479	3,745	3,976	1.28	1.30	1.28
Latin America..............	1,239	5,966	5,723	1.07	2.07	1.84
Africa and Middle East.......	799	2,987	3,501	0.69	1.03	1.13
Unallocated production.......	−417	816	−1,160	−0.36	0.28	−0.37

Source: See Table A-4 which gives demand by countries.
* Author's estimates.

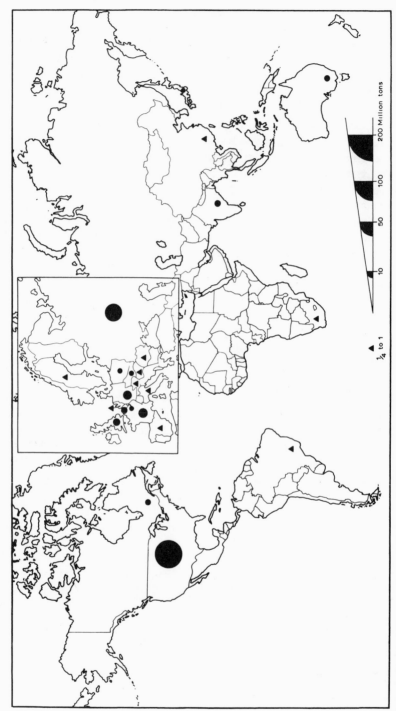

FIGURE 10. World iron ore demand (Fe content), 1950.

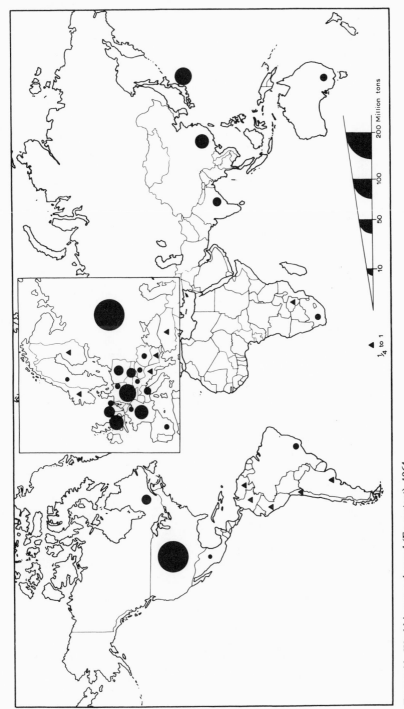

FIGURE 11. World iron ore demand (Fe content), 1964.

the other hand, in North America there was a tendency for the ratio to fall; it nevertheless still remained higher than that of Western Europe, and as a consequence ore demands there in 1964 stood at 72 million tons of contained iron ore. The particularly high Eastern European ratio persisted throughout the period; in fact, there was a small rise from 1:1.04 to 1:1.09. By 1964 the apparent consumption of iron ore in Eastern Europe totaled significantly more than in either Western Europe or North America; it had reached the level of 87 million "c" tons. In Asia, the ratio of pig iron production to apparent ore consumption also remained generally stable, and the demands for ore there grew tenfold, from 4 to 43 million "c" tons. The apparent consumption of ore in the rest of the world was very small indeed; although it had nearly quadrupled since 1950, it was still only 13 million "c" tons in 1964.

By the end of the period, a dozen countries were consuming over 5 million tons of contained iron ore per year, compared with only 5 countries fifteen years earlier. The U.S.S.R. had overtaken the United States as the largest national market for ore; these two countries individually demanded quantities of ore far in excess of any other country. Their apparent consumption in 1964 was 69.7 and 67.1 million "c" tons, respectively. The countries of the European Economic Community together used 50.6 million "c" tons; the largest national markets among them were West Germany (21.1 million tons), France (13.8), and Belgium (6.9). The British iron and steel industry made use of 15.3 million "c" tons of ore and was the fifth largest ore market in the world. It was in Asia, however, that two new and very large centers of demand emerged on the map. By 1964 the apparent consumption of the Japanese iron and steel industry had reached just under 20 million "c" tons, while that of the Chinese industry was estimated at just under 15 million "c" tons. The Indian market required 6 million "c" tons of ore. Of the other three outstanding national demands for ore in 1964, two were in Middle Europe: Czechoslovakia (5.8 million tons) and Poland (5.5 million tons). The third was in Canada (4.8 million tons). Some of the national and regional details of this new geography of iron ore demands are recorded in Table A-4.

Not only did the quantity and the geography of ore demands change during the period, but the quality of ore requirements shifted as well. In a competitive steel market, the quality of steel products steadily improved. This in turn necessitated that pig iron and steel manufacturers should pay greater attention to the removal of impurities from their products. And there was a natural feedback to the market for iron ore, in which those grades and types with a better and more uniform chemical composition were increasingly sought by blast-furnace managers. Ores with a high or variable silica content, for example, were increasingly rejected by purchasers, and ores with a high phosphorus content were only accepted with increasing discounts. Further, the amount of iron contained in a ton of delivered ore also assumed greater importance. Whereas many blast-furnace managers in 1950 regarded ores with 50 percent iron as a quite satisfactory raw material, and sometimes referred to them as "high grade," their counterparts fifteen years later frequently rejected such ores as too lean and increasingly demanded ores of 63 percent iron and above.

Iron ore quality has yet a third dimension. Ore can be fed into the blast furnace unsized, in 35-millimeter lumps, in the form of sinter or as pellets. Each of these types of ore (and their variants) gives a somewhat different performance. Ore that is unsized makes, on the whole, for a somewhat inefficient use of blast-furnace capacity; sinter gives a better performance than most well-sized ores; and pellets possibly give the best performance of all, although this still remained an open question at the end of the period (see Chapters 3 and 8). As a result, the better forms of blast-furnace feed, in terms of their physical characteristics, were demanded increasingly during the period, often at premium prices. It was a premium worth paying, particularly if a country, a region, or a steel plant was short of blast-furnace capacity.

In sum, by 1965, with the iron and steel industry paying more attention to the chemical composition, the iron content, and the physical structure of iron ores than had been the case fifteen years earlier, any understanding of the world market for iron ore has to recognize not only the increasing quantity of iron ore demands but also their changing quality. The response to these demands is examined in Part II.

part II

---

*Trends in the Supply of
Iron Ore, 1950–1965*

CHAPTER 7

Location Factors in the Supply of Iron Ore

It is through the mechanism of the market that the complex demands for iron ore are able to interact with the various alternatives available for their satisfaction, and that the patterns of iron ore trade and production are normally determined. In no country, however, has the market for iron ore ever been given a physical expression in the form of a commodity exchange in which buyers and sellers can meet to do business. One reason for this contrast with so many other raw materials and commodities can be found in the fact that historically the iron and steel industry has located close to its raw material sources. For many years, purchases of iron ore were generally made from local supplies, and therefore an ore exchange was simply not required. Furthermore, the considerable expense involved in the construction of an iron and steel works persuaded many managements of the economic desirability, if not necessity, of ensuring the long-term availability of their raw materials, and frequently they achieved this end by backward integration into iron ore production, through either a complete or a partial ownership of one or several iron ore mines. In such circumstances, there was no need for many iron and steel manufacturers to enter the open market for iron ore in order to procure their ore supplies. Finally, while the chemical and physical variety of iron ores does not deny accurate description, it certainly makes dealings in "futures" more than a little difficult. Thus another traditional justification for the appearance of a commodity exchange is absent in the case of iron ore.

THE ARCHITECTURE OF THE MARKET

Lacking a formal institutional framework, the market for iron ore must be understood primarily through an examination of its chief attributes, which are manifested particularly in (1) the market places, (2) the market regions, and (3) the market supply areas.

The market contains a large number of *market places*, through which (and occasionally within which) bargaining for ore is conducted and deals are concluded. Among these, a number have a key importance, since the contracts and prices on which they have agreed tend strongly to influence dealings in other market places. Thus the West German iron and steel industry purchases most of its foreign ores through two organizations— Rohrstoffhandel GmbH and Erzkontor GmbH, located in Düsseldorf and Essen, respectively. The bargains they strike with suppliers usually refer to ore *frei Ruhr* ("f.o.b. the Ruhr River")—that is, to ore delivered to the principal West German market place in and around Duisburg. The ore prices agreed on by the German steelmakers through their ore importers naturally influence the price of ore throughout the Ruhr area and in other nearby market places. Ore delivered to Rotterdam, for example, will generally have the same price as ore delivered to the western Ruhr, less a transfer charge for the barge haul up the Rhine. And the Rotterdam price has a considerable bearing on the price of foreign ores delivered to the nearby Dutch steelworks at Ijmuiden and to the Belgian and French works at Ghent and Dunkirk.

Such a relationship between neighboring market places underlies the *market regions*. Ore prices within a region are closely comparable, whereas between market regions price relationships are unevenly attenuated. Thus it is possible to recognize a set of closely related prices for iron ore in the market places around the North Sea, extending up the Rhine to the Ruhr and stretching inland to other large steel-producing centers. One can also recognize a similar group of market places along the east coast of the United States. But for a variety of both economic and institutional reasons, the price of ore in these two groups of market places is sufficiently different to justify their interpretation as separate market regions.

The relationship between a market region and the various places from which it satisfies its needs for iron ore can be described as the *market supply area*. Sometimes the system of suppliers and consumers is self-contained. But insofar as many producing countries—such as Brazil, Canada, Chile, and Liberia—send supplies to more than one market region, the system is more frequently to a greater or lesser extent open. When purchasers in two or even three market regions compete for limited supplies of ore from the same mines, a distant price relationship can clearly exist between different market supply areas. As the costs of bulk transport have fallen, and as iron and steel producers have reached out over ever-increasing distances to obtain their ore, the once separate market supply areas have tended increasingly to overlap. The relationships between iron ore prices throughout the world have thus been gradually extended over space and strengthened (see Chapter 12).

These three features of the architecture of the market for iron ore are embellished by a great variety of detail in its full design. In each market place or market region, the buyers have a considerable range of iron ore needs, depending on such factors as their existing ore contracts, the equipment they have available for the processing of ore, and the type of steel they propose to produce. Something of the variety of ore demands was noted in Chapter 3. Buyers, therefore, are bargaining not so much for "ore" as for particular types, grades, and qualities of ore, and for supplies delivered over differing periods of time. The patterns of trade in market supply areas are also strongly influenced by the existence of "captive" or "tied" mines, from which ore moves regularly to the furnaces of their owners. The market is also less than perfect when ore producers, particularly in times of ore scarcity, exploit their quasi-monopolistic position to increase prices; or when consumers, particularly in times of ore abundance, introduce an element of collusive monopsony into price bargaining. It also has to be remembered that a considerable trade in iron ore is conducted on a barter basis and with government support.

Moreover, within the fully planned economies of Eastern Europe and Asia there are no market places in the classical sense of the term, but only points of consumption. To these points, various quantities and types of ore are allocated by the planning authorities, and the prices of ore are determined by them. These administered prices are related to the *costs* of producing and transporting the ore, rather than to any assessment of its *worth*. As a result, the prices paid for even identical ores from different sources at a particular point of consumption are liable to considerable variation according to the mine of origin. However, when ore exchanges take place between a fully planned economy and a mixed or market economy, the discipline of market forces and prices is allowed to assert itself again. Because of these and many other complexities in the market for iron ore, generalizations about its overall design at a world or macroregional level must of necessity be rather crude. Yet it is only through such generalizations that the market's essential nature can be grasped.

Regarding the question of the broad pattern of trade, the key commercial price is that of ore delivered, c. & f., to the blast furnace. All other things being equal (it has to be remembered that sometimes they are not), those ores that can meet all the technical specifications and requirements of a particular consumer and can be delivered at the lowest price to his iron and steel works, will normally be purchased to satisfy demands. It follows that the price paid for the ores at or near their source or sources (that is, the f.o.b. price) will be the c. & f. price minus the relevant transfer charge.

The latter is the freight rate, or rates, paid for transporting the ore, plus any related insurance, loading, transshipment, or other expenses. Iron ore, in other words, has no intrinsically fixed value at the mine, any more than it has an inherent value in the ground. Ore is only worth what a consumer is prepared to pay for it.

If it is assumed that there are several blast furnaces located in the same vicinity (as they are around the North Sea, Tokyo Bay, or the Inland Sea of Japan); if it is further assumed (though this is not the case in the aforesaid examples) that their ore requirements are identical as a result of similar steelmaking intentions, similar ore preparation facilities, and the like (that is, if a common demand curve can be ascribed to them); and if it is assumed that similar ore transport and ore-handling facilities are available at or near each of their blast furnaces, thus making transfer charges to each of them the same, then it is clear that at any one time the same c. & f. price would be paid for ore at each furnace. There would clearly be no point in one blast-furnace operator paying more for his ore than his neighbor, any more than it would make much sense for an ore supplier to accept less from one of the adjacent purchasers than from another. In other words, the aggregate demands of the nearby works, in relation to existing supplies of ore and transfer charges at any one time, would generate a recognized price for any particular type of ore purchased under identical contractual arrangements.

This does not mean, of course, that all the pig iron producers in such a market region would necessarily be paying exactly the same price for their ore supplies. They would strike their bargains at different times, for different qualities and quantities of ore, and for different periods of time. But it does mean that the bargaining for any identical supplies of ore being negotiated simultaneously would be based on the same assumptions of demand and supply. Hence such ores would have the same c. & f. price, regardless of their origin.

If iron and steel works in the same market region do not have the same transport facilities, the situation would be rather different. Let us assume that the works can be divided into two groups—one with deepwater port facilities and the other without. It is immediately apparent that those blast furnaces with deepwater facilities would have the possibility, through the use of larger ships with their lower ton-kilometer freight rates (see Chapter 9), of reaching out to a much wider range of ore sources than those furnaces with only shallow-water facilities. In all probability, the more distant sources would have a different set of supply costs from the nearer mines, and the possibility would exist for at least some of them being able to undersell some of the nearer ores. But even if the supply costs of all the deposits were the same, the number of ore sources competing to satisfy the demands at the deepwater ports would be so much larger than those at the shallow-water ports that—granted ore was not in short supply—the former would be able to bargain for and obtain ore at lower prices. There would in effect be two market prices for ore—one for blast furnaces with deepwater facilities and one for those without.

These prices would, of course, be closely related. Assuming that only one mine served the two groups of works and that the difference in the transfer charges to them was $0.75 per ton, then the difference in the c. & f. prices for ore at the two groups of works would be unlikely to differ by much more (or much less) than that amount. For example, if the ore at the shallow-water ports was priced at $1 per ton more than at the deepwater ports, there would be a $0.25 advantage for the ore producer to sell at the former. He would therefore offer more ore for sale there, and presumably the price would fall. At the same time, less ore would be offered to the deepwater ports, its price would rise, and only when the difference in the ore prices at the two groups of works differed by $0.75 would an equilibrium be achieved.

A somewhat more diverse set of transport circumstances than simply deep- and shallow-port facilities can readily be imagined. A number of alternative iron ore sources can be postulated. The considerable variety of transfer charges to the market area is, thus, obvious. And with this variety goes an infinitely more complex market structure than has been described. However, the point to be stressed is that, provided the nearby iron and steel works have identical transport facilities and ore transfer costs, the c. & f. price of ore, *ceteris paribus*, will be the same at each of them.

In contrast, it is unrealistic to think in terms of a single f.o.b. price for iron ore at a particular deposit or a group of neighboring deposits. If, for the sake of illustration, the price of ore in two market places (say, Rotterdam and Yokohama) is the same, and if the transfer charges from one particular source (Liberia, for example) to these two markets differ, then there will be at least two f.o.b. prices for the same quality of Liberian ore. Alternatively, if the price of ore in the two market places differs, and if the transfer charges from an ore source (say, South Africa) are the same, once again there will be two f.o.b. prices. Thus, Chilean ore destined for Japan in 1965 commanded a lower f.o.b. price than the same Chilean ore shipped to the United States. And Venezuelan and Canadian ores loaded for Baltimore at Puerto Ordaz and Sept Iles, respectively, had in 1965 a higher value than identical ores loaded for Western Europe. Where a source of ore (such as the Liberian or Brazilian mines) is able to find customers in three major market places (such as Rotterdam, Baltimore, and Yokohama), it is reasonable to think in terms of three basic f.o.b. prices. In reality, of course, there will be a much greater range of prices, depending on such matters as the grade of ore shipped, the size and length of the contract, or the transport arrangements available.

Arising out of such a geography of prices is the embarrassment that results when one consumer develops and provides the primary market for a new ore deposit, and then a second consumer moves in, after the exploration and development risks have been taken, to purchase ore at a lower price. For example, the Japanese industry, having provided the initial market and some of the capital for the development of the West Australian fields, was able to purchase the ore at an attractive price, which subsequently allowed the Japanese to bargain down the ore prices of other supplies (see Chapter 12). However, if the Australian mines are to diversify their outlets and sell their ore in Western Europe, they will have to accept lower f.o.b. prices for their European than for their Japanese sales. Although some ore producers have tried to insist on a fixed f.o.b. price, regardless of market circumstances, the more usual reaction to such a situation is for the original consumers to accept the logic of the market pricing but to insist on a c. & f. price equivalent to their own as the minimum that can be contracted with other consumers.

At root, this set of price relationships between ore markets and their raw-material sources is unstable. On the supply side, the mining companies will strive to increase their income by trying to sell a larger proportion of their ore in what to them is the most profitable market place—in other words, the one that offers them the highest f.o.b. price. And on the demand side, with identical ore moving to different markets at varying f.o.b. prices, those consumers paying the highest f.o.b. price will inevitably urge some price reduction for themselves. However, an equilibrium can theoretically be conceived, and it is toward this state that the market and price mechanisms appear to be working. Equilibrium will be achieved when the c. & f. prices are the same for identical ores in the market places for ore. Then, no inducement will exist for consumers to switch purchases from one ore source to another. At the same time, equilibrium will also require the f.o.b. prices of identical ores from any mine or group of adjacent mines to be the same to all of their markets, thereby eliminating the temptation for ore producers to shift their sales from one market to another. Equilibrium will further require the differences between the c. & f. and the f.o.b. prices of all ore flows to be equal to the transfer charges along these routes. The maintenance of such an equilibrium depends on an unchanging resource base. It also assumes that the production of ore at all mines is subject to increasing costs, with the marginal costs of production equaling the f.o.b. price of ore in each case, which would make any further increase in ore production unattractive. Finally, equilibrium rests on stable transfer charges. Were all these conditions to be satisfied, no incentive would exist for any shift in the pattern of ore movements to take place, and a condition of market equilibrium would be achieved and could be maintained. The parallel with the market for oil is clear (Adelman, 1964).

Undoubtedly, market pressures keep pushing the economic geography of iron ore *toward* this equilibrium. Simultaneously, however, other forces are disrupting the adjustment. The size of the market for iron ore and the resource base of the industry, for example, are constantly changing. The relationship between demand and supply varies continually, yet a full knowledge of this relationship is not accessible to the buyers and sellers of iron ore. Transfer charges, too, are subject to considerable fluctuations; even if they were not, the world's iron ore flows are not decided by a linear program. Moreover, the c. & f. prices for the same grade of iron ore sometimes differ slightly in the same market place. For example, premiums can be paid on ore purchases for strategic or political purposes; and commitments to "captive" deposits are often associated with relatively high c. & f. prices for accountancy, if for no other reason. Similarly, the f.o.b. prices for identical ores frequently differ, since what are potentially their most attractive markets have already been largely preempted by either captive deposits or long-term contracts. Mining companies often sell their ores cheaply in some markets in order to diversify their outlets and lessen their dependence on one or two major customers. It is also clear that certain mining operations exhibit (at least temporarily) decreasing costs. In order to exploit these economies, mine owners are often anxious to sell in markets that do not necessarily yield the highest f.o.b. returns.

Factors such as these prevent the market from ever reaching a state of equilibrium, and during a period of ore surplus the disruptive forces tend to be stronger at the mine than at the market. Just as posted prices for oil in the Middle East and the Caribbean are only a shadow of the real worth of oil there, so the published f.o.b. quotations of, say, the Indian National Minerals Development Corporation are the point at which the Indians prepare to start bargaining—rather than the price that all purchasers are required to pay.

While the c. & f. price provides the key to any understanding of the market for iron ore, it also, together with the geography of transfer charges, basically determines which ore deposits can be economically exploited. When a mining operation cannot make a profit out of a given pattern of c. & f. prices less the relevant transfer charges (short, perhaps, of a public or some other form of subsidy), it is priced out of the market. Whether or not it can make a profit, of course, depends on its costs.

THE STRUCTURE OF DELIVERED ORE COSTS

The main elements in the delivered costs of ore are (1) the costs of mining (including labor, royalties, taxes, etc.); (2) the costs of preparation; and (3) the costs of transport. The proportions and the breakdown of each vary considerably from case to case and from country to country.

150 TRENDS IN SUPPLY OF IRON ORE

The level of *mining costs* is affected by the nature of the physical and economic environment, which in turn influences the costs of providing and maintaining essential supplies, such as food, equipment, water, and electricity. The nature of the ore body—whether it can best be exploited by open-pit or by underground methods of working—also affects both the level and the breakdown of mining expenses. Robie (1964) demonstrated that the average open-pit mine in Minnesota, in 1959, yielded ore at a cost of just under $5.03 per ton, whereas the figure for the underground mines was $8.68 (Table 31). The major factor accounting for this difference was the expense of the particularly high labor inputs in the underground mines, a point also noted by Montague (1961).

It might be tempting to assume that labor costs in iron ore mining vary even more internationally, and in favor of the developing countries of the world. This proposition is, however, highly suspect, since the lower wages per capita in the developing world are frequently offset by lower levels of productivity. The definition of a mine's labor force is somewhat elastic. Yet it is significant that, in 1965, the Erie mine of Ogleby-Norton in the United States produced 24 million actual tons of crude ore and 8 million actual tons of pellets with a labor force of 2,100, while the Marampa mine in Sierra Leone, which employed a slightly larger force (some 2,600), produced only 4.75 million actual tons of crude ore and 2.75 million actual tons of concentrate. Of course, some mines in the developing world are highly productive—for example, the Lamco project in Liberia, which in 1965 produced some 7.5 million actual tons of ore with a labor force of only 2,500.

Scale economies apart (see Chapter 8), a further major variable in the costs of mining iron ore is the level of taxes and royalties. Taxes have been one of the largest cost items in the mining industry. In Minnesota, local and state taxes in the early sixties represented about 25 percent of the total cost of production (McComb, 1963, p. 6). In Canada, iron ore developments have a variety of taxes to pay at the local, provincial, and federal levels. The broad structure of these taxes and the associated allowances are

TABLE 31. AVERAGE IRON ORE MINING COSTS IN MINNESOTA, U.S.A., 1959

(*Dollars per actual ton*)

Item	Open Pit	Underground
Labor and supplies	0.939	4.532
Development	0.749	0.303
Administration, beneficiation, depreciation, etc.	1.761	1.916
Royalty	0.428	0.781
Taxes	1.152	1.152
Total	5.029	8.684

Source: Robie, 1964.

designed to encourage mineral development. Nevertheless, these taxes remove between 35 and 50 percent of the industry's pretax profits. Lower than those of Minnesota, the Canadian taxes are not out of line with those levied in Chile and Venezuela, where the governments also take about 50 percent of the mining companies' profits in tax. Royalty payments are, of course, much smaller. In West Australia, mining companies pay royalties on a basis of 7.5 percent of the f.o.b. value of direct-shipping ores of 60 percent Fe and over (with a minimum figure of 40 cents per actual ton); fine ores carry a smaller royalty of 3.75 percent (with a minimum of 20 cents per actual ton). In sum, the principal elements and variables in the actual costs of mining are the various supplies required, labor, the scale of operations, and taxes.

The *costs of ore preparation* depend on the type of ore being exploited and the nature of the blast-furnace feed being prepared. Where a direct-shipping ore requires only a certain amount of crushing and screening, the cost might only be 60 to 75 cents per actual ton; but where a taconite is crushed, beneficiated, and then agglomerated into pellets, the cost can be as high as $4 to $4.10 per actual ton (Pfleider and Yardley, 1963). The most important variable in these costs is the amount of capital required and the cost of servicing it. For a simple separation process, the investment required might be only $5 per actual ton of annual capacity. But for pellet manufacture the capital cost can be as high as $35 to $40 per actual ton. Other major expenses are the costs of electricity and fuel. The different cost structure of four concentration processes is shown in Table 32.

The *costs of transport* vary enormously. They fluctuate with time (United Nations, 1949, pp. 55–56), with changes in technology, and with the rates charged for moving ore (see Chapters 9 and 10). Much depends on the proximity of the mine to its markets and on the type of transport facilities available. But once a blast furnace is located away from an ore deposit, then it is clear that the transfer charges can powerfully affect which ores are the most competitive. For Lorraine ores, the transfer charges to the local blast furnaces are negligible; at Jœuf, the ore is transferred from the mines to the blast furnaces only a few kilometers away by overhead conveyors. On the other hand, ore from the mines of Minnesota, in 1965, carried transfer charges equal to just under half its delivered value in Pittsburgh. And ores from the Quebec-Labrador deposits had to bear rail and water freight rates equivalent to something like 65 percent of their delivered value in the same Pittsburgh market. Even higher was the share of transfer charges in the value of Brazilian ores c. & f. Japan (over 70%) and of Schefferville (on the Quebec-Labrador boundary) ores c. & f. South Wales (over 75%). While Table 33 breaks down the costs of pellets delivered to a steelworks located on the shores of Lake Erie, these costs in no sense represent a norm.

TABLE 32. COST STRUCTURE OF FOUR METHODS OF IRON ORE PREPARATION, CIRCA 1964

Item	Unit of measurement	Calbecht plant West Germany	Pegnitz plant West Germany	Olenyogorsk plant U.S.S.R.	NKGOK* plant U.S.S.R.
Type of ore		Brown hematite	Brown hematite	Magnetite-hematite	Magnetite iron quartzites
Concentration method		Washing, heavy-media separation and high-intensity magnetic separation	High-intensity magnetic separation	Low-intensity magnetic separation and gravity separation	Low-intensity magnetic separation
Ore output capacity of plant	1,000 tons/day	18.0	1.5	22.5	30.8
Iron content of ore	% Fe	30.0	30.0	32.0	33.0
Iron content of concentrate	% Fe	37.8	39.0	61.3	62.5
Iron recovery	%	91.0		78.5	70.0
Final size to which ore is ground	0.074 mm			55–65	90–95
Cost of operations:					
Coarse crushing of ore	%	11.9	6.8	5.2	8.0
Drying of ore	%		32.2		
Average crushing	%	3.7	4.7		
Fine crushing	%			10.6	16.0
Grinding	%		18.0	34.8	51.0
Washing	%	23.2			
Screening and dehydration	%	17.4		1.0	
Heavy media concentration	%	12.6			
Magnetic separation	%	15.4	25.1	6.2	8.1
Gravity separation on tables	%			8.4	
Dehydration and filtering of concentrate	%			4.2	7.0
Drying of concentrate	%			9.5	
Storage and removal of concentrate	%			4.5	
Transport and storage of tailings	%	6.2	7.2	16.6	3.7
Other expenses	%		1.0		6.2
Overheads	%	9.6	5.0		
Total costs	%	100.0	100.0	100.0	100.0
Cost per ton of ore:					
Electric power	kwhr	8.7	18.9	14.2	16.9
Water	m³	2.5	0.13	2.97	3.9
Number of workers		293	80	715	829

Source: United Nations, 1966, p. 55.
* New Krivoy Rog Mining Combines.

152

TABLE 33.   BREAKDOWN OF COSTS OF PELLETS DELIVERED TO LAKE ERIE, 1959

(*Dollars per actual ton*)

Item	Crude	Pellets	Percentage
Mining and transportation to plant (Mesabi magnetic taconites mined in open pit).....................................	0.55	1.65	11.9
Crushing and storage...................................	0.20	0.60	4.3
Beneficiation..	0.70	2.10	15.2
Agglomeration (2-million-tons capacity per year)...........		1.50	10.8
Overhead and management.............................		0.60	4.3
Royalties...		0.75	5.4
Local and state taxes..................................		0.30	2.2
Amortization of capital................................	0.85	2.55	18.4
Total estimated costs at pellet plant...................		10.05	72.5
Transport charges......................................		3.80	27.4
Total delivered costs at Lake Erie..................		13.85	100.0

Source: Pfleider and Yardley, 1963.

Mines that have the lowest combination of mining, preparation, and transport costs in relation to a particular ore market will have the greatest advantage in satisfying demands there. *Ceteris paribus*, at the very least they should be able to obtain the largest profits per ton. However, *ceteris* are not always *paribus*, and there are several other factors that are influential in the profitability and the geography of iron ore exploitation.

DIVERSE INFLUENCES ON THE GEOGRAPHY OF ORE SUPPLIES

Granted a static geography of ore demand, an unchanging geological knowledge, and a fixed technology of ore exploitation, those deposits that are easiest and cheapest to mine will be exploited first of all. Only when they are exhausted (or when the costs of winning their ore increase) will more expensive deposits be utilized. To this extent, iron ore mining is at root an increasing-cost industry. However, although all these conditions may occasionally exist simultaneously, most of the time the geography of demand is changing, geological knowledge is increasing, and the technology of ore mining and preparation advances. The result is the steady creation of new circumstances in which new ore deposits become available to the mining and the iron and steel industries. Yet these deposits are rarely exploited to the full, and apparently higher cost mines remain in production. The reason lies in the size and economic valuation of capital sunk in existing operations.

The amount of capital sunk in a mine can be considerable. In the case of the Lamco project in Liberia (7.5 million actual tons), some $200 million was invested even before the installation of pellet facilities (Table 34). To protect such investments, the iron ore mining industry has responded principally in two ways:

TABLE 34. PERCENTAGE BREAKDOWN OF INVESTMENT OUTLAYS FOR THE LAMCO PROJECT,
CIRCA 1961
(Annual capacity, 7.5 million actual tons)

Item	Percentage
Mine with drilling and loading equipment, roads, belt conveyors, crusher, ore bins, workshops, stores, laboratories, mine office, etc..............................	14
Railroad with rails, rolling stock, service road, CTC system, etc...............	30
Harbor (including commercial harbor) with storage and loading facilities, power station, workshops, stores, etc..	19
Townships with dwellings, water, drainage, electricity supply, hospitals..........	10
Ore stocks, material stores, cash...	5
Prospecting, investigation work, planning, consultants, inspection and administration (during the planning and construction period)........................	18
Miscellaneous items and general allowance for unforeseen outlays..............	4
	100

Source: Waldenstrom, 1963.

1. It has negotiated long-term supply contracts with the iron and steel industry for periods of up to twenty-one years, and it has also encouraged that industry to take a financial stake in mining ventures (see Chapter 8). Consequently, the purely speculative development of an iron ore deposit has come to be progressively less common. Once an iron and steel company has tied itself to a particular ore deposit or a group of deposits, a certain inflexibility is introduced into the geography of ore supply. And existing sources may be given preference over inherently more attractive sources. For example, after the United States Steel Corporation had invested in its Venezuelan Cerro Bolívar mine and its Canadian Cartier mine, it had committed itself to use those deposits for many years, even though there was some evidence later that alternative sources of ore (say, Brazilian or Liberian) would have been cheaper.

2. Another response of the iron ore mining industry to the size of its investments has been the manipulation of ore prices in order to ensure the continuity of demand at particular deposits. When a mine is threatened with the loss of its markets as a result of changed economic circumstances, it is often in the interest of the company to reduce its prices to a level that merely covers the working costs of the mine and makes no contribution to the cost of the overhead—rather than go out of business altogether. Alternatively, when a mine owner wants to make fuller use of existing infrastructure investments such as a railway or a port facility, or to take advantage of scale economies in mining and ore preparation, it is possible for him to manipulate his prices in order to command a larger share of the market. Thus, in any full understanding of the pattern of ore supplies, recognition must be given to the pricing strategy adopted by mining companies.

One final factor bearing to some extent on the geography of iron ore supply (but by no means as powerfully, or as pervasively, as it affects the pattern of iron ore demands) is the political one. It affects the pattern of both national and international investment, and it influences the competitive position of particular deposits. In any iron ore exploitation, domestic or foreign, there is bound to be some degree of political risk—risk of higher taxation, risk of nationalization, risk of expropriation. However difficult these uncertainties are to quantify, they must nevertheless be taken into account by those making investment decisions.

The 1964 Minnesota "Taconite Amendment" illustrates the way in which political factors can influence the geography of iron ore supplies within a country. The preceding ten years had seen the demise of a large number of the direct-shipping ore mines in the iron-range area of the state. At the same time, large tonnages of low-grade taconite were known to exist in the same district. But the larger iron and steel and iron ore mining companies feigned reluctance to invest the huge sums of capital required to exploit these deposits while there was a risk that iron ore mining taxes, which had tended to creep up over the years, would exceed the general level of taxation. This gave impetus to a proposal for the amendment of the state constitution to guarantee that for twenty-five years taxes on the production of taconite would not exceed the general level of company tax in the state. Its approval by the voters of Minnesota immediately brought announcements from both the United States Steel Corporation and the Hanna Mining Company that they would soon start the construction of large-scale commercial pellet plants using the taconite ore. These investments might well have been made in any case. Nevertheless, the episode clearly demonstrates how the removal of a political uncertainty can, at the very least, accelerate the revival of a district's mining fortunes.

At the international scale, the degree of political stability and investment risks varies from country to country, influencing iron ore investment decisions and thus helping to mold the changing geography of iron ore supply. When a mining company, in developing an ore deposit, has a choice between a country with a stable political tradition and one without, it will tend to choose the former even if the associated costs of mining, preparing, and transporting the ore are marginally higher. Put another way, the company will demand a higher rate of return on its capital in the politically less stable location. In Venezuela, the government's withdrawal of certain mining concessions, its insistence on part ownership of foreign mining companies, and its attempts to manipulate ore prices helped to curtail foreign investment there after the period in the late forties and early fifties when developments were rapid and production rose swiftly. The slow development of the considerable mineral wealth of Brazil was also partly the result of government policies that insisted on certain controls over foreign companies. In contrast, the posture of the Chilean, Peruvian, and Liberian governments was such as to encourage the development of their ore resources. And in the case of Canada, the somewhat variable quality of its ore resources and the, at times, rather high costs of exploitation were quite positively offset by the government's mineral development policies and the country's political stability.

Political factors influence not only broad investment decisions in iron ore supply but also delivered costs of the ore. In mineral resource development, governments frequently play the role of surveyor, scientist, landlord, proprietor, revenue collector, transport agent, and educator. The way in which they fulfill these roles and allocate the associated costs has a considerable bearing on the competitive position of particular deposits. With their control over concessions and royalties and their decisions about taxes, governments have a variety of weapons with which they can influence the geography of the industry through its production cost. And in their supervisory role over national transport systems, their influence over transport investment priorities, their subsidy of particular facilities, and their influence on rating policies, they have an additional effect on the transport component of the delivered costs of iron ore.

In the case of the fully planned economies, governments can more directly influence the pattern of iron ore trade, both within their countries and between them and the mixed economies. With exchange rates kept at artificial levels and barter trade a commonplace, this is inevitably the case. The much lower price of Soviet iron ore exports to countries in the Dollar-Sterling area than to the countries of Middle Europe, for example, reflects not only the bargaining strength of the Soviet Union's interests within COMECON (Council for Mutual Economic Assistance) but also its needs for hard currency. On the other hand, the deliberate expansion of Middle European ore imports from countries in the "uncommitted" world—India, Guinea, Brazil, Tunisia, and Morocco—undoubtedly represents a political decision of the late fifties rather than any immediate commercial advantage.

Generally speaking, however, international trade in iron ore is remarkably free of governmental interference. Outside the fully planned economies, universally there are no import duties or tariff barriers to hinder the "economic" flow of ore. So easily could it have been otherwise. In the United States, West Germany, France, and Britain, from the late fifties onward, ore imports have increasingly displaced domestic production and have created serious social and economic difficulties in many mining districts. Had these countries elected to protect their iron ore industries through quotas, tariffs, and other impediments to trade—such as were provided for the Western European coal and the United States oil industries—the magnitude and the pattern of world trade in iron ore would have been very different indeed. In a negative sense, therefore, political attitudes have been critically important in the evolution of the pattern of iron ore supplies throughout the world.

Outside the fully planned economies, there have been relatively few examples of governments imposing a complete ban on iron ore exports. Currently, a ban does exist in Mexico. Historically, the most celebrated case has been that of Australia, where for many years the government in Canberra insisted on the need to conserve the country's iron ore reserves for its domestic iron and steel industry. However, the gradual realization of the enormous wealth of the subcontinent's iron ore resources—now rated among the largest in the world (see Chapter 11)—led to the removal of the embargo in 1960. Immediately there followed the speedy development of several of the deposits, almost overnight transforming the supply situation of Japan's iron and steel industry. International trade in iron ore, unlike oil, has also been unimpeded by attempts on the part of the ore-producing countries to create some form of supranational control over iron ore exports. In 1962 the Venezuelan government tried to create an iron ore counterpart to the Organization of the Petroleum Exporting Countries (OPEC) with the objective that all exporting producers should coordinate their marketing and investment strategies. However, as a consequence of the divergent self-interests of the many ore exporters, plus the considerable financial involvement of the steel industry in many mining operations, the proposal attracted very little support.

In summary, any interpretation of the changing geography of iron ore supplies must recognize, in addition to what can broadly be described as market and cost factors, the role of contractual and ownership relationships between the iron ore and the iron and steel industries; of pricing policies adopted by the mining industry; and of a variety of political influences and policies. All these factors operate within the industry's changing technological framework. The next chapter examines the most important developments in the technology of iron ore mining and preparation during the period 1950 to 1965.

CHAPTER 8

Technological Progress

The growing demands for iron ore between 1950 and 1965, plus a changing supply situation (see Chapter 11), generated a significant technological response in virtually all aspects of the iron ore mining industry. And there were parallel developments in the modes and the cost of transporting the ore to its markets (see Chapters 9 and 10). In the actual mining operations, the scale, the efficiency, and the productivity of each phase of the operations were steadily increased; and unit costs fell. The drilling of an ore body for blasting, for example, is subject to important scale economies. Hollingsworth (1964) showed that it cost 0.6 cent per meter to drill a hole with a diameter of 26 cm., whereas it cost only 0.4 cent per meter to drill a hole with a diameter of 38 cm. Similarly, there are economies in using larger shovels and lifting equipment, with the result that shovels of 11.5 cubic meters are able to move ore at 72 percent of the cost of shovels with 7 m³ capacity. Throughout the period the size of loaders, stripping shovels, and draglines gradually increased. Whereas in the early fifties shovels of 1.5 to 4.5 cubic meters were in regular use, fifteen years later they had been replaced by shovels of 7 to 12 m³. And for the removal of overburden, very much larger machines were developed; some of these by 1965 were able to handle up to 90 cubic meters in each shovel, and yet they could still be operated by one man. In a like manner the capacity of vehicles used for hauling ore within the mine increased from 5 and 10 tons to 100 tons. As a consequence of all these developments, the annual capacity of individual mines was gradually increased. Whereas mines of over 1 or 2 million actual tons per year were rare in 1950, fifteen years later mines producing 5 or 10 million actual tons of ore were increasingly common, and even larger ones were being developed. The Reserve Mining Company at Silver Bay, Minnesota, for example, had to extract over 25 million tons of rock to produce its 9 million actual tons of pellets each year, while the UGOK mine in the Krivoy Rog mining district in 1965 handled 25 million tons of crude magnetite to produce 11.4 million actual tons of concentrate each year.

PROGRESS IN ORE PREPARATION

It was in the sphere of iron ore preparation, however, that the greatest changes were recorded during the period. The first stage in iron ore preparation is the crushing and grading of the ores. These are processes that have been used for many centuries; they produce a lumpy product of improved size for feeding into the blast furnace. The slightly more advanced processes of grinding and screening were also well established at the beginning of the period. The subsequent processes of blending, bedding, beneficiation, and agglomeration, on the other hand, have been subject to considerable technological development, and they have also become much more widely used (Roe, 1957; United Nations, 1966).

The purpose of blending ores is to ensure that their physical and chemical composition is uniform when they are fed into either a blast furnace or any subsequent preparation process. As Percival (1959, p. 4) put it: "If an irregular diet is provided, the blast furnace is as prone to indigestion as a human being." The need for blending and the extent to which it is used depends on the composition and qualities of the iron ore or iron ores in question (this in turn is a function of the methods used to extract it, and the number of mines from which it is won). The need for blending also depends on the permissible range of physical and chemical variations in the ore, which is determined by the subsequent processes and/or the end products. In the case of low-grade British ores, the calcareous ores of North Lincolnshire have traditionally been blended with the siliceous ores of Northamptonshire to produce a useful (though still low-grade) self-fluxing burden for the "lean ore" blast furnaces or sinter plants; and increasingly these home ores are further blended with high-grade imported ores in order to raise the iron content of the blast-furnace burdens. In other circumstances, various grades of ore are put into stockpiles in level layers, and then removed in slices taken through the pile in order to get an even mixture of the several components for daily use or shipment. Given suitable conditions, such bedding procedure ores can reduce the variations of iron content of ores in a mine from 3 to 5 percent when recovered to ±0.5 percent when ready for the furnace; this in fact happens at the Magnitogorsk combine in the Soviet Union.

It is generally by means of beneficiation or concentration that the iron content of ores is significantly increased. A considerable and still increasing variety of processes have gradually been developed to this end. They range from relatively simple washing processes, in which clays and sandy materials can be removed, to heavy media separation, jigging, spiral separation, magnetic concentration, and electrostatic separation or concentration. The appropriate beneficiation technique for any ore will be determined by its exact properties, especially its mineral composition, hardness, grain size, and the like. At the two largest beneficiation plants in Canada—Lac Jeannine (20 million actual tons) and Carol Lake (17.5 million)—natural ores of 30 and 37 percent Fe, respectively, are crushed and ground, and then beneficiated in spiral separators to produce concentrates of 66 percent Fe. At the Soviet Union's Olenyogorsk mine, on the other hand, an ore body with an average iron content of 32 percent Fe is treated by a wet magnetic separation process and then by a flotation process to produce a magnetite concentrate of 69 percent and a hematite concentrate of 64 percent Fe.

The final group of ore preparation processes embraces those known as agglomeration. The two principal techniques are sintering and pelletizing, both of which are essentially concerned with improving the physical structure of ore burdens in the blast furnace. Their development since 1950 has meant that blast-furnace burdens averaged between 40 and 50 percent sinter in 1965, compared with 10 to 20 percent only a few years earlier. In the case of sinter, fine-sized particles of ore (below about 12.5 mm diameter) are mixed with flue dust, burnt pyrites, and coke breeze into a coherent cinder-like agglomerate through incipient fusion. The first sinter plants were developed to make use of blast-furnace dust and waste fines accumulating at steelworks. But from this relatively auxiliary function, sintering gradually became a major element in iron ore preparation, since the physical and chemical properties of a charge—its size, hardness, reducibility, flexibility, and chemical stability—can usually be improved by the process, especially if the materials are less than 12 mm in diameter. Table 35 gives a good indication of the way in which the volume of sinter production increased during the decade 1955–64. At first, sinter was made solely from essentially iron-bearing materials. With time, however, producers began to add minerals such as limestone, chalk, and dolomite in order to produce self-fluxing sinters of almost any required basicity. By 1964 the U.S.S.R. produced more than 103 million actual tons of sinter, of which 98 percent was of the self-fluxing variety. This development meant not only that the calcination of the fluxes was transferred to the sintering strand (where cheaper fuels than blast-furnace coke could be used), but also that the greater part of the work of preparing the ore burden for pig iron production was removed from the blast furnace with a consequent increase in its efficiency.

The other method of iron ore agglomeration—pelletization—achieves the same end. It was fundamentally the result of a large and costly research and engineering program in the United States, designed to meet the

162

TRENDS IN SUPPLY OF IRON ORE

TABLE 35.   RECORDED CONSUMPTION OF IRON ORE IN THE PRODUCTION OF SINTER AND OTHER
AGGLOMERATES, 1950 AND 1964

(Thousands of contained tons)

Region and country	1950	1964
WORLD	18,210	164,665
NORTH AMERICA	7,800	51,700
Canada		6,700
United States	7,800	45,000
WESTERN EUROPE	3,993	40,968
EEC	1,465	25,864
Belgium		2,900
France	87	6,773
Italy	60	1,237
Luxembourg		1,652
Netherlands		1,534
West Germany	1,318	11,768
Austria	328	1,085
Britain	1,430	9,887
Finland		450
Norway		440
Portugal		127
Spain		800
Sweden	770	2,060
Turkey		265
EASTERN EUROPE	5,961	59,066
Middle Europe	261	6,566
Bulgaria		190
Czechoslovakia	200	2,850
Hungary	61	740
Poland		2,786
U.S.S.R.	5,700	52,500
OTHERS	456	12,931
Australia		2,180
Japan	456	10,100
Peru		651

Source: United Nations, 1968-A.

growing deficiency in the country's direct-shipping ore resources. Pelletization consists in balling high-grade fine ores or concentrates to various sizes
(from 8 to 30 mm in diameter), and subsequently hardening them by high-
temperature firing. When it is well prepared, the resultant product has a
uniform lump size; it has physical strength to withstand breaking in both
handling and the blast furnace; it has good reducibility; and it has a high
iron content and a uniform chemical composition. Consequently, it affords
as good a blast-furnace input as sinter, and at best it provides an economically more attractive feed. It was not without significance that the Yawata
Iron and Steel Company, in planning its new Sakai works, elected not to
build sintering facilities but rather to depend heavily on Californian and
Peruvian pellets. The first commercial-scale pellet plant, at Silver Bay,
Minnesota, using low-grade magnetic taconites, came on-stream in 1956.
Within ten years, the pellet capacity of the United States had reached 32
million actual tons, and capacity in Canada reached 16 million. Addition-

TABLE 36. PELLET CAPACITY, IN USE AND PLANNED, 1960 AND 1965

(*Millions of actual tons*)

Region and country	Capacity 1960	Capacity 1965	Under construction or firm plans, end of 1965
WORLD	15.6	54.8	49.5
NORTH AMERICA	15.1	47.7	25.4
Canada	1.4	15.6	5.5
U.S.A.	13.8	32.1	19.9
WESTERN EUROPE	0.5	3.9	4.5
EEC		0.3	
Italy		0.3	
Finland	0.2	0.2	
Norway		0.6	
Sweden	0.3	2.8	4.5
EASTERN EUROPE		1.0	
U.S.S.R.		1.0	
ASIA AND OCEANIA		1.2	8.8
India			0.5
Japan		1.2	1.0
Philippines			0.8
Australia			6.5
LATIN AMERICA		1.0	6.5
Peru		1.0	6.5
AFRICA AND MIDDLE EAST			4.3
Liberia			3.5
Morocco			0.8

Sources: American Iron Ore Association; Erzkontor Ruhr GmbH.

ally, in North America there were 25 million actual tons of capacity either under construction or firmly planned. Elsewhere in the world, 7 million actual tons of pellet capacity were in existence, and 24 million were in prospect (Table 36).

Most pellets in the first instance had an iron content of between 62 and 68 percent. There is, however, no reason why the latter figure should represent an upper limit. Experiments have been conducted, and pilot plants built, to reduce the iron oxide in the ore still further in order to produce a blast-furnace feed of 80 or even 90 percent iron (see Chapter 3). Such "pre-reduced pellets," if they could be manufactured at low cost, and if they could be handled and stored without significant reoxidation, would further underline the advantages and the geographical implications of the recent advances in ore preparation.

SPATIAL IMPLICATIONS OF ORE PREPARATION

The increasing use of iron ore preparation resulted in certain important reassessments of iron ore needs and resources. The introduction of sinter, for example, reduced the waste of blast-furnace dust; as a consequence, the yield of iron ore was marginally increased and, relative to pig iron output, less ore had to be mined. Even more important was the use (for the first time) made of fines, which are produced in very large quantities in some ore operations and which previously had been unable to find a market. The value of the mines that produced fines was immediately increased. However, not all types of ore are equally amenable to a preparation process. As a consequence, differential reassessments came to be made of the worth of certain deposits. Some low-grade ore bodies, for example, could be used after preliminary beneficiation for the first time; they therefore assumed a new economic importance. Other ore bodies, which had previously had a value but for which no economical beneficiation process was developed, began to lose their markets and value.

In the United States and the Soviet Union in particular, several key deposits of high-grade, lumpy blast-furnace ore bodies, which had been exploited for many years, were nearing exhaustion (or presenting mounting extraction and preparation costs) by 1950. As a result the iron and steel industries of both countries sought to develop technologies whereby lower-grade deposits, which were known to be available, could be economically concentrated and agglomerated. In the United States, it was the low-grade taconites and jasperites of the Lake Superior region (containing *in situ* 24 to 26% Fe) that attracted attention; through the new preparation technologies, they were of commercial interest to the iron and steel industry for the first time. The waning fortunes of that traditional mining district of the United States thereby came to be revived. Similarly, in the Soviet Union, exploration drilling after 1945 established the existence of huge deposits of magnetite (37% Fe) in the quartzite rocks of the Krivoy Rog area; to exploit these deposits, one of the largest and most advanced concentration plants in the country—UGOK—was opened in 1956.

In contrast, the competitive position of other ore bodies deteriorated when their products were found to be unsuited to the new preparation and beneficiation processes. The bedded oolitic ores of the southern Appalachian Mountains, for example—ores which for many years had fed the blast furnaces of Birmingham, Alabama, and which were very similar to the Minette deposits of eastern France—were in this category. They came under increasing competition from foreign ores, and mining finally ceased when all attempts at developing an economic beneficiation process failed. In Western Europe, too, the lean ore resources of several major steel-producing countries came to be relatively less attractive. These differential results of the new iron ore preparation technology called for a reassessment of the world's ore resources; something of this reassessment is recorded in Chapter 11.

A second implication of the increasing use made of iron ore preparation technology was the further encouragement of spatially concentrated production in order to take advantage of the technological scale economies exhibited by each of the various forms of ore preparation. In the matter of ore blending, the economies to be derived from the use of larger equipment —where capital costs dominate total costs—were demonstrated by Maertens (1963), who showed how the cost of depreciation fell from $2.50 per actual ton to $0.75, with an increase in plant size from 0.07 to 1.6 million actual tons per year. High investment costs similarly dominate the economics of sintering. In West Germany in 1963, they represented about 38 percent of the total costs (with labor costs making up 15%, energy 22%, and maintenance 23%). Once again, the process has pronounced technological economies of scale (Lehmkuhler, 1963). While the capital costs of small plants varied between $13 and $14 per actual ton of annual capacity, those of larger plants ranged between $11.50 and $12.50. Some scale economies of pellet plants are shown in Table 37.

To these technological scale economies of ore preparation plants, plus those of the actual mining operations, were added the internal and external scale economies of the large mining complex, such as its engineering workshops, transport facilities, and the infrastructure of townships. During the period, all these scale economies tended to increase. Strong economic pressures were therefore generated to close down many small mines and to extend the larger ones. The 1950 situation in the United States, where three mines each had an annual capacity of over 5 million actual tons of ore, was somewhat exceptional. Generally speaking, the annual output of a single mine rarely exceeded 1 or 2 million actual tons; and even such famous mines as Tunisia's Djerissa and Spain's Marquesade reached their peak levels of production with 990,000 and 550,000 actual tons, respectively, in 1960 and 1961.

By 1965, the scale of mining operations had been completely transformed. The Cerro Bolívar mine in Venezuela, for example, had an annual capacity of nearly 14 million actual tons of salable ore; the Lamco mine in Liberia was capable of producing 10 million actual tons; and the Quebec Cartier mine had a capacity of 8 million actual tons of concentrates per year. Even larger were the mines planned for 1970 and beyond. In the

TABLE 37. SCALE ECONOMIES IN PELLET PRODUCTION, CIRCA 1962

| | Cost of production (*dollars/ton*) | | |
Capacity: tons/day of actual pellets	Shaft furnace	Continuous strand	Grate kiln
100	4.14		
500	2.97		
1,000	2.24	2.67	2.62
5,000	1.87	1.83	1.78
25,000	1.76	1.68	1.63

Source: Astier, 1963.

U.S.S.R., the Lisakov and Sokolovsk-Sarbaisk "C" plants are scheduled to be expanded to produce 36 and 30 million actual tons of crude ore, which will yield about half that tonnage of concentrates; and in the United States the possibility has been reported of the United States Steel Corporation expanding its pellet-manufacturing facilities at Iron Mountain (Minnesota) to 18 million actual tons, an output which would involve the mining of about 50 million actual tons of taconite (Table 38). The undoubted advantages of such large units of ore production and preparation have to be set against the other cost factors. Given a geography of ore demands, a more centralized pattern of ore production creates higher aggregate costs for transporting the ore to its markets. Sometimes the economies of the large mine can be offset at smaller pits by lower extraction costs as a result of differing geological conditions or cheaper labor. And particular grades and types of ore can sometimes only be found, and are sometimes only needed, in small quantities. Many small mines were thus able to survive profitably until 1965, and they also had hope of being able to continue in production for many years to come. Nevertheless, the impress of increasing scale economies on the geography of iron ore mining and preparation throughout the period was to be seen in every continent and showed no signs of weakening.

TABLE 38.   OUTPUT AND/OR CAPACITY OF SOME OF THE WORLD'S LARGEST IRON ORE MINES, 1965

(Millions of actual tons)

Mine	Fe content	Production of marketable ore	Capacity
CANADA			
Carol Lake...............................	65%		7.0
Quebec-Cartier..........................	65	9.1	
U.S.A.			
Erie Mining..............................	61–62	7.5*	
Minntac.................................	65		4.5* (1967)
U.S.S.R.			
Magnitnaya Gora.........................	56–60	10.7	
Southern Combine, Ukraine.................	63	11.4	
BRAZIL			
Cía. Vale do Rio Doce, Caué mine............	67–69	5.4	
CHILE			
El Algarroba.............................	56–64	3.7	
Cía. Minera Sta. Fe.......................	63–65	3.6	
PERU			
Marcona................................	60–67	4.2	
VENEZUELA			
Cerro Bolívar............................	63	13.7	20.0
LIBERIA			
Lamco..................................	65	8.2	10.0
MAURITANIA			
Fort Gouraud...........................	60–69	10.7	

* Pellets.

Such a shift in the size of individual mining operations also prompted a critical reassessment of the value of different ore bodies. Some small ones, which in the past would have attracted the attention of the mining industry, were henceforth neglected. Large deposits that were formerly unattractive were reassessed for large-scale exploitation: the economics of the industry for the first time justified the opening of a mine, the establishment of a township, and the provision of the necessary transport facilities.

A third implication of the growth of ore preparation stemmed from the high and increasing capital costs of the processing plants. For an open-cast mine, the investment required in the mid-sixties (including all the costs of equipment, construction, financing, preproduction expenses, and the like, but excluding long-distance transport facilities, harbors, etc.) was in the order of $15 to $20 per actual ton of annual capacity. Plants comprising beneficiation facilities for magnetic or gravity separation required an investment in the order of $30 to $35 per actual ton of annual capacity, which for a 5-million actual ton mine implied an initial cost of between $150 and $175 million. Production facilities for pellets were even more expensive, demanding the investment of about $40 per actual ton of annual capacity. In addition, a mining company frequently has to provide the capital for a mining township, a railway, harbor facilities, a power station, and other items of infrastructure (see Table 34).

This huge scale of capital investment meant that mining companies became increasingly reluctant to invest in new extraction and preparation facilities without some assurance of a continuing market for their output. In fact, under the market conditions of the early sixties, it was only by working their facilities fairly close to their capacity that any hope could be entertained by mining interests of meeting the considerable interest charges on capital, amortizing their plant, and getting a reasonable return on their investment. The result was a growing commitment of iron ore production to particular markets, either through the negotiation of long-term contracts or as a result of investments by the iron and steel industry in mining operations. The iron and steel industry of the United States had traditionally been assured of its ore supplies through such means; only about 20 percent of U.S. iron ore is generally sold on the open market. But for the Western European and the Japanese iron and steel producers, this was a development that contrasted with their traditional practice of satisfying the greater part of their ore needs through regular annual purchases on the open market.

It was Japan, more than any other single country, that accepted the need for, and saw the financial advantages of, long-term ore-supply contracts. By 1966, its iron and steel industry was committed to receive from seven different countries (Table 39) nearly 30 million actual tons of ore each year

TABLE 39. LONG-TERM CONTRACTS FOR IRON ORE SUPPLIES TO JAPAN, 1965

Country	Source	Contract period	Annual delivery (*millions of actual tons*)
Australia...............	Hamersley	18 yrs. from 1966	3.6
Australia...............	Mt. Goldsworthy	7 yrs. from 1966	2.3
Australia...............	Western Mining	1966–73	0.5 to 0.7
Australia...............	Francis Creek	8 yrs. from 1967	3.0
Australia...............	Mt. Newman	21–22 yrs. from 1969	5.0
Australia...............	Robe River	Under negotiation	
Australia...............	Savage River	Under negotiation	
Brazil...................	Rio Doce	15 yrs. from 1966	5.0
Chile...................	Santa Fe	10 yrs. from 1961	1.0
Chile...................	Algarrobo	11 yrs. from 1962	0.8
India...................	Chowgule (Goa)	5 yrs. from 1964	1.0
India...................	Chowgule (Goa)	6 yrs. from 1966	3.3
India...................	Rourkela	10 yrs. from 1964	2.0
India...................	Kiriburu	10 yrs. from 1965	2.0
India...................	Bailadila	15 yrs. from 1966	4.0
Peru....................	Marcona	7 yrs. from 1963	0.8
Swaziland..............	Ngwenya	10 yrs. from 1964	1.2
U.S.A..................	Kaiser (Eagle Mt.)	10 yrs. from 1962	1.0

(compared with its total imports of just under 40 million actual tons in 1965). And additional supplies were either agreed upon or under negotiation with Australian mining interests. All these bargains invariably included a "10 percent clause," which permitted increases in the volume of shipments at the same price and at very short notice. Most of these contracts were straightforward commercial arrangements; the exports from the United States to Japan fell into this category. Others, however, involved reciprocal help from the purchasers in the form of financial and engineering assistance to open up a particular deposit. Japan's financial aid program assisted the exploitation of India's Kiriburu deposit, and the Brazilian government negotiated a large credit for locomotives from Japan, the loan to be paid back over ten to fifteen years in shipments of iron ore.

Although American and the Western European iron and steel producers did not eschew the long-term contract as a means of securing their ore supplies and encouraging mining developments, they both reacted more characteristically to the changing technology and economics of iron ore mining by following the traditional American pattern and becoming closely associated with mining activities. With a rather easier access to capital than their Japanese counterparts (and in the American case with valuable domestic iron ore resources), they sometimes initiated new mining enterprises. On other occasions they provided both the financial backing and a guaranteed market for national and international mining companies.

In the case of the Pilot Knob development in Missouri, the mine and the pellet plant (750,000 actual tons/year) were financed jointly by the Hanna Mining Company and Granite City Steel (to which all the products are shipped). The Pioneer pellet plant at Eagle Mills (Michigan) was developed jointly by three American steel corporations and a merchant ore company, the Cleveland-Cliffs Iron Company. On the international scale, the United States Steel Corporation undertook the development of the Cerro Bolívar deposit in Venezuela. The Lamco development in Liberia, on the other hand, is jointly owned by the Liberian government (50%), Swedish mining interests (37.5%), and the Bethlehem Steel Corporation (12.5%). And the open-pit mine at Fort Gouraud (Mauritania) is jointly owned by the British Ore Investment Company, Finsider (of Italy), Gewerkschaft Exploration (West Germany), USINOR, MM. de Rothschild Frères, the Bureau de Recherches Géologiques et Minières (France), and the government of Mauritania itself; it is operated by the Société Anonyme des Mines de Fer de Mauritanie (MIFERMA).

Although in part a response to the steel industry's need for security of raw-material supplies, these long-term supply contracts and the growing financial commitment of the steel industry to iron ore mining can also be interpreted as a response to the changing technology of the mining industry and the increasing scale of investment required. The gains were, of course, mutual. And simultaneously with the lessening of the risks taken by the mining industry, both the proportion of ore sold on the open market and the medium-term flexibility of ore movements were significantly reduced.

LOCATION OF PREPARATION FACILITIES

With an increasing proportion of iron ore subject to some form of preparation, the question of the best location at which to perform these operations became progressively more important. The several processes used in ore preparation essentially involve the application of energy—both mechanical and thermal—to iron ores in such a way as to remove their impurities, to concentrate the amount of iron within a given weight of ore, and to improve their physical structure for use in the blast furnace. In the process they generally lose weight, although sometimes there is a weight gain. And the ease with which they can be handled is often significantly increased. In a sense, therefore, the locational problem resolves itself into measuring the geographical differentials in energy costs against differences in the costs (and the convenience) of transporting prepared as opposed to unprepared ores.

There are often strong transport-cost inducements to locate preparation plants as close to the mine as possible, or at a nearby break-of-bulk point or transport interface. Whenever there is any beneficiation in the preparation process, the transport costs per unit of iron are inevitably lower with a mine orientation. The greater the concentration, the stronger the pull. Thus, when an ore like taconite or jasperite is beneficiated, and three actual tons of ore have to be drilled, blasted, and mined in order to obtain one actual ton of pellets, the preparation facilities are invariably sited at or near the mining operations. Such is the case at the Erie mine in the United States, where some 24 million actual tons of taconite and 13 million of waste have to be mined each year to produce 7.5 million actual tons of pellets. On the other hand, where a high-grade (perhaps 63 percent Fe) magnetite ore is being mined, the locational pull toward the mine is much less, since the transport costs of the concentrate are much the same as those of the natural ore. A further advantage of mine-oriented preparation facilities is the fact that the haulage of prepared ore is sometimes physically easier (and hence cheaper) than the transport of many natural ores. Pellets, for example, can be shipped with little or no degradation of quality throughout the year, even in those parts of the world that have a particularly severe winter. With a low water content, they do not freeze together and become immovable when subjected to subzero temperatures. In contrast, the natural ores of, say, Schefferville have a rather high water content, and as a result they freeze solid in winter and cannot be moved. This necessitates a costly seasonal stockpile on the St. Lawrence, and in turn limits the efficiency with which the Quebec and North Shore Railway can be operated.

In many parts of the world the major disadvantage of ore preparation at the mine is the high cost of energy there. Mines that are located in relatively inaccessible and/or cold places often have to pay a high price for fuel oil. Occasionally, however, when the railways serving a mine are owned by the mining company itself, a relatively low rate is charged for the haulage of fuel oil on the assumption that only the operating costs of the haul need be covered. In the case of the Iron Ore Company of Canada's Carol Lake development, the location of the pellet plant near the mine has been justified by the low rate allocated by the company for the movement of fuel oil over its own railway from the St. Lawrence. Although the nearby mining venture of Wabush Lake is linked to the St. Lawrence by the same railway, that company is charged a higher freight rate for the movement of its supplies, including fuel oil, north from the St. Lawrence; consequently, it elected to concentrate its 36.5 percent Fe ore at the mine, but to pelletize on the St. Lawrence at Pointe Noire, where lower-cost fuel oil was available.

In addition to these matters of transport costs, the location of preparation plants near the mine has several other advantages. It frequently affords the possibility of exploiting scale economies in ore preparation that would not be available to a facility located at an integrated steelworks. A pellet plant sited near a mine can serve several iron and steel works, whereas the size of one located near its market is generally limited by the scale of pig iron production there. Technically, too, there are advantages in material-oriented preparation facilities, since they normally require careful adjustment in handling the distinctive physical and chemical characteristics of the crude ore. Sintering apart—a process that is technically highly flexible and easily adapted to a variety of ores—this adjustment can best be accomplished at the mine, where variations in the quality of the crude ore are likely to be least, rather than at the blast furnace, where a variety of ores are normally assembled to produce a chemically satisfactory metal as well as an efficient furnace feed. Occasionally a further encouragement to mine-oriented preparation stems from political pressures within an ore-producing country or region. There are obvious local advantages in being able to export a product worth perhaps twice as much as untreated ore per ton. Political forces can also work in the opposite direction, as will be noted later.

The location of some preparation facilities at an integrated iron and steel works is widely recognized as an advantage. Certain preparation processes simply have to take place there. The screening of ores after transport, and the blending of ores from different sources, are two examples. A third is the sintering of blast-furnace dust and of ore fines produced in the handling of ore. Granted that a sintering plant is to be built at an integrated steel works for these ores, there is a clear case for making it large enough to prepare in addition feedstocks such as low-priced fines, which are frequently available on the world market. In the ensuing larger scale of sinter production, scale economies are naturally forthcoming. The location of a sinter plant at the iron and steel works affords other advantages too. Coke breeze, needed for the process, is more readily available there. Energy is normally cheaper at an iron and steel works, partly because the location is more accessible than that of many mines, and partly because inexpensive waste heat is on hand. This latter economy is particularly important for sintering, since the process requires more heat than most pelletizing techniques—200,000 to 300,000 kcal/ton compared with 120,000 to 170,000 kcal/ton. Labor costs and materials also tend to be cheaper at a steelworks than at a remote iron ore mining site. And some North American evidence suggests that there is a significantly higher capital cost for sinter capacity in the more remote ore mining areas of Canada (between $9 and $11 per actual ton of annual capacity) compared with the cost in the Midwest of the United States (between $6 and $8 per actual ton of annual capacity).

Sinter is a blast-furnace feed that needs to be handled and transported with considerable care. It does not lend itself to shipment by sea, since there is a tendency for it to break up both in handling and in transit. It can be railed considerable distances. In 1962 some sixteen out of the Soviet Union's twenty-nine sinter plants were located at mines, and their product was railed, in specially built wagons, up to 300 kilometers to their blast-furnace markets. But there is inevitably some decrepitation in the process, and in North America and Western Europe most sinter plants are sited adjacent to the blast furnaces they feed. Technically very flexible, these market-oriented preparation plants can draw upon the ores of several mines; hence they have the advantage of being able to switch their ore sources should it become either economically attractive or strategically necessary. The same applies to facilities constructed at break-of-bulk points near their markets. For example, the 1.5-million actual ton pellet plant built on the Adriatic at Bakar was initially based on an agreement between the Yugoslavian Association of Port Enterprises of Rijeka and the Brazilian Cia. Vale do Rio Doce, with the latter supplying the necessary ore and the former manufacturing the pellets and distributing them to iron and steel plants throughout Middle Europe. The economics of this particular locational decision was influenced in the first place by the high iron content of Brazilian ores (which keeps their unit transport costs as low as those of pellets) and by the foreign exchange shortages of the receiving countries. The longer-term advantages of the site, however, clearly include the possibility of drawing ore from alternative sources.

One final factor that in the future could encourage the market orientation of preparation facilities is political in nature, and its importance is restricted to the international scale. When preparation facilities are located near their ore source in foreign countries, there exists a certain risk of expropriation and nationalization. Situations could exist in which a market orientation for a plant is chosen in order to avoid such risks. Particularly does this apply to expensive pelletizing facilities. By 1965, however, apart from experimental pellet plants in France and Japan, only the Kobe Steel Company in Japan (at Nadahama) and the Hoogovens management at Ijmuiden had announced firm plans to construct pellet facilities adjacent to their blast furnaces. A Rotterdam pellet plant (one of up to 15 million actual tons, designed to serve the West German, Belgian, and possibly British markets) has been suggested in the technical press and given careful consideration, but it has not materialized at the present writing. Generally speaking, therefore, the risks of expropriation to date appear to have been discounted in pellet-plant location decisions.

In sum, the balance of locational advantage in the case of ore preparation facilities appears to vary not only with different types of ore preparation processes but also with the distinctive geographical and economic circumstances associated with each investment decision. Transport costs are once again one of the most influential factors. It is to an examination of the costs and organization of iron ore transport that this study now turns.

CHAPTER 9

Changes in Ocean Transport

The technical response to changes in the demand for and supply of iron ore was not limited to advances in mining and ore preparation. Transfer charges—that is, loading and unloading costs, freight rates, transshipment costs, port charges, demurrage and brokerage charges, and the like—often play an important role in determining the f.o.b. value of ore (see Chapter 7), and hence have a critical role in molding the changing geography of iron ore production. The present chapter and the next tell of the enormous advances made during the 1950–65 period in the techniques for transporting ore, and the resultant changes in the costs of moving it. In terms of the tons of ore involved and the ton-kilometers of ore moved, it was the changes in ocean transport that were the most important.

It has been estimated that the amount of crude iron ore moving by sea in international trade in 1950 was little more than 30 million actual tons (United Nations, 1953, p. 66). By 1955 this traffic had expanded to 60 million actual tons, by 1960 to 101 million, and by 1965 to 152 million. In terms of distance as well as weight, the growth of ocean ore trade was even more dramatic, for between 1950 and 1965 it increased from about 120 thousand million actual-ton-kilometers to 843 thousand million; and between 1960 and 1965 it more than doubled (Fearnley and Egers, 1966). Such an extraordinary expansion of ocean ore movement was a function of all the factors making for change in the geography of ore supplies. But more particularly it was a response to the very low and falling ton-kilo-meter rates offered by ocean vessels for the carriage of ore.

In 1962 Dubnie (p. 109) estimated that the relative Canadian rates of the different transport media available to carry ore concentrates were 0.6 mill (that is, 0.06 cent) per actual-ton-km for ocean freighters, 1.2 mills for coastal steamers, and 8 mills for rail shipments. While these rates for the major means of ore transport were by no means universally applicable, their relative orders of magnitude were widely confirmed in many parts of

173

the world. By 1967, however, Canada's Department of Energy, Mines, and Resources suggested that a rule-of-thumb guide to comparative transport costs was 1.6 mills per actual-ton-km for ocean transport, 4.2 mills for inland waterways, and 16 mills for railways (Gauvin and Schneider, 1967, p. 68). In fact, many ocean ore freights were well below the 1.6 mills level. For example, at times ore could be shipped in large vessels from Sept Iles on the St. Lawrence to Baltimore for 0.75 cent per actual ton, or 0.32 mill per actual-ton-km; and from Liberia to Philadelphia a typical rate was $1.87 per actual ton, or 0.24 mill per actual-ton-km (see Table 48). It is clearly impossible for any other mode of ore transport to compete with such low rates. Thus, although the terminal costs of ocean transport are relatively high (on occasion they can equal or even exceed the line-haul rates), the economic advantages of its use where physical circumstances permit remain unchallenged for all except the shortest hauls.

TECHNICAL AND ECONOMIC CHARACTERISTICS

Ocean ore carriers are expensive pieces of transport equipment. In 1965, a 25,000-dwt vessel cost $3.4 million and a 65,000-dwt vessel $6.5 million. Yet this scale of investment, in terms of its carrying capacity, affords an extremely inexpensive mode of transport. The ratio of capital to operating costs for ore carriers is, of course, subject to considerable variations. It fluctuates with the size of the vessel, the characteristics of the route (especially the length of the haul), and the ground rules set for depreciation. Nevertheless, it is not unreasonable to think in terms of capital costs representing, in 1965, about 40 percent of the total costs of small vessels on short voyages, and 45 percent for large vessels on long hauls (Table 40). There was a time when these percentage figures were considerably higher.

Between 1950 and 1965 the costs of new vessels fell dramatically. In part this was a response to an increasingly competitive shipbuilding market, but mainly it followed from the exploitation of new shipbuilding technology. Japanese yards set the pace. Exactly comparable costs of new

TABLE 40. DAILY COSTS OF SHIPS, IN PORT AND AT SEA, 1965

Size of ship (dwt)	9,000	15,000	25,000	35,000	45,000	65,000
Capital cost (millions of dollars)	2.25	3.1	3.6	4.5	5.3	7.0
Daily costs (dollars)						
Capital charges	615	850	985	1,230	1,450	1,920
Operating costs	764	935	1,077	1,202	1,305	1,484
Fuel cost in port	25	38	51	59	68	76
Fuel cost at sea	260	385	555	765	930	1,250
Total cost in port	1,404	1,823	2,113	2,491	2,823	3,480
Total cost at sea	1,639	2,170	2,617	3,197	3,685	4,654

Source: United Nations, 1968-A.

vessels over time cannot be quoted, since the specifications and the size of vessels tend to change. A 30,000-dwt ore carrier ordered for delivery in 1951–52 would have cost circa $7.5 million ($250 per ton). Its price fell throughout the early years of the decade, rose dramatically around the time of the Suez crisis, and then continued its downward trend until by 1965 a new 30,000-dwt ore carrier could be purchased for about $3.75 million ($125 per ton). Unit costs of larger ships were lower still. Vessels of 80,000 dwt were not built at the beginning of the period under study, but by 1965 they were available from Japanese yards at prices of circa $95 to $100 per ton, with further falls imminent. The cost of vessels naturally varied with their specifications and with the country of construction. Western European shipyards tended to quote higher prices than their Japanese counterparts, and American prices were noticeably out of line with the international market, sometimes 100 percent higher. Between 1950 and 1965, however, the capital cost of bulk carriers generally fell by about one-half at current dollar prices.

The capital costs of ore carriers fell in another sense. In the late fifties and early sixties, the world shipbuilding industry responded to competitive conditions by offering increasingly generous credit facilities to prospective purchasers. In the early fifties all orders were placed on a sliding-scale basis, and buyers were required to meet any rise in costs between the time of placing a contract and a ship's delivery; in addition, all contracts called for payment of the full cash price by the time of delivery. By the early sixties, in contrast, all orders were being quoted on a fixed-price basis, with no provision for escalating costs, and virtually all were accepted with generous credit terms—generally 80 percent advances with repayments spread over periods of eight to ten years at a low rate (5.5%) of interest.

The economic advantages of ocean carriers and their low ton-kilometer costs were based on a relatively high degree of vessel use. The more revenue ton-kilometers a ship can be worked, the lower become its ton-kilometer costs. In an increasingly competitive shipping market, therefore, it was natural that the owners and operators of ore carriers should go to considerable lengths to intensify the use they made of capacity. Thus, to the falling capital costs of ships could be added the further economy of falling capital costs per ton-km. One traditional means of achieving this end was to encourage shippers to make use of a vessel over longer periods than a single voyage, by offering freight rate discounts for long-term charters. At first, such arrangements were for periods of three months, six months, or a year. However, in time term charters and contracts of affreightment of up to fifteen years came to be commonly agreed upon between shippers and shipowners. By transferring many of the risks of shipowning to the shipper in this way, exceptionally low freight rates became possible by the standards of the spot-charter market, reflecting the fuller use made of capital investment.

A second way in which the shipping industry intensified the use it made of ore carriers was to encourage, through its freight rate structure, faster port operations. Their expense, never small, varies with the nature, the size, and the efficiency of the facilities available. By 1965, for example, a number of ore-loading ports still were able to handle only between 200 and 500 actual tons per hour, compared with a reasonable rate of 2,000 to 3,000 tons; and some ports were equipped to load 8,000 tons/hr (see Table 44). Although discharging is inherently a slower process, the poorest facilities (as a consequence of the readier availability of capital in the ore-importing countries) were rated at between 600 and 1,000 tons/hr (see Table 45). A more normal rate was between 2,000 and 2,500 tons/hr, and the fastest facilities were rated at 6,000. These loading and discharging facilities are all subject to scale economies (Table 41). In 1965 an average charge for loading ore was 50 cents per actual ton; the most efficient facilities had charges as low as 20 to 25 cents, but some ports charged as much as 80 cents. Unloading charges, on the other hand, although inherently more expensive, had a somewhat narrower range, from 25 to 50 cents per actual ton. In addition to these charges, ore passing through a port could be charged another 25 cents per actual ton for intermediate storage, and the costs of wharfage could add yet another 50 cents per actual ton at each end of the haul. These port operations and charges can add anything from $1.50 to $2.50 per actual ton to the line-haul freight rate for shipping ore. At this level they represent more than twice the freight rate for some vessels plying between Sept Iles and Philadelphia. In some places there are no modern port facilities. This is the situation facing Malaysian and Philippine ore exports, for which lighters are used to load ore carriers anchored some kilometers offshore. With such grossly inefficient loading and discharging conditions, terminal costs can be very high indeed. At Madras, for example, where the average loading time in 1965 was 8.8 days (Table 42), the loading and port charges alone were $3.25 per actual ton (India, Planning Commission, 1965).

Quite apart from the considerable loading, discharging, wharfage, and demurrage charges incurred in port, a ship not at sea is an investment failing to earn a return. In port, a vessel incurs about three-quarters of its expenses at sea (see Table 40). Where port facilities are such as to require ships to spend a considerable time waiting to be loaded or discharged, a vessel's earning opportunities are reduced and its ton-km costs are raised. The rates to and from that port tend therefore to be adjusted upward by the shipping industry. Whereas in the early fifties it was normal for 15,000-dwt ore boats to be in and out of the port of Vitória (Brazil) in two days,

TABLE 41. THEORETICAL PORT LOADING AND DISCHARGING COSTS FOR ORE, 1965

(Actual tons of ore)

LOADING

Annual exports (tons/yr)	Suitable loading rate (tons/hr)	Number and rated capacity of loaders (tons/hr)	Equipment capital costs (millions of dollars)	Capital charges (cents/ton)	Operating costs (cents/ton)			Total cost (cents/ton)
					Labor	Power	Maintenance	
2,000,000	4,000	2 at 3,000	2.0	10.0	7.0	1.0	4.0	22.0
5,000,000	6,000	2 at 4,000	2.5	5.0	3.0	1.0	3.0	12.0
10,000,000	9,000	2 at 6,000	3.5	3.5	1.5	1.0	2.0	8.0
20,000,000	12,000	3 at 6,000	5.0	2.5	1.0	1.0	2.0	6.5

DISCHARGING

Annual imports (tons/yr)	Suitable discharging rate (tons/hr)	Number and rated capacity of unloaders (tons/hr)	Equipment capital costs (millions of dollars)	Capital charges (cents/ton)	Operating costs (cents/ton)			Total cost (cents/ton)
					Labor	Power	Maintenance	
1,000,000	1,000	2 at 850	2.5	25.0	19.0	1.0	5.0	50.0
2,000,000	1,500	2 at 1,250	3.6	18.0	9.0	1.0	4.0	32.0
5,000,000	3,000	3 at 1,700	5.7	11.0	5.0	1.0	3.0	20.0
8,000,000	4,000	4 at 1,700	7.0	9.0	3.0	1.0	3.0	16.0

Source: United Nations, 1968-A, pp. 117, 120.

TABLE 42. TURNAROUND TIME OF ORE AND BULK CARRIERS IN MAJOR ORE PORTS, 1965
(*Average number of days per call*)

LOADING PORTS		DISCHARGING PORTS	
Pointe Noire	1.5		
Port Cartier	0.9	Sydney, Nova Scotia	2.7
Sept Iles	1.2		
Wabana	1.1	Baltimore	2.0
		Mobile	1.6
Long Beach	2.3	Philadelphia	2.5
Kirkenes	1.1	Antwerp	3.5
Narvik	2.3		
		Dunkirk	2.8
Luleå	2.0		
Oxelösund	2.4	Bagnoli	3.5
		Genoa	6.0
Goa	12.2	Taranto	1.6
Madras	8.8		
		Amsterdam	2.4
Dungun	7.1	Ijmuiden	3.7
Kuala Rompin	6.2	Rotterdam	2.6
Tumpat	5.8		
		Bremerhaven	2.4
Rio de Janeiro	13.3	Emden	3.0
Vitória	8.2		
		Cardiff	2.2
Guayacan (Coquimbo)	2.8	Glasgow	2.3
		Hartlepool	4.0
Annaba	2.5	Immingham	3.1
		Liverpool	3.1
Lobito	6.4	Middlesbrough	3.7
Luanda	7.2	Newport	4.2
		Tyne	3.6
Conakry	4.3		
		Gdynia	5.0
Buchanan	1.4		
Monrovia	1.6	Chiba	5.4
		Hirohata	2.7
Port Etienne	1.2	Kobe	4.2
		Muroran	2.7
Lourenço Marques	6.5	Nagoya	1.8
		Wakayama	2.7
Pepel	1.8	Yawata	2.0
		Yokohama	3.1
Port Elizabeth	4.2		
		San Nicolás, Argentina	3.7

Source: Fearnley and Egers, 1966, p. 25.
Note: For location of ports see Tables 44 and 45.

it was not uncommon a decade later, when larger vessels of 25,000 dwt called, for well over a week to elapse between a ship's arrival and its dispatch. The relatively high freight rates out of Vitória in the sixties reflected this situation, as did the decision to build a new port at Tubarão. Table 42 illustrates for 1965 something of the variety in turnaround time of ore carriers at the world's major loading and discharging ports. The figures reflect both the average size of vessel and the efficiency with which it was handled.

A third way in which the shipping industry responded to its need to intensify the use made of its vessels was to search for suitable return cargoes. By the early fifties more ore was being transported in specially designed ore carriers, as opposed to tramp vessels. But, as the distances over which the ore moved lengthened, so did the time during which the carriers had to steam in ballast, without earning any return. Trading opportunities for direct return cargoes were rare. Those existing in eastern North America, where ships carrying Canadian ore to Philadelphia or Baltimore could pick up coal at Hampton Roads and transport it north on their return journey to the St. Lawrence, were unusual. However, the shipping industry soon found it quite possible to develop triangular and quadrangular dry bulk cargo trades, in which revenue-earning traffic could be hauled along at least two legs of a three-legged route. For example, the movement of Liberian or Canadian iron ore to the east coast ports of the United States was combined with the shipment of American coal from Norfolk and Newport News to Western Europe; only the return leg (to West Africa or the St. Lawrence) was sailed in ballast. Again, the export of Chilean ore to the United States came to be associated with the shipment of American coal from Hampton Roads to Japan. By 1965 it was even possible to consider hauling Brazilian and Venezuelan ore to Japan, ballasting to West Australia, and then hauling Australian ore to Western Europe before returning to South America for more ore.

The chief limitation of this type of triangular trade was the geographical imbalance of dry bulk commodity flows. Whereas in '65 the United States imported 31 million actual tons of ore by sea and exported 31 million tons of coal, Western Europe and Japan were large net importers of both these raw materials. In response to this problem, vessels were designed that could carry either ore or oil. The first such ships were introduced into the Swedish ore trade in the fifties. They suffered somewhat from being able to carry only a part load of each commodity in each direction. Naval architects, however, were soon able to design vessels capable of transporting full loads of either commodity. As a consequence, there emerged new triangular and quadrangular bulk commodity trades. Ore exports from southern California to Japan came to be moved in vessels that ballasted to the East Indies, where they picked up a return load of crude oil for the Los Angeles market. Similarly, iron ore shipments from Chile and Peru to Japan were combined with oil movements from the East Indies to the United States; and the intermediate and shorter trips from Japan to Sumatra and from California to Latin America were run in ballast. Such procedures allowed the payload-to-distance ratio to be increased well above the 50 percent of the direct ore (and ballast) services. By 1965 there were about one hundred ore/oil carriers in the world ocean fleet, as compared with about 350 specialized ore carriers.

Yet a further step toward ensuring that the capital invested in bulk carriers would yield a high rate of return was the development by the Japanese of multipurpose carriers, which were capable of transporting ore, coal, bauxite, grain, or oil—subsequently dubbed OBOs. By building into ocean vessels an additional versatility in this way, the slightly higher costs of construction could be more than offset by additional revenue-earning capabilities. New backhaul trades could be exploited. And, with the intensity of trade along many routes subject to some degree of fluctuation, the multipurpose vessel was easily adaptable to changing trading opportunities, and so could take advantage of the most profitable traffic available at any one time. Such a flexibility was of particular importance because the rates of growth of various bulk trades vary considerably. While iron ore accounted for 75 percent of the tons and 70 percent of the ton-kilometers moved by bulk carriers (i.e., ships over 14,000 dwt) in 1960, five years later the figures had fallen to 53 and 50 percent, respectively (Fearnley and Egers, 1965, p. 5).

The degree to which the ore trades made fuller use of the capital invested in ships by such transport arrangements was often reflected in the rates negotiated for ore transport. By 1965 studies had been made in Japan of the possibility of importing Brazilian ore in ore/oil carriers that would sail in ballast to the Middle East, pick up crude oil for Western Europe or the United States, and then return in ballast to Brazil. The cargo-haul distance was estimated as rather more than 35,000 km out of a total round trip of nearly 53,000 km, a payload-to-distance ratio of 66 percent. The rate calculated for moving ore from Tubarão, Brazil, to Japan in 70,000-dwt ships on a direct shuttle service was as low as $5.50 per actual ton; but, with the introduction of similar-sized ore/oil carriers on the quadrangular run, it was expected that the freight rate could be reduced even further, to $4 (Nippon Kokan, *Japan Steel Notes*, November 1965).

Thus, by offering freight discounts on time charters, by encouraging more efficient loading and unloading port procedures, and by reducing ballast hauls through the search for return cargoes, the shipping industry was able to intensify the use made of its capital equipment, and so significantly to reduce the ton-kilometer costs of hauling iron ore.

These were not the only developments reducing the shipping industry's costs. Equally important was the exploitation of scale economies in ore movements (Jones, Bardelmeier, Clements & Co., 1965; Benford *et al.*, 1962). Over a 16,000-km return journey (that is, for an 8,000-km ore haul), the estimated 1962 cost to a ship operator of using a 15,000-dwt vessel (Figure 12) was $4.25 per actual ton (0.5 mill per ton-km). The cost of a 35,000-dwt vessel, on the other hand, was $2.50 (0.3 mill); and of a 65,000-dwt vessel, $2 (0.25 mill). In other words, per actual ton of ore carried, the 65,000-dwt vessel incurred one-half of the total expenses of a 15,000-dwt vessel. The greatest gains in the scale economies of ocean bulk carriers are undoubtedly to be obtained in sizes up to about 30,000 to 35,000 dwt. Above the latter size, the gains tend to become progressively less, but they are nonetheless real.

The major savings in the use of large ships stem from their lower unit capital costs (a characteristic noted in Table 40); hence their lower interest charges per ton-km. In addition, the annual cash operating costs of large vessels per ton-km are lower than for smaller ones. These costs, it will be recalled, represented between 55 and 60 percent of the total in 1965. In matters such as wages, fuel, insurance, repairs, maintenance charges, administration and ship's stores and provisions, the economies of scale are considerable. At 1965 prices (assuming an 8,000-km direct shuttle service), the annual operating costs of a small 15,000-dwt vessel were

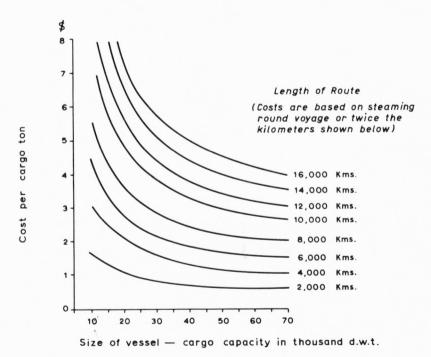

FIGURE 12. Scale economies in ocean ore transport, circa 1962. (From Jones, Bardelmeier, Clements & Co., 1965.)

$340,000, or $23 per ton; those of a 35,000-dwt vessel, $380,000, or $11 per ton; and those of a 65,000-dwt vessel, $440,000, or $7 per ton (Jones, Bardelmeier, Clements & Co., 1965). One of the major elements in operating costs of larger vessels was, of course, their labor charges. These varied with the nationality of the crew and the wage levels they could demand. In 1962, a Japanese vessel of just under 50,000 dwt, with a crew of fifty-nine, cost its owners $139,000 per year in wages; a comparable American ship, with a rather smaller crew of forty-four men, cost its owners $550,000. But independent of national wage rates and manning practices and also of any effects that increasing automation might have on the size of ships' crews, the fact remains that the number of men required to man a ship of 20,000 dwt was basically about the same as that required for one of 60,000 dwt. The cost of labor per ton or ton-km was thus considerably lower in larger ships. Repair and maintenance, insurance, and general administration costs were lower, too.

As a consequence of these scale economies, the average size of vessels carrying ore increased steadily during the fifties and sixties. In the early fifties, most ore was carried in small tramp ships. Unlike the ore carriers on the Great Lakes, which were the first to be designed especially for the ore trade, the tramps were general-purpose vessels. Loading and discharging ore from tramps was both a relatively inefficient and a costly exercise. There were some exceptions, such as the four 24,000-dwt ore carriers built by the Bethlehem Steel Corporation in 1945–48 to ship El Tofo ore from Chile to Sparrows Point. But generally speaking, the ore ship of the time was below 10,000 dwt.

As seaborne ore traffic increased during the fifties and as the average distance of the ore hauls increased, more specialized ore carriers were constructed, and their average size was increased. Although as early as 1953 the Hanna Mining Co. ordered two vessels of nearly 60,000 dwt, most of the new ones at this time were in the 10,000- to 25,000-dwt range. For a time Japanese shipyards made a specialty of enlarging ("jumboizing") Liberty ships for the ore trade, and a considerable number of redundant tankers of up to 25,000 dwt were converted into bulk carriers. For some years the size of vessels on many ore routes was restricted by conditions at both the loading and discharging ports, such as the width of a lock entrance, a limited turning circle, or, more usually, shallow water. By the early sixties, however—after the development of new sources of ore around the world and the construction of "green field" coastal steelworks—larger ports gradually became available, and vessels of 35,000 and 40,000 dwt (and larger) were introduced on an increasing number of ore routes. Although by 1965 ore and bulk carriers had not yet reached the size of the largest tankers (some of those on order were over 300,000 dwt), a growing number of ore carriers were between 50,000 and 60,000 dwt, and the largest was nearly 90,000 dwt. In addition, there was an OBO carrier of 144,000 dwt. The changing size characteristics of the world's ore carriers between 1950 and 1969 are summarized in Table 43.

From the viewpoint of the naval architect, no technical reason exists why ore carriers of 300,000 or 400,000 dwt should not be built. Their development, however, is halted by the following factors:

1. Existing blast-furnace practice tends to mix ore from several fields, and as a result many steelworks do not want to receive too much ore from any one source at any one time. This practice is changing, but for some time it has proved to be a conservative influence over patterns of iron ore flows.

2. Although production and internal scale economies can be derived from iron and steel works as large as 10 or 12 million tons per year (see Chapter 4), the geographical pattern of steel demand and the historical and existing structure of the industry have all militated against the construction of many works with an annual capacity exceeding 3 or 4 million tons. Yet it is only works over this size that can readily handle loads of 100,000 or 150,000 actual tons of ore.

3. The existing loading and unloading technology inhibits a fast turn-around for very large carriers. Possibly the experimental shipments of iron ore as a slurry being tested on the Peru-Japan run will remove this obstacle.

4. The depth and width limitations of the Panama and Suez canals (the former can only take certain 65,000-dwt bulk carriers).

5. There are only a limited number of ports in the world capable of handling really large ships in the 80,000- and 100,000-dwt class (Tables 44 and 45).

The number of sites at which thirteen or fourteen meters of water are naturally available near either exploitable ore deposits or major markets for ore is very few indeed. There are both technical and economic constraints on the provision and maintenance of channels and ports of that depth. Whereas it is relatively easy to provide facilities for loading and discharging oil tankers (they can use underwater pipes) in many locations, ore carriers present a vastly more difficult engineering problem. Much more complex equipment is required, particularly for unloading, and inshore deep water is essential. Obviously, large ore carriers cannot possibly have the same flexibility of route and trade opportunities as their smaller counterparts. The construction of large carriers, as a consequence, has usually been the result of anticipated ore haulage opportunities along specific routes.

To some extent the depth limitations of particular ports can be overcome by operating medium-sized vessels at rather less than their design

TABLE 43. GROWTH AND CHARACTERISTICS OF THE WORLD ORE FLEET, 1950 TO 1969

Size (*dwt*)	Before 1950	1950/54	Year of Construction 1955	1956	1957	1958	1959	1960	1961	1962	1963	1964	1965	1966	1967	1968	Fleet at Jan. 1, 1969
Under 10,000																	
Ore carriers	5	31	4	3	5	10	8	6	2	3	2		4	3	2		88
Ore/oil and OBO carriers	1	1			3		1	2		1							9
Total	6	32	4	3	8	10	9	8	2	4	2		4	3	2		98
10,000–29,000																	
Ore carriers	16	5	5	6	12	25	6	33	28	21	17	3	4	7	6	3	217
Ore/oil and OBO carriers	4	10	5	4		3	2	2	1				3			2	36
Total	20	15	10	10	12	28	8	35	29	21	17	3	7	7	6	5	253
30,000–39,000																	
Ore carriers			2	2	5	4	2	3	2	4	2	1		1	2		28
Ore/oil and OBO carriers				2	2		2	2				1		1			12
Total			2	4	7	4	4	5	2	4	2	2		2	2		30
40,000–49,000																	
Ore carriers				3	1	2	1			4	1		1	1	2	2	10
Ore/oil and OBO carriers									2				2	1	2	2	13
Total				3	1	2	1		2	4	1		3	2	2	2	23

Deadweight tonnage												Total
50,000–59,000												
Ore carriers	3	4		1	1	4	1	11	7	2	2	36
Ore/oil and OBO carriers		2	2		1	5	3	2	4	4		23
Total	3	6	2	1	2	9	4	13	11	6	2	59
60,000–69,000												
Ore carriers									5	1		6
Ore/oil and OBO carriers	1	1				1	3	2	5	4	4	21
Total	1	1				1	3	2	10	5	4	27
70,000–79,000												
Ore carriers									3	1	1	5
Ore/oil and OBO carriers					2	1		2	2	16	6	29
Total					2	1		2	5	17	7	34
80,000–89,000												
Ore carriers							1	2		1		4
Ore/oil and OBO carriers							1	2		9	2	14
Total							2	4		10	2	18
90,000–99,000												
Ore carriers												
Ore/oil and OBO carriers										6	13	19
Total										6	13	19
100,000 and over												
Ore carriers										1	1	2
Ore/oil and OBO carriers											5	5
Total										1	6	7

Source: Maritime Transport Research, London.

TABLE 44. PRINCIPAL ORE-LOADING PORTS

Country and port	1965 Conditions*			Subsequent and future planned conditions		
	Maximum draft (meters)	Largest ship (dwt)	Maximum loading rate (t/hr)	Maximum draft (meters)	Largest ship (dwt)	Maximum loading rate (t/hr)
NORTH AMERICA						
Canada						
Bell Island	11.3	36,000	5,000			
Contrecoeur	10.0	40,000	1,850			
Harriet Harbour (Jedway)	10.0	27,000	1,120		35,000	
Pointe Noire	13.7	60,000	5,000		100,000	
Port Cartier	15.0	100,000	6,000			
Prince Rupert	11.0	40,000				
Sayward		52,000	1,000			
Sept Iles	12.0	65,000	8,000		150,000	
Tasu		52,000	2,500			
Texada	13.0	60,000	2,000		80,000	
Toquart Bay	11.5	45,000				
Zeballos		20,000			50,000	
U.S.A.						
Long Beach	12.8	80,000	3,000		100,000	
Los Angeles	15.9	60,000	2,500			
Stockton	9.0	24,000	1,600			
WESTERN EUROPE						
Norway						
Kirkenes	11.6	35,000	2,000		65,000	
Narvik	13.0	65,000	8,000		100,000	
Sweden						
Luleå (Svarto)	11.5	40,000	8,000		65,000	
Oxelösund	13.0	60,000	3,000			
Spain						
Almería	9.0	15,000	800			
Sagunto		15,000				
Vigo	11.5	40,000	2,000		70,000	
EASTERN EUROPE						
U.S.S.R.						
Murmansk	9.1	13,500	3,000		15,000	
Novorossiak	9.2	24,000			35,000	
Odessa	13.0	24,000			35,000	
ASIA						
India						
Haldia					60,000	3,000
Madras	9.0	25,000	600			1,500
Mormugão	8.5	10,000	600		65,000	
Paradip	13.0	60,000	2,500		65,000	5,000
Vizagapatam	9.0	33,000	2,600		150,000	
Malaysia						
Dungun	10.0	26,000	500			
Sura-Lanjut		300-ton lighters				
Tumpat	9.0	20,000				
Philippines						
Calambayagon		11,000				
OCEANIA						
Australia						
Brickmakers Bay					65,000	
Cockatoo Island	10.5	35,000	1,500			
Geraldton	8.7	35,000	500		45,000	2,000
King Bay		65,000	6,000		100,000	

TABLE 44.—Continued

Country and port	1965 Conditions*			Subsequent and future planned conditions		
	Maximum draft (*meters*)	Largest ship (*dwt*)	Maximum loading rate (*t/hr*)	Maximum draft (*meters*)	Largest ship (*dwt*)	Maximum loading rate (*t/hr*)
Kooland Island...............	14.0	70,000	3,000			
Port Hedland.................	11.9	50,000	2,000		100,000	5,000
Whyalla......................	11.8	45,000	3,000			
LATIN AMERICA						
Brazil						
Macapá......................		15,000				
Rio de Janeiro...............	10.5	32,000	1,000			
Septiba......................					100,000	
Tubarão......................	14.5	100,000	6,000	16	130,000	12,000
Vitória......................	10.9	45,000	3,600		65,000	2,900
Chile						
Caldera......................	12.2	55,000	2,000			
Chañeral.....................	12.4	55,000	2,000		80,000	
Cruz Grande.................	11.5	35,000	3,000			
Guacolda Island (Huasco).......	13.0	50,000	3,000		100,000	
Guayacan (Coquimbo)...........	12.1	56,000	3,500		60,000	
Peru						
San Juan.....................	12.8	50,000	2,500		80,000	3,000
San Nicolás..................	15.2	100,000	3,600		125,000	
Venezuela						
Palua........................	20.0	45,000	3,000	20.0	60,000	6,000
Puerto Ordaz.................	20.0	60,000	6,000			
AFRICA						
Algeria						
Algiers......................		14,000	200			
Annaba......................	8.5	20,000	1,200			
Bône........................	9.1	25,000	2,000			
Bougie......................	9.3	14,000				
Angola						
Lobito......................	10.4	27,000	450		35,000	
Luanda.....................	10.0	20,000			35,000	
Moçâmedes.................	13.0	37,000	3,000		100,000	12,000
Guinea						
Conakry.....................	9.0	20,000	1,200			
Liberia						
Buchanan....................	13.0	65,000	6,000	14.0	75,000	
Monrovia...................	10.7	50,000	4,200		70,000	
Mauritania						
Port Etienne.................	12.5	65,000	3,000		100,000	6,000
Morocco						
Casablanca...................	8.5	15,000				
Melilla......................	11.3	11,000	1,000			
Mozambique						
Lourenço Marques..............	12.0	65,000	3,500		80,000	
Sierra Leone						
Pepel........................	6.4	38,000	2,750		100,000	
South Africa						
Durban......................		24,000	350		45,000	
Port Elizabeth................	11.5	45,000	1,500		50,000	
Tunisia						
La Goulette..................	8.5	16,000	1,500	10.4	30,000	4,500

Sources: United Nations, 1968-A, pp. 115–16; and others.
* Including some 1966 and 1967 improvements.

TABLE 45. PRINCIPAL ORE-UNLOADING PORTS

Country and port	1965 Conditions*			Subsequent and future planned conditions		
	Maximum draft (*meters*)	Largest ship (*dwt*)	Maximum unloading rate (*tons/hr*)	Maximum draft (*meters*)	Largest ship (*dwt*)	Maximum unloading rate (*tons/hr*)
NORTH AMERICA						
Canada						
Contrecoeur....................	10.0	28,000	1,600		35,000	
U.S.A.						
Baltimore.....................	12.0	65,000	2,000		75,000	
Baton Rouge (Burnside)..........	11.6	50,000	2,400			
Houston......................	10.7	35,000	1,000			
Mobile.......................	12.0	60,000	1,100			
Morrisville...................	10.5	60,000	2,000			
Newport News.................	12.0	60,000	3,600		85,000	
Philadelphia..................	12.0	60,000	6,000			
WESTERN EUROPE						
Belgium						
Antwerp......................	11.6	50,000	2,000		70,000	
Zelzate.......................	8.0	10,000			60,000	2,000
France						
Dunkirk......................	12.2	50,000	3,000	13.3	125,000	
Le Havre.....................		35,000	1,000		60,000	2,000
Italy						
Bagnoli.......................	11.3	45,000	2,400		55,000	
Genoa........................	13.0	60,000	2,400			
Piombino.....................	11.3	45,000	2,400			
Taranto.......................	13.0	45,000	3,600		100,000	
Trieste.......................		35,000	1,000			
Netherlands						
Amsterdam...................	11.5	45,000	2,000		100,000	6,000
Ijmuiden......................	10.3	35,000	1,500		100,000	
Rotterdam....................	11.5	50,000	2,000	18.9	225,000	
Europoort....................	12.5	60,000	2,000	18.9	225,000	
West Germany						
Brake........................	10.4	30,000				
Bremen.......................	9.5	22,000	1,000		25,000	2,000
Bremerhaven..................	11.9	45,000	1,000		100,000	3,000
Emden........................	11.0	40,000			80,000	
Hamburg......................	11.0	40,000			60,000	
Hordenham...................		33,000			80,000	
Britain						
Birkenhead....................	8.7	17,000	1,100			
Cardiff.......................	8.5	20,000	1,500			
Dagenham....................	8.5	12,000	750			
Glasgow......................	10.0	25,000	1,800		65,000	
Grangemouth.................	7.5	9,000				
Hartlepool....................	9.0	16,000	800			
Immingham...................	9.5	27,000	800		65,000	
Irlam........................	8.0	10,000	600			
Manchester...................	8.0	10,000	750			
Middlesbrough (Teesside)........	9.5	24,000	1,000		65,000	
Newport......................	9.5	26,000	750			
Port Talbot...................	7.7	10,000	1,000	15.5	150,000	4,000
Tyne Dock....................	11.0	37,000	1,500			
Workington...................	7.5	10,000	700			
Yugoslavia						
Bakar........................		40,000				5,000
Bar..........................		30,000			60,000	
Rijeka.......................		32,000			100,000	
EASTERN EUROPE						
Poland						
Gdansk.......................	9.0	20,000			27,000	
Gdynia.......................	10.0	27,000			65,000	
Szczecin......................		23,000				

TABLE 45.—Continued

Country and port	1965 Conditions*			Subsequent and future planned conditions		
	Maximum draft (meters)	Largest ship (dwt)	Maximum unloading rate (tons/hr)	Maximum draft (meters)	Largest ship (dwt)	Maximum unloading rate (tons/hr)
ASIA						
Japan						
Chiba..........................	12.0	50,000				
Fukuyama.....................		100,000	1,500			
Hirohata......................	12.0	50,000				
Innoshima.....................	12.0	50,000				
Kamaishi......................	10.5	30,000				
Kawasaki......................	12.0	50,000				
Kobe..........................	13.5	50,000			60,000	
Mizushima....................	13.5	65,000			100,000	
Moji..........................		50,000				
Muroran......................		65,000				
Nagasaki......................		45,000				
Nagoya........................	11.5	48,000				
Oogishima....................	13.0	65,000	2,000			
Osaka.........................	11.5	15,000			40,000	
Tobata........................	13.5	65,000	2,000		80,000	
Tokyo.........................	11.5	48,000				
Wakayama....................	14.0	70,000				
Yawata........................		65,000				
Yokohama....................		55,000				
OCEANIA						
Australia						
Darwin........................		35,000	1,000			
Newcastle.....................	8.5	12,000	1,000		50,000	
Port Kembla..................	10.8	48,000	1,100		55,000	

Sources: United Nations, 1968-A, pp. 117–18; and others.
* Including some 1966 and 1967 improvements.

draft. For a number of years, 35,000-dwt vessels (which fully laden have a draft of just under 11 meters) have been used to deliver ore to Glasgow, where there are only about 10 meters of water. They carried only 25,000 actual tons of ore, but they proved to be more economical than the 20,000-dwt ships normally drawing between 9 and 10 meters of water when fully laden. The limitations of an ore-loading port can also be overcome by only partially loading a ship in the harbor, and then "topping up" its cargo in rather deeper water offshore. In the case of ore shipments from Lourenço Marques (Mozambique), the 77,000-dwt vessels used for the Japan run cannot be fully loaded (with Swaziland ore) in port; they are only partly filled there, and the loading is completed some 50 km offshore with the help of a 13,000-dwt self-unloading vessel. The economics of this type of operation is highly controversial. Not only does it extend the time of loading operations, but it also prevents the supplementary loading vessel from being fully employed except in occasional circumstances. In the case of the Mozambique-to-Japan run, transshipment and ship under-employment costs had to be set against the relatively limited gains of increasing the size of vessel for the main haul from 65,000 to 77,000 dwt.

Certainly this approach was rejected in two cases of unloading ports. Only for a short while were 30,000-dwt self-unloaders used to deliver ore to the lower reaches of the River Plate, where they were partly unloaded for the final stages of their journey upriver. Experimentally, a similar vessel brought ore to Milford Haven in South Wales, where its cargo was unloaded into small 9,000-dwt carriers for delivery to Port Talbot; again, it proved to be too costly.

The effects of scale economies are naturally evident in the structure of iron ore freight rates. In 1964 the rate from Narvik to the British east coast was $2.59 per ton in a 9,000-dwt vessel; $2.24 in a 15,000-dwt vessel; and $1.89 in vessels above that size. The rate from Chile to the U.S. east coast circa 1960 was at least $5 per actual ton for ore shipped in vessels of 10,000 dwt; $3.25 in vessels of 25,000 dwt; and $2.75 in vessels of 50,000 dwt. Some 1963 estimates of the Japan Iron and Steel Federation relating to scale economies in ore shipments from Peru and Angola to Japan are given in Table 46. Where iron ore ports are shallow and, as a consequence, the size of ore carriers small, the absence of scale economies inevitably means that the ton-kilometer costs of shipping to and from those ports are relatively high. One of the major difficulties facing Indian authorities in their attempts to expand the country's ore export trade on a larger scale is the shallow nature of their harbors and the high freight rates carried by their ore shipments. In 1965 the rate from Calcutta, Madras, and Mormugão to Japan stood at $6.75 per actual ton, thus posing considerable difficulties for those seeking to market Indian ore in the highly competitive steelmaking centers of the world.

A final aspect of the changing technology and costs of ocean ore transport was the increasing advantage taken of the economies of the long haul. Because the proportion of time a vessel spends at sea (earning a return on capital) increases with longer journeys, tapering rates have always been a fundamental characteristic of ocean freights. If one assumes that it takes two days to load and two days to discharge an ore carrier efficiently, a vessel shuttling on a line-haul taking four days can theoretically earn a return on its capital for 33 percent of the time. However, if the line-haul

TABLE 46. SCALE ECONOMIES IN WATER TRANSPORT: ESTIMATED FREIGHT RATES FOR HAULING IRON ORE IN VESSELS OF DIFFERENT SIZES FROM PERU AND ANGOLA TO JAPAN, 1963

Vessel size (dwt)	Peru (San Juan) to Japan (16,376 km)	Angola to Japan (17,680 km)
45,000	$6.24 (0.38 mill/ton-km)	$7.64 (0.43 mill/ton-km)
60,000		7.04 (0.40 mill/ton-km)
76,500	5.44 (0.33 mill/ton-km)	
85,000	4.93 (0.30 mill/ton-km)	5.97 (0.34 mill/ton-km)
100,000	4.61 (0.28 mill/ton-km)	5.43 (0.31 mill/ton-km)

Source: Japan Iron and Steel Federation.

distance is lengthened to eighteen days of sailing, the potential earning capacity of the vessel is theoretically increased to 45 percent of the time. Thus, Jones, Bardelmeier, Clements & Co. (1965) showed that for a 40,000-dwt carrier (at 1962 prices) the ton-kilometer cost of hauling ore fell from 0.37 mill for 1,000 km to 0.31 for 4,000 km; and for a 15,000-dwt carrier, 0.66 mill to 0.55 mill, respectively. These cost variations were also reflected in the freight rates for ore. The charge from Puerto Ordaz to Philadelphia in 1961 was $3 to $4 per actual ton, or 0.71 to 0.95 mill per ton-km; yet from Puerto Ordaz to Rotterdam, which is nearly twice the distance, it was only $5.50 to $6 per actual ton, or 0.68 to 0.75 mill per ton-km (Table 47).

TABLE 47.   APPROXIMATE LEVEL OF FREIGHT RATES ALONG MAJOR OCEAN ORE ROUTES, 1965

From	To	Rate/actual ton (dollars)	Rate/actual-ton-km (mills)
NORTH AMERICA			
Canada			
British Columbia.................	Japan	3.50–4.50	0.40–0.52
Sept Iles........................	Philadelphia	0.75–1.00	0.33–0.44
Sept Iles........................	Rotterdam	2.50–3.50	0.46–0.65
WESTERN EUROPE			
Norway			
Narvik..........................	Rotterdam	1.00–2.50	0.48–1.19
ASIA AND OCEANIA			
Australia			
King Bay.......................	Japan	2.20–4.25	0.33–0.63
India			
Mormugão......................	Japan	5.50–7.00	0.52–0.67
Mormugão......................	Rotterdam	5.50–7.00	0.45–0.58
Vizagapatam....................	Japan	5.00–6.50	0.52–0.67
Vizagapatam....................	Rotterdam	6.50–7.50	0.46–0.53
Malaya..........................	Japan	4.50–5.50	0.83–1.02
Philippines......................	Japan	3.00–3.50	0.91–1.05
LATIN AMERICA			
Brazil			
Tubarão/Vitória.................	Baltimore	3.25–5.50	0.38–0.65
Tubarão/Vitória.................	Rotterdam	2.50–7.00	0.27–0.75
Tubarão/Vitória.................	Japan	4.00–8.00	0.19–0.38
Chile			
Coquimbo.......................	Philadelphia	4.00–4.50	0.49–0.56
Coquimbo.......................	Japan	4.00–7.00	0.23–0.41
Venezuela			
Puerto Ordaz....................	Philadelphia	3.50–4.00	0.83–0.95
Puerto Ordaz....................	Rotterdam	5.00–6.00	0.62–0.74
AFRICA			
Liberia			
Monrovia.......................	Baltimore	1.80–5.00	0.23–0.64
Monrovia.......................	Rotterdam	1.80–4.00	0.29–0.64
South Africa			
Durban..........................	Japan	7.00–7.50	0.49–0.53
Durban..........................	Rotterdam	5.50–6.00	0.42–0.46

Sources: Canada, Department of Energy, Mines and Resources; *Metal Bulletin;* industry sources.

An important corollary of both the scale and the long-haul economies of ocean ore transport is that for any given length of haul there is theoretically at any one time an ideal size of carrier. As the length of a haul increases, and as the proportion of time a vessel spends in ports falls, so the potential degree of vessel use at sea rises and shipowners are prepared to accept the higher capital costs of larger vessels. For short distances, on the other hand, the relatively large amount of time a vessel must inevitably spend in port makes it imperative for shipping operators to minimize their capital costs, even at the expense of higher working costs. Thus, small carriers still have a role to play in short-distance ocean ore shipments, especially those that may be relatively old, with their capital costs heavily written down. For such ore movements as Narvik to Rotterdam, or the Philippines to Japan, at the 1965 speeds of loading and unloading, there appeared little advantage in using carriers of more than 30,000 dwt; and for the longer 6,690-km haul between West Australia and Japan, in spite of the large tonnages of ore to be moved, it was decided that ships of 65,000 dwt would be large enough. Naturally, improvements in the speed of vessel turnaround, and variations in the relationship between the capital and working costs of bulk carriers, will in the long run change the optimum size of vessels for any particular haul.

In sum, the main technological developments affecting the costs of ocean ore transport during the 1950–65 period were the falling costs of ship construction; the measures taken to increase the use of vessels, especially by increasing the payload-to-distance ratio; the construction of larger ore carriers; and the exploitation of long-haul economies.

Changing Organization

In order to take full advantage of the changing technology and the new economic potential of large ocean carriers, major changes became necessary in the organizational structure of the ore shipping industry. At the beginning of the 1950–65 period, most iron ore movements about the world were arranged on the open tramp market, a market which also catered for the shipment of coal, grain, fertilizers, and other bulk commodities. Single or multiple voyages were chartered through brokers, especially on the Baltic Exchange in London. The ships were jacks-of-all-trades. They were expected to call at a large number of ports throughout the world, and this fact alone kept their size down to less than 10,000 dwt.

The economics and the organization of this transport market proved to be increasingly unsatisfactory for the iron and steel industry. Bigger works demanded larger supplies of ore on a regular basis. Iron and steel makers also wanted to ship ore over longer distances—distances over which the small tramp movements were both irregular and rather costly. And the growing sophistication of iron and steelmaking processes and products demanded a more rigorous control over the quality of raw materials, which in turn implied the need for guaranteed supplies of particular types of ore from particular deposits at particular times. But with shipping space generally in short supply, and periodically in very short supply, the open tramp market could only guarantee these requirements at a very high price. If grain or coal suddenly offered more profitable hauls than ore, then the iron and steel industry had to be prepared to bear a higher freight charge for ore or do without it. The result was constant and considerable fluctuation in the freight rates for ore in phase with the changing supply of and demand for tramp tonnage. The rate from Goa to the "near Continent," for example, stood at $19.25 per actual ton during the Korean war; by 1953 it had dropped to $6.79; it nearly doubled again during the winter of 1954, hitting a peak of $28 at the time of the Suez crisis; and then it slipped back within twelve months to $7 per ton. With iron ore valued at perhaps $8 to $12 per actual ton f.o.b., such fluctuations—even allowing for the introduction of complicated "freight equalization accounts"—proved to be increasingly unsatisfactory for a cost-conscious steel industry. It became clear that the industry's ore transport needs could no longer continue to be met efficiently in this way.

Just after World War II, the spatially fragmented characteristic of an iron and steel industry that consumed small quantities of ore from a variety of sources prevented any significant rationalization of the industry's ore transport arrangements. The major producers of the United States were the one exception. But in the early fifties, new factors began to impinge upon the ore-shipping situation. First there was an increasing centralization of ore-purchasing arrangements, with large organizations bargaining for, and contracting to purchase, considerable quantities of ore. Sometimes national bodies were created, such as the British Iron and Steel Corporation (Ore) Ltd. (BISCORE). Elsewhere, private companies emerged to purchase ore on behalf of groups of iron and steel makers; Erzkontor Ruhr GmbH and Rohrstoffhandel GmbH were two such associations in West Germany. A gradual extension of the activities of these purchasing groups into the field of raw material transport followed. At a later stage they even moved into the realm of iron ore exploration and mining. Such central buying and cartelization not only strengthened the bargaining hand of the ore-importing nations in price negotiations, but also made it possible for the iron and steel industry to recast its shipping policies.

In order to overcome the problems presented by the open tramp market, many ore importers in Western Europe, America, and Japan followed the pattern established first by the oil industry in the thirties. They began covering most of their transport needs by "contractual tramping"—that is, by chartering bulk cargo vessels on terms of five, ten, or even fifteen years. Other importing bodies decided to finance the construction of their own vessels; they then either placed them in the hands of experienced shipping managers or operated them through subsidiary companies. Although both of these types of arrangement were satisfactory, the lack of expertise in shipping management within the ore and steel industries prompted them eventually to turn increasingly to medium- and long-term contracts of affreightment as an even better means of solving their ocean transport problems. Under these highly competitive contracts, shipping companies agreed to haul specified quantities of ore, at set intervals, for a number of months or years, between particular ports. The mining and steel industries were thereby relieved of the responsibility of either chartering or owning vessels. Although by 1965 the open tramp market had not been completely abandoned for ore movements, its importance had been severely eroded to a mere 5 percent or so of the industry's shipping needs; and resort was made to it only to cover marginal ore requirements or to meet emergency situations.

BISCORE was one of the first of the new organizations set up to rationalize ore purchasing and transport arrangements on a national basis. Immediately, by eliminating competition between the British iron and steel companies for the use of limited ore-shipping space, it was able to bargain for lower freight rates on ore imports. Gradually it put most of its transport operations on a time-charter basis. In 1953 it relied largely on the open tramp market and had only two vessels on time-charter, but by 1965 BISCORE had completely transformed the situation. The corporation then had seventy-four vessels on time-charter and a considerable capital interest in rather more than one-third of them; only occasionally did it make recourse to the open tramp market. Although the British iron and steel industry gained considerably from this rationalization initially, its ore freight rates in the sixties were relatively high by international standards. This was partly because the corporation had chartered many of its vessels on a long-term basis during the mid-fifties, when worldwide shipping shortages generated particularly high freight rates; and, more especially, because the country's outdated port facilities severely limited the size of vessels the corporation could charter. In 1965, twenty-four of its ships were a mere 9,000 dwt, designed for the small lock entrance to Port Talbot; forty-four were between 13,500 and 18,500 dwt; and six were between 21,000 and 28,000 dwt.

In Italy, a state shipping agency—Sidermar, established under Finsider (the national steel corporation)—was made responsible for the handling of all ore imports of the country. It elected to own about one-third of its fleet, charter another third on long term, and charter the rest on short term (Ferraro, 1961). The German and the French steel industries also put their ore imports on a time-charter and own-vessel basis. But by far the most spectacular developments took place in the Far East. Virtually without an ore fleet in the fifties, the Japanese iron and steel industry was operating the largest national ore fleet in the world by 1965. It comprised 82 ore and bulk carriers, among which were 12 of 50,000 dwt and 7 of 70,000 dwt—reflecting the fact that by the mid-sixties Japan was by far the largest importer of ore by sea. In 1965 Japan imported 39 million actual tons of iron ore, compared with 31.2 million by the United States and 30.6 million by West Germany. The importance of Japan's ore trade was even greater on a ton-kilometer basis, for in the same year the Japanese iron and steel industry used 341 thousand million ton-kilometers of ocean ore-carrying capacity, while West Germany used 152, the United States 130, and the rest of the world 221 (Fearnley and Egers, 1966, p. 6).

The emergence of new national ore fleets was one of the results of the changing organization of shipping during the fifteen years. At the beginning of the period, when most ore was carried in tramp vessels, the greater part of iron ore tonnage was shipped in vessels flying the flags of the "traditional" shipping nations—Britain and Norway in particular. As the period progressed, vessels flying either flags of convenience or national flags assumed a much greater importance. The shift toward flags of convenience was fundamentally a response to the lower taxes and labor costs of vessels with such a registration, but it was also a means whereby the scarcity of engineers in the British mercantile marine could be overcome by tapping Italian sources in particular. The move toward national flags and the decision of many countries to build up their own merchant marine had rather different origins. There were undoubtedly both strategic and chauvinistic objectives behind this development, and government subsidies certainly supported it. In addition, the argument was properly employed that the ownership of an ore fleet (by exporters such as Brazil and Peru or importers such as Italy and France) was a means of either earning or saving scarce foreign exchange. The steps taken by the Indian government, for example, to develop an Indian flag merchant marine, mainly through interest-free loans and other financial assistance, together with efforts to give priority to their own ships in the export of iron ore, basically represented a genuine effort to earn foreign exchange.

The tendency of iron ore importers or producers to ship an increasing quantity of their ore requirements and exports in their own vessels was, however, checked by two factors in particular. The first was the need for shipowners and ship operators to have specialized knowledge and expertise plus worldwide shipping contacts, if their bulk shipping practice was to be efficient. The second was the increasingly competitive condition in the bulk freight market—a situation in which it proved to be progressively more difficult to match the falling level of freight rates secured in independent or bilateral arrangements. Certainly the mistakes of BISCORE were a warning. Thus, both the need to ensure that the large bulk carriers were operated near their full capacity and, more especially, the advantages of exploiting multicommodity OBOs, gave the larger of the old and experienced international shipping operators—and the contract of affreightment—an important role in the ore freight market. The existing shipping lines moved slowly into the specialized bulk transport field, and carriers such as National Bulk Carriers and Marcona Mining initially set the technological pace. But by the mid-sixties, new bulk shipping consortia (such as Associated Bulk Carriers, formed out of Anglo-Norness and Peninsular and Orient interests) were also firmly established in the trade. Operating large fleets of bulk carriers, usually on medium- and long-term contracts to the major ore consumers in Western Europe, Japan, and the United States—and flying the Liberian, the Panamanian, or other flags of convenience, as well as the traditional shipping flags—these companies were in a strong position to share with the new national fleets the rapidly expanding market for shipping iron ore.

THE FALLING LEVEL OF FREIGHT RATES

The impact of all these developments in the technology, costs, and organization of ocean bulk shipping found its full expression in the changing level of iron ore freight rates. Although these are by no means the total transfer charges for ocean ore movements, as has been noted, they generally are the dominant element, and between 1950 and 1965 many rates plunged dramatically. The charge for moving ore between Brazil and Japan in the mid-fifties varied between $16 and $20 per actual ton of ore; these were rates negotiated on the open tramp market in years of relative shipping scarcity, and usually paid following a spot charter of a vessel of 10,000 to 15,000 dwt. By the early sixties, however, such charter rates for vessels of up to 20,000 dwt, in a weaker shipping market, had fallen to $7 or $8 per actual ton. Even lower were the rates for ore shipments after the opening of the new deepwater port at Tubarao in 1965. For example, the 70,000-dwt vessels on a direct shuttle service between Brazil and Japan permitted a rate of $5.50 per actual ton; and plans for similar-sized ore/oil carriers anticipated the further falling of the rate to $4 per actual ton (Nippon Kokan, *Japan Steel Notes*, November 1965). Such a drop in freight rates from $20 to $4 in fifteen years may reflect an extreme case. Yet reductions of 50 and 60 percent along other routes are not particularly difficult to find. An actual ton of Liberian ore hauled from Monrovia to Baltimore in 1958 cost circa $5.50; by 1965, large vessels on term-charters were carrying ore between the same ports for $1.88 per actual ton (some spot charters were slightly above this figure). Similarly, the iron ore freight rate between Sept Iles and Baltimore in 1958 was $1.63 per actual ton, and by 1965 some rates were as low as $0.75 per actual ton.

The rates for transporting iron ore also declined in another sense. Ocean freights are negotiated irrespective of the quality of the ore to be shipped. Thus, if a rate is fixed for $3.30 per actual ton, it represents a charge of $6.60 per ton of contained iron in the case of a 50 percent Fe ore, and $5.08 in the case of a 65 percent Fe ore. Therefore, as the iron content of ores sold internationally increased throughout the period, the freight rates for contained iron in effect fell even faster than the rates for actual tons of ore.

The freight rates for ocean ore shipments in the late fifties and early sixties were characterized not only by their tendency to move downward but also by their continuing and considerable variety. The rate charged for any particular haul is a function of a variety of factors, but in particular it reflects the size of the vessel, the length of the charter, the distance of the haul, the efficiency of the ship's use, and to some extent the ownership and the flag of the vessel. In addition, it is affected by the state of the market for bulk commodity tonnage at the time of the charter. The longer the charter, the closer does the rate tend to approximate the ship's costs plus a reasonable profit. The shorter the charter (the shortest being the single "spot" voyage), the greater become the variations from the cost-plus level. In times of shipping scarcity, shipowners naturally bargain for rates as high as the market will bear. But in times of shipping abundance, the shipowners are willing on some occasions to accept rates that cover no more than their operating costs, simply in order to get a ship into a more favorable geographical location (where it can pick up a profitable traffic), or perhaps to buy time until the market improves. Occasionally it becomes necessary to accept a rate lower than the operating costs of a carrier, if the losses thus incurred are less than the costs of laying up the carrier for a short time.

The range of ocean freight rates is therefore considerable. Table 47, drawn from a variety of sources, suggests the range that was operative in 1965 for the movement of ore along major routes. The rates are, of course, representative, and the charges actually made for particular hauls could vary somewhat from the figures in the table. The width of rate variations along any particular route was greatest when vessels of differing sizes and with differing lengths of charter were used. Conversely, rate variations were smallest when a route was served by only one size of vessel and one type of charter. Table 48, in fact, lists a number of actual ore freights accepted in 1965. The lowest rate shown is the $0.75 per actual ton agreed upon for

TABLE 48. SOME OCEAN IRON ORE FREIGHTS, 1965

From	To	Vessel size (dwt)	Rate/actual ton (dollars)	Rate/actual ton-km (mills)
LONG-TERM CHARTERS AND CONTRACTS OF AFFREIGHTMENT				
Tubarão, Brazil*...............	Japan	70,000†	4.00	0.19
Chanaral, Chile...............	Japan	55,000†	4.00	0.23
Monrovia, Liberia..............	Philadelphia	50,000†	1.87	0.24
San Nicolás, Peru.............	Japan	55,000†	4.00	0.24
Tubarão, Brazil................	Japan	70,000	5.50	0.26
Chanaral, Chile...............	Rotterdam	55,000	4.00	0.29
Sept Iles, Canada.............	Baltimore	65,000†	0.75	0.32
San Nicolás, Peru.............	Rotterdam	55,000	4.00	0.33
King Bay, Australia...........	Japan	65,000	2.20	0.33
Coquimbo, Chile..............	Baltimore	55,000†	3.25	0.41
Lourenço Marques, Mozambique...	Japan	77,000	5.75	0.41
San Nicolás, Peru.............	Baltimore	55,000	3.25	0.47
Puerto Ordaz, Venezuela..........	Baltimore	50,000	3.75	0.89
SPOT AND SHORT-TERM CHARTERS				
Bougie, Algeria................	Rotterdam	10,000	1.78	0.45
Mormugão, India..............	Rotterdam	10,000	5.45	0.45
Macapa, Brazil................	Japan	10,000	9.75	0.45
Narvik, Norway...............	Rotterdam	10,000	1.14	0.55
Pepel, Sierra Leone............	Rotterdam	17,000	3.22	0.55
Vitória, Brazil.................	Italy	16,000	5.45	0.59
Vitória, Brazil.................	Dunkirk	15,000	5.45	0.59
Mormugão, India..............	Gdansk	10,000	7.90	0.59
Vitória, Brazil.................	Rotterdam	19,000	5.81	0.63
Vitória, Brazil.................	Rotterdam	18,000	6.30	0.68
Conakry, Guinea..............	Gdansk	12,000	4.86	0.68
Vitória, Brazil.................	Dunkirk	10,000	6.30	0.69
Vizagapatam, India............	Japan	10,000	6.75	0.69
Vizagapatam, India............	Baltimore	10,000	11.00	0.70
Monrovia, Liberia.............	Baltimore	10,000	5.75	0.74
Luleå, Sweden................	Amsterdam	10,000	1.96	0.80
Monrovia, Liberia.............	Bremen	15,000	3.65	0.91
Narvik, Norway...............	Middlesbrough	15,000	2.24	1.22
Sept Iles, Canada.............	Port Talbot	9,000	5.95	1.23
Narvik, Norway...............	Port Talbot	9,000	4.27	1.69
Rotterdam....................	Port Talbot	9,000	2.73	1.94

Sources: Metal Bulletin; Canada, Department of Energy, Mines and Resources; industry sources; and others.

Note: Tolls included (rate per actual ton): Panama, $1.00; Suez, $0.95; Venezuela, Boca Grande Canal, $0.85.

* From 1967.

† Ore/oil or OBO carriers.

the 2,300-km haul from Sept Iles on the St. Lawrence to Baltimore—a rate that reflects the use of large vessels on either long-term charters or contracts of affreightment, as well as the further economy of being able to combine the ore shipments with coal exports from Hampton Roads to Canada and to Western Europe. The highest rate shown is $11 per actual ton for spot charter on the open market of a 10,000-dwt vessel hauling ore between India and the United States, a distance of about 16,000 km via the Suez Canal. (Table 49 lists some representative ocean shipping distances.)

TABLE 49. SOME OCEAN SHIPPING DISTANCES

From	Distance (kilometers)	From	Distance (kilometers)

To the U.S. East Coast (Baltimore) from:

From	Distance (kilometers)	From	Distance (kilometers)
Sept Iles, Canada	2,300	Vitória, Brazil	8,500
Puerto Ordaz, Venezuela	4,200	Moçâmedes, Angola	11,100
San Juan, Peru*	6,500	Mormugão, India*	15,700
Conakry, Guinea	7,200	Vizigapatam, India*	16,800
Freetown, Sierra Leone	7,300	Mormugão, India	21,100
Narvik, Norway	7,500	Vizagapatam, India	22,200
Monrovia, Liberia	7,770	Port Hedland, Australia	22,500
Coquimbo, Chile*	8,100		

To the North Sea (Rotterdam) from:

From	Distance (kilometers)	From	Distance (kilometers)
Bilboa, Spain	1,600	Moçâmedes, Angola	9,700
Narvik, Norway	2,100	San Juan, Peru	11,900
Luleå, Sweden	2,600	Mormugão, India*	12,100
Bône, Algeria	3,800	Durban, South Africa	13,000
Sept Iles, Canada	5,400	Coquimbo, Chile*	13,500
Conakry, Guinea	5,700	Vizagapatam, India*	14,100
Freetown, Sierra Leone	5,800	Mormugão, India	19,800
Monrovia, Liberia	6,200	Vizagapatam, India	21,000
Puerto Ordaz, Venezuela	8,100	Port Hedland, Australia	21,200
Vitória, Brazil	9,300		

To Japan (Tokyo) from:

From	Distance (kilometers)	From	Distance (kilometers)
Manila, Philippines	3,300	Durban, South Africa	14,200
Singapore, Malaya	5,400	San Juan, Peru	16,400
Port Hedland, Australia	6,700	Puerto Ordaz, Venezuela*	17,100
Vancouver, Canada	8,700	Coquimbo, Chile	17,100
Los Angeles, U.S.A.	9,000	Moçâmedes, Angola	17,700
Vizagapatam, India	9,700	Monrovia, Liberia	20,900
Mormugão, India	10,500	Vitória, Brazil	21,300
Lourenço Marques, Mozambique	14,000	Puerto Ordaz, Venezuela	25,200

Source: Hutchinson, 1958.
* Via the Suez or the Panama Canal.

On a ton-kilometer basis, the rates take on a somewhat different perspective, and two overlapping groups of rates are distinguished in Table 48 on this basis.

The first group, consisting entirely of medium- and long-term charters or contracts of affreightment for large ore carriers and OBO carriers of 50,000 dwt and over, includes the very lowest rates for ocean transport, ranging from just under 0.2 mill to rather more than 0.4 mill per actual-ton-kilometer. The lowest rates in the group are afforded by the bulk and OBO carriers on long and medium hauls, such as the runs from Brazil and Chile to Japan (21,300 and 17,100 km) or from Liberia to the United States (7,700 km). In the middle of the group are some rates for medium-distance direct shuttle services, such as those between Western Australia and Japan (6,700 km) or between Brazil and Rotterdam (9,300 km). The highest rates in this group are sometimes associated with the use of large vessels either on relatively short journeys (such as Sept Iles to Baltimore, about 2,300 km) or on routes where vessels are regularly subject to slow turnarounds at their loading or discharging ports. Carriers using the port of Lourenço Marques, which complete their loading offshore, are in the latter category. And some rates in this group are for trades involving the use of a ship canal, which necessitates the payment of a toll. The Panama Canal, for example, which currently limits vessels passing through it to about 65,000 dwt, imposes a toll of just under $1 per actual ton, and pushes up the rate from the west coast of South America to the east coast of the United States to $3.25; the ton-km rates from Chile and Peru are therefore relatively high at 0.41 mill and 0.47 mill, respectively. Similarly, ore shipments from Venezuela to the United States bear an unusually high rate for large vessels, which reflects both the relatively short distance involved and a toll of $0.85 per actual ton for the Boca Grande Canal in the Orinoco Delta.

The second group, a much wider group of freight rates, includes spot voyages and very short-term (six months) charters of smallish vessels (9,000 to 20,000 dwt) on the open market. In 1965 there was a weakening demand for these carriers, and as a result their rates tended to move downward throughout the year. Those listed in the table range from about 0.4 mill to nearly 2 mills per actual-ton-kilometer. Predictably, the highest rates were charged for ore carried in the smaller vessels on the shorter runs. By ocean transport standards, many of these rates were very high indeed. Some were above those generally pertaining on the Great Lakes of North America, and a number were even above those charged for the most efficient inland waterway hauls.

The modes of transport for ore on the Great Lakes and other inland waterways are examined in the next chapter. In their case, too, a downward drift in the range of freight rates followed their changing technology and economics.

CHAPTER 10

Changes in Inland Transport

ORE TRANSPORT ON THE GREAT LAKES
AND THE ST. LAWRENCE SEAWAY

Developments in the shipment of iron ore along the North American Great Lakes and up the St. Lawrence Seaway in many respects parallel the changes in ocean ore haulage. There are, however, certain important differences. As far as the Great Lakes are concerned, the first contrast to be noted is the failure of ore traffic to expand significantly over the years since 1950. Indeed, the primary characteristic of lake ore traffic has been its fluctuating volume. In 1950 it stood at 80 million actual tons, and by 1953 shipments had risen to a record 98 million. By 1959, they had slumped to 48 million actual tons from the ports of the upper lakes, plus another 4 million tons that came up the St. Lawrence Seaway. Five years later, they had expanded again to 68 million actual tons from the upper lakes and a further 12 million from the Seaway, a total of 80 million actual tons (the same figure as for 1950).

These fluctuations were to some extent reflected in the size of the Great Lakes ore fleet. At the beginning of the period there were some 266 vessels serving the trade. There followed a burst of shipbuilding and ship-renovating activity in the early fifties. But after 1954 only a few new vessels were built, and the average age of the 170 vessels in the 1964 fleet was forty-one years (Reno, 1965, p. 472). It is fortunate that the fresh water of the lakes does not corrode the ships' plates as rapidly as salt water.

A second contrast between ore transport on the Great Lakes and the oceans stemmed from the limitations on the size of vessel that could be used on the lakes. Most of the ore boats at the beginning of the period were quite small, having an average carrying capacity of less than 10,000 dwt. In addition, there were several larger vessels of just under 18,000 dwt, and a new Inland Steel carrier 21,000 dwt (Vines, 1961). In terms of vessel size, therefore, the fleet was not markedly different from the tramps carrying ore across the oceans. From 1951–54, the shipyards on the lakes kept pace with world developments, building new vessels of up to 25,800 dwt and at the same time reconstructing and jumboizing some of the existing carriers. A number of significant improvements were also made in the operating performance of the lake vessels, as modern diesel engines were installed and their operating speeds increased. Assuming a 220-day season, one of the new 25,000-dwt ships traveling at 27 km/hr could carry close to 950,000 actual tons of ore each year, a figure that compared favorably with the 300,000 actual tons carried annually by a slower 10,000-dwt lake vessel. The greater efficiency of the new ships did not mean, however, that they necessarily exhibited lower costs than their smaller predecessors. Through inflation, the capital costs of the new vessels—even expressed in terms of their annual carrying capacity—were eight times those of the older 10,000-dwt vessels; and their much higher capital charges kept up their total costs.

This burst of shipbuilding activity ended in 1954. After that, very few additional ships were constructed (consequent upon the fluctuating but generally downward volume of traffic), and there was no further significant increase in vessel size. A new Canadian self-unloader, commissioned in 1965, was still only 28,000 dwt. The reasons were twofold: First, an upper limit of vessel size had been reached as far as the docking (including dry docking) facilities of the lakes were concerned. Only considerable capital investments in new harbor facilities could have permitted the effective use of yet larger ships. These investments were simply not forthcoming in a fluctuating and uncertain market. Second, most of the shipping routes passed through the St. Marys River, where the locks could not handle vessels over about 26,000 dwt.

The future could portend the construction of larger ships for the Great Lakes ore trade. New locks on the St. Marys River at Sault Ste. Marie (commissioned in 1967) now allow vessels of 45,000 to 50,000 dwt to pass between Lakes Superior and Huron. Self-unloading vessels could limit the additional investment required at the terminals of the lower lakes. On the other hand, the costs of the Great Lakes ships are relatively high by international standards, and the need for some major harbor improvements remains. Whether these will be forthcoming in the light of railway competition remains to be seen. In 1967, however, the Pittsburgh Steamship Division of the United States Steel Corporation ordered the first new lake carrier since 1960, a self-unloader of 38,000 dwt.

A third distinguishing feature of the Great Lakes ore trade follows from the natural and geographical circumstances of the waterway, which prevent a high degree of vessel use. The winter freeze, for example, limits the Great Lakes shipping season to seven or eight months in the year. When the Baltic freezes, Swedish ore carriers can easily be switched to Narvik, but there exists no alternative to a winter lay-up for the Great Lakes carriers. Many techniques have been suggested to keep the lakes open for a longer season —techniques such as modified ship design, more powerful icebreakers, and the release of compressed-air bubbles from the floor of harbor entrances to keep them ice free—but they all demand considerable capital investments, which are not readily forthcoming. It is quite possible, however, that one of the most effective ways to improve the economics of the Great Lakes fleets would be to lengthen the shipping season. A set of calculations by Thiele (1963) has shown that on the Escanaba-Chicago run (which represents about 10 percent of Great Lakes traffic) the annual capacity of existing vessels could be increased from 5 to 9 million actual tons by extending the shipping season to ten or eleven months in the year. Meanwhile, the winter lay-up remains, and for four or five months in the year the only return on the capital invested in the ore carriers comes from their occasional use as grain or coal stores. Another natural condition that affects the efficiency with which the Great Lakes ore fleet can be operated— and hence the level of its costs—is the variation in water level (this also occurs on the Rhine and many other navigable rivers). During those seasons or years when the river is low, the carrying capacity of the ore carriers is considerably reduced. In 1964, for example, an unusually severe fall in the water level of the Great Lakes reduced the seasonal carrying capacity of the ore fleet by as much as 15 percent.

A circumstance of economic geography has further prevented the achievement of high load factors in the operation of Great Lakes ships— namely, the virtual absence of return cargoes. Some coal is, of course, transported from the ports of the lower lakes westward. However, the volume is small; most of it is destined up-lake only as far as Detroit. And, because of the rather ancient coal-loading and discharging facilities, it is a traffic available only to very small vessels and therefore tends to move in returning limestone carriers (Benford *et al.*, 1962, p. 25). Moreover, with the railways offering low through-rates between the Appalachian coalfields and the Midwest coal markets, lake coal shipments showed an absolute decline throughout the latter part of the period.

A final characteristic of the Great Lakes ore trade stemmed from the fact that most of the ore was carried coastwise between U.S. ports and harbors. As a consequence it was subject to detailed public control and political influences unknown to the ocean ore trades. American law demands that ore be carried between American ports solely in American vessels, and that these be built in American shipyards (where construction costs in 1965 were about twice those in Western Europe and Japan). For a few years in the fifties, middle sections of carriers were constructed in Western Europe and then floated across the Atlantic to be used for the enlargement of existing lake vessels in the Great Lakes yards; but even this procedure was finally stopped by Congress at the insistence of domestic shipbuilding interests. In addition, American ships have to be manned by American crews. This means that high wage rates are added to the internationally high capital costs of the lake vessels, which can only partly be offset by automation.

Some traffic on the Great Lakes was, of course, between Canadian and American ports. It was therefore international in character, and the same political restrictions did not apply. This trade was rather more competitive. It was increasingly captured by Canadian companies, partly because their shipbuilding costs (through government subsidies) were lower, and partly because of the lower wage rates of the Canadian merchant marine. By 1965 the United States had only one company engaged in the international ore trade on the Great Lakes, although a number of U.S. interests were in fact operating through Canadian subsidiary companies.

The total effect of these characteristics of the Great Lakes ore trade was a relatively high-cost transport situation, even acknowledging the short distances involved. Especially was this the case toward the end of the period. In 1950 the rate for moving ore from the head of Lake Superior to Cleveland was $1.35 per actual ton; with the distance just under 1,400 km, this represented a rate of rather less than 1 mill per ton-km. By 1965, however, unlike international rates, which had generally fallen substantially, the rate had increased to $1.90 per actual ton, or 1.42 mills per ton-km (Table 50). The Canadian rate from Port Arthur to the ports of the lower lakes was slightly lower, at $1.78 per actual ton. And on the much shorter Escanaba-to-Chicago haul, a distance of just over 400 km, the rate rose between 1950 and 1965 from $0.81 to $1.14 per actual ton (from 1.8 to nearly 2.6 mills per ton-km). To a small extent these increases were offset by a gradual increase in the iron content of the ores moving down-lake, as beneficiation increased and pellet production expanded.

The necessity for several ore transfers between rail wagons and the Great Lakes vessels added to the comparatively high line-haul charges of the trade. All ore moving on the lakes was transferred a minimum of three times (from rail to dock, to ship, and then to blast-furnace stockyard); and

TABLE 50.   FREIGHT RATES FROM LAKE SUPERIOR TO LAKE ERIE PORTS, 1950–1965

Year	Line-haul rate/ actual ton	Line-haul rate/ actual-ton-km	Unloading rate/actual ton
1950	$1.35	1.00 mill	$0.20
1955	1.70	1.27 mill	0.23
1960	2.00	1.49 mill	0.28
1965	1.90	1.42 mill	0.28

Source: Cleveland-Cliffs Iron Company.

some consignments were transferred six times (from mine truck to rail, to dock, to ship, to lakeside stockpile, to rail, and finally to a blast-furnace stockyard). Each transfer not only generated additional fines to lower the value of the ore, but also added between 20¢ and 50¢ per actual ton to the total transfer charge. For example, ore moving between Duluth and Cleveland in 1965 carried charges of 19¢ per actual ton for loading, 28¢ for discharging from the ship's hold to the rail of the vessel, and 22¢ for the completion of unloading from the rail of the vessel to a railroad car. If the ore was transferred from the rail of the vessel to a stockpile, and then from the stockpile to a railway wagon, there was a further charge of 80¢ per actual ton plus a storage fee.

Moreover, the rail rates for moving ore from the mines to the loading berths, and then from the lower lakes ports to inland steelworks, were rather high; in 1965, they were $1.47 per actual ton from Mesabi to Duluth (including handling), and $2.73 from Cleveland to Pittsburgh (Table 51; see also Table 56). In sum, there were total freight charges of $6.60 per actual ton between Mesabi and Pittsburgh (3.9 mills per ton-km), assuming direct loading to railcars at Cleveland. From Menominee to Youngstown via Marquette and Cleveland, including the use of a stockpile at the latter, the charges were at least $6.73 (5.8 mills); and for the short haul from Marquette to Chicago via Escanaba they were $3.35 (6 mills). Although the published rates for all-rail hauls between the upper lakes ore deposits and the lower lakes consuming centers were somewhat above these rail/water rates, they in no way reflected the potential strength of railway competition for the ore traffic of the Great Lakes (see pp. 210–22).

By 1965 the shipment of ore on the Great Lakes was beginning to look

TABLE 51. TRANSPORT CHARGES ON THE GREAT LAKES ORE ROUTE, 1965

(*Dollars per actual ton*)

Range	Loading port	Destination	Rail freight	Han-dling[a]	Lake freight	Un-loading[b]	Total[c]
Marquette............	Marquette	Lower lakes	0.72	0.17	1.71	0.28	2.88
Marquette............	Escanaba	Lower lakes	1.25	0.19	1.43	0.28	3.15
Marquette............	Escanaba	Chicago	1.25	0.19	1.14	0.28	2.86
Menominee..........	Escanaba	Lower lakes	1.25	0.19	1.43	0.28	3.15
Menominee..........	Escanaba	Chicago	1.25	0.19	1.14	0.28	2.86
Menominee..........	Marquette	Lower lakes	1.69	0.17	1.71	0.28	3.85
Menominee..........	Ashland	Lower lakes	2.25	0.19	1.90	0.28	4.62
Gogebic.............	Ashland	Lower lakes	0.82	0.19	1.90	0.28	3.19
Gogebic.............	Escanaba	Lower lakes	1.37	0.19	1.43	0.28	3.27
Gogebic.............	Escanaba	Chicago	1.37	0.19	1.14	0.28	2.98
Mesabi.............	Duluth-Superior	Lower lakes	1.28	0.19	1.90	0.28	3.65
Vermilion...........	Two Harbors	Lower lakes	1.28	0.19	1.90	0.28	3.65
Cuyuna.............	Superior	Lower lakes	1.28	0.19	1.90	0.28	3.65
Atikokan............	Port Arthur	Lower lakes	1.45	0.19	1.78	0.28	3.70

Sources: Cleveland-Cliffs Iron Company; and others.
[a] Slightly lower for pellets at several ports.
[b] From hold to rail of vessel.
[c] Add: Rail of vessel to car—0.22; rail of vessel to dock stockpile—0.49; dock stockpile to car—0.31; dock storage per month—0.0125.

like a distinctly high-cost operation. Only the conservatism of railway managements had prevented an earlier challenge to its continuing importance. Any revitalization of the competitive position of the trade demanded the injection of large amounts of capital into new facilities and a fundamental change in the ground rules on which the ore fleet was required to operate. It was clearly imperative that the greater part of the fleet should gradually be replaced and that the capital and operating costs of the carriers should be reduced. One of the most obvious and effective ways to achieve this end lay in the removal of the embargo on foreign-built ore carriers; together with a fairly rapid rate of depreciation, this would certainly bring the capital charges of Great Lakes transport down to competitive levels. The case for the use of larger ships has been well made by Benford *et al.* (1962), Thaeler (1964), and others. Experience elsewhere in the world suggests that vessels of at least 35,000 dwt could be used profitably over the longer Great Lakes hauls, although it is doubtful whether a sufficiently rapid turnaround could be achieved to justify very much larger ore carriers. Larger vessels would inevitably demand the simultaneous investment of a considerable amount of capital in more efficient loading and discharging equipment and in devices to lengthen the trading season to ten or eleven months in the year. Another means of reducing transport costs on the Great Lakes lay in the possibility of opening up at least part of the ore trade to vessels flying foreign flags; in turn, this would allow the use of cheaper foreign labor and so lower the costs of operating at least some of the vessels. Any estimate of the benefits of such developments turns finally upon a series of political decisions. The decision-makers had to weigh the advantages of maintaining healthy competition with the other media moving ore between the upper lakes deposits and the Midwest blast furnaces against the alternative of keeping the movement of ore entirely in American hands and possibly seeing an increasing share of the ore movement captured by the railways. And inasmuch as the cost of transport strongly influences the size of market an ore source can command, these decisions would ultimately affect the size of the upper lakes iron ore mining industry.

The St. Lawrence Seaway was opened for navigation early in 1959 (Hill, 1959). From the viewpoint of iron ore traffic, it is a physical and to some extent an economic extension of the Great Lakes system. By 1966, ore movements up the Seaway had reached nearly 14 million actual tons. Like shipping costs on the Great Lakes, the costs of (and hence the rates for) moving ore along the Seaway were relatively high by ocean freight standards. The size of the ore carriers was restricted; in fact, it was even more restricted than on the Great Lakes, since the 8.4-meter channel could only handle vessels of up to 17,000 dwt. The shipping season was severely limited by the winter freeze. Return cargoes were few. And, unlike the Great Lakes where the use of locks was free, the Seaway levied a toll of about 50 cents per ton. However, its ore freight rates were approximately in line with those on the Great Lakes, since the shipments of ore originated in Canada and were largely destined for the United States; this made them international in character, and allowed the trade to be dominated by Canadian rather than U.S. shipping companies.

Even before the Seaway opened, ore was moved from eastern Canada to the U.S. Midwest and to Canadian steel industries by water. It had to be transshipped at Contrecoeur into small canal vessels, and the rates were high. The charge from Sept Iles to Ashtabula in 1957 was $3.39 per actual ton; and ore moving as far as Toledo was even more costly, with the rate standing at $5.25. With the opening of the Seaway, the Sept Iles to Ashtabula rate (including the toll) fell to $2 per actual ton (1.48 mills per ton-km). High though this was by the changing ocean standards, it permitted the rapid expansion of the Quebec-Labrador ore shipments into the United States by landing them competitively against the upper lakes ores on the shores of Lake Erie. However, potential competition from all-rail transport between the south bank of the St. Lawrence and the ore markets of the Midwest (after barging the ore across the river), plus the growing use of ocean transport from the St. Lawrence to Philadelphia and Baltimore, followed by rail haulage inland, raised doubts about the future attractiveness of the Seaway for ore shipments.

The 1965 rates for moving ore by the Seaway and rail to Pittsburgh and Johnstown were $4.95 and $5.24 per actual ton, respectively; the ocean/rail route on the other hand (assuming a sea freight of $0.90) was $5.16 and $4.90, and occasionally 15 cents cheaper still (Table 52). Quite apart from the ocean route's advantage of a year-round flow of ore, improvements in the efficiency of the eastern railroads would allow them to penetrate further into the interior and would present real problems to those anxious to see a growth in Seaway ore movements.

Plans existed for the deepening of the Seaway to allow the passage of ships up to 25,000 or 30,000 dwt. Such vessels would probably be the maximum economic size for the shipping distances involved and would certainly allow further reductions in ore freight rates. Extension of the shipping season by the application of the same type of technology as had been mooted for the Great Lakes would also permit economies. However, such developments would be both extravagant of capital and slow to implement. Undoubtedly, the quickest solution to the difficulties of the Seaway lay in the reduction or abolition of its tolls, but this was a matter on which Canadian and U.S. opinion and practice in 1965 were divided. It was a solution that raised far-reaching questions about the economics of such major transport investments.

TABLE 52. FREIGHT RATES FROM SEPT ILES TO PITTSBURGH, JOHNSTOWN, AND WHEELING, BY
ALTERNATE ROUTES, 1965

(Dollars/actual ton)

By sea	Rate	By St. Lawrence Seaway	Rate
Sept Iles to Baltimore*	0.90	Sept Iles to Ashtabula†	2.00
Unload	0.50	Unload	0.22
Baltimore to Pittsburgh	3.76	Ashtabula to Pittsburgh	2.73
Total	5.16	Total	4.95
Sept Iles to Baltimore*	0.75	Sept Iles to Ashtabula†	2.00
Unload	0.50	Unload, stock, load	0.80
Baltimore to Pittsburgh	3.76	Ashtabula to Pittsburgh	2.73
Total	5.01	Total	5.53
Sept Iles to Baltimore*	0.90	Sept Iles to Ashtabula†	2.00
Unload	0.50	Unload	0.22
Baltimore to Johnstown	3.76	Ashtabula to Johnstown	3.02
Total	5.16	Total	5.24
Sept Iles to Baltimore*	0.90	Sept Iles to Ashtabula†	2.00
Unload	0.50	Unload	0.22
Baltimore to Wheeling	3.96	Ashtabula to Wheeling	2.73
Total	5.36	Total	4.95

Source: Hanna Mining Company.
* Normal rate, $0.90; special charters, $0.75.
† Sept Iles to Ashtabula line haul, $1.60/actual ton; St. Lawrence Seaway toll, $0.40/actual ton.

CANAL AND RIVER TRANSPORT

The two outstanding contrasts between canal and river ore transport on the one hand, and ocean or Great Lakes ore transport on the other, are the size of vessels and the allocation of indirect (overhead) costs. As to the first point, the width and depth of channels available for canal and river navigation in 1950 generally restricted the size of barges to only 500 or 1,000 tons. Subsequently, the capacity of individual barges was increased to 1,500 tons, and at the same time the size of loads grew to about 5,000 actual tons (on the Rhine) and 10,000 actual tons (on some American rivers) by means of grouping barges together and pushing them with powerful tugs. Engines large enough to move up to 40,000 actual tons of ore have in fact been developed, but the number of inland waterways on which, say, thirty barges of 1,500 tons each might be pushed or hauled together is very few indeed. There clearly are upper limits to the opportunities for exploiting the economies of scale on canal and river waterways. Even by 1965, the largest loads of ore moving up the Rhine to the Ruhr were only about half the tonnage of the average tramp vessel in the ocean ore trade fifteen years earlier.

On the second point, it is worth recalling the distinction made by Dubnie (1962, p. 31) between the direct and the indirect costs of water transport. In most countries, as he pointed out, "Governments spend considerable sums annually on inland waterways and seaport facilities. These indirect expenditures are generally borne by the taxpayers at large. Users of waterways and harbours pay fees for the use of the facilities provided; however, the charges generally cover only a portion of the cost of facilities." In the United States, the costs of improving inland waterways are carried by the Federal Government, and the users make little or no contribution to the costs of building and maintaining either the improved channels or the port and harbor facilities. In France and Germany, the construction of the Moselle Canal was part of a larger political and economic arrangement between the two countries; and no attempt has been made to allocate to its users the costs of construction in order to ensure, for example, the liquidation of the capital over a period of fifty years, which is the basis of the St. Lawrence Seaway tolls. Until a serious attempt is made to assess the effects of these hidden subsidies in much of inland water transport, it will be difficult to confirm or refute the claims of competing carriers that the costs of water transport (as opposed to the rates charged) are rarely as low as they might seem (Curran, 1964; Blackwell, 1964).

Those are the contrasts. In other respects, there are similarities in the various forms of water haulage. Just as the winter freeze on the Great Lakes causes a lay-up of carriers, the freezing of canals and rivers in many countries prevents a year-round flow of ore, thereby making equipment seasonally idle and demanding a costly buildup of ore stockpiles during the summer and autumn months. Natural variations in the level of the water can also lead to a temporary reduction in the carrying capacity of rivers and again raise transport costs. There are certain times of certain years when the ore barges plying between Rotterdam and Duisburg cannot carry full loads because of the low water level on the Rhine. Another important characteristic that barge transport shares with ocean and Great Lakes haulage is the low ton-kilometer cost of its capital equipment. Partly for this reason, where navigable rivers are available to meet an ore transport need, and where the distances involved are over, say, 400 or 500 km, highly competitive ton-kilometer rates are generally assured. However, where the distances are shorter, or, especially, where the provision of inland waterway facilities involves considerable capital investment—for example, the dredging of a channel, the construction of locks, or the digging of a canal—the competitive status of freight rates is much less predictable.

The rates charged for the haulage of iron ore by inland waterway—constrained as they frequently are by the rates offered by alternative media—have in fact only a moderate range. In the examples contained in Table 53 they vary between $0.37 per actual ton for shipment in multiple push barges up the Rhine from Rotterdam to Duisburg (in 1965) and $4 for the Baton Rouge, Louisiana, to Chicago run (in 1960). On the other hand, the ton-kilometer rates show a much greater variation. Where distances are considerable, where scale economies are extensively exploited, and where user charges are small (as on the Mississippi), the ton-km rate can be as low as

TABLE 53.   SOME IRON ORE FREIGHT RATES ON INLAND WATERWAYS, 1960–1965

From	To	Date	Rate/actual ton (*dollars*)	Rate/actual-ton-km (*mills*)
Baton Rouge, Louisiana...........	Chicago	1965	3.00	1.47
Baton Rouge...................	Chicago	1960	4.00	1.96
Baton Rouge...................	St. Louis	1960	3.07	1.84
Rotterdam.....................	Ruhr*	1965	0.37–0.49	1.75–2.32
Rotterdam.....................	Ruhr†	1965	0.84	3.98
Rotterdam.....................	Ruhr†	1960	0.93	4.40
Salzgitter......................	Ruhr†	1960	0.95	4.55
Emden.........................	Ruhr (east)	1965	1.30	5.20
Antwerp.......................	Liège	1960	0.85	6.75
Antwerp.......................	Charleroi	1960	1.50	12.50
Sanvorden.....................	Mormugão	1960	0.98	22.00

Sources: Canada, Department of Energy, Mines and Resources; and others.
Note: Unloading from ship and loading onto a barge at Rotterdam, $0.60 to 0.80 per actual ton; unloading at Ruhr, $0.30 per actual ton.
* Multiple push barges.
† Single barges.

the rates on the Great Lakes or the rates charged for small tramp vessels on short ocean routes. The 1965 rate from Baton Rouge to Chicago was equivalent to only 1.47 mills per actual-ton-km. Slightly higher were the ton-km rates in Western Europe—for example, between Rotterdam and the Ruhr, where the shorter distance and smaller groups of push barges resulted in a line-haul rate varying between 1.75 and 2.32 mills per ton-km. These international rates were not subject to government regulation; as a result, they fluctuated in response to the supply of and demand for barge tonnage. They were naturally lower than the single barge charge (around 84 cents), or the government-regulated barge rates for transport entirely within West Germany. Higher still were the rates for the very short hauls within Belgium. And exceptionally high was the rate for the 50-km barge journey between Sanvorden and Mormugão in India, where the $0.98 per actual ton charge represented 22 mills per ton-km.

In any consideration of the ton-kilometer rates charged for the haulage of ore on inland waterways, it is noteworthy that rivers in particular, but also canals, do not always follow the most direct route between two points. Most barge rates in the United States are in the vicinity of 2.5 mills per ton-km; Vigrass (1962) has suggested that when this is coupled to an average 50 percent circuity of the waterways as against overland routes, the adjusted figure would be equal to 3.75 mills per ton-km. It is against such adjusted figures that the railways had to compete if they were to win ore traffic from the inland waterways. Their ability to do so is explored in the next section.

ORE MOVEMENT BY RAIL

Comparative statistics of the volume of iron ore moved by rail and by other transport media are not available. Whereas it is probable that the ton-kilometer movements of ore are greater by sea than by rail, it is certain that the actual tonnage of ore handled by the world's railways is appreciably larger than that of any other transport system. For in addition to the considerable tonnages of ore railed directly from mine to blast furnace, most of the ore transported to and from ports for sea transport is also handled by rail.

The costs and the rates of rail transport have as wide a range as those of other transport media. The costs of providing railway services vary with the nature of the terrain, the volume of traffic, the public regulations surrounding the operation, the type of equipment used, and the distance of the haul—to name just a few of the many variables. Basic to railway economics is the need to provide and to maintain a specialized track or track network for the exclusive use of the railway company. This involves a considerable capital expenditure. A new line in a less developed country, for example, might cost somewhere in the order of $60,000 to $160,000 per kilometer. And capital is also required for the rolling stock and terminal facilities. When fully exploited, however, capital costs of rail transport per ton-km fall quite low. And running costs, when high-capacity rolling stock is used, can be equally attractive.

Data available on the Quebec, North Shore and Labrador Railway provide a useful insight into the cost structure of at least one type of railway. The QNSL Railway Company was created solely for the transport of iron ore, although its tracks are used for the shipment of mining supplies and fuel oil as well. The initial line links the ore field at Schefferville on the Quebec-Labrador boundary with the St. Lawrence at Sept Iles, a distance of 570 km. In 1960 the company maintained a fleet of some 3,000 ore wagons (short gondolas of 97 tons capacity), and through efficient terminal arrangements it was able to unload up to 1,000 cars each day at Sept Iles during the peak season. The line, however, is only operated for about seven months in each year. Partly this is because the ore contains a good deal of moisture, which presents problems of freezing, and partly because ore movement up the St. Lawrence Seaway is seasonal, with most vessels being laid up from about the beginning of December. Vigrass (1962) has estimated that the total costs of the QNSL Railway in 1960 were nearly 4 mills per ton-km (Table 54). Of this total, 1.31 mills (33 percent) represented capital charges; 1.87 mills (47 percent), the cost of maintaining the track and equipment; and 0.3 mill (nearly 8 percent), the other overhead costs. The cost of the actual haulage operations was 0.48 mill, about one-eighth of the total.

Because of both the limited season for the railway's activities and the difficult terrain over which the line had to be laid, the QNSL Railway is inherently a relatively high-cost operation. It does, however, usefully characterize one type of railway facility—namely, the line that is constructed

TABLE 54.   COST STRUCTURE OF THE QUEBEC, NORTH SHORE AND LABRADOR RAILWAY, 1960

Item	Cost (Mills/ton-km)	Percent
Operating costs...................................	0.48	12.1
Maintenance of equipment..........................	0.59	14.9
Maintenance of track..............................	1.28	32.3
Other costs, e.g., administration.....................	0.30	7.6
Capital costs.....................................	1.31	33.1
Total...	3.96	100.0

Source: Vigrass, 1962.

most commonly in the less developed regions and countries of the world and is used almost exclusively for mineral haulage. On such lines, the allocation of capital costs to each ton of ore traffic for rate-making purposes is a relatively straightforward exercise. In the majority of circumstances, however, financial allocation of overhead costs is a more difficult exercise, since railways compete for and are offered a considerable variety of traffics—general merchandise and passengers as well as minerals. Obviously, an "accurate" allocation of part of the joint overhead costs to each of these traffics is impossible, and a cost breakdown for a common carrier railway (comparable to that calculated for the QNSL Railway) simply cannot be produced. Rate-making for this type of railway must find an alternative basis.

From the late fifties onward, while the more fortunate railway managements continued to bask in the profitable comfort of their ore transport monopoly along many routes, the growing severity of competition in the markets for iron ore exerted pressures on other railway operators to reduce at least some of their rates. Not unlike the shipping industry, the railways sought to lower their costs by making fuller use of their capital equipment, by exploiting the economies of large-scale operations, and by taking advantage of the economies of long-distance hauls. In order to utilize their tracks more fully, managements tried to attract additional traffic and occasionally to concentrate commodity flows along fewer tracks. A single-line mineral railway can comfortably handle somewhere between 20 and 25 million actual tons of ore each year. Yet very few lines, especially mineral lines, are required to handle such tonnages. There is, therefore, almost universally, a surplus of track capacity, and obvious economies are to be gained from the attraction of more traffic. When, for example, many of the high-cost Gogebic (Michigan) mines were threatened with closure, the North Western Railroad estimated that if all the ore were shipped through Escanaba the rail rate could be reduced from $2 to $1.45 per actual ton (Hussey, 1961).

Furthermore, in seeking to make greater use of their rolling stock, railway managements raised their demurrage rates in order to discourage the slow turnaround of ore wagons. Similarly, loading and unloading procedures were speeded up considerably by the installation of more automatic equipment capable of handling ore trains while they are still moving. Thus, the Erie Mining Company, which hauls ore to Taconite Harbor, unloads its trainloads of 10,000 actual tons of ore in six and a half minutes while the trains are still moving at 16 km/hr (Thomte, 1963).

Equally important in the reduction of railway costs was the development and exploitation of unit-train technology. The unit train (called the "merry-go-round" train in Britain) is a semipermanently coupled train of wagons. It is operated on regular schedules between two fixed places, where loop arrangements of the track at the termini not only obviate marshaling but also minimize the number of locomotive changes. The economies of the system derive from the high degree of use to which the rolling stock is put, together with reductions in labor and operating costs. In the United States, where unit trains were more widely used for the haulage of coal than for ore, a further advance in railway technology—the integral train—was conceived to help the competitive position of the Lake Superior ore mines (the research was financed by railways interested in that traffic). This concept of railway engineering was surprisingly neglected by a generally complacent and institutionalized ore trade. The integral train is basically characterized by the disposition of locomotives at regular intervals along the length of the train—that is, between groups of four to seven wagons. The power units are centrally controlled, and their position along the train allows both higher speeds and larger loads. Kneiling and Kauffield (1965) have suggested that integral trains could operate at speeds of 80 to 90 km/hr, with payloads of at least 25,000 actual tons of ore. Such developments, however, are for the future. Although the necessary technology was already available by the early sixties, the organization and the mood of the railway industry by 1965 still prevented its application.

Paralleling this search to utilize capital equipment more fully, the railway industry also sought to take advantage of the lower costs of larger units of haulage. At the time of the Anglo-American Council on Productivity (1952), average American rail wagons each carried somewhere between 40 and 65 actual tons of iron ore, and were hauled in trains of between 50 and 60 wagons. Between 2,000 and 4,000 actual tons of ore were thus handled in a single consignment. In contrast, by 1965 it had become common for American companies to reinvest in larger wagons, with 85 or 100 actual tons carrying capacity, and to group as many as 100 or 120 of these together to make trainloads of 10,000, 12,000, or even sometimes 15,000 actual tons of ore. Articulated railway wagons of some 200 tons were by that time also on the drawing boards.

By no means did all railway systems in the world adopt trainloads as large as those in the United States. Many large and modern ore mines had railways capable of carrying axle loads of 25 tons or more; their trains, hauled by three or four powerful locomotives, carried up to 14,000 actual tons of ore. But elsewhere smaller wagons and smaller trains were more usual. In the ECSC countries, for example, individual wagons even in 1965 rarely carried over 60 tons. In Britain, most wagons hauled only 30 tons, although a few of 57-ton capacity did exist. Nevertheless, in Western Europe also the general trend was toward larger units of haulage. While in the late forties the capacity of British ore wagons was often only 12 to 15 tons each, and the locomotives hauled only 250 to 500 actual tons, loads of twice that size were common by the end of the period.

Many of the traditional movements of iron ore by rail were over quite short distances. Mesabi to Duluth is about 110 km; Ashtabula to Pittsburgh, 200; Lorraine to Luxembourg, 100; and Kiruna to Narvik, 180. But since one of the most significant items in railway costs is the loading and unloading of the ore, plus the preparation and marshaling of trains, and since all shipments must make some contribution to the system overheads, costs per ton-km tend to fall significantly with increasing distance. The sixties saw the exploitation of these economies of the long haul. Such routes as Schefferville to Sept Iles (570 km), Lac Jeannine to Port Cartier (910 km), Belo Horizonte to Vitória (685 km), Fort Gouraud to Port Etienne (660 km), and Orissa to Vizagapatam (720 km), all became increasingly important in the ore trade (Table 55).

The rates charged for iron ore transport by rail are obviously influenced to a considerable extent by the many factors that have a bearing on the

TABLE 55. SOME RAIL TRANSPORT DISTANCES, FROM MINE TO PORT

From	To	Dis-tance (km)
NORTH AMERICA		
Canada		
Carol Lake	Sept Iles	419
Labrador City	Pointe Noire	440
Lac Jeannine	Port Cartier	910
Schefferville	Sept Iles	571
Steep Rock	Port Arthur	225
Texada, B.C.	Foquart Bay	1
Wabush	Pointe Noire	130
U.S.A.		
Eagle Mountain	Long Beach	385
WESTERN EUROPE		
Norway		
Sydvaranger	Kirkenes	8
Sweden		
Grangesberg	Oxelösund	250
Kiruna	Narvik	170
Svappavaara	Luleå	300

TABLE 55. Continued

From	To	Distance (km)
ASIA AND OCEANIA		
India		
Baladilla	Vizagapatam	480
Goa	Mormugão	70
Rourkela	Vizagapatam	720
Malaysia		
Bukit Iham	Lanjut	80
Australia		
Hamersley	Cape Preston	110
Mt. Goldsworthy	Port Hedland	112
Mt. Newman	Port Hedland	380
Mt. Tom Price	King Bay	270
LATIN AMERICA		
Brazil		
Belgo Mineira	Tubarão	560
Belo Horizonte	Vitória	658
Parapoeba	Rio de Janeiro	500
St. John del Rey	Septiba	400
Chile		
El Romeral	Guayacan	39
El Tofo	Cruz Grande	25
Peru		
Acarí	San Juan	85
Marcona	San Nicolás	10
Venezuela		
Cerro Bolívar	Puerto Ordaz	144
El Pao	Palua	55
AFRICA		
Angola		
Cassinga	Moçâmedes	630
Gabon		
Mékambo	Owendo	560
Liberia		
Bomi and Bong	Monrovia	70
Mano River	Monrovia	150
Nimba	Buchanan	270
Mauretania		
Fort Gouraud	Port Etienne	660
Sierra Leone		
Marampa	Pepel	85
Swaziland		
Ngwenya	Lourenço Marques	275
Tunisia		
Djerissa	Tunis	200

costs of operating a line or a system. For example, the response of one carrier to the economies of large-scale and regular movements of ore can be seen in the 1965 rates for ore shipments between Mesabi and Granite City, a distance of about 1,120 km. The normal rate was $5.88 per actual ton (5.2 mills per ton-km). When more than twenty wagons were moved at the same time on the same bill of lading, the rate was reduced to $4.98 (4.5 mills). And when the annual tonnage of a shipper exceeded 150,000 tons, and not less than 6,000 tons were shipped on one bill of lading, the rate was reduced still further, to $4 per actual ton (3.6 mills per ton-km), which is the lowest rate per ton-km in Table 56.

In the case of lines concerned largely or entirely with the haulage of ore,

TABLE 56. SOME RAILWAY IRON ORE FREIGHT RATES IN NORTH AMERICA, 1965

From	To	Distance (km)	Rate/actual ton (dollars)	Rate/actual-ton-km (mills)
Mesabi	Granite City	1,120	4.00	3.6
Gogebic	Granite City	960	3.50	3.7
Marquette	Granite City	1,000	4.00	4.0
Gogebic	Birmingham	1,800	7.15	4.0
Gulf Coast	Chicago	1,500	6.40	4.3
Mesabi	Chicago	880	4.00	4.5
Fillmore County, Minn.	Birmingham	1,500	6.80	4.5
Fillmore County	Granite City	720	3.26	4.5
Gulf Coast	Granite City	1,100	5.05	4.6
Gogebic	Escanaba	300	1.37	4.6
Gulf Coast	Birmingham	400	2.13	5.3
Schefferville	Sept Iles	570	3.00	5.3
Iron Mt., Miss.	Birmingham	900	4.92	5.5
Upper New York	Pittsburgh	900	4.95	5.5
Fillmore County	Chicago	500	2.80	5.6
Erie, Pa.*	Sparrows Point	700	3.92	5.6
Eagle Mountain	Fontana	260	1.46	5.6
Wyman	Hamilton	530	3.00	5.6
Baltimore	Middleton	800	4.52	5.6
Baltimore	Chicago	1,100	6.40	5.8
Gogebic	Weirton	1,350	8.02	5.9
Gogebic	Pittsburgh	1,400	8.33	5.9
Mesabi	Pittsburgh	1,600	8.33	5.9
Lowphos	Depot Harbor	240	1.45	6.0
Baltimore	Ashland	700	4.25	6.1
Copper Cliff*	Welland	540	3.36	6.2
Atikokan	Port Arthur	230	1.46	6.3
Mesabi	Pittsburgh	1,600	10.23	6.4
Hilton*	Hamilton	450	3.06	6.8
Mesabi	Cleveland	1,440	9.78	6.8
Mormora*	Hamilton	280	2.00	7.1
Lake Erie	Ashland	400	2.93	7.3
Copper Cliff*	Sault Ste. Marie	280	2.28	8.1
Philadelphia	Pittsburgh	460	3.76	8.2
Gulf Coast	Lone Star	450	3.75	8.3
Baltimore	Youngstown	480	4.03	8.4
Steep Rock	Port Arthur	220	1.87	8.5
Baltimore	Weirton	460	3.76	9.9
Baltimore	Pittsburgh	350	3.76	10.7
Mesabi	Duluth	110	1.28	11.6
Ashtabula	Aliquippa	195	2.39	12.2
Mormora*	Hamilton	280	2.00	12.3
Iron Mountain	Granite City	150	1.88	12.5
Cleveland	Pittsburgh	200	2.73	13.6
Cleveland	Weirton	190	2.73	14.4
Ashtabula	Youngstown	100	2.08	20.8
Ashtabula	Warren	75	2.08	27.8
Wawa*	Michipicoten	13	0.70	53.8

Sources: Hanna Mining Company; Canada, Bureau of Mines; and others.
* 1961.

a direct relationship between railway costs and rates can be seen. On the common carrier lines, however, the level of freight rates is influenced in addition by a variety of commercial, historical, and political criteria. As their overhead costs cannot be accurately allocated among their different traffics, these companies in the first instance charge or bargain for what they consider to be the highest rate the traffic can bear. Thus it is found that rates tend to fall as competition from other transport media increases, or as the very existence of an ore traffic is threatened by an increasingly competitive situation in the market for the ore. For example, in 1965 the low rates per ton-km to Granite City, Illinois (Table 56) were in considerable measure a response to cheap water transport opportunities on the Mississippi and the growing attractiveness of South American ores for use in the blast furnaces of the St. Louis district. The low rate from Mesabi to Chicago at $4 per actual ton (4.5 mills) represented the growing challenge of the railways to the traditional ore flows by Great Lakes carrier.

As some circumstances led to highly competitive and falling railway rates, there were at the same time situations in which the rates charged for hauling ore became institutionalized and to some extent inappropriate to contemporary transport costs and conditions. Such rates were to be found especially in industrially mature regions and countries, where, largely as a consequence of a Victorian legacy of public controls surrounding railway operations, inertia characterized both the operations and the rate structure of certain lines and commodities. In the United States, for example, throughout the period, the rates for hauling ore away from the lower ports of the Great Lakes were particularly high, despite the rather short distances involved. The 1965 rate between Cleveland and Pittsburgh, a distance of about 200 km, was $2.73 per actual ton, or 13.6 mills per ton-km; the rate between Ashtabula and Youngstown was $2.08 per actual ton, or 20.8 mills per ton-km, for a distance of 100 km. As can be seen from Table 56, these rates were noticeably higher than the general level of ore freight rates between the mines and the upper lakes ports, and between the eastern seaboard and inland consuming centers. They demonstrate the way in which many of the common carrier railways operating along traditional ore routes charged rates that have been handed down from long-irrelevant historical circumstances. As a result, gross inequalities can be found in the price paid by different steelworks for quite similar transport services. By the same token, the competitive position of particular ore deposits was often arbitrarily stifled.

In the early and mid-sixties, however, the majority of rail freight rates for iron ore in North America stood at between 4 and 8 mills per actual-ton-km. In contrast to ocean freight rates, these figures, in current dollar terms, were no lower than (and sometimes were above) the rates that had been in effect fifteen years earlier. In real dollar terms, they were virtually all somewhat lower. For example, the charge for hauling ore from Eagle Mountain, California, to the Kaiser steelworks at Fontana in 1951 was $1.22 per actual ton; by 1965, in spite of the much greater tonnage using the tracks (both private and common carrier), the rate had increased to $1.46 per actual ton. This represents an increase from 4.7 to 5.6 mills per ton-km over the 260-km journey. Similarly, the rate from Mesabi to Duluth, a distance of 110 km, increased from $0.98 to $1.28 per actual ton between 1950 and 1965 (that is, from 8.9 to 11.6 mills per ton-km). In the case of one of the upper lakes railways, however, although the rate for ore haulage rose throughout the early years of the period, by the late fifties it had reached its peak, and by 1965 it had begun to fall. This was the rate from Gogebic to Escanaba, a distance of 300 km; it stood at $1.50 per actual ton (5 mills per ton-km) in 1950, rose to $2 (6.7 mills per ton-km) by 1958, and fell to $1.37 (4.6 mills per ton-km) in 1962, where it remained until 1965.

By 1965 the pressures to reduce railway rates in North America were steadily mounting. In particular, cheaper overseas ores and falling ocean rates were challenging many of the traditional ore movements, and the pressures on the iron and steel industry to reduce its costs were growing fast. Fortunately for the railways, new technology was available to achieve this end, and the successful reduction of coal freight rates in the early sixties by anything up to 50 percent had powerfully demonstrated its commercial feasibility. The rates charged for the haulage of coal by unit trains had been reduced to 2.5 and 3 mills per ton-km in many instances, and even these rates represented no more than response to competition from barges, pipelines, and transmission wires. When rates at this level were offered, severe penalties were written into the haulage agreements between the shipper and the railway company, in order to minimize the disruption of regular commodity flows. Should a shipper fail to provide the agreed quantities of a mineral for haulage at the agreed time, or in any other way hinder the smooth operation of the trains, his expenses rose dramatically, perhaps by as much as $1 per ton per hour. Applied to ore shipments, freight rates of 2.5 and 3 mills per ton-km could conceivably bring the charge for the Mesabi-to-Granite City haul down from its 1965 level of $4 per actual ton to $2.40–$2.70 per actual ton.

It appeared in 1965 that the railways could sustain, and indeed in places would be forced to accept, even lower ton-km rates for mineral traffic as competition intensified in the American energy market. Moreover, development of integral train technology seemed likely to permit further cost savings, thus making the rate reductions more acceptable. Kneiling (1964, 1965) suggested that ore could be transported from Baltimore to Pittsburgh for $0.70 per actual ton, or 1.4 mills per ton-km, and that the Silver Bay (Minnesota) to Middletown (Ohio) haul could be reduced to $1.40 per actual ton. Such a level of railway efficiency and rates would allow Atlantic City (Wyoming) pellets, with a freight charge as low as $3 per actual ton, to compete for the first time in the Pittsburgh market; it would allow Quebec-Labrador ores to move into the Midwest via rail from the south bank of the St. Lawrence, thereby providing an alternative to transportation via the Seaway and Great Lakes; and it would sharpen considerably the competition in the ore markets of the Midwest generally through the new inland accessibility it would offer to African and South American ores.

This background is essential to an understanding of the serious challenge (toward the end of the period) by all-rail transport to the traditional pattern of ore movements via Great Lakes carriers from the upper lakes to the Midwest. The advantages of hauling ore directly to the blast furnaces were increasingly evident. First, such direct hauls meant a reduction in the number of authorities concerned with the transport operation. However, the all-rail arrangements were by no means perfect, since a division of ownership between the several railway companies of "the old North West" and of the Midwest still remained. Second, they offered to eliminate the costly intermediate transshipment operations, which also caused a degradation in the quality ore. Third, provided pellets were being shipped, all-rail transport permitted a year-round flow of ore, which allowed the regular utilization of loading and unloading facilities and of rolling stock and eliminated the costly seasonal stockpiles at the lower lakes or the steelworks. Over a year, these stockpiles could add about 50 cents to the cost of an actual ton of ore. In spite of these advantages, the all-rail rate from Mesabi to Pittsburgh, published by the railways in 1965, was as high as $10.23 per ton, compared with $6.60 per ton for the rail-lake-rail haul. Equivalent to just under 6 mills per ton-km, the all-rail rate reflected the conservatism of the relevant railway companies and their surprising lack of interest in the traffic, rather than the inherent inability of the medium to compete with the Great Lakes carriers. In fact, the U.S. Area Redevelopment Administration in 1964 spelled out in some detail the economic advantages of the all-rail haul.

The ARA study sought a means of reducing the cost of transporting ore from Minnesota to Pittsburgh in order to improve its competitive position in that market. It embraced the unit-train concept as the most appropriate means of achieving this end. Adopting an all-rail rate of under 4 mills per ton-km, the study assumed that the line-haul rate between Mesabi and Pittsburgh could be as low as $6 per actual ton. Although only 60 cents less than the rail-lake-rail rate, the real gain to a shipper using the all-rail route was as much as $1.14 per actual ton through lower stockpiling costs (Table 57). The rate of $6 was based on the assumption that the ore trains would return empty to Minnesota. But if the returning wagons could be used to haul Appalachian coal in the opposite direction (as suggested by the

TABLE 57. COMPARISON OF COSTS FOR MOVING 5 MILLION ACTUAL TONS OF TACONITE PELLETS FROM THE MESABI RANGE TO PITTSBURGH BETWEEN RAIL-LAKE-RAIL ARRANGEMENTS AND ALL-RAIL UNIT TRAINS, CIRCA 1962

Item	Rail-lake-rail	Unit train
Shipping season via Great Lakes and rail..............	237 days	360 days
Total return on investment cost in seasonal stockpiles...	$2.60 million	
Handling cost at upper lake dock ($0.19 per ton).......	0.95 million	
Handling costs at lower lake dock ($1.08 per ton)......	2.06 million	
Annual dock stockpile storage cost..................	0.07 million	
Annual transport cost for 5 million tons..............	29.65 million	$30.00 million
Handling from mill stockpile to mill storage..........	0.09 million	0.38 million
Annual amortization of unloading facilities required with unit train..		0.20 million
Total annual cost.............................	36.28 million	30.58 million
Total annual savings with unit train..............		5.70 million
Total annual savings per ton with unit train.......		1.14

Source: United States Area Redevelopment Administration, 1964, p. 13.

ARA), the rate could be reduced still further, to $5 per actual ton. And, of course, integral-train technology prospectively offered a further 50 percent reduction.

By 1965 the potential competitive strength of the all-rail haul from the upper lakes to Pennsylvania, West Virginia, and inland Ohio was undoubted. And at Chicago, where the lake shipments were denied the advantages of even a medium-length haul, all-rail movements were in theory extremely attractive. Even along the shores of Lake Erie, where the lake haul has the advantage that the carriers can sometimes unload directly into the ore stockyards of the iron and steel works, an all-rail rate of $4 to $4.50 per actual ton would be both competitive and not out of line with 1965 unit-train (coal) rates. Although only a very small proportion of Minnesota and Michigan ore was moved all-rail by the mid-sixties, it appeared likely that, as the large taconite pellet plants of the upper lakes began to expand their output, massive all-rail shipments would characterize this particular ore trade in the future.

Despite the considerable potential for a further reduction in the general level of ore freight rates on North American railways, their charges at the end of the period stood up well to international comparisons. This was particularly relevant in the case of mineral lines. The QNSL Railway, for example, charged $3 per actual ton for its 570-km haul (5.3 mills); and from Steep Rock to Port Arthur in 1965 the rate was $1.45 (6.3 mills). As can be seen from Table 58, these rates were very similar to those pertaining in the developing world, where national and international capital had opened up ore deposits with the construction of new railways and ports. In 1960 the rate for the very long haul from Minas Gerais to Vitória was $3.42 per actual ton (4.5 mills), and that from Cerro Bolívar to Puerto Ordaz, $1.17

TABLE 58. SOME RAILWAY IRON ORE FREIGHT RATES IN WESTERN EUROPE AND THE REST OF
THE WORLD, 1960-1965

From	To	Date	Distance (km)	Rate/actual ton (dollars)	Rate/actual- ton-km (mills)
WESTERN EUROPE					
Rotterdam.............	Duisburg	1965	220	1.02–1.08	4.5–4.8
Salzgitter...............	Ruhr	1960	260	1.27	4.9
Lorraine...............	Ruhr	1960	365	2.88	7.9
Northamptonshire........	Teesside	1965	300	2.52	8.4
Rouge.................	Caen	1965	245	2.32	9.5
Lorraine...............	Charleroi	1965	205	3.17	12.7
Lorraine...............	Liège	1965	240	3.08	12.8
Antwerp...............	Liège	1965	130	1.62	12.9
Antwerp...............	Charleroi	1965	110	1.50	13.8
Rouge.................	Nantes	1965	75	1.37	18.3
Lorraine...............	Esche-Bevel	1960	100	2.04	21.3
Newcastle..............	Consett	1965	37	1.00	27.0
REST OF THE WORLD					
Minas Gerais............	Vitória	1965	760	3.42	4.5
Postmasburg............	Vander- bijlspark	1965	700	4.20	6.0
Cerro Bolívar...........	Puerto Ordaz	1965	180	1.17	6.5
Bomi Hills..............	Monrovia	1960	70	0.52	7.5
Orissa.................	Calcutta	1960	390	3.30	8.5

Sources: Canada, Department of Energy, Mines and Resources; and others.

(6.5 mills); even the short 70-km haul from the Bomi Hills mines to Monrovia at $0.52 per actual ton was only 7.5 mills per ton-km.

In Western Europe the rates for ore haulage by rail on a ton-kilometer
basis were rather higher, and in many respects reminiscent of the situation
pertaining at the lower lakes of the Great Lakes (Table 58). Scale economies
were neglected, and the rates had become rather institutionalized. Ore shipments between Lorraine and Liège, for example, in 1960 were charged
$3.08 per actual ton (12.8 mills), and those between Lorraine and Esche-
Bevel, $2.04 (21.3 mills). Distance for distance, railway rates in Britain
tended to be even higher. Only where there was effective competition from
water transport in Western Europe did railway rates show the potential
economies of rail transport. From the Salzgitter mines to the Ruhr, for
example, the rate in 1960 was $1.27 per actual ton (4.9 mills); and from
Rotterdam to Duisburg in 1965 the rate fluctuated between $1.02 and $1.08
per actual ton (4.5 to 4.8 mills).

In the fully planned economies of Eastern Europe, of course, railway
rates were manipulated to fulfill the broader economic and geographical
objectives of state planning (see Chapter 5). In the Soviet Union, rates per
ton-km generally tended to vary directly rather than inversely with distance,
in order to minimize the attractions of road transport over short hauls and
to encourage the use of water transport over longer distances (Clark,

1956-A; Hunter, 1957; Williams, 1962). Consequent upon administrative decisions during the period, there was a tendency for iron ore rail rates to rise more rapidly than coal rates; as a result, steelworks located near the sources of coal were increasingly placed in a less advantageous position compared with their ore-based counterparts. The changing pattern of railway rates between the Urals and the Kuznetz industrial areas is recorded elsewhere (see pp. 103–4).

Such a manipulation of rail rates was not unique to the planned economies. Even in the mixed economies, railway rates were modified to suit the broader goals of economic planning. The Indian government, for example, in order to ensure the competitive position of iron ore exports, placed a differential on the rates for hauling ore to the domestic blast furnaces and to the ports for export. While a 12 percent surcharge was levied on ore moving to inland steelworks in 1965, the surcharge on ore transported to the ports for export was only 5 percent (India, Planning Commission, 1965, p. 21).

There were, then, considerable national differences in the levels of railway rates for iron ore transport. While many of the actual tonnage rates (and more especially the ton-km rates) were quite high, it is clear that railway costs and rates, if full advantage were taken of modern technology, could be brought down to a level at which the alternative land transport media would generally be uncompetitive. There are, however, some circumstances when ore transport by pipelines, conveyors, and roads, with which the following survey is concerned, has a role to play.

PIPELINES, CONVEYORS, AND ROADS

For the very short distance movement of iron ore concentrates and tailings, pipelines have a fairly widespread use. But over distances of more than one or two kilometers their role in the transport of ore has, to date, been rather restricted and largely speculative. The short-lived technological, if not economic, success of coal pipelines, however, does demand that ore pipelines be given serious consideration. The essential characteristics of this medium of transport are its high proportion of capital to total costs (a proportion that varies with the nature of the terrain through which the pipeline passes) and its considerable scale economies. The competitive position of pipelines is therefore strongest when high load factors and large volumes of ore shipment are contemplated. Pipelines are most attractive economically when the costs of alternative transport media are unusually high. This condition is ideally met in Tasmania, where a singularly rough terrain would have necessitated a lengthy and costly railway between the iron ore mine at Savage River and Brickmakers Bay. Instead, a 112-km pipeline passes directly over the ridges and carries ore concentrates to a pellet plant on the coast. The details of this Tasmanian development illustrate two other requirements for the successful application of pipeline technology to the transport of iron ore. First, the composition of the ore must not be too abrasive, in order to minimize damage to the line; and, second, the ore must be carried in the form of a slurry. If in fact a slurry that is suitable for pipeline transport is created during a beneficiation process, a pipeline is likely to be more competitive; but if a slurry has to be mixed especially for the transport operation, the cost of mixing must be added to the pipeline costs in any comparative transport analysis.

Constantini (1963) has suggested that ore pipelines could be used by the Canadian iron ore industry in certain circumstances, since the pipe would be buried below the frost line and so would permit easier year-round transport. In addition, if the ore were piped from a mine to a harbor on the Great Lakes in the form of a slurry concentrate, there would be a saving in the cost of moving large quantities of fuel oil to the mine, since the agglomeration process could then most advantageously be performed on the lakeside. Constantini's costings suggest that a 40- to 45-cm diameter pipe laid over 800 km could be used to move 10 million actual tons of ore at a cost of between $3 and $4 per ton, depending on the ground rules set for capital charges; this is equivalent to 4 or 5 mills per ton-km. Attractive though such figures might at first sight appear, it must be remembered that the number of mines producing 10 million tons of concentrated ore per year is very limited indeed. But even if there were more mines of that size, these are rates that can quite easily be met by a modern railway system. Moreover, since in most circumstances the capacity of many railways is seriously underutilized, it is very much in their interest to offer rates attractive enough to capture additional traffic that might otherwise go to a pipeline facility.

The prospects for ore pipelines are also limited by the fact that when new ore deposits are being opened up for exploitation in the developing world, the host government will generally be inclined to favor a railway rather than a pipeline in the hope that the former might help to stimulate other economic developments. While it is not uncommon for proposals to be made for the construction of iron ore pipelines (such as the 640-km pipeline of 15.25-cm diameter suggested to carry 1 million actual tons of ore annually from the Peace River region of Canada to the west coast, or the 460-km pipeline proposed to carry 4 million actual tons of ore from Minas Gerais to Rio de Janeiro), the advantages of the Tasmanian situation would appear to be the exception rather than the rule. As a consequence, unless there are major developments in the ocean transport of ore slurry, it appears unlikely that pipelines will make anything other than a small contribution to the overall pattern of medium- and long-distance ore transport in the foreseeable future.

Like pipelines, the overhead cable with buckets and the conveyor belt are continuous means of transport. Both are efficient and competitive for the movement of ore under special circumstances. They are particularly valuable for the transfer of ore over short distances. For example, ore is moved from the mines of Lorraine to the blast furnaces at Jœuf by overhead bucket conveyors; at Wabana (Newfoundland), the Dominion Steel and Coal Corporation uses a trans-island belt conveyor to move beneficiated ore nearly 3 km from stockpiles to the dock area; and at the Texada mines in western Canada the ore, after concentration, is transferred by a short conveyor belt to ships at the docks. The cost of these movements—perhaps 25 to 50 cents per actual ton—is quite low, but their wider use over distances longer than, say, 15 km would appear to be most unlikely. A major disadvantage of both pipelines and conveyors, even for short-distance ore movements, is their route inflexibility. Once aligned between two points, they are costly or impossible to move.

In contrast, road transport has considerable route flexibility. For this reason it is frequently used to transport ore within opencast mining complexes, between the (moving) mining face and the screening and beneficiating facilities. Moreover, the simplicity of handling ore in lorries and trailers means that they have relatively low loading and unloading costs. Thus, where the distance for ore shipment is short, and where terminal charges would normally represent a large percentage of the total costs of a transport operation, a strong case often exists for the use of road haulage. The linehaul costs of road transport are, however, very high. Dubnie (1962, p. 77) records that the cost of transport in northern Canada by diesel vehicles of 10 to 20 tons capacity is 20 to 60 mills per actual-ton-km. These costs might be lowered slightly with year-round operations in more accessible locations and through use of larger trucks and trailers. By 1965 some trucks had a capacity of 100 or even 160 tons. But over more than 20 or 30 km, the more rapid decline in the ton-km costs of alternative media made road transport generally unattractive.

The exploitation of the main iron ore resource at Marcona in Peru illustrates a conventional application of modern road-haulage technology. The deposits are only about 2 km from the port of San Nicolás, but the difference in elevation is 600 meters, and therefore the annual production of 4 million actual tons of ore is initially hauled 7 km by road in 60- to 80-ton truck trailers to a conveyor belt, which then carries the ore 2,424 meters downhill to storage bins. Until 1967 trucks were used to haul the ore from the bins over a final 7-km journey to San Nicolás, and over the 17-km journey to the alternative port at San Juan. But in that year the San Nicolás leg of the final haul was replaced by a conveyor system capable of handling 2,000 tons of ore per hour. The use of road transport to move ore 85 km from the other major Peruvian deposit at Acari to San Juan must be regarded as somewhat exceptional; negotiating singularly mountainous terrain, it is clearly a response to distinctive local transport opportunities and costs.

As a consequence of the rapid advances and the falling costs of ore transport between 1950 and 1965, the geographical distance between blast furnaces and the mines that feed them has become progressively less important. The quality, the speed, the capacity, and the cost of the transport links between them, on the other hand, have assumed a new role in the economic geography of the iron ore industry. Due to the rapid strides made in ocean transport and the extraordinary declines in ocean freight rates, iron ore deposits and mines situated fairly close to deepwater port facilities have been given a new competitive advantage over ores dependent on either inland water transport or long rail hauls to reach their markets. This is but one aspect of the changing assessments made of the worth of particular ore resources during the period under review. Some of the other aspects are discussed in the next chapter.

CHAPTER 11

A New Resource Base

CHALLENGE AND RESPONSE

In the years immediately following World War II—quite apart from the shortage of ore-producing capacity in many parts of the world resulting from a failure to provide or renew the necessary mining and transport investment during the hostilities—there was a growing sense of the inadequacy of existing ore resources. This was especially true in North America and Western Europe, where serious questions were being raised about the future ore supplies for a steadily expanding iron and steel industry. In 1950, for example, the U.S. Bureau of Mines suggested that the American iron and steel industry could well be faced with a shortage of ore within twenty years, and that it would have to hold back production unless alternative supplies could be found. During the war the Lake Superior district, the main source of supply for American blast furnaces, had yielded some 340 million actual tons of its richest and most easily worked ores, and, with the rate of exploitation quickening, it was clear that they would not last indefinitely.

In partial response to this situation, U.S. iron and steel manufacturers began to import ore for the first time on a considerable scale. They began to buy from some of the traditional suppliers to the Western European market, such as Sweden and North Africa. The consequent shortage of mining capacity at those deposits caused a rise in prices and a degree of alarm in Western European steelmaking circles. Percival (1959), in retrospect, coolly averred that these purely local and temporary changes gave rise to fears of a world shortage of iron ore, but that there was no basis for apprehension. However, during the previous decade these fears were seriously considered and widely expressed. Pounds (1963, p. 34) more accurately reflected the mood of the fifties when he observed that "there is, locally at least, a shortage of ore in the world today, and it is certain that future generations will face a real scarcity."

227

One United Nations estimate of the world resources of contained iron ore, published in 1950 on the available evidence, put probable reserves at 27 thousand million tons (Table 59). Just under 10 percent were in North America. The United States had reserves of 1.7 thousand million tons. Its blast furnaces consumed well over 50 million tons each year, and, with their demands steadily increasing, the reserves appeared to be only slightly above the minimum level of twenty-five to thirty years' supply, which most iron and steel producers sought to have available if they owned their own iron ore mines. The reserves of Western and Middle Europe were more substantial at 5.6 thousand million tons. Swedish reserves, at 1.4 thousand million tons, were considerable, but not so large as the French reserves, which, at 2.5 thousand million tons, represented over 45 percent of the

TABLE 59. WORLD IRON ORE RESERVES, BY REGIONS AND SELECTED COUNTRIES, 1950 ESTI-
MATE

(*Millions of contained tons*)

Region and country	Reserves	Potential reserves
World	26,719	102,119
North America	2,640	25,069
Canada	930	1,291
U.S.A.	1,710	23,778
Western and Eastern Europe	5,562	3,771
Britain	672	246
France	2,546	1,330
West Germany	256	584
Spain	360	270
Sweden	1,408	194
Yugoslavia	26	172
Poland	21	40
U.S.S.R.	2,027	2,318
Asia	6,988	5,936
China	810	405
India	5,608	4,664
Indonesia	49	671
Japan		38
Oceania	130	86
Australia	126	72
Latin America	5,763	11,327
Argentina		32
Brazil	4,095	6,712
Chile	43	109
Cuba	1,200	4,200
Mexico	189	
Venezuela	216	274
Africa	3,609	53,612
Algeria	44	
Rhodesia	1,142	49,529
South Africa	1,275	3,814

Source: United Nations, 1950-A.

region's total. Even larger reserves, according to this 1950 estimate, were to be found in Asia and Latin America. India had 5.6 thousand million tons, and Brazil 4.1 thousand million. The total reserves of Asia, Africa, and Latin America came to 16.4 thousand million contained tons—over 60 percent of the world total—but it was by no means clear how these reserves could be economically exploited for the North American and Western European iron and steel industries, which needed them most.

Two of the responses to the fears about the adequacy of iron ore reserves have already been discussed—namely, the development of techniques that would allow the economic use of ores previously unacceptable in the blast furnace (see Chapter 8), and the improvement of transport to reduce the costs of long-distance ore movements (see Chapters 9 and 10). There was a third and equally important response in the form of a vigorous search for new sources of ore. During the middle and late forties, the iron and steel industries of both the United States and Western Europe embarked on a major exploration program overseas to ensure the future adequacy of their ore supplies. That program took their geologists into Canada and Latin America, into Africa and Asia. Their effort, aided by new mineral exploration technologies, such as the airborne magnetometer, gradually reaped a lush harvest. A large number of either new or newly proved ore deposits were mapped out, initially on both sides of the North and South Atlantic and later further afield.

It was natural that those reserves fairly close to their prospective markets (close in the sense of transport costs rather than geographical space) should attract the lion's share of investment in the first instance. El Pao, the Bethlehem Steel Corporation's mine in Venezuela, started shipping ore in 1951; the Bomi Hills deposit in Liberia was opened up in the same year; 1953 saw the start of production at Conakry in Guinea and by the Marcona Company in Peru; the United States Steel Corporation opened its Cerro Bolívar mine in Venezuela in 1954; and the new Schefferville mine near the Quebec-Labrador border started up production a few months later. In fact, the American and Western European geologists discovered ore deposits far in excess of their nations' requirements. Huge ore sources in Bolivia and Gabon, for example, were proved, but their relative inaccessibility precluded immediate development. In the case of Gabon, the Société Anonyme des Mines de Fer de Mékambo (an American, French, German, Belgian, Italian, and Dutch consortium) drew up plans to mine annually 10 million actual tons of ore and to pelletize 2 million actual tons from the Belinga deposit, but the project remained "under consideration" until market conditions improved and the construction of port facilities and a 560-km railway could yield a reasonable return on any capital invested.

All other things being equal, iron and steel producers prefer to rely on domestic rather than foreign ores when the former are available. It was therefore logical that steelmakers with unexplored terrain, especially the larger new producers, should embark on major domestic ore exploration programs. By far the most successful quantitatively was the U.S.S.R. (see Table 62). Although only a limited contemporary economic significance could be accorded to many of the deposits found in the more remote parts of the country, there were enough accessible deposits to satisfy the needs of Russia's rapidly growing steel industry, to meet most of the requirements of the Middle European industries, and (by the end of the period) to offer ore for sale on the world market. China and India also explored for, and succeeded in finding, additional domestic supplies of ore for their expanding iron and steel industries. With reserves well in excess of its domestic requirements, India embarked on a vigorous export program.

On top of these developments were the efforts of the developing countries to exploit their natural resources in their search for economic growth. Providing both nonagricultural employment and a source of foreign exchange earnings, mining developments were looked upon favorably by many of these countries. Their governments sought to marshal capital from all available sources—domestic and foreign, public and private—in order to ascertain the extent of their iron ore (and other mineral) wealth. They proceeded to encourage the more detailed prospecting of any finds and the later mining developments. Not infrequently, the United Nations and its development agencies gave technical assistance as well as capital loans for the exploitation process. Liberia provides one example of the leading role which national governments in the developing countries can play, for, with the establishment of the Bureau of Natural Resources and Surveys in 1948, a quickening interest in the country's mineral resources was assured. Its policy was to provide mining companies with preliminary geological information on individual deposits of likely economic interest, and to encourage the investment of capital in prospecting for and developing the country's ore resources. In Swaziland the government's Geological Survey proved the existence of high-grade ore deposits in commercial quantities. This led first to an interest in the deposits by the Anglo-American Corporation of South Africa, which set about proving the ore body. Subsequently, in 1958, the Swaziland Iron Ore Development Company was formed, with financial backing by Anglo-American, the British Guest Keen and Nettlefold Company, and the Commonwealth Development Corporation.

Both the technological advances and economic changes in ore preparation and transport—plus the efforts made by the traditional iron and steel producers, the new iron and steelmaking countries, and the developing world to discover and exploit new deposits—created a new outlook for iron ore resources. Within a few years, estimates of reserves were revised upward. The 1950 United Nations estimate, it will be recalled, was 27 thousand million contained tons. The *Survey of World Iron Ore Resources*, published by the United Nations in 1955 (one of the most thorough studies of the subject), raised the estimate of what were termed "resources" to 42 thousand million contained tons. Within another four years, Percival (1959) increased the United Nations total by a factor of three, by adding data on the additional reserves that were by then known to exist in the Soviet Union and West Africa, and—most important of all—by including the low-grade taconites of North America. By 1959 these ores had become widely recognized as being suitable for economic beneficiation and agglomeration; they were already being used on a small scale by the U.S. iron and steel industry. Thus the size of the world's ore reserves in 1959, according to Percival, was 132 thousand million contained tons, nearly five times the 1950 figure.

As new ore deposits continued to be found in the sixties, from the Yukon Territory to Uruguay, and from the Ukraine to Angola, it was clearly necessary to continue amending any estimate of reserves upward. However, in a survey of world ore resources made by the United Nations in 1966 (United Nations, 1968-A), although the actual tonnage of reserves was put at 256 thousand million tons, the iron content of those ores was put at no more than 114 thousand million tons (see Table 62). Such a surprising downturn in the estimates of world ore reserves, during a period when new discoveries and technological advances were apparently adding lavishly to the ore deposits at man's disposal, throws doubts on whether those concerned with the surveys at different times were agreed on a definition of what constitutes an iron ore reserve. It is to this question that we now turn.

ESTIMATING THE RESOURCE BASE

While somewhere between 4 and 5 percent of the earth's crust is composed of iron, only occasionally can pure metallic iron be found in nature. Usually, iron is found in combination with oxygen and smaller quantities of phosphorus, silica, chrome, nickel, alumina, and other substances. The ores of iron, in terms of their iron content, their chemistry, and their physical structure, exhibit a considerable variety. For the iron and steel industry, the cheapest to reduce to pig iron are generally the *magnetites* (Fe_3O_4), some of which contain nearly 70 percent of metallic iron (pure magnetite contains 72.3 percent metallic iron and 27.7 percent oxygen). Almost equally attractive are the *hematites* (Fe_2O_3), which in their purest form comprise 70 percent metallic iron, but which are more usually found with a slightly lower iron content. The *limonites* ($2Fe_2O_3 \cdot 3H_2O$), or brown ores, are a hydrated form of hematite ore; in addition to their somewhat lower metallic iron content, usually around 60 percent, they have rather more variable composition than the hematites. Even lower in iron content are the *siderites* ($FeCO_3$), which are a carbonate of iron and contain at the most 48 percent metallic iron. There are in addition other types of ore, such as *ilmenite* ($FeO \cdot TiO_2$), *iron pyrites* (FeS_2), *chamosite*, and certain *laterites;* but the commercial significance of these ores is relatively small (United Nations, 1955).

In any assessment of the commercial value of an ore, the percentage of metallic iron contained within it is an important matter. *Ceteris paribus*, those ores with a relatively low percentage of iron demand the application of more energy per actual ton of ore in either a blast furnace or a preparation plant—in order to separate them from the gangue—than do higher-grade deposits. The cost of preparing and smelting a hard and cherty rock in which grains of magnetite and hematite are disseminated—a rock such as the taconites found in Minnesota, which has an iron content varying between 25 and 35 percent Fe—is much higher than the cost of preparing and smelting, say, a lumpy Brazilian ore from Minas Gerais with an iron content of 68.5 percent.

The metallic content of an ore is by no means the sole criterion of its worth. Its physical structure (or texture) and chemical composition are important as well.

The *physical structure* of an ideal ore would be evenly sized so as to give ample interspaces for an effective flow of hot reducing gases in the blast furnace; at the same time the pieces of ore must be small enough to maximize the surface area they present to the attack of those gases. If in addition the ore is porous, so much the better. The parent rocks of an ore also affect its value. Some of them make an ore particularly difficult to win. They are hard and demand blasting and crushing before they can be used in a preparation plant or blast furnace. The ores of Cockatoo Island and Kooland Island in Yampi Sound, Western Australia, are of this variety. Other ores, by contrast, are found in a somewhat earthy and granular form; they can easily be removed from their source with simple excavating equipment. However, although the actual mining operations for such ores are inexpensive, their friable nature prevents them from being used directly in the blast furnace, since they would either block the flow of gases or blow out of the top. Only with sintering can such ores be made suitable for pig iron production.

The other aspect of ore quality is its *chemical composition*—in particular, the quantity and range of its "impurities." Silica and alumina, magnesia and lime, sulfur and phosphorus, vanadium, zinc, copper, and arsenic are all found in varying quantities in the ores of iron. Most of them have to be removed in order to produce a pig iron and steel of an acceptable quality. The method of removal is either by oxidizing the impurities and removing them with the exhaust gases or by producing in the blast furnace a slag whose chemical properties can be carefully controlled (see Chapter 3). Sulfur, for example, is oxidized into sulfur dioxide and lost into the atmosphere. Silica and alumina are removed by the addition of lime, which fuses with them to form a slag, which in turn separates out from the iron. But the oxidization of impurities and the production of a molten slag require a great deal of heat, and for this reason the fewer the impurities found in an ore, the cheaper it is to reduce the ore to pig iron. The extent to which these minerals and elements have to be removed depends on the use to which the pig iron and steel are to be put. For the manufacture of fine castings, a large quantity of phosphorus is desirable, since it gives the iron a fluid quality. And foundry iron can be rich in silicon. Generally speaking, however, ores that are low in phosphorus, silica, alumina, and sulfur are at a premium on the market; those with large proportions of these "impurities" bring a lower price. Some sample analyses of marketable iron ores are given in Table 60.

In sum, "The grade of the ore is far from being the only factor of importance in assessing the value of an ore. Its physical texture and the nature and proportion of all the slag-making constituents are of vital importance. It is they which so often make it necessary for a country rich in ore to import others for blending purposes" (Pounds, 1963, p. 37).

Of equal importance in the evaluation of an ore body are judgments concerning the implications of its size and location. As was pointed out in Chapter 8, small deposits of ore, regardless of their iron content, are of little interest to a modern mining concern anxious to exploit the economies of large-scale mining, preparation, and transport of ore. Inaccessible deposits, on the other hand, pose problems to the large and small mining

TABLE 60. SOME IRON ORE ANALYSES, 1965

Source	Iron	Phosphorus	Silica	Manganese	Alumina	Lime	Magnesia	Sulfur
Mesabi Range, U.S.A. (St. Paul)	52.00%	0.060%	7.50%	0.68%	1.53%	0.18%	0.19%	0.020%
Old Range (Marquette), U.S.A. (Mather)	54.62	0.091	6.70	0.32	2.31	0.24	0.50	0.014
Marquette Range, U.S.A. (Empire pellets)	63.24	0.010	7.74	0.08	0.31	0.24	0.31	0.003
Michipicoten District, Canada (Algoma sinter)	50.20	0.010	11.23	2.80	1.93	3.66	7.44	0.100
Itabira District, Brazil (Lump ore)	68.38	0.025	0.35	0.04	0.62	Trace	Trace	0.012
Nimba, Liberia	66.80	0.044	2.00		0.89			0.005
Kiruna D, Sweden	59.80	1.500	4.58	1.15	0.83	5.28	0.09	0.045

Sources: Cleveland-Cliffs Iron Company, Cliffs Iron Ore Analysis; United Nations, 1968-A.

concern alike; often they have little more than a cartographic value. The huge and easily beneficiated Bolivian deposits of Lake Superior–type ore (53 % Fe) were discovered as early as 1826, but since they are located some 2,000 km from the Latin American coastline or any industrial center of significance, their estimated 21 thousand million contained tons of ore have no contemporary worth and are unlikely to offer possibilities of exploitation for some time to come. Whether these ores can legitimately be regarded as reserves for the world iron and steel industry is a moot point.

Had such a size and quality of ore body been located in Britain or West Germany, there can be little doubt that it would have been extensively exploited, and that any untapped ores would have been rightly classified as reserves. Had it been located in France, the Minette ores of Lorraine might not have become so famous or, indeed, been worked at all. Contariwise, if South Africa and India had not possessed large deposits of high-grade ore, the former might today be mining and beneficiating its large deposits of banded hematite-quartzites, and India would probably be crushing and concentrating its magnetite-quartz rocks in Madras (as do the ore miners of Sydvananger in Norway).

On what grounds should an ore body be classified as a reserve? With almost identical ores being given different evaluations by the steel and mining industries in different places and at different times—evaluations that change with new mining and steelmaking technologies, with movements in transport costs, and with shifts in the geography of ore demand and supply—it is clear that some recognition of these variables should be built into any evaluation of an ore deposit's worth. This, however, is no simple matter, since there are inherent limitations to the accuracy with which the many factors influencing the present and future value of an ore field can be quantified. In resource appraisals, there are geological, economic, technological, and political indeterminates that cannot properly be ignored.

The geological aspects of an ore appraisal must rest on a series of plausible assumptions concerning the underground geology of the district containing a deposit. Some of these assumptions are liable to be proved inaccurate in the event of fuller exploration and prospecting. However skillfully a geologist performs his task in estimating iron ore reserves, even from a purely geological viewpoint, at the end of his search only a rough estimate qualified by many uncertainties can possibly be produced. Certainly the margin of error inherent in a preliminary geological investigation is too great for a mining company, which will always insist on a series of mining tests and more positive information before it commits itself to an investment in mining plant, transport facilities, and the like.

Such tests are costly, and since they can only be justified by the intention of a mining company to initiate exploitation, any broad geological estimation of iron ore reserves in a country or continent must be made without them.

The purely economic component of an appraisal suffers from much the same problems and even more. Existing economic conditions provide at least one reasonably accurate bench mark for resource assessment. Granted a particular set of market prices for particular types of ore, and granted an existing pattern of iron ore freight rates, it is possible to suggest the range of prices that the ore will command at the mine, and hence the maximum level of costs if the venture is to show some profit. But such a set of costs could only be reasonably produced after a detailed mining test. At this point the economist is confronted with much the same type of problem as the geologist. In addition, it would be unrealistic for an economic evaluation of an ore body to be based solely on contemporary economic conditions. A series of judgments must therefore be made concerning the future growth of ore demands, the development of supply, the trend in prices, and the movements in freight rates, in order to estimate the prospective markets of a particular deposit (see the discussion of this aspect in Part III). The precision of such forecasts and the accuracy of resource appraisals from an economic viewpoint are obviously limited.

Closely related to the economic factor are the indeterminates presented by changing technology. On the demand side, technological changes can cause a revision to be made of the worth of particular ores. For example, the worldwide growth in the popularity of L.D. oxygen steelmaking has considerably reduced the prospective demand for Swedish high-phosphorus ores. Although the future of a substantial Swedish iron ore industry would seem to be assured, its prospects are by no means as unclouded as they were in the heyday of open-hearth steelmaking. On the supply side, technological progress in beneficiation and transport can alter the competitive position of particular ore deposits in particular markets. Suggestions that taconite should be pelletized for the U.S. Midwest market, and that large quantities of Brazilian ore should be shipped the 21,000 km to Japan, would have been received with not a little skepticism in 1950. The problems of assessing the resource implications of future technological changes are legion, and they are matched by political uncertainties.

Canberra's decision to allow the export of ore from Western Australia could not have been anticipated in the mid-fifties, yet its effect on resource assessments elsewhere has been considerable. Again, should both the U.S.S.R. and China elect in the future to sell large quantities of low-priced ore in Western Europe and Japan (and should their offers be accepted), the worth of the iron ore reserves of, say, Brazil and West Africa would be adversely affected. Certainly, such an occurrence would diminish the already faint prospect of the Mékambo ore project coming to early fruition, and hence would demand some reassessment of Gabon's contribution to the ore reserves of the world. Whether the U.S.S.R. and China will opt for such a trading strategy is of course uncertain. At root it is a political matter, although the decision could also be influenced by foreign exchange considerations.

Not only must a realistic evaluation of iron ore resources relate to a reasonably articulate set of market circumstances in time and place—circumstances defined within an intricate system of economic, technological, and political constraints—but it must also recognize the indeterminates of resource appraisal by acknowledging the varying degrees of accuracy with which the worth of individual ore bodies can be measured. This implies the need for a taxonomy of resources, which in fact the earliest resource appraisals did have. Their categories, however, reflected primarily the interests of geologists and mining engineers, who were basically concerned in such studies with underscoring the indeterminate nature of much of the world's underground geology. The terms used to describe ore reserves in the early appraisals—terms such as "proved," "probable," and "possible" (Leith, 1938, pp. 47, 48)—clearly reflect this emphasis. Therefore the suggestion of Blondel and Lasky (United Nations, 1955, p. 169 ff.), that the term "reserves" should be applied solely to those deposits that appear capable of being profitably exploited under existing economic conditions, represented a distinct conceptual advance, even though they failed to stress the equally important technological and political constraints in resource appraisal.

Iron ore "reserves," then, can be defined as those ore bodies that are judged to be suitable for profitable exploitation under existing economic, technical, and political conditions. And those other deposits that appear to be capable of profitable development only if the conditions change (for example, if costs become lower or prices are raised) can be classified separately as "potential reserves." In addition, each of these two categories can be subdivided. Of the reserves of ore, it is useful to distinguish between deposits whose size has been carefully "measured" and deposits whose size has been "inferred" from less precise evidence. Similarly, there is a case for distinguishing between potential reserves that are marginal and those that are submarginal. The former can be defined as deposits that appear to be capable of profitable exploitation with a slight (say, 10%) increase in ore prices or a small (say, 10%) fall in production and distribution costs. Submarginal deposits, however, would only be exploited following a substantial change in market and other conditions. They are nevertheless judged to be rather more valuable than those potential resources that are the least attractive ore bodies remaining in the world's resource base (Figure 13). Some of the definitions within this broad taxonomy may lack precision, yet they usefully stress both the need to appraise ore resources within their economic-technical-political system and the differing degrees of accuracy with which they can in fact be measured.

The practicability of adopting such a taxonomy in resource appraisals depends largely on the scale of the review. At the local and regional level, and perhaps at some national levels, its application appears to be perfectly feasible. But at the world scale (even assuming a static market framework), such a degree of detail is out of the question, however loosely the categories are defined. The size of the task, to say nothing of the survey costs, makes such an approach impossible. In answer to global questions, therefore, much more generalized resource evaluations have to suffice, but they must be interpreted with great caution. An examination of the several attempts in recent years to measure the world's resources of iron ore reveals that they all lack rigorous definitions of the terms used, especially the word reserves. Hence the disparity between results, as noted earlier.

The one noteworthy (yet still only partial) exception is a study that was conducted by Arthur D. Little, Inc. (Hyde *et al.*, 1962), in which an attempt was made to determine the iron ore reserves of the world on the basis of narrow yet explicit criteria. The researchers sought to establish from secondary sources the world pattern of iron-bearing materials that could be used at the time of their study and in the foreseeable future (defined as thirty years), under current and expected cost and market price conditions, and assuming no demand limitations for iron and steel. They were simply interested in reserves of ore, and they neglected the potential reserves (as defined in a preceding paragraph). They concluded that there were 71 thousand million tons of contained ore immediately available to

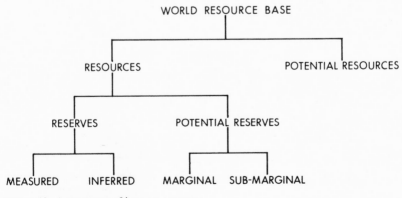

FIGURE 13. A taxonomy of iron ore resources.

the world iron and steel industry. Of this, the reserves of the U.S.S.R. (14.8 thousand million), Brazil (10.3 thousand million), India (9.9 thousand million), and the United States (8.6 thousand million) were outstanding, while Canada, China, and France each had reserves of between 4 and 5 thousand million tons (Table 61).

The strength of the Arthur D. Little appraisal lies in its clear recognition of economic and technical, as well as geological, considerations in the estimation of reserves. It also recognized that what constitutes an ore varies not only with time but also from place to place. And it displayed an independence of judgment in interpreting the evidence available on particular national and regional iron ore deposits, before deciding on the most realistic reserve estimate.

TABLE 61. WORLD IRON ORE RESOURCES, 1962 ESTIMATE

Region and country	Millions of contained tons	Region and country	Millions of contained tons
WORLD	71,169	Hong Kong	4
NORTH AMERICA	13,162	India	9,949
Canada	4,566	Indonesia	8
U.S.A.	8,596	Japan	24
WESTERN EUROPE	10,126	Malaysia	29
EEC	5,649	Philippines	19
France	4,062	Thailand	13
Italy	39	OCEANIA	1,208
Luxembourg	81	Australia	1,208
West Germany	1,467	LATIN AMERICA	12,129
Austria	115	Argentina	84
Britain	1,001	Brazil	10,285
Finland	152	Chile	287
Greece	80	Colombia	48
Norway	504	Mexico	150
Spain	578	Peru	332
Sweden	1,901	Venezuela	939
Switzerland	20	Others	4
Turkey	36	AFRICA AND MIDDLE EAST	4,063
Yugoslavia	90	Algeria	76
EASTERN EUROPE	15,249	Angola	197
Middle Europe	432	Egypt	83
Bulgaria	94	Cameroons	40
Czechoslovakia	79	Gabon	378
Eastern Germany	12	Guinea	1,430
Hungary	10	Ivory Coast	130
Poland	184	Iran	34
Romania	53	Israel	5
U.S.S.R.	14,817	Liberia	343
ASIA	15,236	Mauretania	95
Communist Asia	5,173	Morocco	92
China	4,679	Rhodesia	126
North Korea	427	Sierra Leone	153
North Vietnam	67	South Africa	795
Non-Communist Asia	10,063	Swaziland	64
Burma	17	Tunisia	22

Source: Hyde *et al.*, 1962.

Such an independence of judgment is lacking in all the United Nations appraisals, including the most recent one (1968-A). Having asked the member countries to supply detailed information on their iron ore reserves and to present it in a particular form, the United Nations compilers of the data would have been undiplomatic to challenge too boldly the estimates they received. Yet many of these estimates look remarkably high. This is not to suggest that some of the ores reported do not in fact exist, but rather to propose that it would be most unlikely for the reporting bodies in the member countries to base their judgments of "reserves" and "additional potential reserves" (Table 62) on identical criteria. At the very least, countries whose mines were faced with contracting markets, and possibly even with the cessation of mining activities, would be reluctant to write down the value of their ore fields in an impartial way. At the same time, the temptation for all the ore-exporting countries to overestimate their market prospects, and hence their ore reserves, was naturally quite strong. As a result, many of the ores classified as reserves might more appropriately have been recorded in the category of potential reserves, or even in a third category of submarginal potential reserves. It is not surprising, in such circumstances of partisan resource evaluation, that the 1966 United Nations estimate of world ore reserves is considerably higher than the Arthur D. Little estimate. In fact, it is approximately twice as large (Table 62).

Of the 114 thousand million tons of contained iron ore available to the iron and steel industry according to the United Nations study, by far the largest reserves are located in the U.S.S.R., which has 44.3 thousand million tons; this is one and a half times the size of Brazilian reserves (28.2 thousand million tons) and more than three times the U.S. reserves (12.7 thousand million tons). These three major sources of iron ore reserves are followed in importance by those of Australia, India, and Canada, each of which has only one-tenth of the reserves of the Soviet Union (Figure 14). There were unfortunately no new statistics available for the United Nations study on the Chinese resource position; as a consequence only some 1945 estimates are included in the "potential reserves" figures. Compared with the Arthur D. Little appraisal, the United Nations figures suggest the existence of much larger iron ore reserves throughout the world, and also point to a quite different distribution between countries. The relative importance of Soviet reserves, for example, is much greater in the United Nations appraisal; Brazilian reserves are calculated to be twice as large as those of the United States and not just a little larger; Australian ores assume a major importance for the first time in a world appraisal; and the reserves of India are judged in a rather more conservative light.

Table 62. World Iron Ore Reserves, 1966 Estimate

(*Millions of tons*)

Region and country	Reserves		Additional potential reserves	
	Fe content	Actual tonnage	Fe content	Actual tonnage
WORLD	114,400	256,000	83,000	205,000
NORTH AMERICA	16,900	52,895	28,400	92,970
Canada	4,200	10,970	6,500	19,030
U.S.A.	12,700	41,925	21,900	73,940
WESTERN EUROPE	7,100	20,034	2,200	5,333
EEC	3,200	9,786	400	230
Belgium		8		
France	2,700	8,017		
Italy		36		
Luxembourg	100	225		70
West Germany	400	1,500	400	160
Austria	100	321		
Britain	800	3,162		
Finland		130		
Greece		70		70
Norway	300	740	400	1,280
Portugal	100	312		
Spain	600	1,240	600	1,223
Sweden	1,800	3,370		
Switzerland		70		10
Turkey		178		80
Yugoslavia	200	655	400	1,000
EASTERN EUROPE	44,800	104,417	4,300	14,182
Middle Europe	200	778		
Bulgaria	100	264		
Czechoslovakia		90		140
East Germany		10		
Hungary		20		80
Poland	100	314		167
Romania		80		70
U.S.S.R.	44,600	103,639	4,300	13,725
ASIA	4,300	8,299	16,200	28,602
Communist Asia		452	1,300	2,375
China			1,300	2,275
North Korea		411		
North Vietnam		411		100
Non-Communist Asia	4,300	7,847	14,900	26,227
Burma		10		69
Hong Kong		10		
India	4,200	7,239	12,600	21,300
Japan		90		
Laos			600	1,000
Malaysia		40	500	1,000
Pakistan	100	300		100
Philippines		127	1,200	2,758
South Korea		18		
Taiwan				
Thailand		13		
Others			large*	large*

TABLE 62.—Continued

Region and country	Reserves		Additional potential reserves	
	Fe content	Actual tonnage	Fe content	Actual tonnage
OCEANIA	4,700	8,152	3,600	7,048
Australia	4,400	7,507	3,300	6,500
New Caledonia		100	large	large
New Zealand	300	545	300	548
LATIN AMERICA	30,600	49,767	22,900	42,092
Argentina	100	184		150
Bolivia			11,100	21,000
Brazil	28,200	45,757	9,600	15,557
Chile	400	683	1,000	2,208
Colombia		55		
Cuba				
Mexico	300	572	1,200	3,000
Peru	200	397		
Uruguay		100		77
Venezuela	1,300	2,000	large	large
Central America			large	large
AFRICA AND MIDDLE EAST	6,000	12,606	5,400	13,929
Algeria	100	150	600	995
Angola	100	130		130
Congo			3,200	5,000
Egypt	100	280	100	284
Gabon	600	1,000	large	large
Guinea	100	200	500	2,000
Liberia	300	578	200	397
Libya	200	390	600	1,400
Mauretania	100	150	100	300
Morocco		70	100	105
Nigeria	100	266		
Rhodesia		90	large	large
Sierra Leone		100		100
South Africa	4,300	8,600	large	large
Swaziland		43		105
Tunisia		50		
Zambia		87		60
Others		673	large*	large

Source: United Nations, 1968-A.

Note: Reserves exclude China; potential reserves include 1945 estimates for China.

* Especially Java and New Guinea in Asia; Cameroons and Central African Republic in Africa.

THREE CONCLUSIONS

There is clearly ample room for disagreement concerning the reserves of particular iron ore deposits and hence of the world as a whole. The considerable geological, economic, technological, and political uncertainties inevitably make this so. To attempt a detailed adjudication between the Arthur D. Little and the United Nations surveys would be a major undertaking. However, three broad conclusions can confidently be drawn from these two (and earlier) appraisals of global iron ore resources: (1)

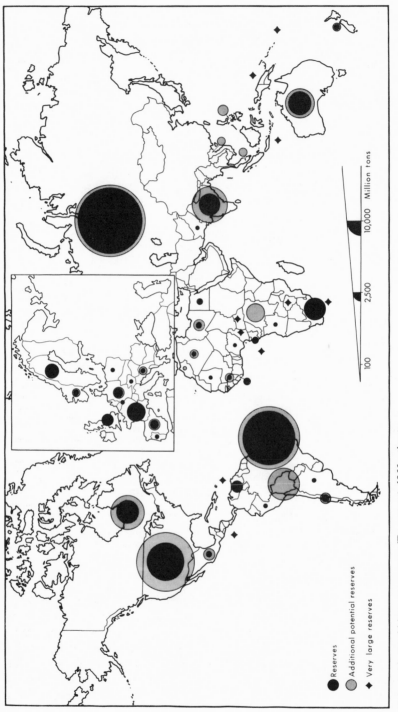

FIGURE 14. World iron ore reserves (Fe content), 1966 estimate.

Reserves
Additional potential reserves
Very large reserves

100   2,500   10,000   Million tons

Over the period 1950 to 1965, despite the ambiguity over the term reserves, the size of the iron ore reserves available to the world's iron and steel industries increased considerably, quite possibly by a factor of three. (2) There was a decisive geographical shift in the pattern of these ore reserves, in particular the huge increments to the reserves of the U.S.S.R. and the declining importance of the iron ore wealth of Western Europe. The United Nations figures also record a decline in the relative importance of Asia's reserves, but this is accounted for largely by the absence of contemporary estimates for China; had they been available, these would undoubtedly have kept that continent's share nearer 20 percent of the world total. (3) By 1965, in spite of the more competitive market conditions and falling prices of ore (see Chapter 12), there were known to exist reserves of ore that could easily satisfy the needs of the iron and steel industry for many years to come. If one takes the low reserve estimate of Arthur D. Little, at the 1965 rate of consumption there were ore reserves available to last over two hundred years. Even granted the prospective rapid growth in iron and steel production and iron ore demands (see Part III)—unlike the situation fifteen years earlier—this could only be regarded as a generous resource base.

CHAPTER 12

Changing Patterns of Iron Ore Supply

The world demand in 1950 for 116 million tons of iron contained in ore (see Chapter 6) was satisfied by the production and transport of 244 million actual tons of marketable ores. Most of them came from mines relatively close to the centers of pig iron production. As was pointed out in Chapter 2, the traditional location of the iron and steel industry was on the site of or near its basic raw materials—iron ore and coking coal. In 1950 the greater part of North American demands for iron ore was still being satisfied from the surface pit workings and underground mines of that continent, and only a small part of the ore consumed in the blast furnaces of Western Europe was being mined outside that region. Nevertheless, some demands for ore were met through international trade, which had developed very slowly as local resources of ore became exhausted, or as their mining costs became too expensive compared with the cost of obtaining distant supplies. When international trade did begin to grow, the relatively high costs of the traditional modes of ore transport restricted it to short distances, such as the haul between Canada and the United States, or between France and West Germany. The major exception was provided by the iron and steel industry of the United States, which from the thirties had developed an efficient bulk transport operation between its works on the east coast and captive ore deposits in Chile. The U.S. industry was also willing to bear the high transport charges on Swedish ore during periods of ore shortage. As the industry's transport arrangements improved, however, and as the location equation swung increasingly in favor of market orientation, the volume of trade in iron ore began to increase rapidly. This was essentially a post-1945 phenomenon. It is to the patterns of the world's iron ore trade and production in 1950 that we first turn.

THE NETWORK OF TRADE AND THE LOCATION OF PRODUCTION IN 1950

World exports of iron ore in 1950 were 21 million tons of contained iron, 42 million tons of actual ore (see Table A-7). These figures are equivalent to 19 and 17 percent of world consumption, respectively. The country importing the largest tonnage of ore was the United States (Figure 15; see also Table A-5), which used just under 5 million contained tons of foreign ore in its blast furnaces. With domestic consumption standing at 53 million contained tons, this import tonnage represented just over 9 percent of the country's needs. The largest shares came from Chile, Sweden, and Canada (see Table A-6), and rather smaller quantities were imported from Brazil, North Africa, and West Africa. To some extent these imports were offset by exports to Canada and Japan, which left the United States as a net importer of only 3.4 million contained tons of iron ore. Canada was also a small net importer in 1950, exchanging 1 million contained tons of exports from the mainly captive mines of the United States' steel corporations for 1.4 million contained tons of Lake Superior ores, which were needed in Canada's own blast furnaces and steel shops. North America as a whole thus had a net import of 3.8 million contained tons of ore.

Western Europe's net imports were much smaller, at 0.6 million contained tons. However, international trade within the region was very vigorous. The constituent countries imported a total of 12 million tons of contained ore. Of this total, Britain took just under 5 million tons. These imports, which were already considerably above Britain's domestic production of 3.8 million contained tons, were used principally in the steelworks of South Wales and Teesside. They came mainly from Sweden, but imports were also shipped in from Algeria, Sierra Leone, Spain, and Morocco in the small tramp vessels that characterized the ore trade of that day.

There were two other large importers in Western Europe. The Benelux countries consumed 3.4 million contained tons of foreign ore, and West Germany imported 2.9 million. These imports represented just over 80 and 50 percent, respectively, of consumption in the two areas. Part of the Benelux imports came from the nearby Minette fields of France, but Swedish and North African ores were also favored. The West German imports were dominated by Swedish supplies, with Spanish and North African shipments playing a subsidiary role. A significant destination of ore imports into Western Europe in 1950 was the Netherlands, which, without home supplies, relied entirely on imports and received most of its 0.4 million contained tons from Sweden. Out of a total Western European consumption of 29 million tons of contained ore in 1950, imports represented more than 40 percent. Sweden and France were the largest suppliers, and two North African countries—Sierra Leone and Spain—shipped in additional quantities.

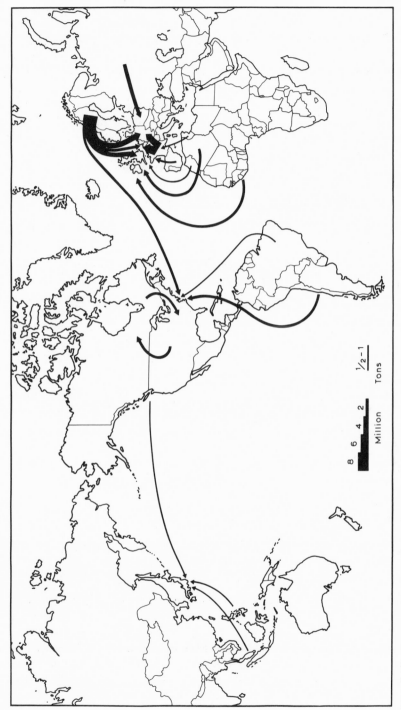

FIGURE 15. World trade in iron ore (Fe content), 1950.

Eastern Europe was essentially a closed economy in 1950, yet its net imports of iron ore, at 1.4 million contained tons, were more than twice those of Western Europe. Its total trade activity on the other hand was on a rather smaller scale. The main flow of ore was from the U.S.S.R. to the countries of Middle Europe. Czechoslovakia and Poland in particular were deficient in ore supplies and imported over 1 million contained tons each. More than half of these imports were transported from the mines of the Soviet Union. Their other major supplier was Sweden.

In Asia, the only ore importer of any significance was Japan. With limited domestic resources of iron ore, the Japanese iron and steel industry imported over 60 percent of its needs, mainly from the Philippines and Malaya.

By far the largest exporter of iron ore in 1950 was Sweden (see Table A-7), with foreign shipments of 7.9 million contained tons. France's exports, in terms of their iron content, came a poor second at 2.4 million tons, although the actual tonnage of ore exported was as high as 7.5 million tons, consequent upon its very low grade. The U.S.S.R., Chile, the United States, Canada, and Algeria, all exported between 1 and 2 million tons of contained ore. This pattern of exports contributed to, but certainly did not dominate, the geography of iron ore production, for 81 percent of the world demand for iron ore was satisfied by domestic mining operations.

Out of a total world production of 116 million contained tons in 1950, some 44 percent was won from the mines of North America. With Canadian output a mere 2 million contained tons, the industry was dominated by activities in the United States, which had the largest iron ore mining industry in the world and produced 49 million contained tons in that year (see Fig. 18 and Tables 72 and A-8). Approximately 80 percent of this ore originated in the ranges of the Lake Superior region, among which the Mesabi was by far the most important. By the standards of the day, this ore, averaging 51 percent Fe, was a reasonably good grade; it was won from both open-pit and more expensive underground mines (see Table 31). Exploiting scale economies of production in an unparalleled way, the industry could boast both low unit costs in winning the ores (mainly direct-shipping ores) and a highly efficient pattern of lake and rail transport to carry its products to the blast furnaces of the Midwest and the Appalachians. The other domestic sources of iron ore for the American iron and steel industry were the relatively small deposits of New York State and Pennsylvania and the very low grade (35% Fe) oolitic fields of the southern Appalachians, which were used by the Birmingham industry. The blast furnaces of the Mountain States and the Far West were served by local ore mines, although in the case of Kaiser's Fontana plant these were 260 km away in the Colorado Desert of California.

This geography of iron ore supply, forged essentially during the first half of the twentieth century, was showing signs of impermanence. The industry was aware of the gradual exhaustion of the Mesabi deposits, and (though it increasingly beneficiated the direct-shipping ores by simple processes) it was highly skeptical of the economics of beneficiating the low-grade taconites and jasperites known to abound in the region. The next decade presented no problems, but the Paley Commission (United States, President's Materials Policy Commission, 1952, p. 14) reflected informed opinion when it concluded that "a serious long-run problem confronts all the mills now served by Lake Superior ore. . . . On the whole, the steel industry in the United States must depend increasingly upon deposits of lower grades around Lake Superior and upon imports from Canada and overseas for future additions to its supply of ore." With nearly four-fifths of the country's blast-furnace capacity located between the Allegheny Mountains and the Mississippi River north of the Ohio, the Commission looked in particular toward Canada for a solution to the long-term ore supply problem.

In 1950 about one-quarter of the world's iron ore was produced in Western Europe, where the largest output came from the mines of France, which yielded nearly 10 million contained tons, making the country the world's third-largest producer. Most of the ore came from the low-grade (28 to 32% Fe) Minette field of Lorraine, where the underground mines served mainly local blast furnaces. The rest of the ore, because of its inevitably high ton-kilometer transport costs per unit of iron, did not have much of a "reach" and was consumed in the nearby blast furnaces of Lorraine and the Saar. The only other noteworthy French deposit was in the western part of the country, near Caen, where a 45 percent Fe hematite was mined for the nearby iron and steel industry. The two other producers of the European Economic Community were Luxembourg and West Germany. In the former, an extension of the Minette field was worked to produce 1 million tons of contained ore. The West German output was three times as large; it was based on a relatively poor natural endowment of low-grade and high-phosphorus ore bodies.

Sweden and Britain, ranking fourth and fifth in world output of iron ore, were the other significant producers of Western Europe. Most of the 8 million contained tons of Swedish output came from the iron mountains of Luossavaara and Kiirunavaara (more than 160 km inside the Arctic Circle), whence the high-phosphorus ores were moved by rail to Luleå on the Gulf of Bothnia during the summer months and to Narvik on the Norwegian ice-free coast during the winter, to meet both domestic and overseas demands. The magnitude of these Swedish exports was such that their delivered price to blast furnaces on or near the North Sea became a key element in the Western European ore market. In Britain, the major source of ore production lay to the south and southwest of the Humber River, in the beds of the Jurassic series. There were three distinct fields within that geological belt, all of which yielded low-grade ores averaging about 28 percent Fe and sometimes only 20 percent. Like the ores of Lorraine, the greater part of this 4 million contained tons of British production was consumed in local Lincolnshire and Northamptonshire blast furnaces. The only other significant producer in Western Europe in 1950 was Spain, where the most important mining district was in the northern provinces near the port of Bilbao. There was also some iron ore mining activity in Austria and Yugoslavia.

The world's second-largest ore producer in 1950 was the Soviet Union, with an output of 22 million contained tons. Although it was abundantly endowed with iron ores, the chemical structure of many of the ores presented problems in the blast furnace, and over one-third had to be beneficiated in some way. The highest-quality ores were mined in the largest center of production (accounting for half the country's output), which is located in the great bend of the Dnepr River in the Krivoy Rog district. These mines supplied the local steel industry plus the larger concentration of works some 300 km away on the Donetsk coalfield. Also in the Ukraine was the much smaller Kerch ore deposit in the Crimea. The other large center of production was in the Urals. There, near Magnitogorsk, a high-grade deposit of magnetite served both the local and the Kusbas iron and steel industry. By 1950, however, the quality of this ore was falling and the costs of extraction were rising; consequently, the Soviet planners were looking for a major alternative to the "iron mountain," which had served them well for so long. Elsewhere in the Soviet Union, ore production was quite small.

Only one-quarter of the ore requirements of Middle Europe were mined there. The most richly endowed countries were Czechoslovakia and Poland, but their deposits were essentially low grade and relatively expensive to mine. A small production in Romania, East Germany, and Hungary helped to increase the output of the Middle European countries by just over 1 million contained tons. Eastern Europe as a whole produced 23 million contained tons, approximately 20 percent of the world total.

The rest of the world mined very little iron ore in 1950. The output of Asia, Oceania, Africa, and Latin America was only 11 percent of the world total—an output that was nearly twice the demands of these macroregions. Of the 4 million contained tons of ore mined in Asia, the largest producer was India, with nearly half the total. Many of the ores had a high iron content (61 percent Fe in India proper and 55 percent Fe in the Portuguese colony of Goa in West India). Most of these ores were consumed in domestic furnaces in northeast India. The other large producer was China, where a highly localized iron ore industry served an equally localized pattern of pig iron production; southern Manchuria was the center of both activities. Elsewhere in Asia, the only notable producers were Japan, the Philippines, and Malaya.

In Australia, mining activities were in the hands of the Broken Hill Proprietary Limited, which ensured the country a self-sufficiency of ore with a production of 1.5 million contained tons from the extremely rich deposits of the Middleback Ranges. The growth of domestic demand for ore during the postwar years had sent the steel industry looking for additional supplies, and by 1950 the deposits at Yampi Sound in Western Australia were being developed (although they had yet to yield their first ore). In Latin America, in contrast, production was dominated by overseas demands; its total output was 3.5 million contained tons. The largest producer (for the American market) was Chile, and the mines of Brazil, mainly in Minas Gerais, came a close second. Venezuela produced very little ore in 1950, although in that year the Bethlehem Steel Corporation opened up a new deposit at El Pao to the south of the Orinoco River. In the continent of Africa (apart from the small output of South Africa), iron ore production at 4 million contained tons was primarily in response to foreign needs. The largest producers were in North Africa, where Algeria, Morocco, and Tunisia mined reasonably good quality self-fluxing ores. In West Africa, Sierra Leone stood as the only producer and exporter.

The relative impermanence of this 1950 geography of ore trade and production was all too clear. Some resources were nearing the end of their economic life; others were in the process of being opened up for the first time. Markets were growing and their geography was changing. Technology and political events were not standing still. What could not have been envisaged in 1950 was the radical nature of the changes that were to take place during the following fifteen years. In that period the demand for ore nearly trebled. Production patterns responded, and trade patterns changed. Central to the transformation was a changing geography of the market for iron ore.

THE CHANGING GEOGRAPHY OF THE MARKET

In 1950 one iron ore market was of outstanding importance—the lower lakes market of the Great Lakes in the United States, with Cleveland as its principal market place. Of much lesser importance were the American east coast market centered on Baltimore and the North Sea market with its multiplicity of centers such as Teesside, Rotterdam, and Antwerp. In the Far East, there was the small market of Japan. During the subsequent fifteen years, however, this simple market system was gradually replaced by a much more complex pattern of ore markets, within which four principal centers of demand and three subsidiary ones were outstanding.

In North America, the lower lakes continued to be an important market for ore, with Cleveland still serving as a major market place for both upper lake and Canadian ores moving into the eastern section of the Midwest. However, by 1965, with the westward shift of iron and steel production and in particular its growing concentration around the southern tip of Lake Michigan, Chicago had become an equally important market place for ore —a fact that was not always formally recognized by the industry (see pp. 258–59). An integral part of this lower lakes market region was the much smaller Ontario market for ore. With the Canadian iron and steel industry to some extent drawing its ore down-lake from U.S. mines, as well as relying on domestic resources, and with the Cleveland and Pittsburgh iron and steel industries increasingly using the ores of eastern Canada, the opportunities for any significant variation of ore prices in this Canadian market from those of the lower lakes were very small indeed.

A second major market for ore by the end of the period was on the east coast of the United States. The rapid expansion of iron and steel production in that section of the country meant that the volume of ore imports into the region from overseas grew larger—for both littoral and increasingly extensive inland consumption. The greater part of the ore that was landed at Baltimore and Morrisville originated from captive deposits. Nevertheless, some market prices were negotiated for the east-coast blast furnaces, and these negotiations were an important component in the world geography of ore prices. The extent to which this market region remained distinct from that of the lower lakes is an open question in the absence of accurate and detailed price data. But as imported ores increasingly displaced Mesabi and other domestic ores farther and farther west—a trend assisted by the falling rates for long-distance ore haulage by rail—a closer relationship between the prices charged for ore on the east coast and in the Midwest was being forged. A single market region for the whole "metropolitan belt" was clearly in the making.

Loosely related to both of these market regions (and especially the market of the east coast) was a small and relatively unimportant one on the Gulf of Mexico coast. As the Alabama iron and steel industry substituted richer and cheaper foreign ores for its local ores, and as small quantities of ore moved inland from the Gulf to the blast furnaces of Texas, Missouri, and even Illinois, the industry came to recognize, if not to publish, a distinctive set of ore prices c. & f. Gulf ports—a market region with a potential importance in the future.

Judging by the size of its regular open-market negotiations for ore, possibly the most important market region by 1965 was that located around the North Sea. It was primarily with reference to the state of supply and demand, and hence the price of ore there, that iron ore prices in West Germany, Britain, Belgium, the Netherlands, and to a small extent

France were determined. Within the region, ore prices varied to some extent. Obviously, the price of Swedish or Liberian ore in the Ruhr was higher than the price at Rotterdam or Ijmuiden. And ore prices in Britain were somewhat above those of its European neighbors as a consequence of its inadequate ports and costly shipping arrangements (see Chapter 9). Nevertheless, the North Sea market region had a growing coherence as the steelmakers were brought together through take-overs and amalgamations, as they embarked on joint ore investment projects overseas, and as, toward the end of the period, their transport arrangements were modernized. Geographical price differentials, therefore, tended to narrow.

Within Western Europe, there was a second, but much less important, market for ore in the Mediterranean. The major demand there originated from the iron and steel industry of Italy, which expanded rapidly during the period and was almost entirely dependent on foreign ores. But as Spanish ores became less competitive, as Spain began to import limited quantities of ore from overseas, and as the countries of Middle Europe increased their imports of ore through the Yugoslavian ports in particular, the possibility of a more important market region in the Mediterranean increased.

The fourth (and last) major market was that of Japan. From almost negligible proportions in the early fifties, iron ore consumption in that country increased to over 20 million contained tons in 1965, most of which was imported. The importance of the Japanese market far exceeded the volume of imports moving into that country. Partly because of the rapid rate of growth of demand for iron ore, but also because of the highly aggressive purchasing policies adopted by their iron and steel industry, the Japanese tended to set the pace and the style of change in the ore markets of the world. Faced with exceptionally high raw-material costs at the beginning of the period, the Japanese steel industry systematically set about to ensure a reduction of its raw-material transport costs. By accepting the responsibility and the economies of long-term and large-scale ore purchases, and by skillful bargaining with its suppliers, Japan by 1965 had established for itself a much admired and an almost enviable position.

Paralleling the emergence of this new set of market regions were equally radical changes in associated market supply areas. At the beginning of the period, most iron ore demands were satisfied from relatively "local" mines. These were rarely more than one or two hundred kilometers away on land, and only occasionally more than two or three thousand kilometers away by sea. The lower lakes market region drew its supplies almost entirely from the mines of the upper lakes. The smaller U.S. east coast market region drew partly on local (eastern states) domestic sources and partly on ore imported from overseas. In fact, by drawing imports from as far away as Sweden, Chile, and Brazil, the east coast had the most extensive supply area of all ore markets at the time. Certainly it was larger than the supply area of the North Sea market region, which relied largely on domestic and Swedish supplies, together with small supplementary imports from North and West Africa. And the minute Japanese market in 1950 drew its ores principally from Malaya and the Philippines. Only in the case of Sweden was there any geographical overlap in the supply areas.

By 1965 this pattern of supply areas had been transformed. Each market during the period reached out farther and farther for its supplies of ore. Consequently, a high degree of market supply area overlap was created. As local ore resources became either impoverished or too expensive, as transport rates fell, and as new reserves of ore were discovered and developed far from the major centers of iron and steel production, a new worldwide and interrelated system of supply areas was consolidated. The lower lakes market region, for example, took its ore supplies from eastern Canada and from the upper lakes. The American east coast market region drew upon the same eastern Canadian ore supplies, and in addition reached out to West African sources and to Venezuela, Brazil, and other Latin American countries. The North Sea market supply area also extended to eastern Canada, Latin America, and West Africa, and was being extended even to Western Australia. And the Japanese market supply area reached out the farthest of all, drawing its ores from virtually every continent.

These changes in the spatial expression of the markets for iron ore were naturally reflected in, and in turn influenced by, the geography of iron ore prices. Throughout the fully planned economies (by 1965 they represented well over one-third of the world's demands for iron ore on a contained iron basis), the satisfaction of demands and the allocation of supplies were determined by the decisions of planners, administrators, and managers, with the assistance of a set of administered prices. And in both the market and mixed economies the satisfaction of iron ore demands was strongly molded by the iron and steel industry's complete ownership of some mines and its financial interest in others. Nevertheless, market prices for ore have a significance considerably beyond the tonnages actually bargained. A knowledge of price changes is crucial to an understanding of the shifting geography of supply. It is with the evidence available on the price of ore that the next section is concerned.

THE PRICE OF IRON ORE

Evidence concerning the geographical pattern and historical trends of iron ore prices remains somewhat elusive, though rather fuller in the sixties than in the previous decade. In part, this is because many of the larger sellers and consumers of iron ore prefer to keep their contracts confidential. There are, however, a number of ore producers (especially those with a prime interest in overseas markets) who regularly publish a "price" for their ores on an f.o.b. basis. Some of these prices are more meaningful than others.

The prices of Brazilian ores (f.o.b. Vitória) and Goan ores (f.o.b. Mormugão), for example, are always publicly available. A number of them are shown in Table 63. But since such prices do not refer to a particular market place or region, they have only a limited meaning if the analysis of Chapter 7 is at all correct. If the ores are shipped to several markets (as in the case of Indian, Moroccan, and Venezuelan ores)—markets to which there are different transfer charges and between which there exist different sets of price levels—f.o.b. quotations of this vagueness have little meaning. At best they offer some indication of the value of the ores when these are sold in the exporter's principal market place; at worst they are deceptive; and in most cases they are the price at which negotiations for ore sales might begin but are unlikely to be concluded. A few f.o.b. price quotations are not subject to negotiation. Some mining companies impose rigid export prices on their ores and refuse to negotiate further. Provided the delivered price of the ore is competitive or the ore is in rather short supply, sales will obviously be achieved. But there have been cases (for example, some Canadian companies selling ore in Western Europe) where such an inflexible policy has caused ores to be priced out of markets in which they previously had a secure foothold.

In addition to the highly generalized f.o.b. price quotations, a number of others are specific to particular markets. For example, published f.o.b. quotations for Algerian ore refer to assumed sales in the British market, and f.o.b. quotations for the famous Swedish Kiruna ores are invariably made on the assumption of Rotterdam sales. Some ores are exported to only one market region (this is the case with exports from British Columbia, all of which are shipped to Japan), and it is consequently a simple matter to relate the f.o.b. price to the ore's c. & f. value through the relevant freight rate. F.o.b. quotations in these cases are both precise and useful.

Equally valuable in the search for an understanding of the market price of iron ore has been the growing tendency for large ore producers (particularly in dealing with Japanese buyers) to make public the financial basis of their long-term contracts. In a weakening market, it was obviously in the interest of the Japanese to stress the falling value of ore in this way. Inasmuch as they increasingly insisted on transporting at least part of these purchases in their own vessels, many of the contracts were drawn up and quoted on an f.o.b. basis, usually with existing freight rates to the market being assumed in the bargaining. Should the improving efficiency of the Japanese merchant marine subsequently permit a fall in freight rates, then advantage would accrue to Japan's iron and steel industry in the form of

256   TRENDS IN SUPPLY OF IRON ORE

TABLE 63. SOME PUBLISHED F.O.B. PRICES OF ORE, 1965

Source	Market	Fe content (%)	Dollars/ actual ton	Cents per iron unit
ALGERIA, f.o.b. Bône	Britain	50	7.30	14.60
			7.40	14.80
ANGOLA, f.o.b. Moçâmedes	Japan	64	8.14	12.72
AUSTRALIA				
Cliffs Western Australian Mining Co. (Robe River), f.o.b.				
Cape Preston, pellets (1968)	Japan	63.6	12.03	18.92
Francis Creek, f.o.b. Darwin, r.o.m. (1967)	Japan	62	8.90	14.35
Hamersley (Mt. Tom Price), f.o.b. King Bay, r.o.m.	Japan	62/64		
30 × 6 mm (1966)			9.92	15.75
100 × 6 mm (1966)			9.66	15.33
Fines (1966)			7.68	12.19
Pellets (1968)			11.66	18.51
Mt. Goldsworthy, f.o.b. Port Hedland, r.o.m. (1966)	Japan	61/64	9.86	15.78
Mt. Newman, f.o.b. King Bay, r.o.m. (1969)	Japan	62/64		
30 × 6 mm			9.37	14.87
100 × 6 mm			9.16	14.54
Fines			7.48	11.87
Savage River Consortium (Tasmania), f.o.b. Brickmakers				
Bay, pellets (1967)	Japan	67.5	10.29	15.24
Western Mining Consort, f.o.b. Geraldton, r.o.m. (1966).	Japan	58/60	8.45	14.32
BRAZIL, f.o.b. Vitória, lump (dry)		68.5	10.40	15.18
R.o.m.		67	8.00	12.50
Fines		67	6.10	9.53
F.o.b. Tubarão	Japan			
R.o.m. (1967)	Japan	64/66	8.00	12.31
Fines (1966)	Japan	64/66	5.70	8.77
CANADA				
F.o.b. British Columbia	Japan			
Texada, Magnetite concentrate	Japan	62/64	9.85	15.63
Orecan, Magnetite concentrate	Japan	62	8.75	14.11
F.o.b. Sept Îles, Carol Lake pellets		65	14.30	22.00
CHILE, f.o.b. Cruz Grande	Japan	65	7.26	11.17
FRANCE, f.o.t. Bazailles		32	3.10	9.68
F.o.t. Giraument		32	3.30	10.31
F.o.t. La Mourière		32	3.53	11.03
F.o.t. Minerai de Sègre		52	9.03	17.37
INDIA, f.o.b. Mormugão lump		56	5.05	9.02
		58	5.45	9.40
		60	6.78	11.30
		62	8.49	13.69
Fines		60	4.20	7.00
		62	4.50	7.26
F.o.b. other ports (1965)		65	10.20	15.69
			10.40	16.00
F.o.b. Vizagapatam, Kiriburu ore (1966)	Japan	60/62	5.85	9.59
F.o.b. Paradip, Tomka ore (1967)	Japan	63/65	7.25	11.33
LIBERIA				
F.o.b. Buchanan, Lamco r.o.m.	Japan	63		
(1966)	Japan		6.55	10.40
(1968)	Japan		6.30	10.00
(1969)	Japan		6.11	9.70
MOROCCO, f.o.b. Casablanca, Rif lumpy		62	10.30	16.61
NORTH KOREA, f.o.b. Musan (1967)	Japan	58	7.50	12.93
SWEDEN, f.o.b. Narvik	Rotterdam			
Kiruna D		59	8.40	14.24
Kiruna B		67	9.03	13.48
Pellets		68	14.00	20.59
U.S.S.R., f.o.b. Jllichutsk, Krivoy Rog fines		60.5	4.00	6.61
VENEZUELA, f.o.b. Puerto Ordaz r.o.m. Orinoco		58	7.88	13.59

Sources: *American Metal Market; Metal Bulletin; Metals Week; Japan Metals Daily;* External Trade News Agency (Japan); United Nations, *European Steel Trends;* Canada, Department of Energy, Mines and Resources; American Iron Ore Association.

lower c. & f. prices. Prices bargained in a number of these contracts—for
example, sales by Angolan, Australian, Liberian, and North Korean producers—are shown in Table 63.

Information on ore prices is not only available on an f.o.b. basis, however. For the world's three major markets, it is also possible to obtain
evidence on the c. & f. value of ore transactions. The most famous price
quotation of all, in fact, relates to American and Canadian ores shipped
down the Great Lakes into the lower lakes market. This is the Lake Erie
base price (see Table A-9). It refers to the value of ore delivered to the "rail
of the vessel" of the lake ore carriers docked at the Lake Erie ports. The
price, which is regularly quoted in such American publications as the
Cleveland *Plain Dealer*, *Iron Age*, and *Steel*, is usually established at the
beginning of an ore shipping season and is based on a substantial sale of
ore for delivery during the forthcoming eight months. The first such sale
is often made by the Oliver Iron Mining Division of the United States Steel
Corporation, or by one of the large merchant ore producers such as the
Cleveland-Cliffs Iron Company or the Hanna Mining Company. The 1965
base prices of unscreened ores, assuming an iron content of 51.5 percent,
are shown in Table 64. The difference between the Mesabi and Old Range
ores is one of physical structure, the latter being a hard and coarse ore, the
former being soft and fine. Scales are published for adjusting the base price
if the iron content varies from the 51.5 percent Fe norm, and for premiums
that are payable on low-phosphorus ores (that is, ores with less than 0.045
percent phosphorus).

Discounts are unpublished, but the iron ore trade recognizes that they
are given on base prices for long-term contracts. In fact, most open-market
sales in the United States appear to be long-term contracts of 4 to 5 years

TABLE 64. LAKE ERIE BASE PRICES FOR IRON ORE, 1965

Ores	Dollars per actual ton	Cents per unit
BLAST-FURNACE ORES		
Mesabi non-Bessemer	10.72	20.82
Coarse, 1.27 cm	11.53	22.39
Fine, 1.27 cm	10.26	19.92
Mesabi Bessemer	10.87	21.11
Old Range non-Bessemer	10.97	21.30
Old Range Bessemer	11.13	21.61
High phosphorus	10.82	20.68
Pellets, 63% Fe basis	16.13	25.60
OPEN-HEARTH ORES		
Marquette lump	12.80	24.85
Vermilion coarse lump	13.36	25.94

Sources: Hanna Mining Company; Canada, Department of Energy, Mines and Resources.

and ranging up to 25 years. It is also admitted that spot rates can often be negotiated in the Cleveland market place appreciably below the base prices. Recent information on the difference between actual selling prices and the published base prices is not available. However, a survey in 1942 by the U.S. Office of Price Administration found that the actual price of ore sales averaged 4.7 percent below the published prices, and that long-term contracts were on the average 7.4 percent below and spot sales 2.6 percent. Inasmuch as these figures refer to a period of fairly tight supplies, it is not unreasonable to assume that the difference between the published and the actual prices of Midwest sales has tended to widen over the years as supplies have become more readily available.

The importance placed on the Lake Erie base as a guide to ore prices in the Midwest must be qualified by the westward shift of the center of iron and steel production toward the Chicago district during the last fifteen or so years. The fact that Chicago's blast furnaces bear a lower transport cost on their ore supplies from the upper lakes mines means, at the very least, that the greater part of the iron ore sold there will be negotiated at c. & f. prices well below the Lake Erie base price. Chicago's importance also confirms the increasing irrelevance of the Lake Erie base price quotations as a guide to contemporary market conditions and to actual prices paid for ore in the Midwest. Moreover, it has to be recalled that the Lake Erie base price refers only to open-market sales. Yet approximately 80 percent of the ore consumed in the United States originates from "captive" mines—perhaps rather more in slack years when consumers prefer to use their own ores, for obvious reasons, rather than use supplementary purchases. Much of this captive ore is transported to the blast furnaces over railways and in vessels owned by the iron and steel producers. Any prices charged in such circumstances are as a consequence in large measure a matter of internal company accountancy, and strongly influenced by the structure of taxation and depreciation allowances on iron ore mining.

Nevertheless, the Lake Erie base still has something of a formal value in the buying and selling of ores in North America. At the very least it offers a useful bench mark at which not completely unrealistic bargaining can begin (especially for pellets that are not in overabundant supply); and it is frequently used in the calculation of such matters as royalties. The price of some Canadian ores, too, is related to the Lake Erie base. For example, the price of Wabush Lake ores at Sept Iles is calculated by multiplying the percentage of iron contained in the ore by 17.25 cents (up to 64 percent Fe, and then any additional Fe percentage by 10 cents). Thus, in 1965, an ore of 62 percent Fe had an f.o.b. price of $10.71 per actual ton. This rule for pricing holds while the Lake Erie base price of Old Range non-Bessemer ore stands at or below $11.89 per actual ton. But if the base rises above that figure, the Sept Iles price is allowed to rise according to a prearranged scale.

The only other market region in North America for which ore prices are regularly published is the east coast of the United States. It is a much less institutionalized market than the lower lakes market. Quotations can be found in the technical press relating to the iron ores mined domestically in upper New York State, New Jersey, and eastern Pennsylvania; and some prices are published for ores imported from Latin America, Canada, Africa, and formerly Sweden. Some ores are quoted c. & f.; others are quoted f.o.b. (at times deceptively, since the freight rate assumptions are unknown). In addition it is possible to obtain through industry sources a general idea of east coast import prices. These have been added to published statistics, converted to a common c. & f. basis, and are presented in Table 65. Although there was some variation in delivered price per iron unit, as a consequence of differences in physical and chemical structure, the prices in the east coast market in 1961 appear to be below those of Lake Erie, whose base price in that year was between 22 and 23 cents per iron unit for blast-furnace ores. Moreover, the higher iron content per ton of the east coast's domestic concentrates and imports offered important economies in blast-furnace costs.

With Swedish exports traditionally dominating the international move-

TABLE 65. PUBLISHED AND ESTIMATED PRICES OF ORE DELIVERED TO THE U.S. EAST COAST MARKET REGION, 1961

Source	Fe content (%)	Price, c. & f.	
		Dollars/actual ton	Cents/iron unit
Domestic ores, concentrates (New York, Pennsylvania).................	56–62	9.52–11.16	17.00–18.00
Domestic ores, concentrates (New Jersey)	62–64	11.16–12.16	18.00–19.00
Imported ores			
Blast-furnace ores			
Brazil (Rio Doce, r.o.m.)...........	66	13.65	20.68
Brazil (Rio Doce, lumpy)..........	68–69	14.96–15.18	22.00
Chile (El Algarrobo)..............	62	12.30	19.83
Chile (Santa Fe).................	62	12.50	20.16
Peru (Marcona, coarse)...........	61	13.65	22.37
Peru (Marcona, pellets)...........	69	15.75	22.82
Sweden........................	60–68	14.64–17.00	24.40–25.00
Venezuela......................	63	13.60	21.58
Sinter-plant fines			
Brazil (Rio Doce)................	64	12.05	18.82
Canada (Lac Jeannine)............	65	13.65	21.00
Liberia (Bomi)...................	62	12.40	20.00
Peru (Marcona).................	59	11.05	18.72
Open-hearth ores			
Brazil.........................	68.5	16.45	24.00
Chile (Santa Fe).................	66	15.65	23.71
Peru (Acarí)....................	65	15.40	23.69

Sources: Domestic ore prices from Iron Age; imported ore prices from industry sources.

ment of ore to the Western European market, it is not surprising that one of the best indicators of West European ore prices is the quotation for the Kiruna B and D grades. The Kiruna B is an ore with a low phosphorus content and 67 percent iron; the Kiruna D has a high phosphorus content and is 59 percent iron. Every year it is the practice of representatives of the West German and British iron and steel industries to negotiate contracts with their Swedish suppliers for part of the following year's ore imports. The other parts either are negotiated on the basis of long-term contracts or acquired by spot purchases in the market. The outcome of the annual bargaining is made public in the form of published prices for the Swedish ores on either an f.o.b. Narvik or a c. & f. Rotterdam basis. Naturally, these quotations are published with the proviso that they are merely a guide to the market value of the ores and that all supplies are subject to detailed price negotiations. Nevertheless, they have historically been an important indication of the state of the Western European market for ore. However, with Swedish ore decreasing in its relative importance in that market (the high-phosphorus Kiruna D grade is less and less favored as iron and steel producers turn to L.D. steelmaking), the contemporary pattern of iron ore prices has to be filled out with information gained from the occasional publication of contract information or from industry sources.

The compilation of Table 66 has necessitated the manipulation of data from a variety of sources. Although the figures are broadly correct, affording a reasonably realistic view of ore prices in the Rotterdam market place in 1962, they are recorded with no pretentions to complete accuracy. In any case, ore prices can vary within a short space of time. Negotiations may be

TABLE 66.   PUBLISHED AND ESTIMATED PRICES OF ORE DELIVERED TO ROTTERDAM, 1962

Source	Fe content (%)	Price, c. & f.	
		Dollars/actual ton	Cents/iron unit
Algeria, Djerissa	54.4	11.09	20.40
Brazil, Rio Doce			
Lumpy	68.5	15.07	22.00
R.o.m.	66	12.54	19.00
Fines	64	10.88	17.00
Canada, IOCC	65	14.88	22.89
Wabana	48	7.68	16.00
India, Goa	60	10.80	18.00
Liberia, Mano River	58	9.28	16.00
Norway, Sydvaranger concentrates	65	10.40	16.00
Sierra Leone, Marampa	64	10.24	16.00
Sweden			
Kiruna D	60	10.88	18.13
Kiruna B	67	13.20	19.17
Malmberget pellets	69	17.94	26.00
Venezuela	63	15.39	24.42

Sources: Swedish ore prices from Metal Bulletin; the rest from industry sources.

conducted in the light of market circumstances, but the bargains that are struck frequently agree upon a particular f.o.b. price on the assumption of a "reasonable" level of freight rates. Should there be any variation in those rates, the c. & f. price is accordingly affected. The main point emerging from the Rotterdam figures is the highly competitive nature of the market there.

The prices at Rotterdam (Table 66) relate to a year later than the prices quoted in Table 65 for the east coast market region of the United States (during 1961–62 the market for ore had continued to weaken). The Rotterdam price for all grades of Brazilian ore was 2 cents per iron unit below that of Baltimore. While the value of good-quality ores ranged between 19 and 22 cents per iron unit on the U.S. east coast, Rotterdam prices were in the 16 to 19 cents range. Large coastal steelworks in northwest Europe with reasonably deepwater berths—works like Ijmuiden and Dunkirk—could obtain their ore at these prices. Those without direct access to deep water, such as the Klockner works at Bremen, had to pay an additional transshipment and rail charge. *Frei Ruhr* prices were about 2 cents per iron unit higher than those of Rotterdam. Brazilian run-of-mine ore in the Ruhr area was valued at 20.5 cents, Liberian Mano River at 18.2 cents, and Kiruna D at 20.1 cents per iron unit. Of course, the less accessible iron and steel works of the eastern Ruhr had to pay even more for their imported ores.

British prices were still higher by 1965 (Table 67). The import of all ore was in the hands of the British Iron and Steel Corporation (Ore) Ltd. It negotiated deals for supplies in response to indicated requirements of individual iron and steel companies, and it arranged for the transport of ore imports. The Corporation manipulated the prices it charged the companies to some degree, subsidizing certain sources of ore and, conversely, penalizing others. It also varied the price of ore with the size of vessel in which the ore was carried, thus affording some advantage to the steelworks located near deeper ports. Generally speaking, however, for reasons noted in Chapter 9, the country's poor port facilities, the small ore carriers chartered long-term, the high freight rates, and hence the somewhat uncompetitive British market situation for ore, together resulted in rather high delivered ore prices. Indeed, they stood at or above those of the U.S. east coast market region five years earlier.

The other principal market region for iron ore in 1965 was that of Japan. Although it was the most recent to assume a key international importance, it had in fact an exceptionally well-documented price structure. This did not stem from the regular publication of a base price *à la* Lake Erie, or from a guidance price comparable to the Kiruna D; rather, it originated from the habit of the Japanese iron and steel industry to publish details of their overseas ore purchases, including the prices bargained for them. From a variety

TABLE 67. PUBLISHED AND ESTIMATED PRICES OF ORE DELIVERED TO BRITAIN, 1965

Source	Fe content (%)	Price, c. & f.	
		Dollars/actual ton	Cents/iron unit
Algeria, Ouenza....................	54.4	13.00	23.9
Zaccar..........................	51.9	11.83	22.8
Brazil, Itabira			
Lumpy.........................	68.5	18.36	26.8
Open hearth.....................	68.5	18.36	26.8
Rubble.........................	65.5	17.03	26.0
Fines..........................	63.5	14.35	22.6
Canada, Labrador...................	54.0	12.20	22.6
Carol Lake pellets.................	65	19.31	29.7
Guinea, Conakry			
Lumpy.........................	53.2	9.79	18.4
Fines..........................	50.6	9.01	17.8
Liberia			
Concentrates.....................	65.4	13.67	20.9
Fines..........................	64.2	16.24	25.3
Mano River fines..................	59.2	12.02	20.3
Nimba..........................	65.8	13.82	21.0
Mauritania, Tazadit			
Fines..........................	62.7	11.91	19.0
Rubble.........................	66.0	15.18	23.0
Open hearth.....................	67.2	16.40	24.4
Norway, Sydvaranger			
Concentrates.....................	65.4	12.56	19.2
Sierra Leone concentrates.............	63.5	12.95	20.4
Sweden			
Kiruna B........................	67	14.47	21.6
Kiruna B fines....................	67	13.67	20.4
Kiruna D........................	60	11.88	19.8
Kiruna D fines...................	60	11.70	19.5
Kiruna pellets....................	65	17.42	26.8
Malmberget pellets.................	69	18.91	27.4
U.S.S.R. concentrates................	62	10.29	16.6
Venezuela, Cerro Bolívar..............	63	13.99	22.2

Source: Industry sources.
Note: Prices refer to ore carried in vessels of between 11,000 and 20,000 dwt; prices were slightly lower for larger vessels and slightly higher for smaller vessels.

of published sources, such as press reports, steel industry statements, and the technical press, it is relatively easy to get a clear idea of the pattern of ore prices in the Japanese market supply area. Some of these prices, for the year 1965, are indicated in Table 68. Naturally, the price of the imports varied with the physical and chemical structure of the ores, as well as their iron content. On average, the Japanese were paying about 22 to 24 cents per iron unit for lump ore with a good physical structure, a low phosphorus content, and a reasonably high iron content; and they were paying less, 20 to 22 cents, for fines. These prices were rather higher than those negotiated in the Rotterdam market place; they approximated the value of ore in Britain in that year. Both Japan and Britain had relatively high transport costs. But while the British prices were the result of poor port facilities and costly transport arrangements, the Japanese prices were achieved in spite of the huge distances over which ores had to be hauled. It was, indeed,

TABLE 68. PUBLISHED AND ESTIMATED PRICES OF ORE DELIVERED TO THE JAPANESE MARKET
REGION, 1965, AND CONTRACTED PRICES, 1966–1973

Source	Fe content (%)	Price, c. & f. Dollars/ actual ton	Price, c. & f. Cents/ iron unit
AFRICA			
Angola (1967)	64	12.16	19.00
Liberia, Bomi Hills	64	12.99	20.30
Lamco, r.o.m. (1967)	66.3	12.64	19.06
Lamco, r.o.m. (1966)	63	12.05	19.13
(1968)	63	11.30	17.94
(1969)	63	10.51	16.68
South Africa	68	17.20	25.29
	65	16.38	25.20
	62	15.55	25.08
Swaziland	62	15.55	25.08
NORTH AND SOUTH AMERICA			
Brazil			
R.o.m.	66	13.00	19.70
R.o.m. (1967)	64/66	12.00	18.46
Fines (1966)	64/66	11.20	17.23
Canada, Ocean mines	63	12.75	20.24
Orecan	62	12.75	20.56
Texada	62/64	13.85	21.98
Chile	65	12.90	19.85
Peru, Marcona pellets	66	17.49	26.50
United States, Nevada			
Pellets	67	17.42	26.00
Lump	58/60	14.22	24.10
ASIA			
India			
Standard grade	65	14.08	21.66
Kiriburu ore (1966)	60/62	11.59	19.00
Ledi ore	62	12.12	19.55
Goa pellets	66	16.50	25.00
Malaya			
Lump	59	11.92	20.20
Fines	60	11.30	18.83
North Korea	58	10.30	17.76
Philippines, pellets	67	16.80	25.07
Thailand	59	11.20	18.98
AUSTRALASIA			
Australia, Cliffs Western Australian Mining Co. (Robe River), pellets (1968)	63.6	14.23	22.37
Francis Creek, r.o.m.	62	11.10	17.90
Hamersley, 30 × 6 mm (1966)	62/64	12.12	19.24
100 × 6 mm (1966)	62/64	11.86	18.83
Fines (1966)	62/64	9.88	15.68
Pellets (1968)	63	13.63	21.63
Mt. Goldsworthy, r.o.m. (1966)	61/64	12.06	18.99
Mt. Newman, 30 × 6 mm (1969)	62/64	11.37	18.05
100 × 6 mm (1969)	62/64	11.16	17.71
Fines (1969)	62/64	9.48	15.05
Savage River, pellets (1968)	67.5	13.50	20.00
(1970)	67.5	12.83	19.01
(1973)	67.5	12.49	18.50
Western Mining, r.o.m. (1966)	58/60	12.60	21.36
EASTERN EUROPE			
U.S.S.R., Krivoy Rog			
Fines	60.5	11.20	18.51
Concentrates	60	11.52	19.2

Sources: Japan Iron and Steel Federation; Canada, Department of Energy, Mines and Resources; Nippon Kokan; *Metal Bulletin; The Economist.*

remarkable that the Japanese iron and steel industry could keep its ore costs so low, when the average length of its ore hauls was over twice that of the Western European iron and steel industries. Moreover, there were prospects for further falls in the general level of its freight rates as larger vessels came into use, and as the nearer ore fields of Western Australia came to be the major source of supply for Japanese blast furnaces.

While the published prices for ore and the information obtainable from industry sources throw considerable light on the markets for iron ore, they suffer from an obvious historical patchiness. It is therefore expedient to supplement them with information on ore values that can be abstracted from the trade statistics of the large exporters and importers and from United Nations publications. For many countries, figures are available for the tonnage and the value of iron ore moving in international trade. For most of them (the United States is an exception, since its import statistics are published on an f.o.b. basis) it is possible to calculate the average value of a ton of iron ore either exported or imported. It is even possible crudely to estimate average f.o.b. and c. & f. values per iron unit, by using estimates of the average iron content of the ores.

For example, the estimated average price in 1962 of West German imports from Sweden, derived from trade statistics, was $12.96 per actual ton, or 22.6 cents per iron unit (Table 69). This compares reasonably well with

TABLE 69.   AVERAGE VALUE OF IRON ORE IMPORTED INTO WEST GERMANY AND JAPAN IN 1962

Origin of ore	Average Fe content	Average f.o.b. value		Average c. & f. value	
		Dollars/ actual ton	Cents/ unit	Dollars/ actual ton	Cents/ unit
	To West Germany				
Brazil....................	66.3%	8.42	12.7	13.93	21.05
Canada...................	48.9	8.26	16.9	12.96	25.00
Chile....................	64.2	7.19	11.2	13.61	21.20
France*..................	29.1	3.52	12.1	4.77	16.4
Goa......................	55.4			12.54	22.6
Liberia..................	63.3	8.61	13.6	11.92	18.8
Peru.....................	60.2	5.60	9.3	12.80	21.3
Sierra Leone.............	60.8	6.70	11.5	11.46	18.8
Sweden...................	57.4	9.36	16.3	12.96	22.6
Venezuela................	58.8	8.00	13.6	15.41	26.1
(Home ore)...............	(27.0)			(2.96)	(11.0)
(Home ore concentrate)....	(37.7)			(8.22)	(21.8)
	To Japan				
Brazil....................	69	9.45	13.7	18.49	26.8
Canada...................	55	9.28	16.9	15.07	27.4
Chile....................	60	6.72	11.2	16.02	26.7
Goa......................	56	10.25	18.3	12.94	23.1
India....................	61	11.16	18.3	17.02	27.9
Malaya...................	60	8.28	13.8	13.08	21.8
Peru.....................	60	5.58	9.3	13.74	22.9
Philippines..............	55	10.07	18.3	11.83	21.5

Sources: National trade statistics; U.N., Commodity Trade Statistics.
* C. & f. Saar.

the prices of Kiruna D and Brazil (Rio Doce) run-of-mine ores c. & f. Rotterdam ($10.88 and $12.54, respectively) plus a barge haul of $0.95 per actual ton up the Rhine to Duisburg. Measured against the price of Swedish ores, the average value of Venezuelan and Brazilian imports into West Germany was somewhat higher, and those of West African ores rather lower; this accords with the figures in Table 66. To some extent these differences in value reflected variations in ore quality. In addition, they were a measure of the longer-term contracts of the West German industry with West African suppliers, the high costs of transport from Venezuela, the price inflexibility of some producers, and, of course, the imperfections of the market. Table 69 confirms the rather higher c. & f. price of ore in the Japanese market that same year.

DEMAND, SUPPLY, AND PRICE

In 1950, as was noted in Chapter 11, fears were expressed about a possible long-term scarcity of iron ore. In the markets of the day, iron ore was in short supply, and prices were being pushed upward. Whereas in 1950 the Lake Erie base price for Mesabi non-Bessemer grade was $7.82 per actual ton, it had risen to $9.86 by 1953, and to $11.63 by 1957, when it reached its peak level (see Table A-9). The unit values of exports and imports moved in the same direction, sometimes faster, sometimes slower (see Tables A-10 and A-11). For most ores there were two peaks in the trend of prices: the first in 1952/53, and the second in 1957/58. The intermediate trough was a response to recession conditions in Western Europe in 1953 and in North America in 1954. The average value for an actual ton of Swedish export ore, for example, rose from $6.04 in 1950 to $11.58 in 1953, slipped back to $9.92 in 1954, and then rose to a peak $11.98 in 1958. Similarly, imports of Algerian ore into Britain rose in value (per actual ton) from $8.34 in 1950 to a peak of $17.21 in 1952, moved down to $14.51 two years later, and then rose to a second peak of $16.94 in 1957.

The rising value of ore throughout most of the fifties was a function partly of ore and shipping shortages, and partly of mining cost inflation. It also contained elements of price discrimination under which mining companies raised their export prices well above the ruling price levels for their home sales. In the case of Swedish ores, the export price f.o.b. Narvik was approximately $7 per actual ton for Kiruna D grade, while the price charged on the home market for the same ore on similar contracts was only about $4 (United Nations, 1949, p. 65). Similarly, in 1949 French producers were charging an export price for Lorraine ores nearly twice the price of their home sales.

The shortages of ore and the upward movement and discrimination in prices did not last long. By the mid-fifties, perhaps a little earlier in the North American market, the supply situation began to ease. By 1958 there were clear indications that the shortages were giving way to adequate supplies, which in turn were transformed into surpluses. Locally, even as late as 1965, there were occasional shortages of particular types of ore as a result of special circumstances. Pellets, for example, were by no means as plentiful as other ores, and their price remained relatively firm. But generally speaking the price of ore began to fall from 1959 onward.

The Lake Erie base price did not increase after 1957 (see Table A-9). Although it did not register a formal decline until 1962, it was widely known that the discounts on the posted price rose from about 5 percent in 1960 to 15 percent in 1962, a decline in value of more than 7 percent. The downward movement of the value of export ores after 1958 is shown in Table A-10. The peak export values of ores from Algeria, Brazil, India, Sierra Leone, and Sweden came in that year, and of other countries shortly afterward. By 1965 the average value of Brazilian ore exports had fallen from $13.93 (in 1958) to $8.09 per actual ton, and Swedish exports from $11.98 to $8.78. Some ore prices reacted more quickly than others to the changing market situation. A common denominator of the countries whose export prices moved only slowly was the fact that their mines were either partly or wholly owned by American iron and steel corporations, and the further fact that they exported chiefly to the United States market. The average value of Canadian exports continued to rise until 1967. Partly this represented an increasing export of prepared ores, especially pellets. But it also reflected (as did the firmer export values of Chilean and Venezuelan ores) the internal pricing policies of the American iron and steel industry rather than the interplay of supply and demand on price.

The downward movement of c. & f. import prices was more impressive, for these included not only a measure of the weakening mine values of ore but also the declining level of freight rates. The value of Kiruna D was $13.20 at Rotterdam in 1958; by 1963 it had fallen to $10.88 and by 1965 to $9.64. Table A-11 illustrates the declining value per actual ton of West German ore imports after 1957. The rather lower value of the higher-grade Liberian and Sierra Leone imports, compared with the poorer-grade Canadian and Venezuelan ores, was a response to the long-term contracts arranged by the West German industry with its West African suppliers. Table A-11 also illustrates a downward trend in the c. & f. value of ore imported into Britain and Japan, with the latter country in particular witnessing dramatic falls in its ore prices. Japanese imports from Brazil fell on the average from $34.07 per actual ton in 1957 to $12.34 in 1967, and imports from Chile fell from $30.69 to $13.79 per actual ton. A further fall in Japanese prices, to be seen especially in the contracts with Western Australia's mining companies, is assured into the early seventies (see Table 68).

In any comparison of the several tables of average values of iron ore imported into different countries, the fact that the unit values c. & f. represent a variety of ores and a wide range of freight rates must be taken into account. A country that purchases poorer grades of ore will tend to have lower c. & f. values than a country importing high-grade ores. In 1965 British imports from Sweden included a substantial proportion of the more expensive low-phosphorus ores. West Germany, on the other hand, imported more of the cheaper high-phosphorus ores. Again, British imports from Brazil and Canada had a slightly higher iron content than West German imports from the same countries. Apart from such subtle interpretations of the tables, the point illustrated by the figures is the steady weakening of the world market for iron ore from the late fifties onward. But for the existence of long-term contracts and a degree of corporate integration between producers and consumers, the price of ore would have reacted much more sharply.

Some of the reasons for this changing market situation have been pointed out. The success of both the technological effort to lower the production and preparation costs of low-grade ores, and the exploration investment to find new sources of high-grade ores, lay at the root of the change (see Chapters 8 and 11). Simultaneously, the falling level of freight rates, which allowed more mines to ship their ores with profit over greater distances, increased the degree of market competition and helped to ease the price of ore downward (see Chapters 9 and 10). There were other reasons, too. Once the mining operations at the new sources of ore had been started, the incremental cost of expanding their capacity was quite small. With railways already built and port facilities already installed, and with both inevitably underutilized, the temptations for the new ore producers to expand their output and lower their prices in the hope of gaining a larger share of the market were very strong indeed. And even if mining had not commenced, once a company had invested considerable sums of money in the exploration and the survey of a deposit, powerful economic forces encouraged its development. This effect was clearly apparent in the mid-sixties in Australia, where several companies had proved the commercial worth of their concessions and were anxious to acquire long-term supply contracts with the Japanese iron and steel industry. In the scramble for markets, the mining interests seriously underestimated the size of contracts the Japanese were willing to negotiate, and the price of ore fell dramatically.

It was in the interest of the ore consumers to encourage the extension of existing mining capacity and even the exploration of new deposits in order to keep the market soft, and so to ease the price of ore yet further down. It is quite possible that some of the investments made by the iron and steel industry in new iron ore mining activities were in fact stimulated by a desire to weaken the market and affect prices in this way. Certainly some of the proposed "paper" mining ventures and some of the widely advertised plans to construct pellet plants, were part of the bargaining position of the iron and steel industry in the weakening market.

The worldwide growth in the demand for iron and steel, together with its steadily changing geographical distribution, created a fundamental element of flux in the markets for ore, and so permitted their easier penetration by many of the new producers. In addition, during the sixties in particular, the fact that steel production in three of the largest importers of seaborne ore— the United States, West Germany, and Britain—did not grow as fast as steel and mining interests had anticipated, added to the quantities of ore looking for a market. It was fortunate for the ore producers that Japanese demands exceeded all expectations.

Yet another factor in the generation of ore surpluses and the falling price of ore was the slow rate of adjustment of many of the existing and higher-cost ore producers to the realities of the market. To be sure, most of them reduced their prices. French Giraumont ore (32% Fe) fell in price at Esche-Bevel (Luxembourg) from $5.57 per actual ton in 1962 to $5.39 in 1965. But the essential fact was that the discovery and exploitation of the many new ore resources, and the new market situation, almost overnight ended the economic usefulness of many existing iron ore mines. Either the grade of their ore was too low, making it uneconomical for preparation and use in the blast furnace, or the chemical qualities of the ore were undesirable (often too much phosphorus) and could not be cheaply rectified. Some of these mines, in West Germany, Britain, France, Algeria, the United States, and Newfoundland, ceased operations. At the same time, there were other marginal producers—and indeed some producers below the margin—who continued to mine ore, its price not having drifted low enough finally to encourage them to close down. Very often these producers were persuaded to remain in production by a variety of noneconomic factors. The prospect of mine closures and the threat of unemployment for substantial labor forces generated a blend of sociological and political pressures and hence subsidies sufficient to keep a number of mines open. And in the ore-importing countries, strategic arguments were often used to suggest the desirability of maintaining at least some domestic ore-producing capacity. To the extent that the closure of these older and more costly mines was delayed, the condition of surplus supplies and steadily falling prices was perpetuated in the markets for ore.

NEW PATTERNS OF TRADE AND PRODUCTION

As was seen in Chapter 6, the world demand for iron ore between 1950 and 1965 increased from 116 million tons of contained iron to 311 million tons. At the same time there were radical shifts in the geography of demand (see Table 30). The North American share fell from 47.53 to 24.34 percent; the Western European component remained approximately constant at just under one-quarter of the world total; Eastern European demands increased from 21.25 to 29.72 percent; and the rest of the world, from consuming a mere 6.51 percent of the world's iron ore in 1950, increased its share to 21.53 percent. The greater part of these demands continued to be satisfied from domestic mines. As the period progressed, however, the proportion of ore production entering international trade grew considerably, from 19 to 38 percent, and a new pattern of trade was forged. The actual volume of ore moving across frontiers rose from circa 40 million tons in 1950 to 199 million tons in 1964; on a contained iron basis, the increase was from 22 to 109 million tons. A considerable share of this traffic, about 75 or 80 percent, was carried in oceangoing vessels. As these became larger, and as the length of ore hauls could be economically increased, the amount of oceangoing ore traffic leaped up from 120 to 843 thousand million actual-ton-kilometers.

Throughout the period, the region importing the largest quantities of iron ore continued to be Western Europe. Although its share of world imports between 1950 and 1964 fell from 54 to 43 percent on a contained iron basis, its dependence on foreign sources of ore to feed its blast furnaces increased considerably (Table 70; see also Table A-5). The iron and steel industries of the European Economic Community, with an increasing proportion of their pig iron production located on or near the coast, increased their imports from 7 to 34 million contained tons; and the percentage of foreign ore in their total consumption rose from 38 to just under 68 percent. West Germany remained the largest importer, taking 2.9 million contained tons in 1950 and 18.4 million in 1964, and the Benelux countries were the second largest. Italy, which imported negligible quantities of ore in 1950, purchased 3 million contained tons on the world market fourteen years later. By that time even France, as a consequence of the rising relative costs of using domestic sources and the location of the country's newest iron and steel works at Dunkirk, imported over 2 million contained tons of high-grade ores. The other major importer in Western Europe was Britain, whose foreign purchases of ore more than doubled, from 5 to 11 million contained tons, and whose dependence on imports rose from 56 to 71 percent.

With steadily rising ore shipments, Sweden remained the major overseas supplier to the Western European iron and steel industry in general, and to the West German and British industries in particular (Table 71; see also Tables A-6 and A-7). However, as competition from new low-cost producers in other continents increased, and as high-phosphorus ores came to be

TABLE 70. WORLD IRON ORE IMPORTS AND EXPORTS, BY REGIONS, 1950 AND 1964

Region	Imports (thousands of contained tons)		Percentage		Exports (thousands of contained tons)		Percentage	
	1950	1964	1950	1964	1950	1964	1950	1964
World................	22,193	108,920	100.00	100.00	21,833	110,578	100.00	100.00
North America........	6,325	29,172	28.50	26.78	2,490	22,662	11.40	20.49
Western Europe.......	12,037	46,414	54.24	42.61	11,405	23,981	52.24	21.69
Eastern Europe.......	3,025	13,970	13.63	12.83	1,648	11,689	7.55	10.57
Asia................	806	18,541	3.63	17.02	842	11,646	3.86	10.53
Oceania.............		135		0.12	3	157		0.14
Latin America........		652		0.60	2,302	24,206	10.54	21.89
Africa and Middle East.		36		0.03	3,143	16,237	14.49	14.68

Source: United Nations, 1968-A. See Tables A-5 and A-7 (herein) for imports and exports by countries.

TABLE 71. TOTAL SEABORNE TRADE IN IRON ORE, 1965

(*Thousands of actual tons*)

Exports \ Imports	U.S.A.	West Germany	Italy	Other EEC	Britain	Japan	Others	Total
Total	31,179	30,560	7,930	16,516	19,174	39,018	7,275	151,652
Canada[a]	9,500	1,000	278	873	3,055	1,950	1,273	16,656
Scandinavia	58	10,979	91	6,830	6,888		168	26,119
Other Western Europe[b]	11	1,582	77	218	1,205	10	1,843	3,271
India		700	190	379		7,922		11,034
Malaysia						6,956	40	6,996
Other Asia[b]			33			3,726	100	3,859
Brazil	2,316	3,357	1,277	1,459	624	915	1,372	11,320
Chile	2,703	456		190		6,929	500	10,778
Peru	972	1,601	290	215		4,532		7,610
Venezuela	12,469	1,944	814	52	1,733	129		17,141
North Africa	52	666	1,578	303	1,559		946	5,104
South and East Africa	19	45	1	78		2,286	25	2,454
West Africa	2,994	8,202	3,180	5,696	3,848	385	774	25,079
Not specified	85	28	121	223	262	3,278[c]	234	4,231

Source: Fearnley and Egers, 1966, p. 6.
Note: Import statistics are used when available.
[a] Exports from Canada to the U.S.A. exclude shipments via the Great Lakes.
[b] Partly estimated.
[c] Mainly from the U.S.A.

271

less acceptable to the iron and steel industry, the Swedish share of the regional market fell. West German importers set the pace, and, by taking advantage of the deepwater facilities of Rotterdam and the economies of ocean bulk carriers, they purchased increasing quantities of ore from Liberian, Brazilian, and Venezuelan sources in particular. Whereas in 1950 some 89 and 80 percent of West Germany's iron ore imports on a contained iron basis came from the rest of Western Europe and Sweden, respectively, by 1964 only 30 percent were purchased from the latter country, and half were shipped in from Africa and Latin America. In the case of Britain, the move away from Swedish ores was slower, although still marked. In 1950, 59 and 45 percent of British imports on a contained iron basis came from Western Europe in general and Sweden in particular. By 1964, however, the Swedish share had fallen to 33 percent, while Canada (18%), Venezuela (14%), Liberia (9%), and Mauritania (8%) had increased their importance. Sweden's exports to Belgium and Luxembourg, on the other hand, not only expanded in volume but also increased its share of the markets there. During the fifties, growing quantities of Lorraine ore were railed to the iron and steel works of Belgium and Luxembourg, but by 1965 this trade had entered a rapid decline, and Swedish ore was imported instead. In Italy (the other major Western European market), Swedish ore sales also increased, although imports from suppliers in Africa and Latin America were equally or more important. The net effect of all these changes was that, while Western European imports rose from 12 to 46 million contained tons, the share originating from Sweden fell from about 47 to just over 30 percent. Simultaneously, the importance of Latin American ores in the Western European market rose from virtually nil to 18.5 percent and African ores from 20 to 27 percent.

Meanwhile North American imports rose from 6 million contained tons (29% of the world total in 1950) to 29 million (27% in 1964). In 1950 the United States imported only 5 percent of its ore needs, but by 1964 it was importing 39 percent. Changes in the sources of American imports were equally radical. In 1950, the three main suppliers were Chile (45% on a contained iron basis), Sweden (26%), and Canada (20%). Fifteen years later, the Swedish flow had ceased, and the Chilean shipments had failed to register any substantial expansion as a result of the exploitation of nearer, larger, and cheaper supplies of ore in Canada and Venezuela. By far the largest overseas supplier to the U.S. iron and steel industry in 1964 was Canada, whose shipments represented just under 60 percent of total imports. Next in importance was Venezuela, which, together with smaller shipments from Brazil and Chile, gave Latin America a 34 percent share of the U.S. market. A further 4 percent came from Liberia.

The most dramatic increase in ore imports occurred in Asia. Japan's needs rocketed from less than 1 million contained tons in 1950 to 19 million in 1964. With only very limited domestic resources, the burgeoning Japanese iron and steel industry became dependent on foreign ores for over 90 percent of its needs, and came to handle 17 percent of the world's imports on a contained iron basis. At the beginning of the period, Malaysian (37%) and Philippine mines (40%) satisfied most of the Japanese demands, and they continued to ship ore to Japan throughout the period. Malaysia maintained a leading role by increasing its tonnage of ore to 4 million contained tons by 1964 and retaining a 21.5 percent share of the market. Among others who shared the Japanese market were India including Goa (21.5%), Chile (18%), and Peru (12%). Considerable tonnages were also purchased by Japan from the United States, Canada, South Africa, and Brazil. In 1965 the first shipments of ore were made from Western Australia, which, with several long-term contracts already signed, was destined in the future to rival all others in the satisfaction of Japanese demands. Although by 1964 Japan was the second-largest ore importer in the world, Asian imports as a whole were still much smaller than those of Western Europe or North America.

The only other major ore importing region was Middle Europe. In 1950 the iron and steel industry there purchased three-quarters of its 4 million tons of contained ore requirements from other countries. By 1965 its imports, having increased to 82 percent of their contained iron ore needs, had grown to 14 million contained tons and represented some 13 percent of world trade in iron ore. Their main supplier was the Soviet Union—in particular its Ukraine and Kursk ore fields. However, the gradual increase in trade between the fully planned economies and the rest of the world, the revival of some old trade associations with Western Europe, and the deliberate fostering of new commercial ties (especially with the developing world), together led to increasing quantities of ore being imported from mines outside the Eastern European bloc. Thus, by 1964, the logic of the proximity of Swedish supplies of ore to the Polish and East German iron and steel industries had gradually overcome the hard-currency objections to their import. Increasing quantities of ore were also purchased from India and Brazil, and the construction of a new deepwater terminal at Bakar near Rijeka (Yugoslavia) in 1965/66 was obviously justified by the assumption that imports would continue to increase from these and other hard-currency sources.

Consequent on the emergence of this new pattern of ore trade, the average length of iron ore haul was extended considerably for most importing regions. For Eastern Europe and Britain the increase was quite modest, but for the EEC countries the length of haul rose from 3,850 km in 1957 to 5,300 km in 1964. Even more dramatic was the lengthening of the ore hauls to Japan, which, at 8,700 km in 1957, had reached an average of 11,350 km in 1964, and some ore was moving to Japan over distances exceeding 20,000 km. In contrast, the average length of iron ore movements into the United States fell from 4,500 to 4,450 km as the more remote Chilean and Swedish ores were replaced by the nearer Canadian and Venezuelan supplies.

The new pattern of trade also meant that Canada, the U.S.S.R., and Venezuela became prominent as iron ore exporters for the first time (see Tables 71 and A–7). Canada, whose overseas shipments rose from 1 to 19 million contained tons of ore between 1950 and 1964, became the largest ore exporter in the world. The Canadian industry, which was financed largely by American capital, was developed mainly to serve the iron and steel industry of the United States, but its ores were also exported to Western Europe (especially to Britain) and to Japan (from British Columbia). The U.S.S.R., whose ore exports rose rapidly from 1.7 to 11.7 million contained tons, became the third largest exporter in the world. Almost its entire tonnage went to the countries of Middle Europe, mainly Czechoslovakia and Poland, but by 1965 small quantities of ore were also exported to Britain, West Germany, and Japan. And, with the ore attractively priced, there was a strong possibility that increasing tonnages would be shipped outside of the COMECON countries in the future. The fourth largest exporter in 1964 was Venezuela. Its overseas shipments in that year stood at rather less than 9 million contained tons; fifteen years earlier they had been nonexistent. Developed entirely by the steel interests of the United States, its major market was predictably in that country, but smaller quantities were also sold to Western Europe and even Japan. Sweden, whose overseas shipments grew from 8 to 15 million contained tons, moved from first to second place. Swedish ore sales contracted geographically as their American market disappeared, and increasingly they were concentrated in the West European market, with small additional quantities moving to the blast furnaces of Middle Europe.

The other exporting countries can be classified broadly into three groups:

1. Countries that were able to expand their exports rapidly, even though at the end of the period their volume was appreciably less than that of the four leaders. In West Africa, for example, Liberia and Mauretania fell into this class, with their main customers in Western Europe. Latin America also enhanced its importance as an ore exporter, through the Venezuelan shipments and the sales of Brazil, Chile, and Peru. Brazil was rather slow to develop its ore export trade, but toward the end of the period its mining interests began to develop the country's huge resources and to exploit its relative proximity to both Western Europe and the United States. The Brazilian iron ore industry indicated its determination to win a larger share of the world market by opening a new deepwater port

facility at Tubarão. Chile and Peru steadily expanded their exports but shifted the main direction of their trade increasingly to Japan. The other country in this group of rapidly growing exporters was India (including Goa), the greater part of whose shipments also went to Japan.

2. Countries whose shipments grew at only a moderate rate, through either economic or resource difficulties. One country in this group was the United States. Its loss of Canadian markets, as a result of the traditional deposits of the Lake Superior region becoming either exhausted or too high in cost, was only partly offset by new contracts won by the ore producers of the Western States to supply the Japanese iron and steel industry. In the Far East, the slow growth and the prospective decline of ore exports from Malaysia to Japan was essentially a function of a limited resource base nearing exhaustion. Similar conditions prevailed in the Marampa mine in Sierra Leone and the many smaller mines in Spain. The most important country in this second group was France. There, the lean Minette ores of Lorraine increasingly became too expensive to be transported out of the country in a progressively more competitive Western European market; by 1965, in fact, it was clear that by and large they would be used only in local blast furnaces in the future, and that France would very soon move into the third category of smaller exporters.

3. Countries whose shipments of ore either stagnated or declined absolutely between 1950 and 1964. The most noteworthy were the countries of North Africa, comprising Algeria, Morocco, and Tunisia. In each country, mining companies increasingly found that they could not place their production profitably in overseas markets. As a result they had to contract their output and eventually, in some cases, to close down. Luxembourg also was in this category.

The net effect of all these changes in the world pattern of iron ore exports was the participation of a much greater number of countries in the international ore trade. In 1950 only eighteen countries exported more than 100 thousand contained tons; by 1964 there were thirty. In 1950, only two countries—Sweden and France—were exporting more than 2 million contained tons; by 1964 there were thirteen (Figure 16; see also Figure 15).

In spite of the growing volume of ore being produced for export, the greater part of the world's ore needs was still satisfied by domestic mines. Throughout the fifteen years, Soviet, Chinese, Indian, South African, and Australian ore requirements were met entirely from home production, and the greater part of the iron ore needs of the United States and France continued to be met from domestic sources. The changing pattern of iron ore production was therefore very different from that of iron ore exports. Between 1950 and 1965 the world output rose from 116 million tons to 311 million contained tons. The number of countries producing more than

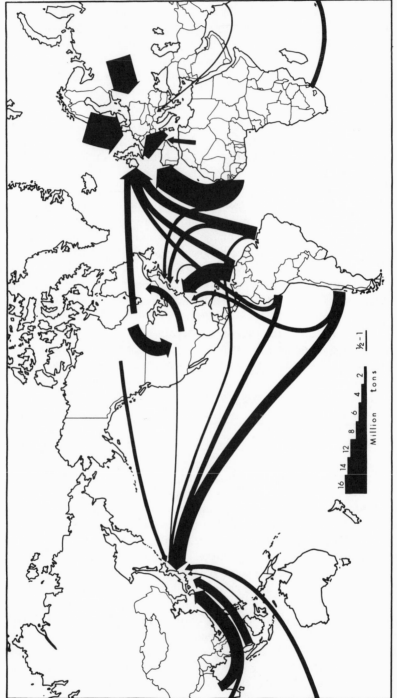

FIGURE 16. World trade in iron ore (Fe content), 1964.

100,000 tons of ore per year increased from thirty-three to forty-nine. And the geography of the industry shifted dramatically (Figures 17, 18, and 19 and Table 72; see also Table A-8).

Contrary to the world trend, the production of iron ore in North America increased only very slowly. This followed largely from events in the United States, where the sluggishness in the growth of demand was paralleled by a rising volume of imports—a circumstance that increased

TABLE 72. WORLD IRON ORE PRODUCTION, BY REGIONS, 1950 AND 1965

Region	Tonnage (thousands of contained tons)		Percentages	
	1950	1965	1950	1965
World..............................	115,582	310,594	100.00	100.00
North America.....................	51,105	68,888	44.22	22.18
Western Europe....................	28,311	51,528	24.49	16.61
Eastern Europe....................	23,181	89,456	20.06	28.80
Asia..............................	4,038	38,160	3.49	12.29
Oceania...........................	1,482	4,586	1.28	1.48
Latin America.....................	3,528	34,486	3.05	11.10
Africa and Middle East............	3,937	23,490	3.41	7.56

Sources: United Nations, 1968-A; and author's estimates. See Table A-8 for contained and actual tonnage, by regions and countries.

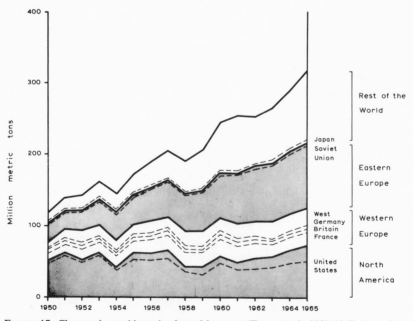

FIGURE 17. Changes in world production of iron ore (Fe content), 1950–1965, by regions and major countries.

North American net imports of ore from 3.8 to 6.5 million contained tons between 1950 and 1964. In addition, the output from the famous Lake Superior ore field initially leveled off and later fell, as a result of its inability to meet the rising quality standards of the market and the gradual exhaustion of many of its mines. Simultaneously, the economic tide turned against the low-grade oolitic ore mines of Alabama and elsewhere, and these also were forced to close down. The shrinking production of these deposits was partly offset (toward the end of the period) by an expansion of ore production in Minnesota and Michigan, based on the development of a combination of new mining and beneficiating technologies for the taconite and jasperite ores. Despite the low iron content of their ore body, the mines producing these ores and the nearby preparation facilities had the advantage of a growing proximity to the westward-shifting iron and steel industry of the Midwest. These mines had another advantage: protection from the competition of imports as a result of the relatively high transport rates for moving foreign ores inland from the east coast and the Gulf Coast ports. An expansion also occurred in the iron ore mining activities of the Far Western states, both for meeting local demands and for export to Japan.

The net effect of these changes was that the total iron ore output from U.S. mines at the end of the period was fractionally lower than at the beginning, 49 million contained tons compared with 49.3 million. It was only as a result of the very rapid growth of the Canadian industry, whose production rose from 1.8 to 19.8 million contained tons, that the continent as a whole was able to record an overall growth in ore production. The Canadian industry was almost entirely concerned with exports. Helped by the country's political stability, together with a favorable tax base, the Canadian iron ore companies in 1965 were still in the process of expanding their capacity. However, two major obstacles to further rapid growth were becoming evident. The first was the fact that the basic costs of iron ore mining in many parts of the country were beginning to appear rather high by international standards. This was a direct consequence of Canadian natural endowments, in particular its geology and physical geography. And the second followed from the fact that the Canadian iron ore mining industry had achieved its greatest marketing success in the United States (to a large extent at the expense of that country's domestic mines). By 1965, competition was stiffening, and it was also clear that the total demand for iron ore in the United States was unlikely to grow very fast. In the light of such circumstances, Canadian producers in 1965 could not read too much from the past when thinking about their future. The rise of North American output from 51.1 to 68.9 million contained tons was, of course, quite modest by world standards. The continent's share of world output fell from 44 to 22 percent during the fifteen years.

In Western Europe, iron ore production expanded rapidly during the fifties in response to the rapid growth of domestic demands. From 28.3 million contained tons in 1950, the industry had nearly doubled its volume to 52.5 million by 1961. However, after that date, while Swedish production continued to expand, the overall level of production first hit a plateau and then turned downward. With the price of iron ore imports falling steadily from 1958 onward, many of the producers of low-grade ores in West Germany, Britain, and France found themselves uncompetitive and unprofitable. Between 1950 and 1964, imports into Western Europe rose from 12 to 46 million contained tons, and net imports from 0.6 to 22.4 million contained tons. At first the domestic producers of low-grade ore were forced only to contract the size of their operations, but later more and more of them were forced to phase out their production. In one important sense, the companies concerned were singularly fortunate in that an earlier phase of blast-furnace and steelmaking location decision-making had given them a substantial local market which they could continue profitably to serve. But as the Lincolnshire iron- and steelmakers began to mix imported pellets and high-grade ores with their traditional ores, and as the canalization of the Moselle beckoned 63 to 67 percent Fe foreign ores into Lorraine, the future prospects of the remaining mines appeared far from bright. By 1965, even the further expansion of the Swedish industry was being questioned as its advantageous proximity to the large Western European market for ore was offset by the iron and steel industry's preference for low-phosphorus ores. Western European output of ore in 1965, therefore, was still only 51.5 million contained tons, of which France and Sweden produced 35.5 million tons. By that date Western Europe's share of world production had fallen from the 25 percent of fifteen years earlier to 16.6 percent.

In Eastern Europe, on the other hand, a growth of net exports from 1.4 to 2.3 million contained tons was paralleled by a rapid expansion of total iron ore production. In 1950 the output of the region was only 23.2 million contained tons, but by 1965 it had increased to 89.5 million tons. Eastern Europe's share of world production as a consequence rose from 20 to mearly 29 percent. Most of this growth was confined to the U.S.S.R., where the industry overcame technical difficulties in preparing its ores for the blast furnace, and where existing and new iron ore mines expanded its output from 22 to 86 million contained tons. The Soviet industry thereby became by far the largest in the world, with very nearly twice the output of the second largest—the United States industry—and with four times the output of the Canadian industry, which ranked third. The largest component of the Soviet industry was to be found in the Ukraine, where the direct-shipping ores, the quartzites, and the Crimean mines together served the regional iron and steel industry and at the same time exported con-

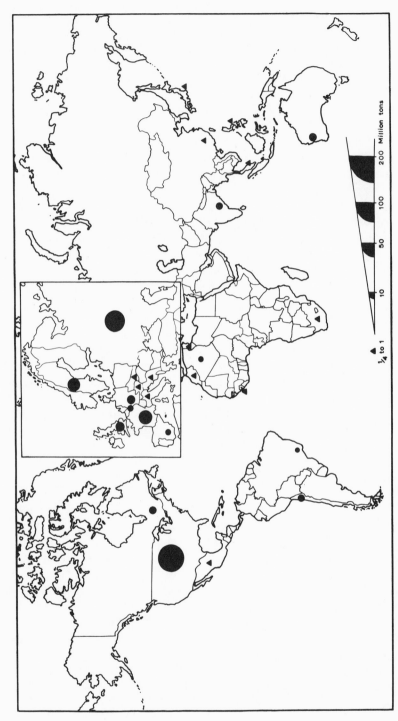

FIGURE 18. World production of iron ore (Fe content), 1950.

280

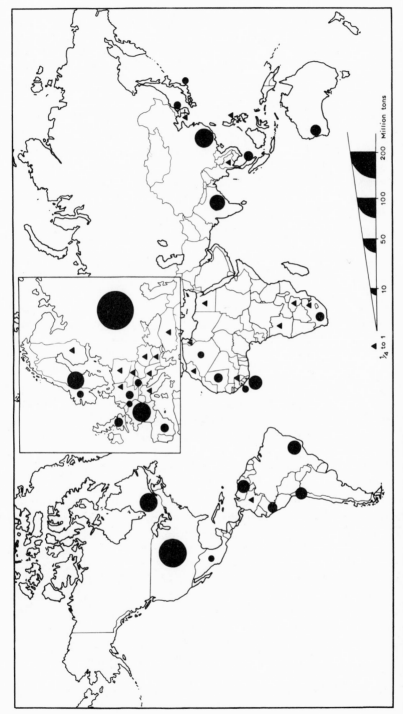

FIGURE 19. World production of iron ore (Fe content), 1965.

siderable tonnages to the countries of Middle Europe. Elsewhere in the western part of Russia, the Kursk magnetic anomaly was being exploited to provide both direct-shipping and quartzite ores for the rapidly developing steel industry of that region; and yet further supplies were being obtained from the mines of the Kola Peninsula. The second-largest source of ore in the U.S.S.R. was still the southern Urals; there the famous Magnitogorsk field was much less important than before, and its supplies were supplemented from deposits in western Siberia, such as the Kachkanov field. The mines of Kazakhstan (by now the third largest Soviet producing region) were being expanded for the local blast furnaces. In Siberia, the ore deposits of Kemerovo, Altai, and Abakan-Korshovnov were being developed for the Kuznetsk iron and steel industry.

During the 1950–65 period, the iron ore industry of the Soviet Union faced and dealt with many severe technical challenges, in particular with regard to the high silica and arsenic contents of some of its deposits. These had been largely overcome by 1965, and the industry was moving forward to a phase in which it would supply the domestic iron and steel works largely with enriched ores having an average iron content of over 60 percent. It was a remarkable performance in a mere fifteen years. In the production of iron ore, the U.S.S.R. completely overshadowed the other countries of Eastern Europe, particularly Czechoslovakia and Poland.

It was in the rest of the world—in Asia, Oceania, Africa, and Latin America—that some of the most rapid developments in iron ore mining took place. In 1950 these macroregions accounted for only 13 million contained tons (11% of the world's production), but by 1965, with their net exports having increased from 4.5 to 32.9 million contained tons (in 1964), they were mining 101 million contained tons, nearly one-third of the world total. The greater part of this growth occurred in Asia and Oceania, where China and India together increased their production from approximately 2.8 million contained tons to 28.6 million. China, of course, was self-sufficient, and its estimated 1965 output of 15 million contained tons placed the country as the sixth-largest iron ore producer in the world. On the assumption that within China's fully planned and relatively underdeveloped economy every effort was made to minimize the distances over which bulk raw materials had to be transported, it is probable that the greater part of this ore was won from the deposits in Manchuria, Hopei, and northern Shansi. In addition, there was probably a considerable geographical scatter of production throughout the rest of the country to meet the needs of small blast furnaces that were satisfying local and regional demands for pig iron. Evidence on the industry is singularly elusive, however.

In contrast to the Chinese situation, India's production was increasingly committed to meeting overseas demands. Its domestic iron and steel industry consumed some 6 million contained tons of ore in 1965, and a further 8 million tons were exported. India's problem as an iron ore exporter (overseas iron ore shipments were becoming an increasingly important element in the country's foreign exchange earnings) lay in the relative inefficiency of its transport facilities. By the mid-sixties the competition in serving both the Japanese and Western European ore markets was stiffening, and delivered prices were falling. The relatively small vessels—with their high freight rates—that had to be used for Indian exports as a result of the country's inadequate port facilities, considerably reduced the profitability of the trade. The devaluation of the rupee in 1966 was to help the situation slightly. Yet the only long-term solution to the iron ore industry's problems lay in the plans to improve the export ports and their associated rail facilities.

Malaysia, Japan, and the Philippines were the other major producers of iron ore in Asia during the period. By the mid-sixties, however, their relative (in the case of Malaysia, absolute) importance was about to decline following the Japanese decision to rely increasingly on cheaper ores from more distant sources, especially Australia. By 1965, production in Australia was still quite modest, at 4.4 million contained tons, and almost entirely for the home market.

Latin America and Africa together produced nearly 19 percent of the world's iron ore in 1965, compared with 6 percent fifteen years earlier. With their home demands still only 3 percent of the world total at the end of the period, the primarily exporting character of their industries is apparent. Two major producers were Brazil and Venezuela. They were responsible for 21 out of Latin America's 34 million contained tons in 1965, while Chile and Peru accounted for virtually all of the rest. The largest African producer was Liberia, which, along with the other West African producers, had only begun to make an impact on world markets in the last few years of the period. Between 1962 and 1965 the mines of Liberia, Mauretania, and Sierra Leone nearly quadrupled their output—from just over 4 million contained tons to 14.2 million. The Republic of South Africa was the only other major producer in Africa. And preparations were well advanced for the large-scale exploitation of the high-grade Angolan deposits through a new port at Moçâmedes. Meanwhile, the output of the high-cost and low-grade North African mines, which had been rather stagnant throughout the fifties, began finally to decline. African production as a whole increased from just under 4 million tons of contained ore in 1950 (3% of the world output) to 23 million tons (7.6%) in 1965.

part III

---

*The Market Prospects for
Iron Ore: Forecasts to 1980*

CHAPTER 13

Trends in the Demand for Iron Ore, 1965–1980

Speculation about the future is always a hazardous exercise. However, it is natural, against the background of the retrospective study of the world market for iron ore, to inquire whether the historical forces that have shaped the demand for and supply of iron ore will continue into the future, and to ask, in the light of contemporary evidence, what their effect will be and what problems (if any) might emerge in the market. Will the rate of growth of demand for iron ore slacken in the seventies, and will its geography change as in the recent past? Can one reasonably anticipate a continuing lengthening of the average haul of iron ore? How will the new technologies of mining and beneficiation affect the geography of the industry? What are the prospects for the price of iron ore? Will it continue to drift downward, or will countervailing forces check this trend of the sixties? The enormous difficulties (and past inaccuracies) inherent in quantitative forecasts over the medium run make it tempting to eschew numbers, and solely to make statements on major tendencies in the relevant industries together with purely qualitative observations about the prospects for the market for iron ore. However, there can be little doubt that, despite their limitations, numerical forecasts, set alongside qualitative discussions, do permit a more focused examination of future changes in the market for iron ore by suggesting a magnitude to various trends exposed. With all the necessary qualifications to the accuracy and reliability of such an approach, the present chapter and the next examine the prospects for the markets for iron ore up to 1980. In the discussion an effort is made to quantify in general terms the changing characteristics of the economic geography of the world market.

GLOBAL FORECASTS

Two basic principles must underlie any attempt to forecast the future demand for iron ore. First, there must be a recognition that the enormous and complex variety of economic forces—which are capable of influencing the trend of demand in any single country or region within it—are to some extent balanced out in a consideration of groups of countries and minimized at the world scale. It is therefore preferable to begin any examination of the future demand for iron ore at an aggregate world level, and then to assay a geographical subdivision of any forecast by groups of countries and, where necessary, by individual countries. Second, it is important to recognize that the roots of iron ore demands lie in the markets for steel. Thus it is expedient to work back from forecasts of steel demand in order to reach a satisfactory estimate of iron ore needs.

Several valuable and sophisticated exercises to forecast the future demand for steel, pig iron, and iron ore have been made by the United Nations—in particular by the Steel Committee of the Economic Commission for Europe. In 1959, in *Long-Term Trends and Problems of the European Steel Industry*, the Committee projected world production from 1957 to the three-year period 1972–75 on the basis of an empirically determined "law" of steel demand growth. Military conflicts and economic crises apart, it was noted that the world's steadily increasing consumption of steel since the third quarter of the nineteenth century displayed, in "normal" years, a regularity that was capable of mathematical description and afforded a reasonable basis for projecting the future growth of steel demands. In a 1968 study, on the other hand, the Committee attempted a steel demand forecast on the basis of several alternative models of the growth of steel production (and hence, on a world scale, of steel demand). It is appropriate to reconsider these models here.

The first was a slightly modified version of the 1959 exercise to understand past and future variations in steel demand as essentially a function of time. Projections were therefore made on the assumption that steel demand developed at a steady rate (with constant income elasticity) in one case, and at a falling rate (with decreasing income elasticity) in another. The second model successfully related variations in steel demand to changes in the standard of living, as expressed by an index of gross domestic product. On the basis of world population projections and the assumption that the world gross national product per head would continue to increase at the same 3.4 percent per annum as between 1950 and 1965, a second pair of figures for 1980 were obtained, again on two assumptions of constant and decreasing income elasticity. A third model of demand growth related to the evolution of what can be termed the "steel stock," although once again the per capita gross domestic product and its growth rate were the key explanatory variables. Given the assumption that the demand for steel is primarily a function of, on the one hand, living standards (or gross domestic product) in any one year, and, on the other hand, the need to replace obsolete steel structures and machinery, it was found statistically possible to isolate historical trends in both these components in order to better understand the prospects for the future. Once again, two projections were obtained on the assumptions of constant and decreasing income elasticity of demand through time.

The 1968 United Nations study, therefore, computed six sets of projections, two for each broad approach to the forecasting problem. For each set, high and low figures were derived on the basis of a forecasting probability of 95 percent (these figures are shown in Table 73). As can be seen, the figures exhibit a substantial range. Even their mean values for the world's steel demands in 1980 range from a low of 720 million tons to a high of 990 million tons. But the considerable resources available to the economists and statisticians of the ECE Steel Committee in making these global forecasts, and the fact that the projections were made publicly available as recently as 1968, mean that the present study would have considerable difficulty in materially improving upon them. Consequently, no new world steel demand forecast is made here, and the best estimate of the size of the world market for steel in 1980 is taken to be the mean tonnage of the six mean values listed in Table 73. The prospect, then, is for a global demand for 830 million tons of steel in 1980.

It is not unreasonable to assume that this demand will be satisfied, and that the resultant steel production will generate demands for pig iron that are capable of estimation. The statistics available necessitate the assumption that all of the pig iron produced in 1980 will be used in steel production. The production for foundry purposes is therefore neglected. The

TABLE 73. FORECASTS OF WORLD CRUDE STEEL PRODUCTION, 1980

(*Millions of tons*)

FORECAST MODEL	Low	High	Mean
I. Extrapolation of historical trend during "normal" years			
a. Assuming constant elasticity	650	995	823
b. Assuming decreasing elasticity	575	865	720
II. Changes in living standards			
a. Constant elasticity	920	1,060	990
b. Decreasing elasticity	727	855	791
III. Development of "steel stock"			
a. Constant elasticity	860	970	915
b. Decreasing elasticity	685	800	742
MEAN FORECAST			830

Source: United Nations, 1968-A.
Note: The forecasts assume a 95 percent probability.

resultant errors introduced into the calculations are clearly quite small compared with the large number of variables that must be acknowledged (and hence the errors that are liable to arise) in world forecasts of this nature. The level of pig iron demand in relation to steel production is subject to considerable variations between plants, localities, regions, and countries, as was seen in Chapter 3. It is affected not only by different and changing steelmaking technologies, but also by the fact that, within many processes, pig iron and scrap can be substituted for each other in response to their relative prices at the place of steel production. Thus, any forecast must recognize that the future replacement of open-hearth steelmaking by L.D. and similar converter processes will tend to reduce the amount of scrap used per ingot ton and so raise the ratio of steel production to pig iron demand. On the other hand, the growing popularity of large-scale electric steelmaking will clearly operate in the opposite direction. And simultaneously the increasing exploitation of continuous-casting processes will tend to make smaller quantities of process scrap available for steelmaking while improved methods of scrap collection, preparation, and transport make larger quantities available.

Although such a variety of changes might initially suggest the impossibility of forecasting the future ratio of steel production to pig iron demand, it has to be recalled that by 1965 many of these developments had already been affecting the consumption of metallics in the iron and steel industry for a number of years. And the available statistics for the previous decade reveal that the ratio (in contrast to its wide historical variations) had been tending to settle down at the level of 1:0.70 to 1:0.72. Moreover, an empirical examination by the ECE Steel Committee (United Nations, 1968-A) of different steelmaking processes and their consumption of metallics showed an increasingly narrow gap between the oxygen and reverberatory processes, and the prospect of that gap being closed at a level of 1:0.71 to 1:0.73.

On the basis of 830 million tons of steel production in 1980, a ratio of 1:0.70 would yield a demand for 581 million tons of pig iron. A ratio of 1:0.73, on the other hand, would imply a demand for 606 million tons. The present study, noting that at either level scrap availabilities would appear to be adequate (United Nations, 1968-A, p. 324), takes an approximate mean value of these two figures as its forecast for world pig iron demand in 1980. There is no reason to believe that this need for 595 million tons of pig iron will not be met. Hence, this figure affords the immediate basis of iron ore demands in 1980.

As was noted in Part I, the relationship between world pig iron production and global iron ore demands is also subject to both temporal and spatial variations. Partly these reflect differences in blast-furnace practice, and partly the inevitably crude nature of iron ore statistics using contained iron as their basic unit. For the purposes of the forecasts, it will be assumed that the ratio of pig iron production to iron ore consumption will fall slightly, over the fifteen-year period, to 1:0.91 as a result of improving blast-furnace practice, smaller losses of flue dust, and a modest increase in the use of scrap. The world demand for iron ore is therefore forecast to increase from 289 million contained tons in 1964 to 540 million tons sixteen years later. It is this global figure that forms the basis of the various regional and national ore demand forecasts in the following section.

REGIONAL FORECASTS

Attempts to disaggregate, on a regional and national basis, forecasts for the future demand for iron ore are inevitably subject to a greater number of pitfalls than the comparable global exercise. So many more variables and uncertainties are involved. Yet the attempt must be made before even the most qualified conclusion regarding future trends in the world market for iron ore can be reached. In order to reduce the variables (and possible errors) to a minimum, it is clearly advisable generally to make forecasts for those groups of countries whose economic systems are closely related and between whom a substantial trade in steel products either exists or could easily develop over a fifteen-year forecast period. Where a country has outstandingly large ore demands, and as a consequence plays a key role in the changing world geography of ore demands, a national forecast must also be made. The geographical basis of the regional ore demand forecast in the present study is shown in Table 74.

Three sets of broad assumptions underlie the forecasting exercise. They relate to the technological, locational, and political characteristics of the emerging world iron and steel industry. The findings of Chapter 3 demand that the projections be based on the expectation that, throughout the forecast period and under most economic and geographical circumstances, the cheapest way to produce pig iron will be provided by the blast furnace; that the most economical means of producing steel (at least tonnage carbon steel) will be in integrated works; and that economies of large-scale production will cause the industry generally to concentrate its output in larger and larger units. Therefore countries and plants that fail to take advantage of these technological imperatives will find their competitive position deteriorating. It is also assumed throughout the forecasts that, to the extent that market forces are allowed to influence the locational decisions of the iron and steel industry, most production will persist either close to large centers of demand or at market-oriented break-of-bulk points until and beyond 1980. Such an assumption follows directly from the

TABLE 74. ESTIMATED CHANGES IN THE PRODUCTION OF CRUDE STEEL AND PIG IRON, 1965–1980, AND IN THE APPARENT DEMAND FOR IRON ORE, 1964–1980, BY REGIONS AND SELECTED COUNTRIES

(Millions of tons)

Region and country	Steel production		Pig iron production		Demand for contained* iron ore	
	1965	1980	1965	1980	1964	1980
World	456	830	335	595	289	540
North America	128	160	89	110	72	96
Canada	9	18	7	13	5	12
U.S.A.	119	142	82	97	67	84
Western Europe	129	165	92	114	74	100
EEC	86	99	64	69	51	62
EFTA and rest	43	66	28	45	23	38
North*	107	124	82	89	67	77
South†	22	41	10	25	7	23
Eastern Europe	120	228	85	160	87	153
Middle Europe	29	48	18	34	17	32
U.S.S.R.	91	180	66	126	70	121
Asia	61	227	56	174	43	156
Japan	41	180	28	126	20	111
China and North Korea	13	32	21	32	17	30
Rest, incl. India	7	15	7	16	6	15
Oceania	5	12	4	9	4	8
Latin America	8	28	5	20	6	19
Africa and Middle East	4	10	4	8	3	8
Unallocated					1	

* North = EEC less Italy, and EFTA less Portugal.
† South = Portugal, Spain, Italy, Greece, Yugoslavia, and Turkey.

locational analyses of Chapters 2 and 5, from the falling volume of blast-furnace inputs for a given quantity of output (Chapter 3), and from the continuing improvement in the efficiency of bulk raw-material transport (Chapters 9 and 10).

At the same time, account has to be taken of the evidence of Chapter 4, which points to the growing efficiency of the transport arrangements for moving steel products to their markets, especially over long distances by sea. This transport efficiency not only implies possible extensions to the market areas of market-oriented plants seeking to exploit the economies of scale, but also permits the shipment of products and the penetration of established markets over considerable distances when substantial differences of steelmaking costs happen to occur. Finally, since the political influences in the determination of product market areas and the political leverage in plant location decisions are certain to persist, they too demand recognition in the forecasts. Their importance varies, of course, with the nature of national and regional economic systems.

The logical procedure for forecasting the demand for iron ore on a subglobal basis is to begin with an assessment of the changing locational pattern of steel demands, trade, and production. Steel demands are primarily a function of population size, living standards, economic structures, and general trading patterns. Steel production is a response to these demands, modified by trade in steel products. The shape of this trade is a response to many influences, including the industry's locational behavior, differentials in steel manufacturing costs, trade barriers, pricing policy, barter agreements between governments, and the like. Since a detailed study of all these many factors would clearly exhaust the resources of this inquiry, an alternative approach to the forecasting problem is required. Once again, a starting point is provided by the work of the Economic Commission for Europe (United Nations, 1968-A), which sought to estimate the broad pattern of steel output through the use of regional and national production coefficients in relation to world output. Countries with the longest tradition of steelmaking were assumed to have a constant coefficient, while variable coefficients were assumed for the more recent arrivals on the steelmaking scene. Such an approach to steel output forecasts is founded on the assumption that the factors influencing the location of steel production change only very slowly, and hence on the notion that the world pattern of steel production is unlikely to undergo any major shifts in a ten- or fifteen-year period.

Valuable though the ECE's forecasts are, they fail to come to grips with two closely related features of the world steel scene noted in Part I of this study. In the first place, they misinterpret the growth of the iron and steel products trade during the sixties. Instead of admitting the emerging differentials in the regional and national costs of producing steel and the geographical aspects of the problem of surplus capacity (see Chapter 6), the ECE Steel Committee interpreted the shifting pattern of steel trade as merely a response to "dynamic short and medium term market effects." It ignored these phenomena in fact, and took as its forecasting base a set of 1970 production estimates submitted by member countries of the United Nations. Naturally, the figures in these estimates represented a number of conflicting national aspirations. In particular, they incorporated a variety of unrealistic assumptions concerning likely trends in the pattern and the magnitude of the world's steel trade. In the second place, the forecasts of the ECE did not embrace what might be termed the "Japanese phenomenon." By this is meant the occasional ability of a country to develop its steel industry on a low-cost and highly competitive basis, and thereby to become capable not only of transforming the overall pattern of world steel trade but also of radically modifying the geography of production in a relatively short time.

The ECE forecasts—based as they were on suspect 1970 data, plus judgments regarding the prospective regional and national coefficients of steel production in relation to global output—demand modification. The regional estimates have therefore been adjusted in the present study, in the light of both recent changes in international steel trade and the evidence (admittedly limited) available on the differential costs of steelmaking in various parts of the world. On this basis, a more realistic set of forecasts can be suggested. And from these steel production forecasts, related expectations of pig iron production and iron ore demands can be determined with relative ease.

In the case of one macroregion—in fact, by 1980, the largest region from the viewpoint of ore demands—very little modification in the ECE figures is required. This is Eastern Europe, where, it must be assumed, an essentially closed economy will persist up to 1980 and beyond. Historically, this region has engaged in steel trade with other regions on only a very small scale. There were steel product exports of circa 1 million tons of ingot equivalent in 1950, and net exports of 3 million tons of ingot equivalent in 1965. Even if one assumes a growing and more liberal set of external trade relationships in the future, especially between the countries of Middle and Western Europe, the overseas trade of the U.S.S.R. would still seem likely to continue as the dominant force in the region's external linkages; and the 1980 net exports of the Eastern European steel industries would appear unlikely to exceed 5 million tons of ingot equivalent. Over the 1965–80 period, an average annual growth rate for steel consumption of 4.5 percent, compared with the characteristically higher rate of 8.5 percent over the previous fifteen years, would result in a consumption of 223 million tons at the end of the period. Therefore a reasonable production forecast for the whole of Eastern Europe in 1980 is 228 million tons. This represents just over 27 percent of the world output in that year, of which the U.S.S.R. will probably produce 180 million tons (see Table 74). Assuming, as did the ECE, that the 1980 ratio of pig iron to steel production in the region will be circa 0.75:1, the forecast of Eastern Europe's pig iron output in that year is 160 million tons. And iron ore demands (on the contained iron basis) are estimated at slightly below this level, at 153 million tons. Historically, Eastern European and especially Soviet production has been based on a somewhat greater ratio of pig iron to iron ore (measured on a contained iron basis). In 1964, for example, the Soviet ratio was 1:1.06. That it will move closer to the projected world average of 1:0.91 is unquestioned. The rate of change, however, does remain open to speculation. In assuming an Eastern European 1980 ratio of pig iron production to iron ore demands of 1:0.96, the forecast makes a reasonable yet bold assumption, which, if wrong, could clearly make an appreciable difference in the actual level of ore demand in the U.S.S.R. in the forecast year, and hence in the relationship of demand and supply. This point will be reiterated later.

North America's prospects are, if anything, more difficult to judge. Its demand for ore will for many years be primarily determined by the performance of the U.S. iron and steel industry, which (as noted in Chapter 6) during the fifties and early sixties experienced a rather slow expansion of home demand followed by a rapid upsurge of imports in the mid- and late sixties. These imports represented in part the effects of "surplus" steelmaking capacity in Western Europe, and a brisk 1964–65 upswing in domestic demands not unrelated to the Vietnam war. At the same time it was clear that the loss of home markets was also a function of lower steel-making costs overseas, especially in Japan (see Table 24). By 1965 steel imports into the United States had reached over 9 million product tons, while the steel trade balance showed a net deficit of nearly 7 million product tons. The import figure represented just under 10 percent of domestic consumption. Three years later, over 16 million tons of steel products were imported, representing approximately 17 percent of national steel consumption. In response, the steel industry exerted mounting pressure on the government to provide some degree of protection, and simultaneously it sought to persuade the international steel community to limit its shipments to the United States. Toward the end of 1968, the steelmakers of Japan and of the European Coal and Steel Community imposed "voluntary" ceilings on their exports to the United States. Britain did not join the ECSC countries in this restriction on exports.

It would be quite unrealistic to assume that the prospective magnitude of steel imports into the United States in 1980 can be scientifically estimated. Therefore the forecast in the present study makes the following (challengeable) assumptions. First, it assumes that the rapidly deteriorating situation (from the viewpoint of the U.S. steel industry) in the mid-sixties will be checked, despite the continuing downward pressure on the real international value of steel products at least throughout the early part of the period. The easing of the situation will be the result of one or more of the following developments: further voluntary international agreements to limit exports to the United States; political action, such as the imposition of tariffs or quotas or some other form of restriction on imports (such measures are, however, difficult to envisage in the light of the General Agreement on Tariffs and Trade [GATT] and the Kennedy Round); significant cost reductions in American iron and steel making; or a revision of exchange rates. At the same time, the inroads of the mid-sixties on the

American market by foreign suppliers will not be easily recaptured by the domestic industry. Without the prospect of a decisive cost and price advantage for the home mills, imports will probably still be entering the American market on a significant scale in 1980. Moreover, in the period up to and beyond 1980 some of the fastest-growing markets of the United States are likely to be in the west and the south of the country. Although by 1965 the steel industry was beginning to locate further capacity there, the existing sites of most U.S. mills and the ease of import into the California and Gulf ports suggest that these steel markets will remain more than usually vulnerable to foreign competition.

In 1965 the whole of North America recorded a deficit of 10 million ingot tons equivalent in its international steel transactions. By 1968 this had more than doubled. The present forecast therefore assumes that this deficit will by 1980 stand at 26 million ingot tons equivalent. This represents nearly 14 percent of the continent's requirements in that year, and is about the same share of North American demands as was satisfied by imports in 1968. North American consumption grew at an average rate of 2.9 percent per annum over the fifteen years up to 1965. In the light of historical trends, and granted the maturity of the economy, it would be overoptimistic to assume that the continent will increase its needs for steel in the years up to 1980 at a rate exceeding an average of 2 percent per annum—even with the prospect of a fairly rapid growth in the population of the United States and the growing importance of Canadian demands. A 2 percent annual growth rate yields a demand for some 186 million ingot tons of steel in 1980. The earlier trade assumptions therefore suggest a 1980 output of 160 million tons. Of this output, all but 18 million tons will be produced in the United States. The high degree of localization of the iron and steel industry in the Middle West, where the major American domestic iron ore resources are at their most competitive, will continue. Including the production of eastern Ontario, this inland zone produced about 70 percent of the continent's iron and steel in 1965. By 1980 the area appears likely still to be producing 65 percent of North American output, which implies an ingot tonnage of 104 million tons compared with 56 million tons elsewhere in the United States and Canada.

Translating these steel production forecasts into pig iron production, a ratio of just under 1:0.69 (compared with 1:0.695 in 1965) yields a North American pig iron output of 110 million tons in 1980. And on the basis of a ratio of pig iron production to iron ore demands of 1:0.87 (somewhat above that in 1964, but still below the assumed world average in 1980), the prospect is for an iron ore market of 96 million contained tons at the end of the period. Of this total, the United States demands will be 84 million tons (see Table 74).

Western European steel demands grew on average at a rate of 6.5 percent per year between 1950 and 1965. Production, even with exports increasing from 8 to 15 million ingot tons equivalent, rose slightly slower, at an annual average rate of 6.2 percent. But the halcyon days of rapid market expansion for the industry appeared to be over by 1965. In the largest and most important countries of the region, national rates of economic growth were quite modest by the mid-sixties (see Chapter 6), and the growth of steel markets was even slower. Moreover, with West Germany, Belgium, Luxembourg, France, and Britain each having a large amount of poorly located, high-cost, and obsolete steelmaking capacity, and with many of the firms sheltered from formal bankruptcy only by skillful accounting devices and government financial support, there appeared to be little medium-term economic reason why many of their export markets outside Western Europe would be retained. The strength of existing commercial channels and trading traditions can only mold the pattern of steel trade for so long. Even the import of steel into Western Europe from Japan on a considerable scale in the early seventies appeared both feasible and, for the Japanese, profitable. Therefore this study assumes that by 1980 Western Europe's 1965 net exports of 15 million tons ingot equivalent will be eroded back to zero, and that there will be a balanced trade account for steel in volume terms.

This does not deny the probability of an increasing amount of trade in steel products both in and out of Western Europe, as specialized products become more important and as problems of surplus capacity generate short-term market responses. Undoubtedly, these trading assumptions would have had to be very much gloomier from a Western European viewpoint but for a recognition of both the emotional role of steelmaking in the public economic mind there, and the regional unemployment implications of a more adverse swing in steel trading patterns. In other words, it is difficult to envisage Western European steelmaking without a great deal more public financial and other support in the period up to 1980, as it undergoes major yet inevitable structural and geographical changes.

Assuming that the demand for steel grows at an annual average rate of just under 2.5 percent between 1965 and 1980, buyers in Western Europe in the latter year will be looking for 165 million tons of steel. This and the earlier trading assumptions suggest a regional output of the same magnitude and imply a production growth rate of circa 1.7 percent per annum (compared with 6.2 percent between 1950 and 1965). This forecast is allocated (see Table 74) between the countries of the EEC on the one hand, and those of the rest of Western Europe on the other. However, a more meaningful breakdown from the viewpoint of ore demand and supply (also recorded in the table) is that between the northern part of the region and the southern part. The northern group of countries produced 90 percent of Western Europe's steel in 1950 and 83 percent in 1965. Yet their steel output between 1965 and 1980 appears likely to grow at an average annual rate of just over 1.1 percent. Their industries are all the "oldest" in the region and are suffering from both structural and geographical problems; they are likely to experience a decline in net export opportunities; and they are primarily serving technologically advanced but slowly growing home markets. On these assumptions, the joint output of the northern group of countries in 1980 appears likely to be 124 million tons, about three-quarters of the Western European total. The southern group of countries (at a lower standard of living at the outset of the forecast period, some with quickly growing economies, and all with a political desire to see the expansion of their iron and steel output) are likely to increase their production to 41 million tons by 1980, at an annual growth rate of circa 4 percent.

If one assumes a ratio of steel output to pig iron production of 1:0.69, these forecasts imply a Western European pig iron output of 114 million tons in 1980. Of this, 89 million tons will be in the northern group of countries, and the other 25 in the south. From these figures, a Western European demand for 100 million tons of contained iron ore can reasonably be forecast for 1980, with the market in the north accounting for 77 million tons of that quantity.

From these forecasts it follows that the rest of the world, outside Europe (both East and West) and North America, will increase its demands for steel from 86 million tons in 1965 to 256 million tons in 1980. This represents an annual average growth rate of nearly 7.6 percent. During the same period, the countries concerned—largely as a result of the highly competitive position of the Japanese iron and steel industry—seem likely to transform a net import of 8 million tons of ingot equivalent in 1965 into a net export of 21 million tons of ingot equivalent in 1980. As a consequence, steel production appears likely to expand at an annual rate of about 8.8 percent, from 78 million tons in 1965 to 277 million tons in 1980.

Any attempt to disaggregate this figure geographically faces more than the usual range of difficulties. The largest single component in the total is Japan, a country whose performance in the matter of steel production could not possibly have been foreseen in 1950. Will its economy and steel industry continue to grow during the next fifteen years at an equally startling pace? Will it be able to maintain its apparent 1965 cost advantage over its chief competitors and so play an ever-increasing exporting role? Or will trade restrictions come to check its penetration of overseas markets? A second large component is the steel industry of China, whose past performance is not exactly clear, owing to poor statistical evidence and limited information. India's iron and steel production has fallen behind the country's original plans. Can it recover? What is the possibility of a Japanese-like performance elsewhere in the developing world during the next fifteen years? The questions are as varied as they are difficult to answer. Yet assumptions have to be made in order to reach working forecasts.

In the case of Japan, it is assumed that the home market will continue its brisk growth of the fifties and sixties (at over 14 percent per annum for steel) and so provide the essential foundation for a vigorous steel industry. It is ventured that this growth (retrospectively based in part on the persistent buoyancy of steel-intensive exports) will afford the steel industry ample opportunities to continue its rapid investment in new and low-cost plant. As a result it will allow the industry a continuing, even growing, cost advantage over its chief competitors. It is further assumed that the trend toward trade liberalization throughout the world will continue, with the result that the Japanese steel industry will be able to increase its exports from an equivalent of 12 million ingot tons in 1965, and 23 million ingot tons in 1968, to 45 million ingot tons equivalent in 1980. The latter tonnage represents a slight decrease in the relative importance of exports to the industry over the period, since the prospect is for the domestic steel demands of Japan to increase at 10.8 percent per annum, from 29 to 135 million tons between 1965 and 1980. Production as a consequence appears likely to grow at an annual average rate of 10.3 percent, and so to reach 180 million tons in 1980. On the basis of an assumed national self-sufficiency in pig iron (which certainly is the medium-term aspiration of the Japanese industry), and a ratio of steel production to pig iron production of circa 1:0.7, this figure suggests a pig iron output of some 126 million tons in 1980. Using a ratio of pig iron production to iron ore demands of 1:0.88, which can reasonably be associated with prospective Japanese conditions, this in turn implies that Japanese iron ore requirements in the forecast year will be 111 million contained tons, 27 million tons more than the forecast demand for the United States at the same time, and only 10 million tons less than the forecast for the U.S.S.R.

Regarding other parts of Asia, if one accepts the United Nations forecast of 1968, there is every reason to assume that there will be a continued growth of iron and steel production in both China and North Korea. Together, they could achieve an output of 32 million tons of steel by 1980. Given the assumption that a steeply falling ratio of steel production to pig iron output will accompany rising living standards and economic development, the steel industry of these two countries is likely to be associated with a pig iron production of 32 million tons and an iron ore requirement of some 30 million tons of contained ore in that year. The rest of Asia, in the meantime, including India, appears likely to have generated demands for about half the latter figure, making the total ore requirements for Asia as a whole some 156 million contained tons.

Table 74 attempts an allocation of the remaining world steel production in 1980 within the global figure of 830 million tons. The greater part of the growth will be in Latin America, where steel production appears likely to rise to 28 million tons and so to generate demands for 19 million tons of contained iron ore—over three times that of fifteen years earlier. The forecast year will also see the ore demands of Oceania and of Africa, together with those of the Middle East, standing each at some 8 million contained tons.

The Demand for Iron Ore in 1980

Figure 20 summarizes the forecast world pattern of steel production in 1980. By that year, 27.5 percent of global output will be in Eastern Europe, and the U.S.S.R. will have increased its share of world production from 19.8 percent in 1965 to nearly 22 percent (Table 75). Meanwhile the relative world importance of steelmaking in North America and Western Europe will have declined. The North American share will have fallen from 27.8 percent in 1965 to 19.3 percent. The industry in the United States will rank as only the third largest in the world, after the joint leaders, the U.S.S.R. and Japan; and it will be producing only 17.1 percent of the world's steel in 1980, compared with the 26 percent it made fifteen years earlier. By 1980 the steelworks of Western Europe, which produced 28.3 percent in 1965, will be pouring only 20 percent of the world's ingots. Nearly two-thirds of this will be made in the present EEC countries, and over three-quarters in the northern part of the region. The output of northern Western European producers will have been exceeded by that of the Japanese industry in the early seventies. Largely as a result of Japan's remarkable performance, the importance of Asia as a steel producer will have risen from 13.9 percent in 1965 to 27.4 percent. On a tonnage basis, Asian steel production will be of equal importance to that of Eastern Europe. Elsewhere in the world, the prospective changes will be of huge importance locally and nationally. Latin American output will more than treble during the period; yet by 1980 its relative importance in the world context will still remain quite small at 3.4 percent.

The resultant pattern of pig iron production in 1980 exhibits broadly the same spatial characteristics and shifts as in the previous fifteen years. The principal exception is the greater share of pig iron production in Asia compared with that continent's steel output. The growing capacities of Chinese and Indian furnaces, which together will produce circa 8 per-

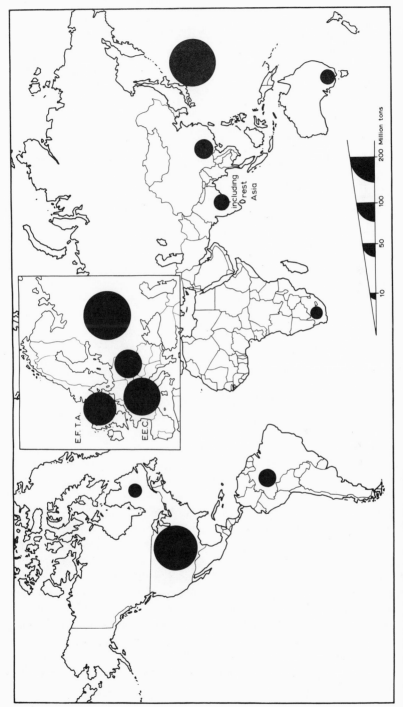

FIGURE 20. Estimated world steel production, 1980.

301

TABLE 75.   ESTIMATED SIZE AND PERCENTAGE SHARE OF WORLD CRUDE STEEL AND PIG IRON
            PRODUCTION, AND APPARENT DEMAND FOR IRON ORE, 1980, BY REGIONS AND
            SELECTED COUNTRIES

| | Steel production | | Pig iron production | | Demand for contained iron ore | |
Region and country	Millions of tons	Percentage	Millions of tons	Percentage	Millions of tons	Percentage
World......................	830	100.00	595	100.00	540	100.00
North America..............	160	19.28	110	18.49	96	17.78
Canada..................	18	2.17	13	2.18	12	2.22
U.S.A....................	142	17.11	97	16.30	84	15.56
Western Europe..............	165	19.88	114	19.16	100	18.52
EEC......................	99	11.93	69	11.60	62	11.48
EFTA and rest..............	66	7.95	45	7.56	38	7.04
North*....................	124	14.94	89	14.96	77	14.26
South*....................	41	4.94	25	4.20	23	4.26
Eastern Europe..............	228	27.47	160	26.89	153	28.33
Middle Europe..............	48	5.78	34	5.71	32	5.93
U.S.S.R...................	180	21.87	126	21.18	121	22.41
Asia......................	227	27.35	174	29.24	156	28.89
Japan.....................	180	21.69	126	21.18	111	20.56
China and North Korea......	32	3.86	32	5.38	30	5.56
Rest, incl. India.............	15	1.81	16	2.69	15	2.78
Oceania....................	12	1.45	9	1.51	8	1.48
Latin America...............	28	3.37	20	3.36	19	3.52
Africa and Middle East........	10	1.20	8	1.34	8	1.48

* See Table 74 for countries included.

cent of the world total in 1980, are especially noteworthy. And these forecasts in turn suggest a 1980 pattern of iron ore demand, which merits
some comments in addition to the visual summary of Figure 21.

Eastern Europe and the U.S.S.R. will be of prime importance, with their
needs for approximately 28 and 22 percent, respectively, of the world's
iron ore in 1980. Global demand, it will be recalled, will by then have
reached 540 million contained tons. Although the Soviet figure represents
the largest national ore market in the world, its percentage share of world
requirements will in fact be slightly smaller than it was in 1964. The relative
decline in ore demands in North America and Western Europe, to 17.8
and 18.5 percent, respectively (from 25.4% and nearly 26% in 1964), will
be rather more severe. Nevertheless, within North America, the United
States will still offer the third-largest national market for iron ore. And the
EEC countries will still generate over 11 percent of global iron ore needs
(compared with over 17 percent fifteen years earlier). More important than
the market of the whole of Western Europe in 1980 will be the market of
Japan. Its prospective level of demand, at 111 million contained tons,
represents over one-fifth of the world total. This will be by far the largest

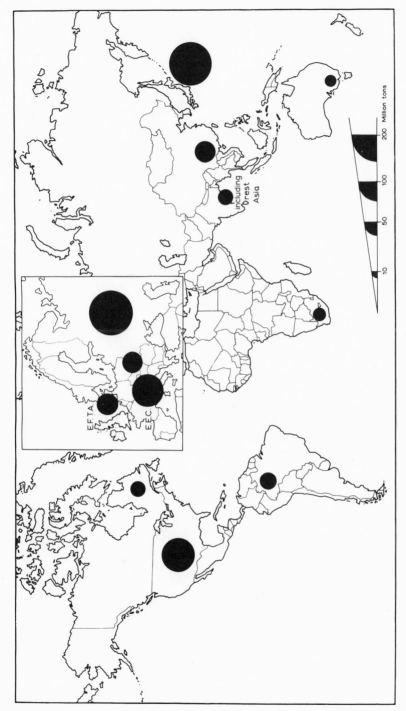

FIGURE 21. Estimated world iron ore demand (Fe content), 1980.

component in the sum of Asian demands, which by 1980 will be slightly larger than Eastern European demands and approaching 30 percent of the world's requirements. In Oceania, Latin America, and Africa the need for iron ore throughout the forecast period will remain very small indeed. Together they will still represent only a little more than 6 percent of the world total in 1980. However, as we shall see in the next chapter, these macroregions will have a much larger role to play in the satisfaction of the world's iron ore demands.

CHAPTER 14

Trends in the Supply of Iron Ore, 1965–1980

AVAILABILITIES IN 1980

Any assessment of the most likely response of the iron ore industry to the growth of demand forecast in Chapter 13 must be rooted in an understanding of the prospective availability of iron ore to 1980. In this regard, three elements in particular merit consideration: the size of reserves, the adequacy of transport, and the availability of production facilities.

As was noted in Chapter 11, there are not likely to be any major constraints on the future supply of iron ore as a consequence of the global magnitude of reserves. On assumptions of world steel production far more optimistic than those in the last chapter, no more than 7 thousand million contained tons of ore will be consumed between 1965 and 1980. However, the world's reserves in 1966 (admittedly loosely defined, yet without recent Chinese figures) were calculated by the United Nations to be 114 thousand million contained tons. On a macroregional basis, also, ample reserves are clearly available. Even the more poorly endowed part of the world, such as Western Europe and Asia (minus China, again), have reserves capable of supporting their steel industries well into the twenty-first century.

As to the second element—ore transport—two questions arise: Will adequate facilities be available, and will competitive rates be offered for the haulage of ore from the mines to the markets? On these questions, it is impossible to make a sweeping global generalization. In certain parts of the world, and between particular mines and particular blast furnaces, transport arrangements could conceivably become congested, inadequate, or too costly, and thus fail the mining industry. But the history of changing transport facilities and costs in the period 1950 to 1965 (see Chapters 9 and 10) suggests that in the future transport developments will generally tend to reduce the delivered costs of iron ore and make larger quantities of ore from a wider range of deposits competitively available to the iron and steel works of the world. It is not unreasonable to assume that the years from 1965 to 1980 will see progressively cheaper rail hauls, faster and more efficient loading and unloading facilities, and a larger size of ore carriers. These are hardly trends likely to constrain the availability of ore at its markets in the period under consideration.

The third element—the size of production facilities—could hamper the availability of sufficient ore to meet demands in 1980. In the long run, this will depend on a variety of complex factors, one of the most important being the price of ore and hence the profitability of production. In a medium run, such as that under consideration, the availability of production facilities has already been broadly decided, since it usually takes more than a decade to establish the complex geological and economic parameters of a mining investment, to come to a commercial decision, to install the necessary plant and transport facilities, and then to get production under way on a large scale. It is highly unlikely, for example, that a deposit not being seriously considered for production in the late sixties will be making a major impact on world ore availabilities in 1980. Therefore the following estimates of *technically feasible* production in 1980 are based on the most recent information concerning the iron ore mining facilities of individual countries and known plans for their development or extension (United Nations, 1968-A). The figures are inevitably crude, and they underestimate what *could* be possible with small judicious investments in particular deposits. However, they are a first necessary step toward answering the question of whether 1980 is likely to have adequate mining capacity. This will subsequently allow judgments to be made about the trends in the markets for ore, changes in its price, shifts in the international ore trade, and hence a probable pattern of production in that year.

In North America, the United States will continue to have a larger capacity than Canada throughout the period up to 1980. All avaliable evidence points to the prospect of a continuing high level of investment in new mine and beneficiating facilities on the taconite and jasperite deposits of the Lake Superior region. There, the Minnesota tax concessions, plus the proximity to the lower lakes market area, appear likely to offset the high capital costs of such developments. By 1980, therefore, the Lake Superior iron ore industry could well have a capacity of just under 50 million contained tons, of which 44 million tons (some 70 million actual tons) would be for the production of pellets. Elsewhere in the country a certain amount of capacity growth can reasonably be expected in Missouri, and more in the Western States, in response to both domestic and Japanese demands. These developments seem likely to push the total capacity of the U.S. industry up to 62 million contained tons (Table 76), of which some 53 million tons will be for the preparation of pellets.

TABLE 76.   ESTIMATED SIZE OF TECHNICALLY FEASIBLE WORLD IRON ORE PRODUCTION, 1980,
BY REGIONS AND SELECTED COUNTRIES

(Thousands of tons)

Region and country	Fe content	Actual tonnage
WORLD	637	1,106
NORTH AMERICA	102	163
Canada	40	63
U.S.A.	62	100
WESTERN EUROPE	60	140
EEC	17	55
France	14	45
Other EEC	3	10
Britain	2	8
Norway	2	4
Sweden	23	37
Others	16	36
EASTERN EUROPE	193	346
Middle Europe	5	16
U.S.S.R.	188	330
ASIA	92	157
Communist Asia	45*	78*
Non-Communist Asia	47	79
India	34	55
Japan	2	4
Malaysia	6	10
Others	5	10
OCEANIA	30	46
Australia	29	45
Others	1	1
LATIN AMERICA	93	147
Brazil	45	70
Chile	17	27
Peru	7	12
Venezuela	18	28
Others	6	10
AFRICA AND MIDDLE EAST	67	108
Angola	4	6
Gabon	10	16
Guinea	6*	10*
Liberia	18	28
Mauretania	6	10
North Africa	7	13
Sierra Leone	3	4
South Africa	7	11
Others	6	10

Source: United Nations, 1968-A, p. 158.
* Author's estimate.

Known investment plans in Canada probably will raise capacity there to 40 million contained tons by 1980. The mines in British Columbia appear unlikely, for purely physical resource reasons, to increase their potential significantly. A modest expansion of mining activity in Ontario can be anticipated in response to the growing needs of the lower lakes iron and steel industry in both Canada and the United States. But by far the largest growth of Canadian production capacity will be located in the eastern provinces—in Quebec and Labrador. There, the installation of beneficiation and pellet facilities is proceeding apace, and by 1980 the facilities of Cartier, Carol Lake, and Wabush will represent the backbone of the Canadian industry. The estimated total capacity of North American mines in that year, therefore, will be slightly in excess of 100 million contained tons. The projected level of North American demands in 1980, it will be recalled, is 96 million contained tons.

The productive capacity of the Western European iron ore industry, on the other hand, is likely to grow at a much slower pace during the years up to 1980. Partly this will result from an actual contraction of mining capacity in certain countries. For example, in the absence of a major technological development that would allow the economic beneficiation of the Minette ores, it would be unwise to assume anything other than a gradual contraction of French output and of mining capacity in Lorraine. The ability of the industry to produce ore is liable to contract more slowly than the willingness of the iron and steel industry to use the ore. Therefore, to suggest that the French iron ore industry will have a capacity to produce 14 million contained tons in 1980 is not meant to imply that all of it will be used. In the same year, it is reasonable to expect that the capacity of the British industry will also have been reduced, to some 2 million contained tons, and that iron ore mining in West Germany will have effectively disappeared.

Although the Swedish industry by 1980 will still be the largest in Western Europe, its capacity will not be expanded in the seventies at a rate comparable to its growth in the fifties and early sixties. The deteriorating market conditions for high-phosphorus ores, plus the relatively high costs of underground mining, are bound to erode profits and slow down investment. On the other hand, the great interest of the Swedish state in the continued prosperity of the industry, plus the possibility of producing more low-phosphorus pellets from the Lapland ores, should ensure a 1980 mining capacity of 23 million contained tons. A further 2 million contained tons of capacity in Norway will bring the Scandinavian total to 25 million tons. Elsewhere in Western Europe, in particular in Spain and Portugal, and in Yugoslavia and Turkey, a continuing expansion of their relatively small-scale mining activities will ensure a total capacity of some 16 million contained tons there in 1980. Total Western European capacity in that year, therefore, appears likely to be 60 million contained tons, compared with a projected demand for iron ore of some 100 million contained tons.

Eastern European mining capacity, on the other hand, appears likely to exceed the region's demands for 153 million contained tons by nearly

40 million tons. If the ratio of pig iron production to iron ore demands there approaches closer to the world average than is assumed in Chapter 13, the excess will be even greater. Most of this Eastern European capacity will be in the Soviet Union, whose plans provide for the establishment of iron ore mining capacity in its far eastern region (in Yakut), and for expansion of capacity in eastern Siberia (at the Ansask and Nizhne-Angara deposits). There are also expansion plans for the northern region, at the Olenyogorsk and Enokovdorsk deposits. By far the most important developments, however, will be more closely related to existing major centers of iron and steel production and ore demand. Thus, in the Ukraine, in the Kursk region, in the Urals, and in Kazakhstan, plans exist for major extensions to the country's iron ore mining capacity. In all, the estimated capacity of the iron ore industry in the U.S.S.R. in 1980 will be 188 million contained tons, of which perhaps 40 million tons will be in the form of pellets. To this figure can be added a capacity of 5 million contained tons in the countries of Middle Europe, where very little expansion of iron ore mining is possible for purely physical resource reasons. The total capacity of Eastern Europe in 1980 is therefore estimated to be 193 million contained tons.

Although the Communist countries of Asia would appear to be able to cover their iron ore needs in 1980, and to have a small amount of capacity available for export, Asia as a whole appears certain to fall into the deficit category. The country with the largest capacity will be India, which has plans for the creation of an iron ore industry capable of winning up to 40 million contained tons. However, in the light of past delays in the implementation of Indian plans, realism demands a reduction of this figure to a more plausible 34 million contained tons. Much smaller by comparison are the anticipated capacities of other Asian countries. Largely because of a poor geological endowment in iron ore, Malaysian capacity will be no more than 6 million contained tons; that of Japan 2 million tons; and that of the rest of Asia—in particular the mines of the Philippines and Thailand —a further 5 million tons. By comparison with the estimated Asian demand for 156 million contained tons of iron ore in 1980, the evidence suggests that only about 92 million contained tons will in fact be available from within the region.

Part of this deficit will be made up from Oceania. There, 1967 plans suggested a 1980 capacity of some 30 million contained tons. This figure could easily and inexpensively be increased, but it is considerably in excess of prospective local needs, which are forecast at a mere 8 million contained tons in 1980. In addition, Asian demands could be satisfied in part by the huge reserves of Latin America and Africa. It is to these that we finally turn.

By far the most important increments to Latin American ore-mining capacity will be in Brazil. Plans are already under way for major extensions to existing capacity, for development of new mines in the Rio Doce and Parapoeba valleys, and for the completion of associated transport facilities for export tonnage. These projects are likely to increase the country's ore-mining capacity to 45 million contained tons by 1980. In Chile, on the other hand, the comparable figure is only 17 million contained tons. Its El Algarrobo and El Romeral mines are likely to expand, but the El Tofo mine will be phased out through exhaustion. In its place there is the possibility of developing at El Laco a new deposit with considerable reserves, provided market conditions are attractive. In Venezuela, after a new deposit has been opened for the domestic iron and steel industry at San Isidro, no major development is to be expected. However, the considerable unexploited potential available at the two existing mines of El Pao and Cerro Bolívar will mean that a total Venezuelan capacity of 18 million contained tons can reasonably be forecast for 1980. The counterpart Peruvian figure, largely dependent on developments at the Marcona mine, is some 7 million contained tons. This is a little above the expected joint capacity of all the other ore producers in Latin America. Therefore the total capacity of the Latin American iron ore industry in 1980, in response to domestic demands of 19 million contained tons and overseas opportunities, appears to be 93 million contained tons.

In Africa, the biggest increase in production capacity will undoubtedly occur in Liberia. There the Lamco Nimba developments will mature, and any decline in the Mano River output can be offset by exploiting the nearby Big Range. By 1980, therefore, Liberia should be in a position to produce 18 million contained tons of ore. The second-largest national capacity in Africa at that time could possibly be a new producer, Gabon, where plans exist to open the Mékambo deposit located some 600 km inland from the port at Owendo. Another significant new producer by 1980 could well be Guinea, whose Nimba and Simandou deposits are so near the Liberian mines that the incremental transport investment required for their exploitation would be small. No major developments are at present expected in Angola, Mauretania, Sierra Leone, Swaziland, and South Africa. In North Africa, with its below-average ores and its falling export opportunities, the condition and capacity of the industry are expected to decline. The prospective capacity of iron ore mining in the various parts of Africa sum to a total of 67 million contained tons. This figure contrasts vividly with the continent's forecast "home" demand in 1980 of a mere 8 million contained tons.

The world's iron ore industry in 1980, then, on the evidence of the late sixties, is likely to have a capacity of some 637 million contained tons— very nearly 100 million contained tons more than the estimated world demand in that year. When geographically isolated markets, tied deposits, and long-term contracts are taken into account, the excess of capacity over uncommitted demands will be even greater. Crude though they may be, these figures strongly suggest that there are likely to be revisions in the expansion plans of the iron ore mining industry, for the cost of such a magnitude of underutilized capacity would be too great for the industry to carry. A tendency toward substantial surplus capacity by the mid-seventies, for example, would cause f.o.b. prices to fall and would almost certainly lead to the postponement or cancellation of some of the projects whose capacity is included in the figures of Table 76. The El Laco deposit in Chile and the Mékambo project in Gabon, both of which have particularly long rail hauls to their prospective ports of export, come readily to mind. Doubts can also be raised about the planned growth of Soviet capacity, which appears likely to be well in excess of Eastern European needs and based partly on a questionable magnitude of exports to the countries of Middle Europe.

Notwithstanding this prospect of iron ore mining capacity being brought more closely into line with the expected growth of demand (and the possibility of temporary and localized shortages as a result of strikes and disasters), other evidence suggests that there is every likelihood of an iron ore buyer's market persisting throughout the greater part, if not all, of the forecast period. With this buyer's market one must associate a steady downward pressure on iron ore prices. Moreover, there is little doubt that advances in the technology of production and improvements in the efficiency of iron ore transport will continue and spread throughout the world. They will not only permit lower haulage rates, but also intensify the competitive challenge of the more distant sources of ore with low f.o.b. costs. In addition, many existing low-cost mines (even some that have no expansion plans) could, with relative ease, be given additional capacity at very low cost, compared with an investment of $30 to $40 per ton of annual capacity in new mines. Existing operations can frequently be expanded for only $5 to $10 per ton. Also, the tendency of major ore consumers to encourage such developments simply in order to keep the market "soft" suggests that it is more reasonable to assume a continuing downward trend in ore prices than to speculate otherwise. There is reason to believe that continuing technological progress (see Chapter 8) will ensure falling unit production costs for the larger and more efficient mines, and so allow them to maintain their profitability in the face of such a weakening of ore prices.

There could, of course, be something of a political rearguard action fought on behalf of the iron ore producers against a continuing fall in the value of iron ore. The countries of the developing world in particular could seek—possibly through the United Nations Conference on Trade and Development (UNCTAD)—to increase their bargaining power and hence their foreign exchange earnings by agreements to raise royalties or attempts to limit supplies. An iron ore equivalent to the oil producers' Organization of the Petroleum Exporting Countries (OPEC) has been mooted. However, the likelihood of such an organization being created and being effective must be regarded skeptically when so much mining capacity to meet export requirements is located in the technologically advanced nations (including the Soviet Union), with their primarily consumer interests. The wisdom of such a move to influence iron ore prices in this fashion must be questioned. For, the first result of higher or even stabilized ore prices would undoubtedly be to prolong the economic life of many of the higher-cost mines in Western Europe, and so to deny to the producers of the developing world a number of markets that might otherwise be theirs.

In sum, there can be little doubt that in the period up to 1980 the market for iron ore will in general be characterized by falling prices, and that these will tend to accelerate the declining importance of the low-grade and high-cost producers. At the same time, the more competitive mines will be afforded an opportunity to increase their share of the market. Before reaching more precise conclusions about the future pattern of iron ore production, it is important first to consider the prospects for international trade in iron ore.

Prospective Patterns of Iron Ore Trade in 1980

The future magnitude and the direction of international trade in iron ore will be molded by four sets of factors in particular.

The first factor is the long-term contractual arrangement for the supply of ore to particular markets. Table 39 lists some contracts for supplies to Japan. A number of these extend well beyond 1980. The Hamersley contract, for example, expires in 1983; the Mt. Newman contract in 1990; the Rio Doce contract in 1981. Between the countries of Middle Europe and the Soviet Union, and between some of the major iron and steel producers of Western Europe and their suppliers, similar long-term agreements exist. Extending up to and beyond 1980, they are clearly one important determining factor in the pattern of iron ore trade for that year.

The second factor influencing ore shipments in the forecast year is the distinctive geography of mine ownership and the considerable investments by iron and steel producers in particular mines and reserves. The investments of the U.S. steel corporations in Canadian, Venezuelan, and Liberian mines, for example, will clearly play an important role in influencing the pattern of American imports in the future, just as they have done in the past. Similarly, Western European investments in the mines of Mauretania, Canada, and Brazil, and Japanese investments in Australia and India, cannot be ignored in any assessment of international iron ore movements in 1980. To be sure, an iron and steel company owning a part interest in a particular mine can elect to sell its share of the mine's production on the open market rather than use the ore itself. And this does happen. It is one of the reasons for the frequent association of merchant iron ore mining companies with developments primarily designed to meet the iron ore needs of an individual iron and steel producer or groups of producers. However, a great number of iron and steel companies prefer the security of supplies and the ore quality control that are associated with their own deposits and preparation facilities, and they are prepared to pay a premium price for that security and product consistency. Moreover, in a market experiencing a glut of ore, it is easy to see why companies with investments in ore mines will generally prefer to maintain mining operations at a reasonable level by using their own supplies, rather than purchase ores at a discount on the open market. Patterns of mine ownership, therefore, cannot be ignored in any forecast of trading patterns.

The third factor demanding recognition is the geographical situations in which the proximity of markets to raw-material sources suggests the virtual certainty of important movements of ore. While the falling costs of long-distance ocean transport have reduced the advantage of Quebec and Labrador ores in the U.S. east coast market, of Swedish ores in the North Sea market, and of Philippine ores in the Japanese market, that advantage of proximity to the respective markets still remains. It remains partly because a small freight advantage will tend to persist, and partly because the accessibility of the mines to their markets is frequently paralleled by loose political affiliations, which also affect the pattern of iron ore trade.

The fourth factor is the more overt political influence on trade. Quite apart from any cost and price advantages, the heavy reliance of the countries of Middle Europe on the mines of the U.S.S.R. is likely to continue for purely political reasons. On the other hand, it is clear that a major obstacle to a vigorous expansion of iron ore trade between China and Japan is the existing and the prospective political relationship between the two countries. The political factor is of importance in both the present pattern of iron ore shipments (see Chapter 7) and the future pattern. Individual blast-furnace operators will doubtless press for a decreasing variety of ores in their furnaces and will move toward the goal of automating their smelting from one or two well-prepared ores; but companies, groups of producers, and countries will simultaneously seek to diversify their ore sources in order to minimize the political risks involved in a major disruption of their supplies. The greater the political stability of a particular source of ore, the less will be the tendency of consumers to diversify away from it. By the same token, most mining companies, when they are primarily meeting open-market demands, will tend to prefer a diversified pattern of outlets, even at the expense of some concessions on price, rather than see themselves dependent on the fortunes and demands of a particular iron and steel producer.

These four sets of factors are somewhat different from, and perhaps less subject to confident quantification than, the so-called "predetermined trade flows" noted by the Economic Commission for Europe in its "theoretical" study of the world's iron ore trade for the year 1975 (United Nations, 1968-A, p. 168). In that study, which excluded China, some 100 million contained tons of trade (about 57 percent of consumer requirements) were allocated on the basis of known trading relationships and anticipated sales contracts. (The Commission, however, appeared strangely eager to allocate "privileged" ore flows from Gabon ore even before the future of the Mékambo deposits had been decided.) These predetermined trade flows fell broadly into two categories. The first included a number of expected 1975 iron ore movements by inland transport—shipments along the Great Lakes and the St. Lawrence, along inland waterways, and by rail. And the second included estimates of certain distinctive ocean movements based on the existence of special relationships between exporters and importers. In large measure the second category comprised anticipated trade in high-phosphorus ores, known long-term contracts between ore suppliers and certain iron and steel producers, and ore movements that could reasonably be expected to follow from the pattern of the iron and steel industry's investments in iron ore mines. In some markets, these predetermined flows made up the greater part of supplies. In the United States, for example, 93 percent of the assumed 1975 imports were allocated in this way. In other markets, such as Britain (29%) or southern Western Europe (10%), the share was quite small.

Outside of these predetermined flows, the remaining markets for iron ore in 1975 were allocated by means of a theoretical model. This was based on a number of broad assumptions concerning the estimated costs of mining and preparing ores in different countries, the costs of railing these ores to the ports of export, and the level of freight rates for iron ore shipments along each of the possible routes to the ports of import. Iron ore production was allocated to the various markets by means of a linear program that assigned to each importing region the most economical ores to the extent that they were assumed to be available. Five alternative forecasts of the nonpredetermined flows of ore were calculated by making small but important changes in the basic cost assumptions. Shipping costs were raised and lowered, for example; mining costs likewise.

Invaluable though the ECE's exercise is in assessing future trading prospects for different iron ore producers throughout the world, it demands interpretation in the light of known geographical variations in mining costs and freight rates. For example, the simplicity of the model meant that all Liberian and Indian ores were assumed to have the same f.o.b. costs, regardless of known differences in the mining costs on different ore fields and variations in length of haul (and hence freight rates) between the mines and the ports of export. Again, the model assumed that ocean freights varied solely with distance. The effects of the growth of backhaul cargoes along particular routes, which are capable of radically lowering the ocean freight rates for iron ore and of significantly altering the competitive position of particular mines or countries (see Chapter 9), had as a result to be overlooked. Moreover, the considerable differences and the variable relationships between the delivered costs of iron ore on the one hand and its market prices on the other (matters that have a considerable bearing on the marketing pattern) simply could not be integrated into the linear program for the nonpredetermined flows.

At the same time, the model demonstrated very effectively certain powerful forces operating on the geography of iron ore trade now and in the near future. The outstandingly advantageous position of Venezuelan ores competing in the U.S. market, of Australian ores in the Japanese market, and of Liberian ores in the North Sea market, clearly emerges from the study. These findings are firmly embraced in the forecasts that follow.

In attempting to reach a reasonable set of forecasts for iron ore trade in 1980, an initial assumption had first to be made for each of the major markets (listed in Table 77) concerning the amount of domestic mining capacity they will use to satisfy their demands. Then, in the light of the four major factors discussed earlier, plus the ECE findings, a preliminary "flow" of ore to some 80 percent of all import markets around the world was determined. This first allocation resulted, not unnaturally, in the prospect of certain mines being worked to full capacity, and in the simultaneous gross underutilization of others. A second allocation of 1980 iron ore flows to the importing countries and regions was therefore made. Some of the original assumptions concerning the use of domestic ores were altered in the light of import availabilities; the other 20 percent of the import market in each country or region was made available; and then, in the light of the evidence embodied in Part II of this study, a judgment was made concerning the prospective marketing and price strategies of the various suppliers in the event of reality approaching the initial allocation. This second set of ore flows still resulted in the prospect of some mines being fully utilized, while in other parts of the world a considerable

TABLE 77. ESTIMATED TRADE IN IRON ORE, 1980

(Millions of contained tons)

Importers Exporters	Estimated capacity available for export	Canada	U.S.A.	Western Europe, North[a]	Western Europe, South	Middle Europe	Japan	Total exports
Canada	30		18	6	1		2	27
U.S.A.	5[b]	2					3	5
Scandinavia	21			12	2	2		16
U.S.S.R.	44			4	2	20	10	36
India	22			0.5	0.5	1	18	20
Other Asian	9[c]						8	8
Australia	36[d]			3			33	36
Brazil and Venezuela	50		9	16	4	3	6	38
Chile and Peru	22		2	2.5	1.5		16	22
West Africa	38		4	17	4	2	9	36
Southern Africa	5			1			4	5
Total		2	33	62	15	28	109	249

a Less Scandinavia.
b Refers to Western States only.
c Excluding China and North Korea.
d Assuming some expansion of capacity beyond that planned in 1967.

share of national mining capacity continued to face the possibility of an unacceptable idleness. A third and final allocation was therefore made.

In one case—Australia—the prospective demands on the country's mines were singularly strong. And since an increase in mining capacity above the level forecast in Table 76 was judged to be both feasible and relatively inexpensive, it was assumed that capacity would in fact be increased and almost fully utilized. Elsewhere, the prospective shipments from fully utilized mines (by the second allocation) were reduced, on the grounds that their commercial managers would be reluctant to lower their prices to the same degree as their underutilized competitors. By the same token, it was judged that mines with large reserves of ore and with considerable sums of capital already sunk in mining plant would be willing to accept narrower profit margins in order to make better use of their facilities. And so a third allocation of export capacity to import markets was determined. The process of allocation was undeniably crude. But what the process lacked in mathematical precision and finesse, it gained through an understanding of the nature and behavior of the world market for iron ore, and through recognition of the limitations of the United Nations linear program. The results are shown in Figure 22 and Table 77. In order to minimize error, the geographical areas are kept as large as possible.

The country importing by far the largest quantity of iron ore in 1980 will be Japan. With a mere 2 million contained tons of ore available from domestic sources, the overseas purchases of its iron and steel industry will reach some 109 million contained tons. Although the mines of Philippine and Malaysian producers are geographically nearer to the Japanese mills than nearly all their competitors, the size of their reserves (together with known investment plans in mines and port facilities) suggests that their exports will actually fall and that they will have a relatively minor role to play in satisfying the Japanese market by 1980. Western Australia, on the other hand, has the advantage of being less than 7,000 km away from Honshu. It has large reserves of ore, plus new ports and railway facilities with surplus capacity, and its producers can already boast a large and assured market in Japan through long-term contracts with various steel companies. Combined, these factors will ensure a paramount role for Western Australia in the satisfaction of Japanese iron ore requirements. On the assumption that Japan will be reluctant to rely on a single country (regardless of a record of political stability) for more than about 30 percent of its ore supplies, and on the premise that the Australian mines can be expanded somewhat in excess of the 29 million contained tons recorded in Table 76 to perhaps 45 million tons, it is forecast that Western Australian exports to Japan will rise from zero in 1965 to some 33 million contained tons fifteen years later. This will be, without doubt, the fastest-growing ore trade route in the world during the forecast period.

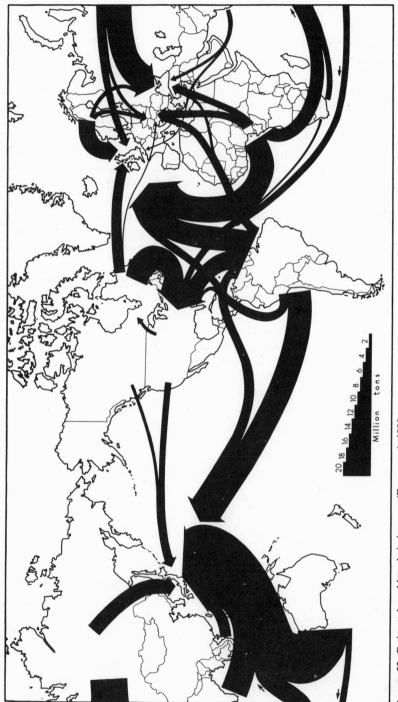

FIGURE 22. Estimated world trade in iron ore (Fe content), 1980.

318

The second-largest share of the rapidly growing Japanese market for iron ore will be taken by Indian producers. However, the forecast 350 percent increase in shipments between 1964 and 1980, and the allocation of 18 million contained tons of the Japanese market to Indian mines, must be qualified by the note that the achievement of such a level of sales will depend heavily on an improvement in India's internal transport arrangements for ore, and the completion of its program for port modernization. The geographical advantage that India could exploit by virtue of its relative proximity to Japan was undermined during the sixties by more efficient transport arrangements between Japan and the west coast of Latin America. In addition to the lower unit costs of larger vessels and the development of economical trans-Pacific backhauls of oil, producers in Chile and Peru have a much shorter rail haul between their mines and the coast than do their Indian counterparts. Chile and Peru are, therefore, together allocated 16 million contained tons of the Japanese iron ore market in 1980, 10 million tons more than in 1964. This 1980 figure could be somewhat higher if the development of the Indian iron ore mining industry does not measure up to international standards of efficiency.

Equally capable of taking advantage of Indian failings will be the Soviet Union. With only a very short sea haul (plus a rather more expensive rail journey), the Russians consider that it would be profitable for them to open up their far eastern reserves on a large scale, provided adequate Japanese markets were assured. The growing interest of the U.S.S.R. in iron ore sales outside the Communist bloc, the increasing use by Japan of Soviet coking coal, and the rising volume of trade between the two countries suggest that prices will be agreed upon and large-scale contracts signed. On this basis, therefore, a figure of 10 million contained tons is forecast for the level of Soviet exports to Japan in 1980, in contrast to their complete absence fifteen years earlier.

Other Japanese ore supplies will originate from Brazil and Venezuela—especially the former, with whose mines long-term contracts have already been signed. Although large ore carriers involved in quadrangular trading movements can reduce the disadvantage of the ocean distances involved, there can be little doubt that the level of ore trade forecast for 1980—some 6 million contained tons, compared with nil in 1965—will only be possible through the acceptance of below-average mine prices and profits on these Japanese sales by the Latin American mining companies concerned.

It is also expected that the mining industries of West Africa (9 million contained tons), the United States, Canada, China, and southern Africa will share in the Japanese market to varying degrees. The total pattern of these ore supplies diverges considerably from what theoretically would be the most efficient flows. It implies the haulage of ores over considerable distances when mines closer to hand, and likely to yield a higher f.o.b. return to their owners, remain underutilized. However, the pattern is based on a recognition of several long-term contracts that will run throughout the period of the forecast. It is also based on the desire of many ore producers to share in the rapidly growing Japanese market (at the expense of lower profits), and on the preference of the Japanese steel industry to maintain a competitive and strategic flow of ore supplies from a wide variety of sources.

In contrast, iron ore imports into the United States will originate from only a few sources in 1980. On the grounds that the mines of the Western States will be able to sell some 3 million contained tons of ore to Japanese iron and steel producers and a further 2 million contained tons to the Canadian industry, and on the premise that about 5 percent of the country's domestic capacity will not be used, it is forecast that some 33 million contained tons of ore will be imported in 1980. This will be only 7 million tons more than in 1965. The patterns of mine ownership by the U.S. iron and steel industry and the known long-term supply contracts suggest that—despite the relatively high average costs of mining, processing, and delivering Canadian iron ores to American furnaces—Canada will remain by far the largest supplier in 1980. The forecast is for a flow of some 18 million contained tons, which represents a growth of only 3 million tons in the fifteen years. Similarly, although on certain freight rate assumptions Venezuelan ores stand in a highly competitive position to serve the United States market, it is largely on the basis of the patterns of mine ownership that the forecast for 1980 is made: 9 million contained tons of imports, mainly from Venezuela and, to a lesser extent, from Brazil. Again, this is a growth of only 2 million tons in fifteen years. Also forecast is a continuing import of 2 million contained tons of ore from western Latin America (especially Chile). These Western Hemisphere sources preempt the greater part of the U.S. ore market open to imports.

As a consequence, the highly competitive position of West African producers will be given very little chance to make any major contribution to U.S. supplies. The 4 million contained tons assigned (twice the 1965 figure, and mostly from the mines of Liberia) considerably understates the inherent attractiveness in the American market of many West African ores. Their sales will suffer from the fact that only about 5 percent of the ore shipments into the United States—in 1980 as in 1965—will continue to be the result of open-market transactions. Fortunately for West African mining interests, alternative markets will be readily available in Western Europe.

The import requirements of the northern group of Western European steelmakers—largely comprising Britain, West Germany, France, and the

Benelux countries—appear likely to stand at circa 62 million tons in 1980. This compares with 33 million contained tons in 1965. The former figure is rooted in the assumption that a continuing downward pressure on iron ore prices throughout the forecast period will leave about 15 percent of the region's high-cost domestic iron ore mining capacity unused. The evidence available on the competitive position of alternative sources of ore suggests that two-thirds of the market will be satisfied from three major sources: West Africa, Latin America, and Scandinavia.

West African mines appear to be in the strongest position, with low mining costs and a relatively short haul to the ports of export. As a result, their shipments to the iron and steel producers of northern Western Europe will more than double, to reach 17 million contained tons by 1980. This trade will be shared between Liberia, Mauretania, and Sierra Leone. However, Brazil and Venezuela, with large ocean carriers and highly competitive freight rates, to say nothing of the high quality of their ores, will be in an equally advantageous position. Provided Brazil in particular can develop an efficient and low-cost inland transport system for the movement of ore to its ports of export (its extravagant plans for the development of its mining industry envisage such an improvement), the prospect is for these two countries to treble their exports to the markets of northern Western Europe between 1965 and 1980. The forecast for 1980 is 16 million contained tons, three-quarters of which will be Brazilian shipments.

Scandinavia has been the traditional source of imports for Britain and West Germany in particular. Its continuing success in these markets during the period up to 1980 depends on two sets of related factors: (1) On the demand side, much will depend on the speed with which the Western European industries change their steelmaking technology to use the L.D. process, and on the extent to which they continue to use open-hearth, high-phosphorus steelmaking plant (or alternatively opt for LD-AC). Decisions on these matters will be influenced by the pricing policy of the Swedish producers of high-phosphorus ores. (2) On the supply side, the fate of the Swedish industry depends heavily on the degree to which its owners are willing to invest in costly pellet plants capable of removing most of the phosphorus from the ores.

The Swedish and Norwegian industries—mining relatively high-cost ore reserves underground, operating under extreme climatic conditions, and experiencing the steady erosion of their traditional freight rate advantages to Western European markets as a result of improved transport technologies elsewhere—are unlikely to have available a ready supply of capital as the delivered and export prices of ore fall. In sum, it is difficult to see how Scandinavian producers can avoid losing some of their markets in northern Western Europe. While they will still satisfy nearly one-fifth of the region's ore needs in 1980, the volume of ore shipments forecast is 12 million contained tons, some 2 million tons less than fifteen years earlier.

Another major supplier to the iron and steel industry of northern Western Europe in 1980 is likely to be the Soviet Union. With a considerable amount of ore-mining capacity likely to be surplus to its domestic needs, with only a moderate length of ocean haul to the North Sea import terminals, and with work already well advanced on several new Black Sea export docks, it is forecast that the U.S.S.R. will be supplying something like 4 million contained tons of ore in 1980 (compared with a negligible tonnage fifteen years earlier). This trade forecast involves a bold political judgment concerning the willingness of the iron and steel producers of Western Europe to become dependent on a Communist country for a significant part of their raw-material supplies. However, the forecast notes the growing interest of the U.S.S.R. in increasing its iron ore exports, an interest expressed by the advertisement of Soviet ores in the technical and trade press of Western Europe; it recognizes the shrewd pricing policies adopted by the Soviet trade organizations in their raw-material exporting activities; it accepts the more fragmented and competitive nature of ore markets compared with oil markets (from which Soviet petroleum has been in large measure excluded); and it assumes that the growing trade between Western and Eastern Europe will accelerate in the years up to 1980 and beyond.

Thirteen million contained tons of the northern Western Europe market for iron ore in 1980 remain unassigned. The forecast assumes that Canada, despite its high mining and beneficiation costs, will be willing to price its ores low enough to double the 3 million contained tons share of the market it held in 1965. Indeed, it can be suggested that the combination of Canadian political stability and existing commercial ties with Western Europe might allow these ores to be sold at a slight premium. On the premise that the producers of Western Australia will become increasingly anxious to diversify their markets, even at the expense of very low f.o.b. prices, some 3 million contained tons are allocated to the blast furnaces of northern Western Europe in 1980, rather more than to Chile and Peru together. Finally, India and southern African countries are allocated a joint 1.5 million contained tons to northern Western Europe. Once again, this is partly as a result of the preference of most purchasers for some diversification of their ore sources, and partly as a result of the ore producers' predictable search for market outlets at the expense of some profitability.

At 23 million contained tons, the demand for iron ore in southern

Western Europe will still be rather small in 1980. If one assumes that only 8 of the 14 million contained tons of domestic mining capacity (some of which is relatively high cost) are used to satisfy these demands, imports totaling 15 million contained tons will be required. This is nearly twice as much as in 1965, yet still only an additional 7 million tons. The two most appropriate sources of ore for the region are the countries of West Africa and the U.S.S.R., which will supply 4 and 2 million contained tons, respectively. Scandinavian producers, although faced with the problem of rather higher f.o.b. costs, have the advantage of being able to integrate some of their ore-exporting activities with a backhaul of Middle Eastern and North African oil shipments. With transport costs "shared" in this way, the forecast is that they will increase their sales in southern Western Europe to 2 million contained tons. Existing arrangements, plus anticipated sales and marketing strategies, will claim a 5.5-million contained ton share of the market for Latin American producers, especially the mines of Brazil. And the remaining 0.5 million contained tons of ore requirements are allocated to Indian, particularly Goan, producers.

Still another importing region is Middle Europe, which has traditionally been supplied by the Soviet Union. On the expectation that it will use 4 of its 5 million contained tons of domestic ore mining capacity, import requirements will double from 14 to 28 million contained tons during the forecast period. The political and economic ties between the countries of COMECON will undoubtedly ensure that nearly three-quarters of the import requirements in 1980 will be supplied by the Soviet Union. The forecast, therefore, adopts the figure of 20 million contained tons. In addition, existing long-term contracts and barter arrangements between the countries of Middle Europe and various non-Communist producers, plus the growing trading relationships between East and West, suggest that the other 8 million contained tons of import requirements can be obtained from non-Soviet sources. The mines of Brazil and West Africa appear to be in a position to win the greater part of this market; they have been assigned 3 and 2 million contained tons, respectively, with Brazil playing a particularly outstanding role. It is also assumed that Sweden will continue to feed some East German, Polish, and Czechoslovak furnaces, doubling sales to some 2 million contained tons by 1980. The other 1 million tons needed by Middle Europe will be supplied by Indian producers.

By 1980, therefore, Australia and the U.S.S.R. will be by far the largest national exporters of iron ore. The increase in their exports presents a contrast: Whereas the Australian export growth will be from zero in 1965 to 36 million contained tons and the ore will be carried entirely by sea, Soviet exports will have trebled from 12 million contained tons and will be carried by rail, river, and ocean transport. Eastern Latin America will also experience an outstanding growth of ore exports during the period. Together, Venezuela and Brazil will be shipping 38 million contained tons of ore overseas. Brazil's exports will have increased fivefold from its 1965 level, to circa 29 million contained tons. Canada will have a smaller export tonnage in 1980—27 million contained tons—but its growth of exports during the period will represent an addition of only 8 million contained tons. West African exports will see a continuing rapid upsurge. From 11 million contained tons in 1964, total shipments will increase over 300 percent to 36 million tons in 1980. This will be half as much again as the overseas sales of Chile and Peru in that year, which are forecast at 22 million contained tons. The two other major ore exporters in 1980 will be India (20 million contained tons) and the Scandinavian countries (16 million). While India will experience a considerable growth of exports during the period, from 6 million tons in 1964, Sweden and Norway will have done no more than maintain their mid-sixties level of exports. The remaining iron ore exporters in 1980—the United States, the smaller Asian producers, and southern Africa—will have a relatively small role to play in the overall pattern of world iron ore trade.

In these trading prospects for iron ore in 1980, three implications are of special significance:

The first is the continuing increase in the volume of international trade in iron ore and the maintenance of its relative importance in the raw-material supplies of the iron and steel industry. As the volume of international ore shipments increases from about 110 million contained tons in 1964 to nearly 250 million in 1980, the proportion of the world's iron ore demands that will be satisfied through this channel will increase from less than 40 to over 46 percent of total demands.

The second implication lies in the prospective growth of the ocean ore, or bulk carrier, fleet. International trade in iron ore appears likely to increase by nearly 140 million contained tons. If one assumes that all of the Soviet exports to Middle Europe, and half of the Canadian exports to the United States, are carried by the various inland transport media, then, in round figures, ocean ore transport will increase nearly threefold, from 80 to 220 million contained tons. The longer average distance over which iron ore will be hauled might be offset to some extent by an improved efficiency in the use of carrier capacity and higher-grade ores. Nevertheless, a substantial increase in the 1965 bulk carrier capacity would appear likely to be required for ore shipments in 1980.

The third implication of the emerging trading patterns in iron ore is that surplus mining capacity appears likely to be distributed somewhat unevenly around the world. While Australian and west coast Latin

American mines will in 1980 be working at or near capacity, and while only small surpluses will exist in West Africa, India, and Canada, the forecast suggests that nearly one-quarter of Scandinavian ore mining capacity available for export will be idle. Even more important in terms of tonnage are the considerable prospective surpluses of capacity in Brazil and Veneuzela (especially the former) and in the Soviet Union. It would appear that the iron ore producers of eastern Latin America have made, and are still tending to make, investment plans on the assumption that they will gain a much larger share of the markets of Western and Middle Europe than is likely to be the case. In their ambition to win a large share of the Middle European import market, they are clearly in the process of presenting the Soviet Union with a major problem, for the Soviet planners have made mining investments on the basis of retaining well over three-quarters of the Middle European market and at the same time making substantial inroads into the Western European market. The Soviet dilemma could be even more acute if its ratio of pig iron production to iron ore demands moved closer to the world average, or alternatively if its iron and steel industry performed more poorly than has been forecast. Moreover, if India's current plans to expand the capacity of its iron ore mining industry were in fact to be fulfilled; if some of the more tentative proposals for the provision of new mining capacity in West Africa, Chile, and Peru were to go ahead; or if one or two of the Western European ore producers, especially France, elected to protect their domestic industries in some way, then the magnitude of the surplus of the world's iron ore mining capacity would be even greater than forecast. The embarrassment of Scandinavia, Brazil, and Venezuela—and especially of the Soviet Union—would be considerable.

In such circumstances, it is difficult to envisage for the forecast period anything other than a continuing fall in iron ore prices. While the larger producers, exploiting the scale economies of mining, preparation, and transport available to their industry, will be able to withstand such a tendency, the smaller and/or higher-cost producers will face a very difficult situation. Some account of this has, in fact, been recognized in the trade projections. A fall in iron ore prices will also influence the total geography of iron ore supplies in 1980, to which we now turn.

THE SUPPLY OF IRON ORE IN 1980

On the basis of the demand and trade forecasts, it is clear that the outstanding producer of iron ore in 1980 will be the Soviet Union (Figure 23 and Table 78). With a large home demand for 121 million contained tons of ore, and exports (again, the world's largest) of 36 million tons, the total production of the country's mines will be 157 million contained tons.

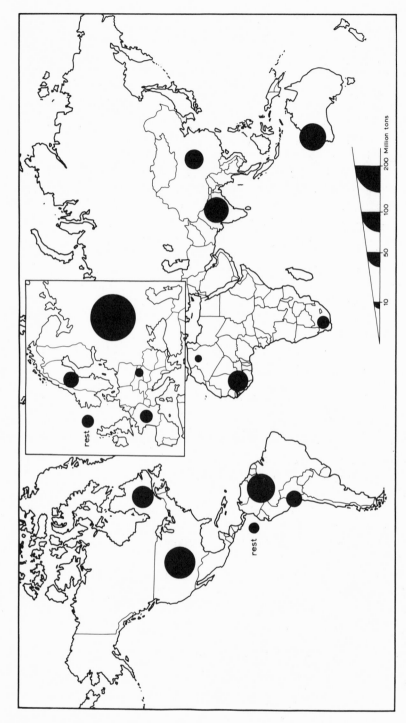

FIGURE 23. Estimated world production of iron ore (Fe content), 1980.

This represents nearly 29 percent of the world output. The production of the countries of Middle Europe will be very small, almost insignificant by comparison. However, their 4 million contained tons will bring the total supply of iron ore in Eastern Europe up to 161 million tons, and thus give the macroregion an approximate 30 percent share of the world output in the forecast year.

The United States will be the world's second largest national producer in 1980, with an output barely more than one-third of that of the leading country. At 56 million contained tons, 5 million tons of which will be exports to Japan and Canada, this production forecast assumes a growing dependence of the country on imports, which will have reached 33 million contained tons. The U.S. iron ore industry will therefore account for only 10 percent of global production in 1980. The other North American producer, Canada, will also have declined somewhat in its relative im-

TABLE 78.   ESTIMATED PRODUCTION OF IRON ORE, 1980, BY REGIONS AND SELECTED COUNTRIES

Region and country	Tons (millions of contained tons)	Percentage
World	540	100.00
North America	93	17.22
Canada	37	6.85
U.S.A.	56	10.37
Western Europe	42	7.78
Scandinavia	20	3.70
France and Luxembourg	12	2.22
Rest	10	1.85
North	32	5.93
South	8	1.48
Eastern Europe	161	29.81
Middle Europe	4	0.74
U.S.S.R.	157	29.07
Asia	73	13.52
Communist Asia	32	5.93
Rest, incl. India	41	7.59
Oceania	44	8.15
Latin America	78	14.44
Brazil and Venezuela	48	8.89
Chile and Peru	24	4.44
Rest	6	1.11
Africa and Middle East	49	9.07
West	37	6.85
Southern	10	1.85
Rest	2	0.37

portance. However, with home sales of some 10 million contained tons and exports of 27 million, total output will have reached 37 million tons, making Canada the fourth largest producer in the world. North America as a whole will be producing a total of 93 million tons of contained iron ore, or 17 percent of the global total.

Another of the larger producers of iron ore in 1980 happens to be the country whose condition and fortunes are among the least predictable. On the basis of the assumption embodied in the forecasts, China by 1980 will have an ore output of some 28 million contained tons. It will be produced largely to satisfy home demands, but a small additional tonnage will be exported to Japan. A further 4 million contained tons of ore is expected to be mined in North Korea, aggregating 32 million tons in the Asian Communist sphere. Elsewhere in Asia, the production of Japan, Malaysia, and the Philippines will remain relatively small. India, on the other hand, with exports of 20 million contained tons, will have made substantial progress in expanding its iron ore industry to the sixth largest in the world, with an output of 32 million contained tons. Taken as a whole, therefore, Asian iron ore mining will total 73 million contained tons in 1980, 13.5 percent of the global figure.

Australasian production in 1980 will have reached 44 million contained tons, to assume the third position in the world league. This largely Australian industry will be based primarily on exporting activities, as indeed will be the industries in Latin America and Africa. The Brazilian total is comprised of a home demand for 6 million contained tons, plus overseas shipments of perhaps 29 million. By adding a further 13 million contained tons for Venezuela, a joint production of 24 million for Chile and Peru, and a further 6 million for other Latin American countries (mainly for home consumption), iron ore production in the whole of Latin America in 1980 is forecast at 78 million contained tons, or over 14 percent of the world total. In Africa, the largest component in the forecast total production is West Africa, with 49 million contained tons—9 percent of the world output. Liberia, Mauretania, and Sierra Leone will be largely responsible for some 37 million tons of contained iron ore; about one-half of this will originate from the mines of Liberia, which by 1980 will have a slightly larger iron ore industry than Sweden. Southern African supplies—principally South African ores for domestic use, but also Angolan and Swaziland ores for export—will total some 10 million contained tons.

Western Europe, with a slightly smaller share of world production than Oceania in 1980, will be the only macroregion to have contracted its iron ore output during the previous fifteen years. The Scandinavian industry, to be sure, will have been expanded to 20 million contained tons, of which

16 million will be for export. But the industries of France and Luxembourg will produce 7 million contained tons less than fifteen years earlier. And other countries of the region—including Britain, West Germany, Spain, Austria, and Yugoslavia—will together be mining only 10 million contained tons. With relatively poor resources and comparatively high costs, most of the producers in these countries will still be faced, even in 1980, with declining profit margins at many of their mines and with the prospect of a still smaller role in the world iron ore industry beyond 1980.

part IV

Summary

CHAPTER 15

Summary

Four themes in particular have run through this study of the world market for iron ore, mainly in retrospect and partially in prospect:

1. The continuing and accelerating technological revolution, which is affecting every phase of the market for iron ore—from the winning of the ore at the mine or pit to the manufacture of semifinished steel products. At the mine, and to an ever-increasing degree, the preparation of the iron and steel industry's raw materials is altering both the quantity and the quality of iron ore required to support the relentless expansion of iron and steel manufacture throughout the world. In transport, on land and ocean, new technologies are permitting the haulage of iron ore to its markets at ever-decreasing ton-kilometer real costs. At the blast furnace, special burden arrangements at the top, and the injection of air and various hydrocarbons at the bottom, are measurably increasing the efficiency and lowering the unit costs of the reduction process. In the melting shop, the economic advantages of making steel with the aid of oxygen in the L.D. furnace have been conclusively proved, and the L.D. process is being increasingly used instead of the older Bessemer and open-hearth processes. At the next stage of production, ingot teeming (known and used for over one hundred years) is faced with the challenge of continuous casting. And the strip mill of the immediate postwar years appears both slow and cumbersome compared with its modern high-speed counterpart.

These and other advances are important in themselves. They are additionally important in having altered the cost structure of both the iron ore industry and the iron and steel industry, thereby playing a major part in influencing the changing locational preferences and behavior of these two industries. Sites close to large markets, for example, with low-cost transport opportunities for hauling raw materials over long distances when this is economically attractive, have come to be valued at an increasing premium

333

for integrated steel production. Large, high-grade, low-phosphorus iron ore deposits within easy reach of deepwater ports and of low-cost ocean transport are now at an unequaled advantage in the satisfaction of the iron and steel industry's demands.

Because the savings afforded by the new technologies have been embraced differentially from country to country, certain tendencies in the geography of the market for iron ore can only be understood through an appreciation of spatial differences in the rates of technological diffusion and the associated international variations in steelmaking costs.

2. The changing scale of the market for iron ore. One of its facets is the total size of the market, which by 1980 will have grown nearly fivefold since 1950. Another facet is the much larger technological scale of the many processes and machines employed by both the iron ore and the iron and steel industries: the larger excavating machines in larger mines, larger beneficiating plants, mammoth ore carriers, larger blast furnaces and large-scale steel plants, larger finishing mills, and larger product trains. This theme is universally the same. The economies of large-scale operations have been relentlessly exploited in the past, and they are likely to be exploited even more in the future. Closely related to the increasing scale of transport operations and the associated falling costs is the geographical extent of the markets for both iron ore and steel, which have become progressively larger with the reduction of the friction of distance. Clearly, this tendency will persist. As West Australian ore is shipped to Wales, as Brazilian pellets are shipped the 21,000 km to Japan, as Japanese steel sheet is sold in Rotterdam and Chicago, and as West European sections and beams meet demands in Buenos Aires and Bangkok, the scale of the spatial markets for both iron ore and steel is seen to approach global proportions.

3. The increasing extent and degree of political influence over ore supply and demand, and the resulting interaction of politics and the market. This phenomenon can no longer be associated with any particular part of the world or particular economic system. To be sure, political priorities are allowed to rank very much higher in a planned economy than in a market economy, and by 1980 the planned economies are likely to represent some 38 percent of the world market for ore. But political factors have also come to be increasingly relevant to an understanding of the market for iron ore in the mixed and market economies alike, whether they are within the advanced or the developing countries. As steelworks are located to meet the objectives of regional planning policies or are subsidized by governments in outdated locations in order to avoid social upheaval; as iron ore mining responds to politically inspired depreciation allowances or exceptionally low royalties; and as the developing countries seek to encourage both iron and steel production and iron ore mining—as all these phenomena occur,

political activities, with and without a logic behind them, come increasingly to shape the geography of iron ore production and consumption.

4. The remarkably rapid geographical changes in the world market for iron ore between 1950 and 1980. To be sure, between 1950 and 1965 the United States and the U.S.S.R. remained the dominant components in the spatial pattern of iron ore demand and supply, and there is every likelihood that they will continue to do so until 1980. However, their relative importance has shifted. Since 1950, iron and steel production in the Soviet Union has slowly approached the level of that in the United States, and the prospect is for it to exceed the output of American mills before 1980. Similarly, while the U.S. steel industry has become increasingly dependent on iron ore imports, the U.S.S.R. not only has satisfied its expanding domestic demands but has also slowly enlarged its exporting activities. These developments mean that Soviet ore production was considerably larger than American output in 1965, and the prospect is for the differential to widen by 1980.

Elsewhere in the world, the years 1950 to 1965 saw the appearance of many new centers of iron ore demand. Japan was undoubtedly the most important, as it grew from insignificance to be the third largest center of demand in the world. In addition, Australia, Canada, China, Czechoslovakia, Italy, India, Poland, and South Africa all emerged as significant manufacturers of iron and steel. Whereas in 1950 only thirty countries were producing steel at an annual rate of more than 100,000 tons, by 1965 (with many new nations searching for national economic growth) there were nearly half as many again. The expectations are that such spatial shifts in iron ore demands will continue throughout the forecast period. Although there is no evidence to suggest that another country will reproduce the experience of Japan, there is every reason to believe that Asian demands will continue to expand as rapidly as in the past, as a consequence of the continuing brisk rate of growth of iron and steel production in China, India, and Japan. And even though Western Europe will still account for about one-fifth of world production in 1980, the relative importance of Australia, Brazil, Canada, and South Africa as steel manufacturers—and as centers of iron ore demand—will have significantly increased.

In response to these changes in the geography of iron ore demands, and assisted by the speedy provision of new and improving iron ore transport facilities, Brazil, Canada, India, Liberia, and Venezuela, between 1950 and 1965, all became major producers of iron ore for the first time. Other producers of ore, such as Britain, North Africa, and Spain, were able to expand their output only slowly, and in some cases were forced to begin closing down their mines.

The net effect of the changes—with many smaller producers also responding to the opportunities of domestic and overseas markets—was that the number of countries producing more than 100,000 contained tons of ore each year rose from thirty-three in 1950 to fifty in 1965. And the same trends can reasonably be expected to persist throughout the forecast period. By 1980, Australia will have developed as an outstanding producer of iron ore. The relative importance of Brazil, China, India, and Liberia seems likely to increase. And a number of smaller new producers, such as Angola and possibly Gabon, will have entered the world market for the first time. At the same time the prospect is for a decline in the relative and possibly absolute importance of Scandinavia, France, Britain, and Spain as producers of ore.

Following these differential shifts in the demand for and the supply of iron ore, new patterns of trade have developed. Between 1950 and 1965, for example, shipments of iron ore from Canada, Brazil, and Venezuela to the United States; from Sweden, West Africa, Brazil, and Venezuela to Western Europe; from the U.S.S.R. to Poland and Czechoslovakia; and from Malaysia, the Philippines, Peru, and Chile to Japan—all increased on a substantial scale. Similarly, major changes in the size and the direction of world trade in iron ore appear to be in prospect. While the size of the flows from Canada to the United States, from Scandinavia to Western Europe, and from Southeast Asia to Japan are likely to be stagnant between 1965 and 1980—or even to fall into decline—other flows will develop strongly. Most important will be those from Brazil and Venezuela to the United States and Western Europe, from the U.S.S.R. to Western Europe and Japan, from West Africa to Western Europe, and from Australia to Japan. Virtually absent in 1965, the Australia-to-Japan flow will be among the largest and most important ore flows in 1980. By that year, of course, the geography of iron ore demand, supply, and trade will be subject to new and as yet unrevealed forces of change, and further shifts will be pending in the world market for iron ore.

Appendixes

A. Appendix Tables

TABLE A-1. WORLD APPARENT CONSUMPTION OF CRUDE STEEL, BY REGIONS AND COUNTRIES, TOTAL AND PER CAPITA, 1950 AND 1965–1967

Region and country	Total apparent consumption (Thousands of ingot tons)				Apparent consumption per capita (Kilograms)			
	1950	1965	1966	1967	1950	1965	1966	1967
WORLD	191,575	455,656	475,916	493,023				
NORTH AMERICA	90,139	138,099	141,116	135,275				
Canada	4,188	10,415	9,802	9,088	303	531	489	446
U.S.A.	85,951	127,684	131,314	126,187	567	656	667	634
WESTERN EUROPE	45,031	115,076	115,674	116,574				
EEC	23,638	67,236	68,879	71,087	248	330	315	422
Belgium and Luxembourg	2,221	3,230	3,110	4,180	156	331	347	360
France	6,670	16,171	17,173	17,941	63	235	273	312
Italy	2,936	12,101	14,175	16,322	165	313	321	327
Netherlands	1,664	3,848	3,959	4,121	205	540	511	476
West Germany	10,147	31,886	30,492	28,523				
Austria	792	2,078	2,065	1,904	115	286	283	260
Britain	14,045	23,131	21,247	21,389	280	424	387	388
Denmark	647	1,719	1,540	1,583	152	361	321	327
Eire	118	232	203	253	40	81	70	87
Finland	420	1,210	1,227	1,257	105	262	264	270
Greece	212	722	839	832	28	85	97	95
Norway	467	1,359	1,415	1,413	143	365	377	373
Portugal	187	679	695	654	22	74	75	69
Spain	850	6,142	6,720	6,035	31	194	211	188
Sweden	2,054	5,272	5,058	4,633	293	682	648	589
Switzerland	703	1,998	1,990	2,045	150	334	331	388
Turkey	307	859	1,013	777	15	27	31	24
Yugoslavia	591	2,441	2,783	2,712	37	125	141	136
EASTERN EUROPE	35,100	117,438	125,393	132,032				
Middle Europe	8,500	30,834	33,104	34,294				
Bulgaria		1,248	1,691	1,856		152	205	223
Czechoslovakia		7,423	7,758	8,337		524	545	583

East Germany		7,483	7,686	7,353		439	450	430
Hungary		2,234	2,377	2,637		220	234	258
Poland		8,528	9,508	10,011		271	300	313
Romania		3,918	4,084	4,100*		206	213	213*
U.S.S.R.	26,600	86,604	92,289	97,738	149	376	396	415
ASIA	7,953	52,802	62,762	80,548				
Communist Asia	1,201	12,288	14,943	17,571				
China	1,201	10,988	13,595	16,105	3	14	17	20
North Korea		1,300	1,308	1,365		100	105	107
North Vietnam*		39	40	101		2	2	5
Non-Communist Asia	6,752	40,514	47,819	62,977				
Ceylon	51	81	90	114	7	7	8	10
Hong Kong	116	573	404	390	50	151	102	102
India	1,756	7,519	6,844	6,405	5	16	14	13
Indonesia	122	320	123	199	2	3	1	2
Japan	4,157	28,841	36,449	51,221	50	294	369	513
Malaysia	143	367	334	387	23	46	40	45
Pakistan	256	827	530	831	3	8	5	8
Philippines	151	765	806	1,070	8	24	24	31
South Vietnam		143	635	744		9	22	25
Taiwan		626	798	895		50	62	68
Thailand		452	806	721		15	26	22
OCEANIA	2,512	6,473	6,156	5,954				
Australia	2,249	5,842	5,508	5,269	274	514	477	448
New Zealand	263	631	648	685	138	239	242	251
LATIN AMERICA	3,681	11,307	11,846	12,147				
Argentina	1,024	2,538	1,909	2,029	60	114	84	88
Brazil	1,038	3,139	4,092	4,005	20	39	49	47
Chile	143	602	630	676	25	70	72	74
Colombia	161	431	514	409	14	24	28	21
Cuba	160	203	200*	200*	30	27	26*	26*
Mexico	707	2,731	2,955	3,285	28	64	67	72
Peru	86	399	396	313	10	34	33	25
Uruguay	136	64	49	30	57	24	18	11
Venezuela	226	1,200	1,101	1,200	46	138	122	128

TABLE A-1.—Continued

Region and country	Total apparent consumption (Thousands of ingot tons)				Apparent consumption per capita (Kilograms)			
	1950	1965	1966	1967	1950	1965	1966	1967
AFRICA AND MIDDLE EAST	3,309	8,509	7,607	8,347	23	23	15	17
Algeria	200	253	188	215	8	3	3*	3*
Congo	122	52	50*	50*		6	6*	6*
East Africa		168	170*	170*		26	27	24
Egypt	372	779	809	745	18	13	5	6
Ghana		103	36	46		13	5	6
Iran	167	710	737	1,330	9	30	29	51
Iraq		213	200*	200*		26	25*	25*
Israel	237	480	397	316	182	187	151	118
Lebanon		253	296	225		111	109	89
Morocco	173	167	204	241	18	13	15	17
Nigeria		312	340	262		6	6	4
Rhodesia	130	255	308	151	33	60	70	33
Saudi Arabia		310	300*	300*		47	45*	45*
South Africa	1,250	4,207	3,355	3,881	102	210	163	186
Syria	181	90	100*	100*	40	16	18*	18*
Tunisia	71	146	107	105	20	31	24	23
Zambia		11	10*	10*		3	3*	3*
Others	406							
Unallocated production	3,850	5,952	5,362	2,146				

Source: United Nations, Statistical Yearbook.
Notes: Apparent consumption = production + imports − exports.
* Author's estimate.

TABLE A-2. WORLD PRODUCTION OF CRUDE STEEL, BY REGIONS AND COUNTRIES, 1950 AND
1965-1967

(Thousands of ingot tons)

Region and country	1950	1965	1966	1967
WORLD	191,575	455,656	475,916	493,023
NORTH AMERICA	93,029	128,081	130,728	124,200
Canada	3,070	9,096	9,074	8,794
U.S.A.	89,959	118,985	121,654	115,406
WESTERN EUROPE	52,538	129,429	126,772	131,631
EEC	31,763	85,998	85,103	89,893
Belgium	3,789	9,162	8,917	9,716
France	8,652	19,604	19,585	19,655
Italy	2,362	12,681	13,639	15,890
Luxembourg	2,451	4,585	4,390	4,481
Netherlands	490	3,145	3,256	3,407
West Germany	14,019	36,821	35,316	36,744
Austria	947	3,221	3,193	3,023
Britain	16,554	27,440	24,705	24,278
Denmark	123	412	405	401
Eire	16	20	27	
Finland	104	362	384	394
Greece	23	210	210	160
Norway	81	686	730	790
Portugal		273	269	316
Spain	805	3,515	3,847	4,335
Sweden	1,456	4,725	4,762	4,768
Switzerland	137	347	428	445
Turkey	91	451	842	996
Yugoslavia	428	1,769	1,867	1,832
EASTERN EUROPE	35,541	119,580	127,438	135,394
Middle Europe	8,212	28,580	30,531	33,170
Bulgaria		588	699	1,239
Czechoslovakia	3,122	8,598	9,124	10,002
East Germany	995	4,366	4,539	4,648
Hungary	1,022	2,520	2,649	2,739
Poland	2,515	9,088	9,850	10,454
Romania	558	3,420	3,670	4,088
U.S.S.R.	27,329	91,000	96,907	102,224
ASIA	6,994	61,321	72,238	81,747
Communist Asia	680	13,371	17,300	12,450
China	680	12,000	16,000	11,000
North Korea		1,371	1,300	1,450
Non-Communist Asia	6,314	49,950	54,938	69,297
Burma		15		
India	1,461	6,408	6,606	6,380
Japan	4,838	41,161	47,784	62,154
Pakistan	4	12		
South Korea		155	216	320
Taiwan	11	192	326	443
Thailand		7	6	
OCEANIA	1,275	5,496	5,890	6,288
Australia	1,275	5,496	5,890	6,288
LATIN AMERICA	1,317	8,121	9,135	9,650
Argentina	130	1,361	1,281	1,325
Brazil	789	2,981	3,782	3,696
Chile	56	442	540	596
Colombia		204	174	207
Mexico	337	2,400	2,750	3,060
Peru		94	61	62
Uruguay		14	10	14
Venezuela	5	625	537	690
AFRICA AND MIDDLE EAST	881	3,635	3,715	4,114
Algeria			21	25*
Egypt	10	200	195	200*
Israel		65	84	100*
Rhodesia	24	130	130	138
South Africa	847	3,240	3,285	3,651

Sources: United Nations, *Statistical Yearbook;* British Steel Corporation, *Statistical Handbook;* United
Nations, 1968-A.
* Author's estimate.

TABLE A-3. WORLD PRODUCTION OF PIG IRON, BY REGIONS AND COUNTRIES, 1950 AND 1965–1967

(Thousands of tons)

Region and country	1950	1965	1966	1967
WORLD	133,651	335,419	347,200	356,737
NORTH AMERICA	62,503	89,142	91,989	87,623
Canada	2,266	6,574	6,714	6,449
U.S.A.	60,237	82,568	85,275	81,174
WESTERN EUROPE	39,183	92,415	84,902	93,787
EEC	26,252	63,510	62,225	66,375
Belgium	3,695	8,366	8,230	8,902
France	7,838	16,020	15,848	15,971
Italy	572	5,625	6,415	7,463
Luxembourg	2,499	4,145	3,962	3,963
Netherlands	454	2,364	2,209	2,579
West Germany	11,194	26,990	25,561	27,497
Austria	886	2,205	2,200	2,145
Britain	9,818	17,740	15,962	15,396
Denmark	51	78	82	76
Finland	64	984	985	1,026
Norway	226	1,080	1,139	1,234
Portugal		275	249	285
Spain	671	2,394	2,186	2,726
Sweden	837	2,446	2,396	2,397
Switzerland	35	27	25	24
Turkey	117	500	736	847
Yugoslavia	226	1,176	1,217	1,256
EASTERN EUROPE	23,825	84,511	89,673	95,991
Middle Europe	4,650	18,327	19,409	21,179
Bulgaria	3	695	903	1,028
Czechoslovakia	1,951	5,927	6,360	6,919
East Germany	333	2,338	2,448	2,525
Hungary	482	1,588	1,640	1,669
Poland	1,546	5,760	5,855	6,581
Romania	335	2,019	2,203	2,457
U.S.S.R.	19,175	66,184	70,264	74,812
ASIA	5,035	56,032	61,542	63,925
Communist Asia	1,030	20,635	21,500	15,750
China	1,030	19,000	20,000	14,000
North Korea		1,635	1,500	1,750
Non-Communist Asia	4,005	35,397	40,042	48,175
India	1,706	7,138	7,199	7,027
Japan	2,299	28,160	32,744	41,040
South Korea		21	23	23
Taiwan		72	71	85
Thailand		6	5	
OCEANIA	1,115	4,356	4,804	5,057
Australia	1,115	4,356	4,804	5,057
LATIN AMERICA	1,223	4,910	5,545	6,100
Argentina	18	663	520	610
Brazil	729	2,400	2,925	3,057
Chile	109	309	433	498
Colombia		242	167	203
Mexico	367	942	1,137	1,279
Peru		20	12	31
Venezuela		334	351	422
AFRICA AND MIDDLE EAST	767	4,053	4,218	4,254
Egypt		200	215	215*
Rhodesia	34	250	260	260
South Africa	733	3,603	3,743	3,779

Sources: United Nations, *Statistical Yearbook* and 1968-A.
* Author's estimate.

TABLE A-4. WORLD APPARENT DEMAND FOR IRON ORE, BY REGIONS AND COUNTRIES, 1950 AND 1964-1967

(Thousands of contained tons)

Region and country	1950	1964	1965	1966	1967
WORLD................................	115,582	288,681	310,594	340,158	339,467
NORTH AMERICA........................	54,940	71,931	75,610	78,019	74,321
Canada............................	2,194	4,797	6,088	6,217	5,972
U.S.A.	52,746	67,134	69,522	71,802	68,349
WESTERN EUROPE......................	28,969	73,537	76,956	74,630	78,374
EEC...............................	18,048	50,554	52,788	51,866	55,377
Belgium.........................	2,332	6,883	7,153	7,037	7,611
France	7,464	13,775	13,729	13,582	13,687
Italy...........................	321	3,425	5,316	6,062	7,053
Luxembourg	1,880	3,587	3,561	3,403	3,404
Netherlands.....................	395	1,829	2,220	2,074	2,422
West Germany	5,656	21,055	20,809	19,708	21,200
Austria............................	652	1,702	1,641	1,637	1,596
Britain............................	8,704	15,265	15,434	13,887	13,395
Denmark...........................		2	2	2	2
Finland...........................	58	488	749	750	781
Greece		181	200*	200*	200*
Norway...........................	33	356	437	461	500
Portugal..........................		129	131	119	136
Spain.............................	720	1,783	2,180	1,991	2,483
Sweden...........................	419	1,536	1,627	1,593	1,594
Switzerland.......................	30	15	15*	13	12
Turkey............................	143	547	682	1,004	1,155
Yugoslavia........................	162	979	1,070	1,107	1,143
EASTERN EUROPE......................	24,558	86,911	92,317	97,998	104,890
Middle Europe	4,102	17,195	18,323	19,443	21,250
Bulgaria........................	14	566	876	1,139	1,296
Czechoslovakia...................	1,765	5,779	5,939	6,373	6,933
East Germany...................	239	1,936	2,004	2,098	2,164
Hungary........................	440	1,517	1,612	1,665	1,694
Poland.........................	1,332	5,540	5,944	6,042	6,792
Romania........................	312	1,857	1,948	2,126	2,371
U.S.S.R..........................	20,456	69,716	73,994	78,555	83,640
ASIA	4,015	42,788	53,671	58,644	58,607
Communist Asia....................	850	16,507	23,978	25,157	18,504
China	850	14,973	21,888	23,240	16,268
North Korea....................		1,534	2,090	1,917	2,236
Non-Communist Asia................	3,165	26,281	29,693	33,487	40,103
India..........................	1,850	6,035	6,389	6,443	6,289
Japan..........................	1,296	19,954	22,979	26,719	33,489
Malaysia.......................		90	100*	100*	100*
Philippines.....................	17	131	150*	150*	150*
South Korea...		20	25*	25*	25*
Thailand.......................	2	51	50*	50*	50*
OCEANIA............................	1,479	3,745	3,976	4,384	4,614
Australia	1,472	3,735	3,964	4,372	4,602
New Caledonia....................	2	2	2*	2*	2*
New Zealand......................	5	8	10*	10*	10*
LATIN AMERICA.......................	1,239	5,966	5,723	6,214	7,219
Argentina........................	16	688	701	550	645
Brazil............................	746	2,211	2,165	2,638	2,757
Chile.............................	203	459	324	455	523
Colombia.........................		292	321	222	269
Cuba.............................		7	10*	10*	10*
Mexico...........................	147	1,249	1,283	1,549	1,742
Peru.............................		585	390	234	605
Venezuela........................	127	475	529	556	668
AFRICA AND MIDDLE EAST..............	799	2,987	3,501	3,627	3,657
Egypt............................		245	250*	250*	250*
Rhodesia.........................	33	338	325	338	338
South Africa.....................	717	2,344	2,926	3,039	3,069
Others...........................	49	60			
Unallocated production†..............	−417	816	−1,160	16,540	7,785

Sources: For 1950 and 1964, United Nations, 1968-A; 1965–67, based on pig iron production (Table A-3) and on 1964 national ratios of pig iron production to iron ore demand.
Note: Apparent demand = production + imports − exports.
* Author's estimate.
† World production minus apparent demand.

TABLE A-5. WORLD IMPORTS OF IRON ORE, BY REGIONS AND MAJOR COUNTRIES, 1950 AND
1964–1967

(Thousands of tons)

Region and country	Fe content		Actual tons				
	1950	1964	1950	1964	1965	1966	1967
WORLD.....................	22,193	108,920	41,883	198,505	214,204	188,965	225,676
NORTH AMERICA..............	6,325	29,172	11,134	48,575	50,668	51,387	47,825
Canada...................	1,431	3,262	2,786	5,315	4,839	4,392	2,439
U.S.A....................	4,894	25,910	8,348	43,260	45,829	46,995	45,386
WESTERN EUROPE..............	12,037	46,414	24,142	90,905	96,588	87,781	90,894
EEC......................	6,831	34,331	15,049	70,378	74,716	68,539	72,194
Belgium.................	2,316	6,863	5,806	15,785	23,745†	21,407†	21,879†
France..................	90	2,090	168	3,602	3,985	4,304	4,889
Italy...................	98	2,989	184	5,038	7,945	8,110	9,926
Luxembourg..............	1,042	2,192	3,209	7,881			
Netherlands.............	420	1,830	812	3,048	3,570	3,451	3,641
West Germany............	2,864	18,367	4,870	35,024	35,471	31,268	31,860
Austria..................	99	562	198	1,081	1,120	1,175	904
Britain..................	4,866	10,774	8,485	18,181	18,608	15,810	15,781
Finland..................	58	308	93	514	968	837	638
Greece...................		150		272	300*	300*	300*
Spain....................	143	56	239	94	362	576	598
Yugoslavia...............		156		260	364	393	128
Others...................	40	87	78	125	150*	150*	150*
MIDDLE EUROPE..............	3,025	13,970	5,162	26,562	26,930	27,135	29,591
Bulgaria.................		249		475	500*	500*	500*
Czechoslovakia............	1,319	4,925⎱	2,300*	9,310	9,553	9,336	10,366
East Germany.............	127	1,441⎰		2,753	2,500*	2,500*	2,500*
Hungary..................	348	1,316	607	2,632	2,481	2,696	2,808
Poland...................	1,097	4,800	1,969	9,087	9,274	9,249	10,056
Romania..................	134	1,239	286	2,305	2,623	2,854	3,360
REST OF THE WORLD...........	806	19,364	1,425	32,463	41,019	46,797	57,566
Argentina.................		652		1,019	1,033	707	880
Australia.................		135		279			
Japan....................	806	18,541	1,425	31,100	38,986	46,090	56,686
Others...................		36		65			

Sources: For 1950 and 1964, United Nations, 1968-A; for 1965–67, United Nations, *Yearbook of International Trade Statistics* and *Commodity Trade Statistics*.

* Author's estimate.

† Belgium and Luxembourg.

TABLE A-6. WORLD TRADE IN IRON ORE, BY REGIONS AND MAJOR COUNTRIES, 1950 AND 1964

(Thousands of tons)

FE CONTENT, 1950

Exporting countries	World	U.S.A.	Importing Countries — Western Europe			Middle Europe	Japan	Other countries
			EEC	Britain	Other countries			
WORLD	18,900	4,800	4,200	4,900	200	2,600	800	1,400
NORTH AMERICA	2,374	945	16	63				1,350
Canada	1,024	945	16	63				
U.S.A.	1,350							1,350
WESTERN EUROPE	9,026	1,261	3,629	2,884	189	1,058		5
France	177			177				
Norway	179		128			51		
Spain	486		86	393	7			
Sweden	7,928	1,261	3,342	2,210	103	1,007		5
Others	256		73	104	79			
EASTERN EUROPE	1,591					1,591		
U.S.S.R.	1,500					1,500		
Others	91					91		
ASIA	818	4	2	6			806	
India	55		2				53	
Malaysia	298			6			292	
North Korea	2						2	
Philippines	330	2					328	
Others	133	2					131	
OCEANIA	1							1
LATIN AMERICA	2,261	2,149	49	12				51
Brazil	590	478	49	12				51
Chile	1,567	1,567						
Mexico	92	92						
Peru								
Venezuela	12	12						
Others								

FE CONTENT, 1964

Exporting countries	World	U.S.A.	Importing Countries — Western Europe			Middle Europe	Japan	Other countries
			EEC	Britain	Other countries			
WORLD	104,700	25,900	28,900	10,800	1,500	15,000	18,700	3,900
NORTH AMERICA	23,675	15,157	618	1,899			2,202	2,799
Canada	18,733	15,157	618	1,899			1,059	
U.S.A.	3,942						1,143	2,799
WESTERN EUROPE	17,072	63	11,382	4,238	605	784		
France	96			96				
Norway	1,007		559	357	17	74		
Spain	759		542	217				
Sweden	14,795	57	10,211	3,568	441	518		
Others	415	6	70		147	192		
EASTERN EUROPE	12,745		257	17	238	12,233		
U.S.S.R.	12,535		257	17	238	12,023		
Others	210					210		
ASIA	11,766	1	860		217	996	9,692	
India	6,065		838		217	986	4,024	
Malaysia	3,973						3,973	
North Korea	568						568	
Philippines	901						901	
Others	259		22			10	226	
OCEANIA	245	1					50	194
LATIN AMERICA	24,282	8,791	6,702	1,453	178	454	5,806	898
Brazil	5,965	686	3,368	364	178	454	281	634
Chile	5,647	1,709	433				3,359	146
Mexico	11	11						
Peru	3,936	365	1,196	100			2,166	109
Venezuela	8,697	6,017	1,691	989				
Others	26	3	14					9

TABLE A-6.—Continued

Fe CONTENT

Exporting countries	1950 — Importing Countries								1964 — Importing Countries							
	World	U.S.A.	EEC	Britain	Other countries	Middle Europe	Japan	Other countries	World	U.S.A.	EEC	Britain	Other countries	Middle Europe	Japan	Other countries
AFRICA	2,887	467	508	1,901		11			15,856	1,897	9,051	3,167	221	501	983	36
Algeria	1,259	266	171	811		11			1,333	10	609	580		134		
Angola									737		648			22	67	
Guinea									345			70	27	242		6
Liberia									7,113	1,751	4,371	941	50			
Mauretania	571	23	140	408					3,021	85	1,990	904		9	33	
Morocco									606		368	120	54	64		
Rhodesia									600						200	
Sierra Leone	652	110	123	419					1,278		898	380			614	
South Africa	3		3						639	11	14					
Tunisia	388	63	62	263					468		146	172	90	30	69	30
Others	14	5	9						116	40	7					
Unallocated exports									76					76		

ACTUAL TONNAGE

Exporting countries	1950 — Importing Countries								1964 — Importing Countries							
	World	U.S.A.	EEC	Britain	Other countries	Middle Europe	Japan	Other countries	World	U.S.A.	EEC	Britain	Other countries	Middle Europe	Japan	Other countries
WORLD	33,405	8,363	7,062	8,485	370	4,914	1,425	2,786	176,440	43,097	47,684	18,181	2,497	27,143	31,100	6,738
NORTH AMERICA	4,741	1,889	32	120				2,700	38,271	25,261	1,030	3,299			3,770	4,911
Canada	2,041	1,889	32	120					31,355	25,261	1,030	3,299			1,765	4,911
U.S.A.	2,700							2,700	6,916						2,005	
WESTERN EUROPE	15,053	2,072	6,035	4,849	349	1,739		9	28,359	105	18,867	7,016	1,018	1,353		
France	386			385					233			233				
Norway	298	1	213			85			1,646		916	581	28	121		
Spain	959		182	762	15				1,518		1,084	434				
Sweden	12,877	2,070	5,488	3,487	169	1,654			24,174	94	16,740	5,768	723	849		
Others	533	1	152	215	165			9	789	11	128		267	383		

APPENDIX A

	1	2	3	4	5	6	7	8	9	10	11	12	13	14
EASTERN EUROPE	3,175			10		3,175	23,192	2	468	29	432	22,263		
U.S.S.R.	3,000			10		3,000	22,789		468	29	432	21,860		
Others	175					175	403					403		
ASIA	1,445	7	3			1,425	19,709	2	1,436		362		16,249	
India	99		3			96	10,108		1,396		362		6,707	
Malaysia	531					521	6,621						6,621	
North Korea	4					4	1,015						1,015	
Philippines	570	4				566	1,501						1,501	
Others	241	3				238	464		40		17		405	
OCEANIA		29			20	75	430	1					88	341
LATIN AMERICA	3,702	3,537	72	18		75	39,455	14,560	10,769	2,365	278	710	9,350	1,423
Brazil	868	703	72	18			9,285	1,072	5,263	533	278	710	439	990
Chile	2,611						9,107	2,756	699				5,417	235
Mexico	194						22	22						
Peru							6,342	589	1,929	155			3,494	175
Venezuela		29					14,632	10,113	2,842	1,677				
Others	29						66	66	35					23
AFRICA	5,287	859	920	3,488			26,853	3,166	15,114	5,472	407	990	1,641	63
Algeria	2,366	502	323	1,521			2,566	20	1,182	1,104		206	109	
Angola							736							
Guinea									1,052	152	57	3		13
Liberia				734			11,910	2,919	7,285	1,622	84	514	53	
Mauretania	1,022	40	248				4,786	135	3,159	208		14		
Morocco				747			1,032		624		92	108	318	
Rhodesia							318							
Sierra Leone	1,140	186	207				2,113	19	1,490	623				
South Africa	5		5				1,066		24				1,023	
Tunisia	726	121	119	486			905	73	284	338	174	59	138	
Others	28	10	18				225		14					50
Unallocated exports	3						168					168		

Source: United Nations, 1968-A.
Note: Intra-EEC trade is not included.

TABLE A-7. WORLD EXPORTS OF IRON ORE, BY REGIONS AND MAJOR COUNTRIES, 1950 AND
1964–1967

(Thousands of tons)

Region and country	Fe content		Actual tonnage				
	1950	1964	1950	1964	1965	1966	1967
WORLD	21,833	110,578	42,069	199,030	191,982	214,113	227,326
NORTH AMERICA	2,490	22,662	4,622	38,035	37,874	38,597	37,520
Canada	1,036	18,630	2,031	30,961	30,676	30,693	31,481
U.S.A.	1,454	4,032	2,591	7,074	7,198	7,904	6,039
WESTERN EUROPE	11,405	23,981	23,156	51,348	49,299	43,770	45,107
EEC	2,668	7,109	8,478	23,305	21,957	19,393	18,641
France	2,376	6,754	7,545	22,070	20,747	18,195	17,537
Italy	4	3	9	7	679	772	718
Luxembourg	244	243	814	935	267	232	293
Netherlands	25	1	58	3	265	194	94
West Germany	19	108	52	290			
Austria	27		59				
Denmark	8	21	23	58			
Finland		120		182	169	142	121
Greece	20		41				
Norway	170	947	283	1,553	1,374	1,437	2,383
Portugal					7		
Spain	467	825	936	1,650	1,234	511	814
Sweden	7,863	14,858	12,944	24,357	24,461	22,287	23,056
Switzerland	27	22	54	56			
Yugoslavia	155	79	338	187	97		91
EASTERN EUROPE	1,648	11,689	3,302	22,611	24,138	26,118	28,685
Middle Europe	34	5	75	11			
Bulgaria		5		11			
Czechoslovakia	34		75				
U.S.S.R.	1,614	11,684	3,227	22,600	24,138	26,118	28,685
ASIA	842	11,646	1,570	19,564	22,432	22,733	22,412
Communist Asia	50	257	182	450	450	450	450
China	50	27	182	50	50*	50*	50*
North Korea		230		400	400*	400*	400*
Non-Communist Asia	790	11,389	1,388	19,114	21,982	21,283	21,867
Hong Kong	92	70	174	132	145	141	170
India	79	6,289	128	10,482	12,269	13,403	13,734
Malaysia	296	3,851	529	6,418	6,741	5,772	5,330
Philippines	325	778	559	1,384	1,398	1,607	1,564
South Korea		329		587	709	641	668
Thailand		72		111	720	720	496
OCEANIA	3	157	5	304	500	2,296	9,195
Australia		7		12	200	1,996	8,895
New Caledonia	3	152	5	292	300*	300*	300*
LATIN AMERICA	2,302	24,206	3,707	39,631	45,101	48,356	49,861
Brazil	605	6,227	890	8,730	12,731	12,910	14,279
Chile	1,568	5,650	2,596	9,114	9,114	10,729	11,095
Cuba	14		29				
Mexico	115	6	192	10	10		
Peru		3,462		5,884	7,246	7,679	8,000
Venezuela		8,861		14,893	16,000*	17,037	16,487
AFRICA AND MIDDLE EAST	3,143	16,237	5,707	27,537	31,422	32,243	34,548
Algeria	1,366	1,456	2,583	2,828	1,647	483	345
Angola		695		1,128	1,128	693	627
Egypt		14		28			
Guinea		337		717	800*	1,000*	1,000*
Liberia		7,440		12,400	15,329	16,000*	17,000*
Mauretania		3,139		4,983	5,961	7,135	7,455
Morocco	726	630	1,265	1,063	957	790	916
Rhodesia		181		287	321		
Sierra Leone	688	1,207	1,161	2,073	2,334	2,218	2,152
South Africa		651		1,085	2,000*	3,000*	4,629
Sudan					35	48	9
Tunisia	363	487	698	945	910	876	775

Sources: For 1950 and 1964, United Nations, 1968-A; for 1965–67, United Nations, *Yearbook of International Trade Statistics* and *Commodity Trade Statistics.*
* Author's estimate.

TABLE A-8. WORLD PRODUCTION OF IRON ORE, BY REGIONS AND COUNTRIES, 1950 AND 1965–1967

(Thousands of tons)

Region and country	Fe content				Actual tonnage			
	1950	1965	1966	1967	1950	1965	1966	1967
WORLD	115,582	310,594	340,158	339,467	244,469	618,098	662,457	637,527
NORTH AMERICA	51,105	68,888	74,689	73,765	102,213	123,386	127,704	123,132
Canada	1,799	19,840	22,480	23,420	3,281	34,207	36,912	38,388
U.S.A.	49,306	49,048	52,209	50,345	98,932	89,179	90,792	84,799
WESTERN EUROPE	28,311	51,528	51,392	49,694	75,602	136,719	125,873	115,580
EEC	13,885	21,879	22,529	20,304	43,497	74,689	69,736	57,459
Belgium	16	30	37	26	48	91	124	88
France	9,750	17,857	17,894	15,997	29,990	59,524	55,056	49,224
Italy	227	266	429	382	499	806	828	737
Luxembourg	1,082	1,579	1,868	1,715	3,845	6,315	6,528	6,300
West Germany	2,810	2,147	2,301	2,184	9,115	7,953	7,200	6,780
Austria	580	1,132	1,099	1,099	1,852	3,536	3,480	3,468
Britain	3,838	4,229	3,747	3,624	13,171	15,662	13,872	12,948
Denmark		14	13	14		41	35	41
Finland		414	409	423		658	631	643
Greece		31	55	63	5	60	128	149
Norway	2	1,478	1,587	2,000	404	2,423	2,448	3,240
Portugal	193	104	93	96		193	191	197
Spain	1,044	2,720	2,417	2,550	2,088	5,788	4,872	5,052
Sweden	8,282	17,691	17,465	17,596	13,611	29,485	27,984	28,332
Switzerland	27	45	26	2	55	113	50	1
Turkey	143	940	928	881	234	1,566*	1,550*	1,470*
Yugoslavia	317	851	1,024	1,042	685	2,504	2,496	2,580
EASTERN EUROPE	23,181	89,456	89,282	94,053	43,216	165,499	173,706	181,319
Middle Europe	1,111	3,776	3,842	3,727	3,565	12,399	13,434	13,067
Albania		135	150*	150*		370	400*	400*
Bulgaria	14	649	815	798		1,804	2,616	2,496
Czechoslovakia	480	720	633	545	1,604	2,572	2,232	1,908
East Germany	112	495	427	407	401	1,650	1,716	1,680
Hungary	92	183	182	176	368	762	746	715
Poland	235	801	831	838	770	2,862	3,048	3,072
Romania	178	793	804	813	395	2,479	2,676	2,796
U.S.S.R.	22,070	85,680	85,440	90,326	39,651	153,000	160,272	168,252
ASIA	4,038	38,160	47,944	40,341	8,334	91,022	116,141	92,836
Communist Asia	900	17,500	25,000	18,650	3,000	55,000	78,000*	56,500*
China	900	15,000	22,000	15,400	3,000	50,000	72,000*	50,000*
North Korea		2,500	3,000	3,250		5,000	6,000*	6,500*

TABLE A-8.—Continued

Region and country	Fe content				Actual tonnage			
	1950	1965	1966	1967	1950	1965	1966	1967
Non-Communist Asia	3,138	20,660	22,944	21,691	5,334	36,022	38,141	36,336
Burma		3				5		
Hong Kong	91	75	77	80	172	134	137	144
India	1,929	13,563	16,545	15,683	3,125	23,385	26,796	25,824
Japan	490	1,436	1,370	1,274	928	2,520	2,400	2,208
Malaysia	284	3,910	3,279	3,044	507	6,982	5,856	5,436
Pakistan		8				23		
Philippines	342	840	860	929	599	1,473	1,464	1,476
South Korea		368	395	349		736	792	696
Taiwan		7				14		
Thailand	2	450	418	332	3	750	696	552
OCEANIA	1,482	4,586	7,626	12,386	2,472	7,113	11,346	17,362
Australia	1,472	4,425	7,504	12,273	2,453	6,807	11,064	17,160
New Caledonia	8	168	121	112	15	300	280*	200*
New Zealand	2	3*	1	1	4	6*	2	2
LATIN AMERICA	3,528	34,486	41,756	39,801	5,597	55,423	64,576	61,566
Argentina	16	45	69	99	40	95	156	226
Brazil	1,351	10,227	15,813	15,163	1,987	15,980	23,256	22,296
Chile	1,771	7,764	7,788	6,853	2,950	12,132	12,204	10,776
Colombia		450	310	300*		750	520*	500*
Cuba	1	7			1	15*		
Mexico	262	1,402	1,481	1,618	420	2,549	2,820	2,988
Peru		4,000	4,877	4,809		6,250	7,776	7,656
Venezuela	127	10,591	11,418	10,959	199	17,652	17,844	17,124
AFRICA AND MIDDLE EAST	3,937	23,490	27,469	29,427	7,035	38,936	43,111	45,732
Algeria	1,361	1,635	916	1,335	2,573	3,144	1,764	2,568
Angola		505	494	712		815	792	1,152
Egypt		254	220	211		508	443	422
Guinea		378	800*	800*		755	1,600	1,600
Iran		30	40	40		60	80	80
Liberia		9,042	11,538	12,575		15,070	16,968	18,492
Mauretania		3,832	4,638	4,846		6,035	7,140	7,452
Morocco	730	561	602	683	1,274	951	1,016	888
Rhodesia	33	824	830	450	57	1,288	1,300*	700*
Sierra Leone	702	1,426	1,382	1,259	1,184	2,377	2,304	2,100
South Africa	717	3,780	4,366	4,910	1,189	5,816	6,792	7,740
Sudan			20	7			40	14
Swaziland		620	1,003	1,098		1,000	1,600*	1,600*
Tunisia	394	603	620	501	758	1,117	1,272	924

Sources: United Nations, Statistical Yearbook and Monthly Statistical Bulletin.
* Author's estimate.

TABLE A-9. LAKE ERIE BASE PRICES, 1950–1969
            (Mesabi non-Bessemer grade)

Year	Per actual ton* (dollars)	Per ton unit* (cents)
1950	7.82	15.18
1951	8.43	16.37
1952 (to July)	8.43	16.37
1952	9.19	17.84
1953 (to July)	9.86	19.17
1953–54	10.06	19.53
1955	10.26	19.92
1956	11.02	21.40
1957–61	11.63	22.58
1962–63 (to August)	10.82	21.01
1963–69	10.72	20.82

Sources: Cleveland-Cliffs Iron Company, Cliffs Iron Ore Analysis; Skillings Mining Review.
* Basis 51.5% Fe, unscreened, delivered to rail of vessel at Lake Erie ports. Premium for coarse ore of 80¢ a ton; penalty for fine ore of 45¢ a ton in 1963–69.

TABLE A-10. AVERAGE F.O.B. VALUE OF IRON ORE EXPORTS FROM SELECTED COUNTRIES,
             1950–1967

(Dollars per actual ton)

Year	Brazil	Canada	Liberia	Malaysia	Sierra Leone	Sweden	Vene-zuela
1950	7.39	6.06		5.76	3.21	6.04	
1951	9.85	6.04		6.92	3.45	7.25	5.85
1952	14.73	6.54		7.34	4.45	10.65	7.79
1953	14.15	7.17		6.63	9.98	11.58	8.60
1954	13.11	7.34		6.37	8.51	9.92	6.81
1955	11.69	7.65	10.38	6.67	7.67	10.01	6.27
1956	12.80	7.99	10.41	6.90	8.32	10.76	6.87
1957	13.55	8.70	10.68	7.27	8.36	11.65	7.43
1958	13.93	8.81	10.43	7.76	8.71	11.98	7.55
1959	10.96	8.74	10.43	8.51	7.51	10.40	7.31
1960	10.24	9.31	11.69	8.19	7.40	10.25	8.56
1961	9.57	9.30	10.41	8.18	7.33	10.19	9.07
1962	9.07	9.31	8.64	8.30	7.11	9.75	8.99
1963	8.50	10.34	6.97	8.62	6.96	8.76	7.94
1964	8.29	10.55	6.60	8.28	7.27	8.55	10.70
1965	8.09	10.67	6.26	7.83	6.54	8.78	10.63
1966	7.76	10.88				8.96	
1967	7.20	11.01				7.93	

Sources: United Nations, Yearbook of International Trade and Commodity Trade Statistics; national trade statistics.
Note: Prices in italics indicate year of highest value per ton.

TABLE A-11. AVERAGE VALUE OF IRON ORE IMPORTS INTO BRITAIN, JAPAN, AND WEST GERMANY, FROM SELECTED ORIGINS, 1950–1967

(Dollars per actual tons)

Year	Algeria	Brazil	Canada	Chile	Goa	India	Liberia	Malaysia	Peru	Philippines	Sierra Leone	Sweden	U.S.A.	Venezuela
IMPORTS INTO BRITAIN														
1950	8.34											8.31		
1951	13.94											9.81		
1952	*17.21*											16.93		
1953	16.39	25.40	10.86				20.84				15.73	16.42		
1954	14.51	20.09	10.71				18.50				14.51	14.51		
1955	15.00	20.96	13.53				18.81				15.34	14.82		15.88
1956	15.89	24.70	16.18				18.36				16.21	16.70		15.34
1957	16.94	*25.12*	*16.46*				*19.10*				*16.36*	*18.41*		16.16
1958	15.84	20.87	14.09				16.66				13.40	17.62		16.24
1959	14.72	20.34	13.92				14.66				12.34	15.88		*16.34*
1960	12.47	18.74	13.46				15.44				12.22	14.59		16.04
1961	12.46	17.63	13.91				15.09				11.85	14.42		15.98
1962	12.36	16.94	14.74				14.15				11.84	14.14		15.41
1963	11.38	15.09	13.94				11.85				11.32	12.35		14.08
1964	11.08	14.90	14.66				11.12				11.69	12.16		13.24
1965	11.03	13.33	14.99				11.20				11.60	12.15		13.83
1966	11.04	13.19	13.89				10.67				10.82	12.60		13.33
1967	10.73	11.66	14.94				10.34				10.30	12.16		12.00
IMPORTS INTO JAPAN														
1952										*15.46*			23.22	
1953										12.75				
1954			13.52		13.18	16.62		12.23		11.69				
1955			16.43		15.31	19.06		14.55		12.43				
1956		28.45	16.91	25.54	20.81	24.65		15.85	29.84	13.87			*20.32*	
1957		*34.07*	*21.90*	*30.69*	*23.01*	*25.82*		*20.12*	*30.39*	14.13			*23.32*	

Year									
1958	26.19	20.70	18.94	19.54	18.40	12.93	30.09	11.53	20.39
1959	18.45	15.78	17.69	12.54	16.06	13.40	14.65	11.72	15.69
1960	18.56	14.91	16.33	13.08	16.18	13.48	15.01	11.82	15.45
1961	18.74	15.02	15.65	12.83	16.66	13.41	14.55	11.73	15.62
1962	18.46	15.07	16.01	12.81	17.01	13.08	13.71	11.83	14.74
1963	16.68	14.31	16.46	11.97	15.66	12.16	12.85	11.48	13.90
1964	16.05	14.24	15.19		15.15[a]	11.75	13.03	11.39	14.02
1965	15.93	14.23	14.89		14.66[a]	11.58	12.99	11.82	14.41
1966	13.54	13.62	14.51		12.77[a]	10.61	12.60	12.11	14.81
1967	12.34	13.08	13.79		12.22[a]		12.54	12.18	14.95

IMPORTS INTO WEST GERMANY

Year									
1950	26.26	12.63	19.38	17.91	19.17		5.21	8.44	14.40
1951	25.36	11.89	14.43	18.61	19.45		12.99	10.39	13.32
1952	23.09	10.60	16.27	16.22	17.76		13.54	15.48	15.34
1953	20.54	10.36	20.24	17.49	16.91		15.96	14.77	16.16
1954	24.18	12.35	23.75	18.47	19.20		13.04	12.93	16.24
1955	26.49	12.59	21.69	16.86	23.08		15.57	12.83	16.04
1956	22.52	14.55	16.05	15.74	17.98	17.69	17.36	13.88	15.98
1957	17.58	14.44	14.55	13.45	14.55	19.27	14.29	14.97	15.41
1958	16.10	13.21	14.26	13.37	14.50	21.82	11.71	14.63	
1959	15.23	12.45	13.61	13.02	12.84	18.27	11.45	13.10	
1960	13.93	12.74		12.54	11.92	14.06	11.53	13.05	
1961		12.66				13.76	11.46	13.39	
1962						14.15		12.96	
1963						12.80			
1964	13.01	11.87	12.01	10.88	10.67	11.46	11.15	10.77	11.76
1965	12.53	10.32	12.56	10.99	10.58	11.66	10.40	10.84	11.18
1966	11.04	10.84	12.18	10.90	10.71	13.35	10.34	10.71	11.21
1967	11.58	14.51	11.53	9.13	10.44	13.54	9.44	9.78	10.44

Sources: United Nations, *Commodity Trade Statistics*; national trade statistics.
Note: Prices in italics indicate year of highest value per ton.
[a] Including Goa.

B. Countries and Regions Covered by Manners' Supplement*

Part One. TRENDS IN THE DEMANDS FOR IRON ORE
    I. North America
        United States
        Canada

    II. Western Europe
        European Economic Community
        West Germany
        France
        Italy
        Luxembourg
        Belgium
        Netherlands
        Britain
        Spain
        Sweden
        Austria
        Yugoslavia

    III. Eastern Europe
        U.S.S.R.
        Poland

* *The Changing World Market for Iron Ore: A Descriptive Supplement Covering the Years 1950–1965* (192 pp., incl. 72 tables) can be obtained in bound manuscript form (Xerox, OP 57522) from University Microfilms, Ann Arbor, Michigan 48106.

Czechoslovakia
East Germany
Romania
Hungary

IV. Rest of World
Bulgaria
China
Japan
India
Australia
Brazil
Mexico
Argentina
Venezuela
Africa

Part Two. TRENDS IN THE SUPPLY OF IRON ORE

I. North America
United States
Canada

II. Western Europe
European Economic Community
France
Belgium–Luxembourg
West Germany
Italy
Netherlands
Britain
Sweden
Norway
Spain

III. Eastern Europe
U.S.S.R.
Czechoslovakia
Poland
East Germany

IV. Rest of the World
China
Japan
India
Australia
Brazil
Venezuela
Chile
Africa

Bibliography

Adams, W., and Dirlam, J. B. (1964). "Steel imports and vertical oligopoly power," *American Economic Review*, 54:626–55.

Adelman, M. A. (1964). "The World Oil Outlook." In Clawson, M., ed., *Natural Resources and International Development*. Baltimore.

Aguirre, F. T. (1963). "Regional Integration of the Steel Industry in Latin America." Technical paper B.23 in United Nations (1963-C).

Alderfer, E. B., and Michl, H. E. (1950). *Economics of American Industry*. New York.

Alexandersson, G. (1956). *The Industrial Structure of American Cities*. Lincoln, Nebraska.

———. (1961). "Changes in the location pattern of the Anglo-American steel industry: 1948–1959," *Economic Geography*, 37:95–114.

———. (1967). *Geography of Manufacturing*. Englewood Cliffs, New Jersey.

American Iron Ore Association (1963). *Iron Ore Industry of the United States and Canada: Facts and Figures*. Cleveland, Ohio.

———. Annually. *Iron Ore News Highlights*. Cleveland, Ohio.

American Iron and Steel Institute (1959). *Steel in the Soviet Union*. New York.

American Steel Industry Delegation (1960). *Iron and Steel in Japan, Report to the Committee on Foreign Relations, American Iron and Steel Institute, on Steelmaking and Utilization*. New York.

———. (1960). *Steel in India, Report to the Committee on Foreign Relations, American Iron and Steel Institute, on the Program "In Step," Other Training Matters, Steelmaking and Utilization*. New York.

Andrews, P. W. S., and Brunner, E. (1951). *Capital Development in Steel*. Oxford.

Anglo-American Council on Productivity (1952). *Iron and Steel*. London.

Association of Iron and Steel Engineers (1964). *Continuous and Pressure Casting*. Pittsburgh.

Associazione Industrie Siderurgiche Italiane (1960). "The iron and steel industry in the postwar period, and its future prospects," *Journal of the Iron and Steel Institute*, 195:16–25.

359

Astier, J. (1963). "Pelletizing." Technical paper A.5 in United Nations (1963-C).
———. (1964). "L'agglomeration en boulettes des minerais de fer," *Revue de Metallurgie*, 61:417–35.
Australian Transport Advisory Council (1959). *Transport Costs in Australia*. Canberra.
Bain, H. F. (1945). *Pattern for Western Steel Production*. Information Circular No. 7315, Bureau of Mines. Washington, D.C.
Bain, J. S. (1956). *Barriers to the New Competition*. Cambridge, Massachusetts.
Bank of Nova Scotia (1956). "Canada's primary steel industry," *Monthly Review*, July, pp. 1–4.
Banks, G. N.; Campbell, R. A.; and Viens, G. E. (1963). *Iron Ore Pelletizing*. Department of Mines and Technical Surveys, Mines Branch. Ottawa.
Bannyy, N. P., Brodskiy, V. B., *et al.* (1960). *Economics of Iron and Steel in the U.S.S.R.* Moscow. Translated by U.S. Department of Commerce, Office of Technical Services, Joint Publications Research Service. Washington, D.C., 1962.
Bardin, I. P. (1955). "The iron and steel industry of the U.S.S.R.," *Eastern Metals Review*, 8:81–84.
Barloon, M. J. (1947). "Steel: The great retreat," *Harpers Magazine*, 195:145–55.
———. (1949). "The question of steel capacity," *Harvard Business Review*, 27:209–20.
———. (1954-A). "The expansion of blast furnace capacity 1938–53: A study in geographical cost differentials," *Business History Review*, 28:1–23.
———. (1954-B). "Institutional foundations of pricing policy in the steel industry," *Business History Review*, 28:214–35.
———. (1965). "The interrelationship of the changing structure of American transportation and changes in industrial location," *Land Economics*, 41:169–79.
Barnett, H. J., and Morse, C. (1963). *Scarcity and Growth: The Economics of Natural Resource Availability*. Baltimore.
Bateman, A. M. (1959). *Economic Mineral Deposits*. New York.
Battelle Memorial Institute (1957). *Final Report on a Survey and Analysis of the Supply and Availability of Obsolete Iron and Steel Scrap*. Columbus, Ohio.
———. (1964). *Final Report on the Technical and Economic Analysis of the Impact of Recent Developments in Steelmaking Practices on the Supplying Industries to the Steelmaking Research Group*. Columbus, Ohio.
Bauchet, P. (1965). *Les Tableaux Économique: Analyse de la Région Lorraine*. Paris.
Belfer, N. (1953). "Some economic effects of the new Morrisville, Pennsylvania, steel plant," *Current Economic Comment*, August, pp. 44–56.
Benford, H. (1958). "Ocean ore carrier economics and preliminary design," *Transactions of the Society of Naval Architects and Marine Engineers*, 66:383–98.
———; Thornton, K. C.; and Williams, E. B. (1962). "Current Trends in the Design of Iron Ore Ships." Paper presented to the Society of Naval Architects and Marine Engineers. Duluth, Minnesota.
Birbragher, L. (1965). "Columbia's Iron and Steel Industry." Master's thesis, University of Chicago.
Blackwell, R. B. (1964). "Toward Improved Cost Data for Inland Waterway

Transportation." Paper presented to Transport Research Forum. Washington, D.C.

Blake, C. (1965). "Supply lags and demand acceleration in the United Kingdom steel market," *Scottish Journal of Political Economy*, 12:62–80.

Boschan, P. (1954). "Productive Capacity, Industrial Production, and Steel Requirements." In National Bureau of Economic Research. *Long Range Economic Projection*. Princeton.

Brisby, M. D. J. (1960). *The Development of a Steel Industry—Affecting the Economics of Steel*. National Metallurgical Laboratory, Council of Scientific and Industrial Research. Jamshedpur, India.

Britain:

Iron and Steel Board (1955, 1957, 1961, and 1964). *Development in the Iron and Steel Industry*. London.

———. Annually. *Annual Report*. London.

Iron and Steel Institute (1956). *The Russian Iron and Steel Industry*. London.

———. (1963-A). *The Iron and Steel Industry of Japan*. London.

———. (1963-B). *Ore Mining and Materials Handling*. London.

———. (1964). *Recent Development in Iron and Steelmaking with Special Reference to Indian Conditions*. London.

———. (1965). *Continuous Casting of Steel*. London.

———. (1967). *Ironmaking Tomorrow*. London.

National Board for Prices and Incomes (1969). *Steel Prices*. Report No. 111, Cmnd. 4033. London.

British Iron and Steel Federation (1958-A). *Account of the Organisation of the British Steel Industry*. London.

———. (1958-B). "The siting of British steelworks," *Steel Review*, 11:26–35.

———. (1959). "Steel in the German economy: A comparison with Britain," *Steel Review*, 14:10–25.

———. (1963). "Structural change in world ore," *Steel Review*, 30:18–30.

———. (1964-A). "Scrap," *Steel Review*, 36:33–40.

———. (1964-B). "Steel in the changing Commonwealth," *Steel Review*, 36:25–32.

———. (1965-A). "World steel surplus," *Steel Review*, 37:33–35.

———. (1965-B). "Location of steel plants in the U.K.," *Steel Review*, 40:30–32.

———. (1966-A). *The Steel Industry: Stage 1 Report on the Development Coordinating Committee* [Benson Committee]. London.

———. (1966-B). "Australian iron ore," *Steel Review*, 41.

———. Annually. *Annual Report* and *Statistical Handbook*. London.

———. Monthly. *Iron and Steel Monthly Statistics*. London.

———. Quarterly, until 1967. *Steel Review*. London.

British Iron and Steel Research Association (1959). "Energy requirements in the iron and steel industry," *Proceedings of the 16th Plant Engineering Conference*. London.

British Steel Corporation (1967). *Report on Organisation, 1967*. Cmnd. 3362. London.

———. Quarterly. *British Steel*. London.

Broude, H. W. (1950). "Location decisions and their relation to industrial development," *Explorations in Entrepreneurial History*, 3:103–34.

———. (1963). *Steel Decisions and the National Economy*. New Haven.

Brown, D. C. (1960). "The what and why of future blast furnace burdens,"

Twenty-first Annual Mining Symposium, University of Minnesota School of Mines and Metallurgy, Minneapolis.

Buck, W. K. (1963). *Mineral Development Policy*. Ottawa.

———, and Elver, R. B. (1963). *The Canadian Steel Industry: A Pattern of Growth*. Mineral Information Bulletin MR 70, Mineral Resources Division, Department of Mines and Technical Surveys. Ottawa.

Burn, D. L. (1940). *The Economic History of Steelmaking, 1867–1939*. Cambridge.

———. (1958). *The Structure of British Industry*. London.

———. (1961). *The Steel Industry, 1939–1959: A Study in Competition and Planning*. Cambridge.

Business and Defense Services Administration (1957). *Industrial Scrap Generation*. Washington, D.C.

Canada:

    Department of Energy, Mines and Resources. Annually, 1967 and subsequent years. *Canadian Iron Ore Industry*. Ottawa.

    Department of Mines and Technical Surveys (1961). *Prospects for the Marketing of Canadian Metallic Products and Iron Ore*. Ottawa.

    ———. Annually, 1965 and previous years. *Primary Iron and Steel* and *Canadian Iron Ore Industry*. Ottawa.

    Royal Commission on Canada's Economic Prospects (1957). *Mining and Mineral Processing*. Ottawa.

Canadian Metal Mining Association (1965). *Canada–U.S.S.R. Exchange Visits: The Iron Ore Industry*. Canadian Group Report. Ottawa.

Carr, J. C., and Taplin, W. (1962). *History of the British Steel Industry*. Oxford.

Carr, M. S., and Dutton, C. E. (1959). *Iron Ore Resources of the United States including Alaska and Puerto Rico, 1955*. Geological Survey Bulletin 1082-C. Washington, D.C.

Cartwright, W. F. (1964). "The Future of Automation in the Iron and Steel Industry." In *United Kingdom Automation Council Record No. 3*. London.

Casetti, E. (1966). "Optimum location of steel mills serving the Quebec and Southern Ontario steel market," *Canadian Geographer*, 10:27–39.

Casey, B. (1963). Speech in the U.S. House of Representatives. *Congressional Record, Proceedings and Debates of the 88th Congress, First Session*, August 22. Washington, D.C.

Chapman, H. H. *et al.* (1953). *The Iron and Steel Industries of the South*. Tuscaloosa, Alabama.

Chardonet, J. (1954). *La Sidérurgie Française, Progrès ou Décadence*. Paris.

Chilcote, R. H. (1968). *Spain's Iron and Steel Industry*. Bureau of Business Research, University of Texas. Austin.

Clark, C. (1940). *Conditions of Economic Progress*. London.

Clark, M. G. (1956-A). *The Economics of Soviet Steel*. Cambridge, Massachusetts.

———. (1956-B). "Soviet iron and steel industry: Recent developments and prospects," *Annals of the American Academy of Political and Social Science*, 303:50–61.

———. (1961). "Economics and Technology: The Case of Soviet Steel." Reprinted by New York State School of Industrial and Labor Relations, from Spulber, N., ed., *Study of the Soviet Economy: Direction and Impact of*

Soviet Growth, Teaching, and Research in Soviet Economics. Bloomington, Indiana.

————. (1964). "Magnitogorsk: A Soviet Iron and Steel Plant in the Southern Urals." In Thoman, R. S., and Patton, D., eds., *Focus on Geographic Activity.* New York.

Cleveland-Cliffs Iron Company. Annually. *Cliffs Iron Ore Analysis.* Cleveland.

Close, A. (1965). "China streamlines her steel," *Far Eastern Economic Review,* 47:365–69.

Coker, J. A. (1952). "Steel and the Schuman Plan," *Economic Geography,* 28:283–94.

Cole, J. P., and German, F. C. (1961). *A Geography of the U.S.S.R.* London.

Constantini, R. (1963). "A case study in pipeline transportation of solids: The challenge and promise with beneficiated ore," *Twenty-fourth Annual Mining Symposium,* University of Minnesota School of Mines and Metallurgy, Minneapolis.

Cordero, H. G. (1952, 1957, 1962, and 1965). *Iron and Steel Works of the World.* London.

Coverdale and Colpits (1964). "India Coal Transport Study." Mimeographed. Surveys and Research Corporation. Washington, D.C.

Craig, P. G. (1957). "Location factors in the development of steel centers," *Papers and Proceedings of the Regional Science Association,* 3:249–65.

Crozier, B. (1959). "China and her race for steel production," *Steel Review,* 15:8–19.

Cumberland, J. H. (1951). "Locational Structure of the East Coast Steel Industry." Ph.D. dissertation, Harvard University.

Curran, C. D. (1964). "The High Cost of Low Cost Transportation." Paper presented to the American Railway Engineering Association. Washington, D.C.

Czechoslovakia, Metallurgical Industry Technical and Economic Research Institute (1967). "Czechoslovakia's iron and steel industry," *Journal of the Iron and Steel Institute,* 205:1–5.

Dastur, M. N. (1963). "Small Steel Plants: Their Influence on Developing Countries." Technical paper A.12 in United Nations (1963-C).

————, and Lalkaka, R. D. (1964). "Layout of Large Integrated Steelworks." In Britain, Iron and Steel Institute (1964).

Davis, J. (1954). "The iron ore industry," *Canadian Geographical Journal,* 49:205–17.

Degeer, G. (1953). "The Swedish iron and steel industry today," *Skandinaviska Banken Quarterly Review,* 34:58–61.

Denton, G. R. (1955). "Investment and location in the steel industry," *Oxford Economic Papers,* 7:272–80.

Dewhurst, J. F. *et al.* (1961). *Europe's Needs and Resources.* New York.

Dick, I. D. (1963). "Technical and Economic Feasibility Planning for a Small Iron and Steel Industry." Technical paper B.12 in United Nations (1963-C).

Dickinson, S. B. (1956). "Economic basis of a South Australian steel industry," *Australian Quarterly,* March, pp. 18–29.

Dittman, F. W. (1965). "Oxygen steelmaking cost comparison: Kaldo vs. LD processes," *Journal of Metals,* 17:372–79.

Doerr, A. H. (1954-A). "Factors influencing the location of nonintegrated and integrated iron and steel centers in Anglo-America," *Southwestern Social Science Quarterly*, March, pp. 39–44.

———. (1954-B). "A quantitative analysis of the locational factors in the integrated and semi-integrated iron and steel industry of the United States and Canada," *Journal of Geography*, 53:393–402.

Dowding, M. F., and Whiting, A. N. (1964). "The Case for 100,000 Tonnes/Year Integrated Iron and Steel Plants for Emergent Countries." In Britain, Iron and Steel Institute (1964).

Dubnie, A. (1961). *Transportation of Minerals in Northern Canada*. Department of Mines and Technical Surveys. Ottawa.

———. (1962). *Transportation and the Competitive Position of Selected Canadian Minerals*. Department of Mines and Technical Surveys. Ottawa.

Earing, F. C. F. (1969). "New ore for old furnaces," *Annals of the Association of American Geographers*, 59:512–34.

Economic Commission for Europe. See United Nations.

Economist Intelligence Unit (1964). *Ocean Shipping and Freight Rates and Developing Countries*. A study for the U.N. Conference on Trade and Development. Geneva.

Einecke, G. (1950). *Die Eisenerzvorräte der Welt und der Anteil der Verbraucher und Lieferländer an deren Verwertung*. Düsseldorf.

Elver, R. B. (1960). *St. Lawrence Seaway and the Canadian Mineral Industry*. Department of Mines and Technical Surveys. Ottawa.

———. (1964). *Economic Aspects of Iron Ore in a Changing Market*. Department of Mines and Technical Surveys. Ottawa.

———; Janes, T. H.; and Walsh, J. H. (1963). *Technical and Economic Factors of Steel Plant Location*. Department of Mines and Technical Surveys. Ottawa.

Er Selcuk, M. (1956). "The iron and steel industry in China," *Economic Geography*, 32:347–71.

Estall, R. C., and Buchanan, R. O. (1961). *Industrial Activity and Economic Geography*. London.

European Coal and Steel Community, The High Authority. Annually. *General Report*. Luxembourg.

Fearnley and Egers Chartering Co. Ltd. Annually. *Trades of World Bulk Carriers*. Oslo.

Federal Reserve Bank of Chicago (1964). *Annual Report*. Chicago.

Federal Reserve Bank of Cleveland (1958). "Geography of steel consumption," *Business Review*, April, pp. 7–12.

Ferraro, F. (1961). "Italian developments in iron ore shipping," *Shipping World*, August 9.

Fink, D. A. (1963-A). "Primary Metals." In Pittsburgh Regional Planning Association (1963).

———. (1963-B). "Location Economics of the Basic Steel Industry of the United States." Unpublished ms.

Fleming, D. K. (1965). "Coastal Steel Production and the European Coal and Steel Community, 1953–63." Ph.D. dissertation, University of Washington.

Foldes, L. (1956). "Iron and steel prices," *Economica*, 23:344–56.

Friedmann, J. (1966). *Regional Development Policy: A Case Study of Venezuela*. Cambridge, Massachusetts.

Gakner, A. (1959). "Battle for steel supremacy: The Soviet Union leads in raw material," *Iron and Steel Engineer*, 36:117–24.

Gauvin, G. J., and Schneider, V. B. (1967). *Canadian Iron Ore Industry 1965*. Department of Energy, Mines and Resources. Ottawa.

Golledge, R. G. (1961). "Decentralisation and reorientation in the Australian iron and steel industry," *Geography*, 46:364–68.

Goodeve, C. F. (1954). "Iron and steel industry of Finland," *Journal of the Iron and Steel Institute*, 178:219–22.

Graff, H. M., and Bouwer, S. C. (1965). "Economics of raw materials preparation for the blast furnace," *Journal of Metals*, 17:389–94.

Gross, G. A. (1960). "The iron ranges and current developments in New Quebec and Labrador," *Twenty-first Annual Mining Symposium*, University of Minnesota School of Mines and Metallurgy, Minneapolis.

Hamilton, F. E. I. (1964). "Location factors in the Yugoslav iron and steel industry," *Economic Geography*, 40:46–64.

Hance, W. A. (1964). *The Geography of Modern Africa*. New York.

———. (1967). *African Economic Development*. London.

Hanna Mining Company. Annually. *Iron Ore Analysis and Data*. Cleveland, Ohio.

Harris, C. D. (1954). "The market as a factor in the location of industry," *Annals of the Association of American Geographers*, 44:315–48.

Hart, J. G. M. (1967). "Future imported iron ore supplies for the U.K." *Journal of the Iron and Steel Institute*, 205:1207–10.

Hartshorne, R. (1928). "Location factors in the iron and steel industry," *Economic Geography*, 4:241–52.

———. (1929). "The iron and steel industry of the United States," *Journal of Geography*, 28:133–53.

Heineman, W. (1963). "The case for rail transport of iron ore," *Twenty-first Annual Mining Symposium*, University of Minnesota School of Mines and Metallurgy, Minneapolis.

Heising, L. F. (1963). *Open-Pit Mining, Milling and Costs, Groveland Mine, the Hanna Mining Company, Dickinson County, Michigan*. Bureau of Mines. Washington, D.C.

Herfindahl, O. C. (1961). *Three Studies in Mineral Economics*. Baltimore.

Hill, T. L. (1959). *The St. Lawrence Seaway*. London.

Holliday, R. W. (1956). "Steel." In *Mineral Facts and Problems*. Bureau of Mines. Washington, D.C.

Hollingsworth, J. A. (1964). "Trends in large excavators," *Twenty-fifth Anniversary Mining Symposium*, University of Minnesota School of Mines and Metallurgy, Minneapolis.

Holloway, R. J. (1952). *The Development of the Russian Iron and Steel Industry*. Business Research Series, No. 6. Stanford, California.

Holmes, C. H. (1959). "Factors affecting development of the steel industry in intermontane America," *Journal of Geography*, 58:20–31.

Holzman, F. D. (1957). "The Soviet Ural-Kuznetsk combine: A study in investment criteria and industrialisation policies," *Quarterly Journal of Economics*, 71:368–405.

Hoover, E. M. (1948). *The Location of Economic Activity*. New York.

Housz, A. H. I. (1960). "The location of modern steel plants on sea coasts," *Stahl und Eisen*, 80:272–76.

Hughes, H. (1964). *The Australian Iron and Steel Industry, 1848–1962*. Melbourne.

Hunter, H. (1957). *Soviet Transportation Policy*. Cambridge, Massachusetts.

Hussey, C. R. (1961). "Transportation, handling, and storage of iron ores from mines to docks in the Lake Superior region," *Twenty-second Annual Mining Symposium*, University of Minnesota School of Mines and Metallurgy, Minneapolis.

Hutchinson, W. M. (1958). *World-wide Marine Distance Tables*. London.

Hyde, R. W., and Bliss, C. (1964). "Impact of Reduced Agglomerates on Steelmaking Technology and World Iron Ore Markets." Paper presented to the 23d Ironmaking Conference, American Institute of Mining, Metallurgical, and Petroleum Engineers. Pittsburgh.

————; Lane, B. M.; and Glaser, W. W. (1962). "Iron ore resources of the world," *Engineering and Mining Journal*, 163:84–88.

India, National Council of Applied Economic Research (1965). *Cost Price Structure of Iron Ore*. New Delhi.

India, Planning Commission, Joint Technical Group for Transport Planning (1965). "Draft Report on Commodity Transport Studies." Mimeographed.

International Bank for Reconstruction and Development (1960). "The Market for Iron Ore in Western Europe." Mimeographed.

————. (1964). "The World Market for Iron Ore." Mimeographed.

Iron Age. Weekly. Philadelphia.

Isard, W. (1948). "Locational factors in the iron and steel industry since the early nineteenth century," *Journal of Political Economy*, 56:203–17.

————, and Capron, W. M. (1949). "The future locational pattern of iron and steel production in the United States," *Journal of Political Economy*, 57: 118–33.

————, and Cumberland, J. H. (1950). "New England as a possible location for an integrated iron and steel works," *Economic Geography*, 26:245–59.

————, and Kuene, R. E. (1953). "The impact of steel upon the Greater New York–Philadelphia industrial region," *Review of Economics and Statistics*, 35:289–301.

Italsider, Sp.A. (1967). "The Taranto works of Italsider," *Journal of the Iron and Steel Institute*, 205:121–41.

Jackson, H. C. (1961). "The influence of taxes on new iron ore investments in Minnesota," *Twenty-second Annual Mining Symposium*, University of Minnesota School of Mines and Metallurgy, Minneapolis.

Janes, T. H. (1959). *Markets for Iron and Steel Products in Western Canada*. Department of Mines and Technical Surveys. Ottawa.

————, and Elver, R. B. (1963). *The Steel Industry of the Prairie Provinces*. Department of Mines and Technical Surveys. Ottawa.

————, and Wittur, G. E. (1962). *The Primary Iron and Steel Industry of Canada*. Department of Mines and Technical Surveys. Ottawa.

Japan Iron and Steel Federation. Annually. *The Steel Industry of Japan*. Tokyo.

Johnson, W. A. (1964). "India's Iron and Steel Industry: A Study of Planned Industrial Growth." Ph.D. dissertation, Harvard University.

————. (1966). *The Steel Industry of India*. Cambridge, Massachusetts.

Jolbrook, D. S. (1958). "Growing Canadian steel industry," *Iron and Steel Engineer*, 35:133–36.

Jones, Bardelmeier, Clements & Co. Ltd. (1965). *Imagination in Bulk*. Nassau, Bahamas.

Joseph, T. L. (1946). "The blast furnace and means of control," *Transactions of the American Institute of Mechanical Engineers*, 167:15–36.

Karan, P. P. (1957). "Iron ore mining industry in the Singhbhum-Mayurbhanj region of India," *Economic Geography*, 33:349–61.

———. (1959). "Locational pattern of the new centres of the Indian iron and steel industry," *Journal of Geography*, 35:151–63.

Keeling, B. S., and Wright, A. E. G. (1962). *The Development of the Modern British Steel Industry*. London.

Kelly, J. M. (1963). "Government as a Dynamic Agent in Mineral Resource Development." In *Natural Resources*, vol. 2. United States papers prepared for the United Nations conference on the application of science and technology for the benefit of the less developed areas. Washington, D.C.

Kennelly, R. A. (1968). "The Location of the Mexican Steel Industry." In Smith, R. H. T.; Taaffe, E. J.; and King, L. J., eds., *Readings in Economic Geography*. Chicago.

Kerr, D. (1959). "The geography of the Canadian iron and steel industry," *Economic Geography*, 35:151–63.

Kikuchi, T. (1967). "Burden preparation for optimum blast furnace performance," *Journal of the Iron and Steel Institute*, 205:606–24.

Kingston, G. A., and Fulkerson, F. B. (1962). *The Pacific Northwest Steel Industry*. Bureau of Mines. Washington, D.C.

Kneiling, J. G. (1964). "The Use of Integral Trains to Produce Competitive Bulk Transport Costs." Paper from the office of T. J. Kauffield, Consulting Engineers. New York.

———, and Kauffield, T. J. (1965). "Integral trains," *Skillings Mining Review*, February 13.

Krause, L. B. (1962). "Import discipline: The case against the U.S. steel industry," *Journal of Industrial Economics*, 11:33–47.

Kyle, D. H. (1958). "BISC(ORE)," *Steel Review*, 9:24–33.

Lake Carriers Association. Annually. *Annual Report*. Cleveland, Ohio.

Landsberg, H. H.; Fischman, L. L.; and Fisher, J. L. (1963). *Resources in America's Future*. Baltimore.

Langley, S. J. (1951). "The location problem in the British steel industry," *Oxford Economic Papers*, 3:113–24.

Leckie, A. H., and Morris, A. J. (1968). "Effect of plant and works scale on costs in the iron and steel industry," *Journal of the Iron and Steel Institute*, 206:442–52.

Lefebvre, A. G. (1953). "Postwar progress and trends in steel manufacture in the Benelux region," *Metal Progress*, 63:84–88.

Lehbert, B. (1961). *Die Entwicklung der Stahlwirtschaft in den Vereinigten Staaten von Amerika und in der Sowjetunion*. Kiel.

Lehmkuhler, H. (1963). "Sintering: A General Review." Technical paper A.7 in United Nations (1963-C).

Leith, C. K. (1938). *Mineral Valuations of the Future*. New York.

Lister, L. (1960). *Europe's Coal and Steel Community*. New York.

Livshits, R. S. (1958). *The Location of the Iron and Steel Industry of the U.S.S.R.* Moscow.

———. (1961). *Production Cost in the Heavy Industry of the U.S.S.R.* Moscow.

Lloyd, R. M. (1960). "Economics and the world iron ore market," *Twenty-first Annual Mining Symposium*, University of Minnesota School of Mines and Metallurgy, Minneapolis.

Lonsdale, R. E., and Thompson, J. H. (1960). "A map of the U.S.S.R.'s manufacturing," *Economic Geography*, 36:36–52.

Losch, A. (1954). *The Economics of Location*. New Haven.

Lutz, V. (1962). *Italy: A Study in Economic Development*. London.

Lydolph, P. E. (1964). *Geography of the U.S.S.R.* New York.

McComb, J. B. (1963). *Iron Ore and Taxes in Minnesota*. Macalester College, St. Paul.

McLachan, D. L. (1959). "Pricing in Ocean Transport." Ph.D. dissertation, University of Leeds.

McLaren, J. (1967). "The future of home ore," *Journal of the Iron and Steel Institute*, 205:905–9.

Maertens, P. (1963). "Operation of a Large Blending Plant." Technical paper A.11 in United Nations (1963-C).

Maizel, D. L. (1957). *Organisation, Planning, and Financing Capital Construction in the Iron and Steel Industry*. Moscow.

Manners, G. (1964-A). *The Geography of Energy*. London.

———, ed. (1964-B). *South Wales in the Sixties*. Oxford.

———. (1967). "Transport costs, freight rates, and the changing economic geography of iron ore," *Geography*, 52:260–79.

———. (1968-A). "Reshaping steel," *New Society*, December 19, pp. 907–8.

———. (1968-B). "Latter-day leviathans for ocean bulk transport," *Optima*, 18:164–73.

———. (1969-A). "New Resource Evaluations." In Cooke, R. C., and Johnson, J. H., *Trends in Geography*. London.

———. (1969-B). "Steel Surpluses: Fact or Fiction?" *Area*, 4:42–45.

Marovelli, R. L. *et al.* (1961). *Lake Superior Iron Resources*. Bureau of Mines. Washington, D.C.

Martin, J. E. (1957). "Location factors in the Lorraine iron and steel industry," *Transactions and Papers of the Institute of British Geographers*, 23:191–212.

———. (1958). "Recent trends in the Lorraine iron and steel industry," *Geography*, 43:191–99.

———. (1961). "Developments in the Lorraine iron and steel industry," *Geography*, 46:242–45.

———. (1968). "New trends in the Lorraine iron region," *Geography*, 53:375–80.

Mason, P. F. (1969). "Some changes in domestic iron mining as a result of pelletization," *Annals of the Association of American Geographers*,59:535–51.

Mayer, H. M. (1964). "Politics and land use: The Indiana shoreline of Lake Michigan," *Annals of the Association of American Geographers*, 54:508–23.

Means, G. C. (1961). *Pricing Power and the Public Interest*. New York.

Metal Bulletin (1965). *Iron Ore*, a special issue. London.

———. Weekly. London.

Miller, E. W. (1958). "Lorraine: Metallurgical center of France," *Mineral Industries*, 28:1–6.

Mills, H. R. (1965). "The shipping of iron ore," *Metal Bulletin* (1965).

———, and Muscroft, K. (1967). "Planning the supply of materials to a steel plant," *Journal of the Iron and Steel Institute*, 205:928–33.

Mining Journal. Weekly. London.

Montague, W. K. (1961). "Impact of labor costs on Lake Superior ore mines," *Twenty-second Annual Mining Symposium*, University of Minnesota School of Mines and Metallurgy, Minneapolis.

Montias, J. M. (1957). "The Polish iron and steel industry," *American and Slavic East European Review*, 16:301–22.

Morgan, L. (1956). *The Canadian Primary Iron and Steel Industry*. Royal Commission on Canada's Economic Prospects. Ottawa.

Murata, K. (1962). "Location Policy and Location of the Private Enterprise." In *Applied Geography*, Annual Report of the Association of Applied Geographers, No. 3. Tokyo.

Murray, L. (1963). "Foreign aid and the steel industry," *Steel Review*, 31:28–33.

Naess, E. D. (1965). *Tanker Industry: Problems and Prospects*. Bergen, Norway.

Nahai, L. (1961). *India's Iron and Steel Industry*. Bureau of Mines, Washington, D.C.

Nardi, G. (1960). "The policy of regional development: A case study, Southern Italy," *Banca Nazionale del Lavoro Quarterly Review*, 70:215–44.

National Council of Association of Iron Ore Producers (1960). *The Iron Ore Industry of Britain*. Kettering.

Netschert, B. C., and Landsberg, H. H. (1961). *The Future Supply of Major Metals*. Washington.

New Zealand Steel Investigating Company Ltd. (1963). *Report*. Wellington.

Nijhawan, B. R. (1963). *Growth Pattern of the Indian Iron and Steel Industry*. National Metallurgical Laboratory, Council of Scientific and Industrial Research. Jamshedpur.

Nikolayev, S. A., and Molodtsova, L. I. (1960). "The present state of the Chinese iron and steel industry," *Soviet Geography*, 1:55–71.

Nippon Kokan. Monthly. *Japan Steel Notes*. Tokyo.

Norris Oakley Bros. (1966). *Iron and Steel Handbook, 1966*. London.

O'Connor, B. (1966). "The Role of the Market in the Economic Geography of Tinplate Production in Western Europe." Ph.D. dissertation, University of London.

Old, B. S.; Hyde, R. W.; and Pepper, E. L. (1963). "The Direct Reduction of Iron and the Less Developed Areas." In *Industrial Development*, vol. 4, United States papers prepared for the United Nations conference on the application of science and technology for the benefit of the less developed areas. Washington, D.C.

Olt, T. F. (1962). "Blast furnace performance using iron ore pellets," *Journal of the Iron and Steel Institute*, 200:87–95.

Organisation for Economic Cooperation and Development (1964). *Continuous Casting of Steel in the U.S.S.R.* Paris.

―――. Annually. *The Iron and Steel Industry*. Paris.

Parrish, J. B. (1956). "Iron and steel in the balance of world power," *Journal of Political Economy*, 64:369–88.

Paterson, J. H. (1956). "Progress of the European coal and steel community," *Geography*, 41:129–30.

Peco, F. (1954). "Progress of the Italian steel industry," *Review of Economic Conditions in Italy*, 8:151–64.

Percival, F. G. (1951; rev. 1959). *The World's Iron Ore Supplies*. British Iron and Steel Federation. London.

Pfleider, E. P., and Yardley, D. H. (1963). "Underground mining of Minnesota taconite: A future probability," *Twenty-fourth Annual Mining Symposium*, University of Minnesota School of Mines and Metallurgy, Minneapolis.

Pickard, J. P. (1968). *Dimensions in Metropolitanism*. Washington, D.C.

Pinot, M. J. (1959). "Location of Steel Industries." In *Iron and Coal*, February 27, pp. 499–502; and March 6, pp. 553–56.

Pittsburgh Regional Planning Association (1963). *Region in Transition, Report of the Economic Study of the Pittsburgh Region*. Pittsburgh.

Pocock, D. C. D. (1963). "Iron and steel at Scunthorpe," *The East Midland Geographer*, 3:124–38.

Political and Economic Planning (1958). "The development of the steel industry," *Planning*, 24:259–74.

———. (1964). "Steel pricing policies," *Planning*, 30:319–75.

Potter, N., and Christy, F. T. (1962). *Trends in Natural Resource Commodities: Statistics of Prices, Output, Consumption, Foreign Trade, and Employment in the United States, 1870–1957*. Baltimore.

Pounds, N. J. G. (1952). *The Ruhr: A Study in Historical and Economic Geography*. London.

———. (1957). "Lorraine and the Ruhr," *Economic Geography*, 33:149–62.

———. (1958). *The Upper Silesian Industrial Region*. Bloomington, Indiana.

———. (1959). "World production and use of steel scrap," *Economic Geography*, 35:247–58.

———. (1963). *The Geography of Iron and Steel*. London.

———, and Parker, W. N. (1957). *Coal and Steel in Western Europe: The Influence of Resources and Production*. Bloomington, Indiana.

Powers, R. E. (1961). "Economic factors in the location of agglomerating facilities," *Twenty-second Annual Mining Symposium*, University of Minnesota School of Mines and Metallurgy, Minneapolis.

Pratten, C. F. (1964). "A comparison of forecast and actual steel production in 1962," *Journal of the Royal Statistical Society*, Series A, 127:242–50.

———, and Dean, R. M. (1965). *The Economies of Large-Scale Production in British Industry*. Cambridge.

Prêcheur, C. (1963). *La Sidérurgie Française*. Paris.

Provisional Board of the New Zealand Steel Company (1965). *Report*. Wellington.

Rawston, E. M. (1955). "Steel production and the East Midlands," *East Midlands Geographer*, 3:21–24.

Reno, H. T. (1965). "Iron." In *Mineral Facts and Problems*. Bureau of Mines. Washington, D.C.

———, and Anderson, S. M. (1960). "Iron in ore in South America," *Twenty-first Annual Mining Symposium*, University of Minnesota School of Mines and Metallurgy, Minneapolis.

Rideau, E. (1956). *Essor et Problèmes d'une Region Française: Houillères et Sidérurgie de Moselle*. Paris.

Robie, E. H., ed. (1964). *Economics of the Mineral Industries*. New York.

Rodgers, A. (1952-A). "Industrial inertia: A major factor in the location of the steel industry in the United States," *Geographical Review*, 42:56–66.

———. (1952-B). "The iron and steel industry of the Mahoning and Shenango valleys," *Economic Geography*, 28:331–42.

———. (1960). *The Industrial Geography of the Port of Genova*. Chicago.

———. (1964). "Coking coal supply: Its role in the expansion of the Soviet steel industry," *Economic Geography*, 40:113–50.

Roe, L. A. (1957). *Iron Ore Beneficiation.* Lake Bluff, Illinois.

Roepke, H. G. (1956). *Movements of the British Iron and Steel Industry, 1720–1951.* Urbana, Illinois.

———. (1957). "Ore supply and the location of the British iron and steel industry," *Northwestern University Studies in Geography*, 2:97–101.

Rotterdamsche Bank (1949). "Steel in Western Europe," *Quarterly Review*, 2:7–28.

Sandbach, E. K. (1963). "The Iron and Steel Industry in a Developing Economy." In *Industrial Development*, vol. 4. United States papers prepared for the United Nations conference on the application of science and technology for the benefit of the less developed areas. Washington, D.C.

Scottish Council (1961). *Inquiry into the Scottish Economy.* Toothill Report. Edinburgh.

Sharer, C. J. (1963). "The Philadelphia iron and steel district: Its relation to the seaways," *Economic Geography*, 39:363–67.

Shimkin, D. (1953). *Minerals: A Key to Soviet Power.* Cambridge, Massachusetts.

Shone, R., and Fisher, H. R. (1958). "Industrial production and steel consumption," *Journal of the Royal Statistical Society*, Series A, 121:269–311.

Silberman, C. E. (1960). "Steel: It's a brand new industry," *Fortune*, 62:122–27.

Sinnhuber, K. A. (1965). "Eisenhüttenstadt and Other New Industrial Locations East of Berlin." In *Festschrift Leopold G. Scheidt zum 60. Geburtstag.* Vienna.

Skillings, D. N. (1961). "Iron ore railroad completed on the Quebec frontier," *Skillings' Mining Review*, vol. 1.

———. (1963). "A review of iron ore in 1962," *Skillings' Mining Review*, vol. 52.

Skillings' Mining Review. Weekly. Duluth, Minnesota.

Smith, W. (1949). *An Economic Geography of Great Britain.* London.

Société des Hautes Fourneaux de Saules (1954). *Les Mines de Fer Françaises.* Paris.

State of Minnesota Legislative Commission on Taxation of Iron Ore (1961). *Report.* Minneapolis.

Stocking, G. W. (1954). *Basing Point System and Regional Development.* Chapel Hill, North Carolina.

Sullivan, G. F. (1958). "Russian steel industry," *Iron Age*, 182:89–104.

Swann, D., and McLachan, D. L. (1965). "Steel pricing in a recession: An analysis of United Kingdom and ECSC experience," *Scottish Journal of Political Economy*, 12:81–104.

Swindell, K. (1967). "Iron ore mining in West Africa: Some recent developments in Guinea, Sierra Leone, and Liberia," *Economic Geography*, 43:333–46.

Thaeler, A. S. (1964). "Ore Movement and Operation with Future 1,000-Foot Great Lakes Ships." Paper presented to the Society of Naval Architects and Marine Engineers, Great Lakes and Great Rivers Section. Chicago.

Thiele, E. H. (1963). "Year-round transportation," *Twenty-fourth Annual Mining Symposium*, University of Minnesota School of Mines and Metallurgy, Minneapolis.

Thomte, W. L. (1963). "Transportation and harbors," *Twenty-fourth Annual Mining Symposium*, University of Minnesota School of Mines and Metallurgy, Minneapolis.

Tumertekin, E. (1955). "The iron and steel industries of Turkey," *Economic Geography*, 31:179–84.

United Kingdom, Secretary of State for Wales, *et al.* (1965). *Iron Ore Imports into South Wales*. Cmnd. 2706. London.

United Nations (1949). *European Steel Trends in the Setting of the World Market* (Economic Commission for Europe). Geneva.

———. (1950-A). *World Iron Ore Resources and Their Utilization*. New York.

———. (1950-B). *Proceedings of the United Nations Scientific Conference on the Conservation and Utilization of Resources* (Department of Economic and Social Affairs). New York.

———. (1953). *The European Steel Industry and the Wide-Strip Mill* (ECE). Geneva.

———. (1954-A). *A Study of the Iron and Steel Industry in Latin America* (Department of Economic and Social Affairs). New York.

———. (1954-B). *Competition between Steel and Aluminium* (ECE). Geneva.

———. (1954-C). *Growth and Stagnation in the European Economy* (ECE). Geneva.

———. (1955). *Survey of World Iron Ore Resources: Occurrence, Appraisal, and Use*. New York.

———. (1958). *Problems of the Steelmaking and Transforming Industries in Latin America* (Economic Commission for Latin America). New York.

———. (1959-A). *Long-Term Trends and Problems of the European Steel Industry* (ECE). Geneva.

———. (1959-B). *Trade in Minerals* (Economic Commission for Asia and the Far East). Document no. E/CN.11/TRADE/L30.

———. (1961). *Formulating Industrial Development Programmes* (ECAFE) Bangkok.

———. (1962-A). *World Trade Trends* (Economic and Social Council). Document nos. E/3629, E/C.N.13/49.

———. (1962-B). *Comparison of Steelmaking Processes* (ECE). New York.

———. (1963-A). *Industrial Growth in Africa* (Economic Commission for Africa). New York.

———. (1963-B). *The Development of the Iron and Steel Industry in Africa* (ECA). Document no. E/CN 14/INR/27.

———. (1963-C). *Technical Papers, Regional Symposium on the Application of Modern Technical Practices in the Iron and Steel Industry to Developing Countries*.

———. (1964-A). *Proceedings, Regional Symposium on the Application of Modern Technical Practices in the Iron and Steel Industry to Developing Countries* (Department of Economic and Social Affairs). New York.

———. (1964-B). *Industrialization and Productivity*. Bulletin 8. New York.

———. (1964-C). *Report on the Conference on Industrial Coordination in West Africa* (ECA and UNESCO). Document no. E/CN.14/324.

———. (1965). *Proposals for the Creation of the Latin American Common Market* (Conference on Trade and Development, Trade and Development Board). Document no. TD/B/11.

———. (1966). *Economic Aspects of Iron Ore Preparation* (ECE). Geneva.

———. (1968-A). *The World Market for Iron Ore* (ECE). New York.

———. (1968-B). *World Trade in Steel and Steel Demand in Developing Countries* (ECE). New York.

———. Annually. *European Steel Market* (ECE). Geneva.

———. Annually. *Statistical Yearbook*. New York.

———. Quarterly. *Quarterly Bulletin of Steel Statistics for Europe* (ECE). Geneva.

United States:

Area Redevelopment Administration (1964). *Transport and Distribution for Selected Industries in Northeast Minnesota and Northern Wisconsin.* Washington, D.C.

Army Engineer Division (1958). "Iron Ore Traffic Analysis." Mimeographed to accompany Great Lakes Harbors study.

Bureau of Mines (1961). *Lake Superior Iron Resources*. Washington, D.C.

———. Annually. *Minerals Yearbook*. Washington, D.C.

———. Quinquennially. *Mineral Facts and Problems*. Washington, D.C.

Department of Commerce (1963). *Preliminary Engineering Studies for the Application of the R-N Process to Lake Superior Region Iron Ores.* Washington, D.C.

Joint Economic Committee of Congress (1963). *Hearings on Steel Prices, Unit Costs, Profits, and Foreign Competition.* Washington, D.C.

President's Materials Policy Commission (1952). *Resources for Freedom* (Paley Commission). Washington, D.C.

Senate Committee on Finance (1967). *Steel Imports*. Washington, D.C.

Senate Committee on Foreign Relations (1953). *Hearings on the St. Lawrence Seaway*. Washington, D.C.

Tariff Commission (1959). *Iron Ore*. Washington, D.C.

Transport Investigation and Research Board (1945). *The Economics of Iron and Steel Transport.* Washington, D.C.

Van der Rest, P. (1958). "Iron and steel in Belgium," *Journal of Metals*, 10:654–55.

Verdoorn, P. J. (1954). "A customs union for Western Europe: Advantages and feasibility," *World Politics*, 6:482–500.

Vigrass, J. W. (1962). "An Evaluation of Multiple Car Volume Rates for Railroads." In *Papers, 3rd Annual Meeting, American Transportation Research Forum*. Pittsburgh.

Vines, F. D. (1961). "Transportation, handling, and storage of iron ore," *Twenty-second Annual Mining Symposium*, Minnesota School of Mines and Metallurgy, Minneapolis.

Vochting, F. (1958). "Considerations on the industrialisation of the Mezzogiorno," *Banca Nationale del Lavoro Quarterly Review*, 68:325–76.

Voskoboinikov, V. G. (1963). "Technical Progress in Iron Making." Technical paper B.1. in United Nations (1963-C).

Vvedensky, G. A. (1959). "Developments in the third and fourth metallurgical centres," Institute for the Study of the U.S.S.R., Bulletin no. 6, pp. 32–37.

Waldenstom, E. (1963). "The Lamco project: A commercial contribution to African economic development," *Annals of the Swedish Ironmasters Association*, 147:437–60.

Waring, H. W. A., and Dennison, T. (1962). "The study of productivity in the iron and steel industry," *Journal of the Iron and Steel Institute*, 200:188–92.

Warren, K. (1959). "The Location of the Iron and Steel Industries of Great Britain and the United States." Ph.D. dissertation, Cambridge University.

———. (1964). "The Steel Industry." In Manners (1964-B).

———. (1967). "The changing steel industry of the European Common Market," *Economic Geography*, 43:314–32.

———. (1969-A). "Recent changes in the geographical location of the British steel industry," *Geographical Journal*, 135:343–64.

———. (1969-B). "Coastal steelworks—a case for argument," *Three Banks Review*, 82:25–38.

Wasmuht, R., and Tschoepke, R. (1963). "Ore Exploration and Exploitation." Technical paper in United Nations (1963-C).

Wheeler, C. R. (1958). "Raw material supplies and the future development of the iron and steel industry," *Journal of the Iron and Steel Institute*, 189:101–9.

White, C. L. (1928). "The iron and steel industry of the Pittsburgh district," *Economic Geography*, 4:115–39.

———. (1959). *Is the West Making the Grade in the Steel Industry?* Business Research Series No. 8. Stanford, California.

Whitman, R. A. (1965). "Steel." In *Mineral Facts and Problems*. Bureau of Mines. Washington, D.C.

Whittington, G. (1965). "Japan's iron ore needs: A catalyst for Indian development," *Tijdschrift voor Economische en Sociale Geografie*, 56:156–58.

Wilbur, J. S. (1960). "The competitive position of Lake Superior ores," *Twenty-first Annual Mining Symposium*, University of Minnesota School of Mines and Metallurgy, Minneapolis.

———. (1961). "Lower lake railroads and the iron ore industry," *Twenty-second Annual Mining Symposium*, University of Minnesota School of Mines and Metallurgy, Minneapolis.

———. (1962). "Iron ore's competitive challenge," *Skillings' Mining Review*, 52:10–13.

Williams, E. W. (1962). *Freight Transportation in the Soviet Union*. Princeton.

Wills, N. R. (1963). "The Basic Iron and Steel Industry." In Hunter, A., *The Economics of Australian Industry*. Melbourne.

Wittur, G. E. (1964). *Postwar Changes in Blast Furnace Technology: The Effect on Pig Iron Costs*. Master's thesis, Pennsylvania State University.

———. (1965). *Canadian Iron Ore Industry, 1964*. Department of Mines. Ottawa.

———. (1967). *The OECD Steel Industry with Emphasis on Europe*. Department of Energy, Mines and Resources. Ottawa.

Wooldridge, E. F.; Mills, H. R.; and Kelly, D. H. (1967). "Specific scope for different means of transport within a works," *Journal of the Iron and Steel Institute*, 205:1018–30.

Woytinsky, W. S., and Woytinsky, E. S. (1953). *World Population and Production*. New York.

Wright, E. C. (1950). "Economics of raw material supplies in the Birmingham district," *Mining Engineering*, 187:1218–25.

Wu, L.-I. (1965). *The Steel Industry in Communist China*. New York.

Wylie, K. H., and Ezekiel, M. (1940). "The cost curve for steel production," *Journal of Political Economy*, 48:777–821.

Zauberman, A. (1964). *Industrial Progress in Poland, Czechoslovakia, and East Germany, 1937–1962*. London.

Zawadki, K. K. F. (1953). "The economics of the Schuman Plan," *Oxford Economic Papers*, 5:179–81.

Zimmermann, E. W. (1951). *World Resources and Industries*. New York.

INDEX

Acme plant, 57
Adelman, M. A., 148
Africa: demand for ore, 300; exports, ore, 272; ore production, 283, 328; ore production capacity, 310
Africa, North: exports, ore, 3, 246; ore production, 251
Africa, South: Iscor ownership, 92; ore production, 283; pig iron production, 134; steel consumption and production, 3, 114, 129
Africa, West: common market, proposed, 89–90; exports, ore, 246, 321, 323, 324; production of ore, 251, 283, 328; steel demand, 89
Agglomerates, 44, 46, 47, 161–63. *See also* Pellets; Sinter
Alan Wood steelworks, 79
Alexandersson, G., 22, 92
Algeria: exports, ore, 246, 248; price of ore, 255, 265
American Iron and Steel Institute, 117
Anglo-American Council on Productivity, 59, 213, 230
Argentina, 100
Armco Steel Corporation, 37
Arthur D. Little, Inc., 237–38, 239, 241, 243
Asia: demand for ore, 299–300, 304, 309; mining capacity, 309; output of leading steel producers, 82*t*; production of ore, 250–51, 282, 283, 328; ratio of pig iron production to ore consumption, 138; steel production, 300
Associated Bulk Carriers, 196
Association of Iron and Steel Engineers, 53
Australia: demand for ore, 111, 317; exports, ore, 273, 317, 323, 334; physical structure of ore, 232; pig iron production, 134; politics and the pattern of supply, 157; price of ore, 148, 267; production of ore, 251, 283; reserves, 239; royalty payments, 151; steel consumption and production, 114, 130; unintegrated blast furnace, 57

Austria, 32, 128
Automation, 64

Bain, J. S., 59
Bannyy, N. P., 54, 57, 101, 102
Barloon, M. J., 17, 22
Batelle Memorial Institute, 48, 49
Belgium: consumption of ore, 138; hot pig iron transport, 57; imports, ore, 3; steel production, 128; transport, 70
Beneficiation of ores, 36–37, 160–61
Benelux countries, 246
Benford, H., 180, 203, 206
Bessemer, Sir Henry, 3
Bessemer process, 29, 32, 49, 333
Bethlehem Steel Corporation, 24, 169, 229, 251; Burns Harbor, 56, 59; Lackawanna, 56, 59; Sparrows Point, 59, 79, 182
Blackwell, R. B., 209
Blast furnace: alternatives, 44–47; description of process, 27–29; location, 1, 41, 151; ore burdens, 36–37, 161; ore diversification, 313; ore quality requirements, 138–39; performances, 40*t*; production costs, 12; technology, 34–35*t*, 36–41, 333; unintegrated, 57
Bliss, C., 44, 45
Bolivia, 229, 234
Bouwer, S. C., 37
Brazil: exports, ore, 246, 273, 274, 320, 321, 323, 324, 328; mining capacity, 310; pig iron production, 134; politics and foreign investment, 155; price of ore, 255, 261, 266; production of ore, 251, 283, 328; reserves, 229, 238*t*, 239, 241*t*; steel consumption and production, 114, 130
Britain: consumption of ore, 111, 138; continuous casting process, 53; economies of scale, 60; exports, 108, 123; flat-product production facilities, 61*t*; imports, ore, 3, 246, 269; labor costs, 116; length of ore haul, 273; manufacturing technology, 33; mining capacity, 308; optimum size of iron and steel works, 67–68; ore fleet, 195; organization to ra-